Diverse
Times,
Sundry
Places

For
Jean

Diverse Times, Sundry Places

DONALD MAITLAND

Foreword by
Sir Edward Heath KG, MBE, MP

THE
*A*lpha
PRESS

2 4 6 8 10 9 7 5 3 1
First published 1996 in Great Britain by
THE ALPHA PRESS
18 Chichester Place
Brighton BN2 1FF

and in the United States of America by
THE ALPHA PRESS
c/o International Specialized Book Services, Inc.
5804 N.E. Hassalo St.
Portland, Oregon 97213-3644

British Library Cataloguing in Publication Data
A CIP catalogue record for this book is available from the British Library.

ISBN 1 898595 17 8

Printed and bound by Biddles Ltd, King's Lynn and Guildford

Contents

Foreword

The Rt. Hon. Sir Edward Heath, K.G., M.B.E., M.P.

HOUSE OF COMMONS

I was both delighted and honoured when Sir Donald asked me to write the foreword to these memoirs.

Sir Donald served me most ably during two of the most important periods of my public life: as my spokesman during the European negotiations of 1961 to 1963, and as my Chief Press Secretary at 10 Downing Street from 1970 to 1973. His devotion, acumen and industry were invaluable assets to me, as I am sure they were to the many other people he has served during an exemplary career.

Finding his inspiration in the sacrifice of his comrades during the Second World War, Sir Donald has committed over half a century of his life to remarkable public service. It is this theme which gives flavour to every page, and which Sir Donald develops fully but without any sense of sanctimoniousness. That is why this book is so relevant, not just to my generation, but more importantly, to those younger people who are in need of inspiration and an antidote to the creeping cynicism which now pervades so much discussion about public life in this country.

Those who look for specific incidents of interest as well as a noble and timeless theme will also find much of interest in *Diverse Times, Sundry Places* - an appropriate title indeed. Sir Donald is a man who has seen it all: from the jungle warfare of Burma and the upheavals of the Middle East to the continuous, real-life dramas of 10 Downing Street. Along the way he offers thoughtful and entertaining insights into the prominent people and issues of historical interest with which he has come into contact.

Edward Heath

4 April 96

Preface and Acknowledgements

The heroes of my boyhood were explorers, rulers, Robert Louis Stevenson, the golfer Henry Cotton and Alan Cobham, the aviator. My father took his botanical skills to Africa in 1910 and, for over twenty years, he passed these on to those who worked with him in Nigeria, the Gold Coast, Uganda and the Cameroons. He encouraged the cultivation of the disease-resistant 'robusta' in place of 'arabica' coffee. He helped to devise methods of controlling locusts and eradicating the tsetse fly. During his long absences from home, his assistants in the botanic gardens, his companions on his journeys on foot and by canoe and on his survey of the grasses on Mount Cameroon, were his surrogate family. His was the acceptable face of colonialism. My mother, who stayed behind, regarded the education of her four sons as her mission in life. She set the highest standards and told us that such talents as we had were a gift which it was our duty to use for the benefit of others. She practised what she preached and her example was a powerful factor in our upbringing.

My three older brothers were born in Uganda during the First World War. By comparison, to have been born in Edinburgh, the city where we lived, seemed mundane and I dreamed of travelling to exotic corners of the world. Within the family it was accepted that, when the time came, we should all seek to make our careers in the service of our country. Two of my brothers joined the army and one the foreign, later the diplomatic, service. My own choice was postponed by the outbreak of the Second World War which took me, once my formal education had been completed, to some of the faraway places on my juvenile list.

I could not have imagined the variety of experiences in store when I was in due course accepted into the foreign service. Few of the tasks I was given were tedious. Some were exhilarating, for instance, my close encounter of an unusual kind with Ernest Bevin, one of the great foreign secretaries of the century, and my making the first foreign contact with a young revolutionary leader in Libya. Some of my assignments were a rare privilege, notably the years spent in the service of a prime minister who believed we were one nation and that our interests required that we play the leading role in creating a new Europe for which our history and genius had equipped us. I enjoyed the dialectic and camaraderie of multilateral negotiation in the United Nations and the European Community. Not all my work was as pleasant. Striving day after day, and night after night, to contain the aggression and tolerate the conceits of an unstable successor of Bevin was not agreeable.

At a later stage I was able to draw on my experiences in the diplomatic service when I penetrated the worlds of energy, of communications and information technology, broadcasting and public health. My youthful appetite for travel has been satisfied. I have seen all seven continents and met people of all sorts and conditions. On the way I have learned much not only about the world beyond our shores, but also about the sort of people we are in these islands and about the way in which we choose to be governed. That the years I spent in the service of the public seldom seemed burdensome was due in great part to the understanding and support of my wife, Jean. The diverse times we have shared in sundry places have been joyful; I owe to her and my family a particular debt for their advice and encouragement during the writing of these memoirs.

The author and publishers wish to thank the following, among others, for permission to reproduce photographs:

John Gilbert, jacket picture; Times Newspapers Ltd [Edward Heath at Battersea]; United Nations/Chen [vote in Security Council]; Secretariat General of the Council of the European Union [the Brussels/Luxembourg photographs]; PIC Photos [self at North Thames Gas].

Every effort has been made to trace all the copyright holders but if any have been inadvertently overlooked the publishers will be pleased to make the necessary arrangement at the first opportunity.

1

Preparation for War

The round green hills of Manipur filled the landscape. From the tents below figures began to emerge and climb the slope, enticed by the siren voice of Elisabeth Schumann singing Schubert. They had not heard such music for months and were taken by surprise. Over the next few days the portable gramophone established my popularity and there were plenty of willing hands to wind it up, turn over the records and sharpen the fibre needles.

There was another reason why my joining the headquarters of 4 Indian Corps on the Burma front in November 1944 was regarded as opportune. A dispute within the intelligence branch had to be settled. My immediate chief, Major Ken Boome, believed that information of military value could be obtained from the civilian population as the advance south gained momentum. He based his argument on advice from civil affairs staff, experience elsewhere and his own judgment. Boome had therefore recommended that the intelligence branch should take steps to exploit this source. However, Derek Holbrook, our colonel, had been sceptical; the information gathered would be of doubtful reliability and the branch had other priorities. In the end he agreed without enthusiasm to an experiment: who better than the new arrival to undertake it? So it was arranged that I should visit the headquarters of 33 Indian Corps – one of the other two corps which composed the Fourteenth Army – to study the techniques they used.

Like many other Anglo-Burmans, Colonel Keely, who advised 33 Corps on civil affairs, had had a distinguished career in the Burma Police. He was in no doubt about the value of intelligence from local sources: the people of Burma were naturally observant, they had an eye for detail and retentive memories. For three years the great majority had been deprived. A high proportion of their crops had been commandeered by the Japanese army and the import of most domestic necessities had stopped. Matches, needles, cloth to make longyis (the Burmese equivalent of the sarong), bandages and medicaments of all kinds had been virtally unobtainable throughout the Japanese occupation. The more they saw of the Japanese in retreat, the sooner would they conclude that the the British would win the war. They would then shed their inhibitions about cooperating with us.

The days I spent with Colonel Keely provided me with insights which were to prove their value over the next several months. On my return to 4 Corps headquarters, I was given an immediate opportunity to practise what the colonel had preached. I was to leave at once to join the 19th Indian Division which had broken out of its bridgehead on the Chindwin river and was on the road to Mandalay.

This, at last, was to be the real test – the moment for which I had been preparing for two and a half years and which my parents, no doubt, had been dreading.

❖

I had left them behind on the platform at Waverley Station. I was excited then and confident, but I could only guess at their feelings at the departure of their fourth son. On leaving university I had enlisted in the army. To streamline the production of officers, those who had acquired a Certificate B in the university training corps were posted direct to officer cadet training units for intensive instruction. During our first month as raw officer cadets at Dunbar in East Lothian we were at the mercy of the archetypal bullying sergeant-major with a heart of gold. He taught us the life and death importance of instinctive reaction and instilled in us fear of 'Return To Unit' – the humiliation of being dismissed from the course as inadequate and posted to an infantry battalion as an ordinary private.

Our training as potential platoon commanders built on what we had learned in the school and university training corps. The difference was that several of our instructors had had recent battle experience and, when our company commander, the much respected Captain Read, told us to 'bum on', we were quick to learn the lesson. Nor were we likely to forget two pearls of wisdom from a Glaswegian sergeant instructor. The first – a warning which fortunately turned out to be superfluous – related to mustard gas: "Wi' this respirator ye'll be all right. But if you get it on your genial organs – aw Jings." The second was an aphorism of universal application: "Ye've gotta cater for the BF in every section."

Throughout the course instruction was systematic and logical. We were told, for instance, that before we could determine which 'battle drill' was appropriate, we had to 'appreciate' the situation. This appreciation had to follow a set pattern. First, the objective to be achieved. Secondly; the factors affecting the attainment of that objective; these were to include the relative strengths of the enemy's forces and our own, the terrain, the amount of time and space available, the weather and the light. Then, the courses open to the enemy and ourselves. And finally, the plan. This procedure soon became instinctive.

Time was also devoted to 'man management' – a novel concept for most of us. The centrepiece was a series of lectures by a veteran of the First World War. He told us that our relationship with our men was as important to efficiency as training and discipline, and this relationship had to be based on mutual respect and confidence. We should, for example, stimulate in our men a sense of unity; we should put their interests first and be their champion. And more in the same vein. On the walk back to our quarters in the former Royal Hotel, my room-mates and I suddenly discerned the Christian message in the advice Captain Innes was offering us.

As a supplement to this part of our course, we were encouraged to read a series of lectures which General Wavell had delivered at Trinity College Cambridge in 1939. These had been published at the moment of his victories over the Italian armies in north Africa in 1941 under the title *Generals and Generalship*. In the first of these Wavell quoted the only apt exposition of the qualities necessary for a general which he had found in his researches. This read: "The general must know how to get the men their rations and every other kind of stores needed for war . . . He must be observant, untiring, shrewd; kindly and cruel; simple and crafty; a watchman and a robber; lavish and miserly; generous and stingy; rash and conservative". What Wavell had appreciated most about this definition was that Socrates – for it was indeed he – gave pride of place to the well-being of the troops.

In March 1942 I went to Bridge of Allan to join the 'Dandy Ninth' – the 7/9 Battalion of the Royal Scots – so called because it was the only battalion in the regiment allowed to wear the kilt. The battalion was soon on the move to Peterhead and Cruden Bay. There were exciting rumours that our division was to undergo training in mountain warfare. I had little time to savour these before I was summoned by the adjutant. He said that I was to take immediate embarkation leave before joining a troopship for India where I would be attached to the Indian Army. Following the entry of Japan into the war, our forces in India had to be built up rapidly and a high proportion of the latest intake of junior officers was being diverted to India for this purpose. He suggested that I might have an opportunity to avenge the loss of the 2nd Battalion of the regiment which had been destroyed the previous December in the fruitless defence of Hong Kong.

With my parents I spent a glorious week in and around Peebles, during which our bonds grew tighter still. Paradoxically this eased the leave-taking at Waverley Station. The fortitude of parents in such circumstances never ceased to astonish me. In London the following morning I saw some of the bomb damage and watched the changing of the guard at Buckingham Palace in the bright May sunshine and, later in the day, arrived at Funtington near Chichester. Here the draft of troops, bearing the code-name RAZAK, which I was to take to India was assembling. We were fitted out with what proved to be quite inappropriate tropical uniforms and were generously entertained by members of the Booth family, who owned Funtington Hall. Within a week the drafts were complete and we marched to Chichester to board a train for an undisclosed port of embarkation; the odds were on Liverpool. The train set off in darkness and stopped on the outskirts of Portsmouth which was being bombed. Some hours later we got down for tea and biscuits at a station we quickly identified as Crewe. The tea was weak, the biscuits hard and the NAAFI staff surly – hardly the intended boost for our morale. Spirits rose in the morning as we marched along the quayside at Greenock and boarded our troopship – the *Otranto* – originally of the Orient Line.

❖

When we were a few days out from Greenock and heading for Iceland, I was put on submarine and mine watch. My instructions were to stand at the starboard end of the lower bridge and call out if I saw any dangerous object. Visibility was poor, the wind gale force and the movement of the ship so violent that within half an hour I would not have cared if the entire U-boat fleet had surfaced alongside us. One of the ship's officers on the bridge saw my plight and had one of the crew take my place – a thoughtful and prudent act on his part.

Otranto was in good company. The convoy was a mixture of troop-carrying vessels, tankers and cargo ships of various shapes and sizes and the importance attached to it was evident from the presence in our escort of two battleships – *Nelson* and *Rodney* – the aircraft carrier *Argus*, an occasional light cruiser and a screen of four destroyers on either horizon. Discipline was rigorous – life-jackets carried at all times, total blackout and waste disposal only at night. The opulence of the ship itself, in contrast to conditions in wartime Britain, bordered on the obscene. Because such ships were able to take on provisions at ports which were either neutral or for other reasons not involved in the hostilities, catering and service were up to peacetime standard.

At Freetown, where the convoy stayed for a week, I had my first sight of the continent where my father had made his career as a botanist and my three older brothers were born. On the run south to the Cape, flying fish and an albatross joined our escort and we cheered one afternoon when an unescorted *Queen Elizabeth* overtook us at high speed some miles to starboard.

We were all looking forward to the next refuelling stop in South Africa, having heard of the hospitality showered on those who had preceded us on their way to the Middle East by the people of Cape

Town and Durban. As we neared the Cape we learned with dismay that Rommel's forces had captured Tobruk on 21 June and we wondered whether this would affect the plans that had been made for us. We did not know then that a major component of the Tobruk garrison of over 30,000 who had surrendered was the 2nd South African Division. In Durban we found a city still in shock. Nor was this relieved by the imposition for the first time of a blackout to counter the threat from Japanese submarines, one of which was said to have shelled the coast nearby during the night. Despite this we were able to stretch our legs and I had the good fortune to catch a glimpse of General Smuts doing his best to revive the spirits of a crowd in one of the city squares.

By 8 July we were on the last stage of our voyage amid persistent rumours of one or more Japanese submarines lurking in the Mozambique channel. A few days later there was a burst of activity by two of our escorting destroyers – rapid changes of direction and the occasional depth charge. The warmer weather and calm seas persuaded three of us to try sleeping on deck. We collected camp-beds, blankets and pillows and set off from our cabins wearing pyjamas. We found that the only access to the boat deck was through the sergeants' mess, which we did not cross unnoticed. Erecting the war-time military camp bed in daylight required close attention; in the dark it frayed tempers. When we were at last settled someone remarked that we would be well placed if we were torpedoed. This brought an oath from the third who had left his life-jacket below. We thought of him with sympathy crossing and recrossing the sergeants' mess. A loud hissing woke me at five o'clock. "Sorry. We have to have all these decks washed down by six." Two weeks later, in late July, we were in sight of the gateway to India.

❖

"Travel, in the younger sort," wrote Francis Bacon, "is a part of education." Quite so. But I had not expected such a bombardment of new sights, sounds and smells. The magnificence of Bombay harbour was matched by the vitality of the city and the splendour of the buildings – both Indian and imperial.

After handing over command of RAZAK, I had to await instructions about language training. During the next few days, thanks to introductions from friends at home, I was able to take a few *Otranto* colleagues to meet members of the British business community in Bombay and their Indian friends. Through these contacts we began to appreciate some of the complexities of the situation in India at that time. The civil disobedience movement launched by Mahatma Gandhi in 1941 had reached the point of crisis with the demand by the Congress party for the immediate withdrawal of British rule from India. This was also the moment – though not even Paul Scott knew it at the time – when

Daphne Manners, the ill-used heroine of his *Jewel in the Crown*, fell
in love with Hari Kumar. By all accounts feelings in many parts of India
were running high.

On the long train journey south from Bombay through the Deccan,
those of us assigned to the training school at Bangalore shared a sense
of mild indignation that our formal education, and what we had read
and learned otherwise, had conveyed so imperfect an impression of this
remarkable subcontinent. If we were to do what was expected of us we
had a mountain to climb. The instructors at the training school seemed
to understand this. They had no more than two months to turn us from
British into Indian Army officers. It was clear that sound thinking lay
behind their methodical approach.

Over the years the lingua franca of the Indian Army had been
reduced to essentials, standardised, simplified, and anglicised where
this was unavoidable. At Bangalore we were taught Urdu in Roman
script, since knowledge of either the Hindi/Sanskrit or the Persi–Arabic
scripts was considered unnecessary at this stage. There was in any case
the question of communicating in Morse code. It followed that Indian
recruits were also required to learn Roman script and the standard
military Urdu vocabulary.

We sat under trees on the spacious lawns of the training school in
groups of three with our 'munshi' – the teacher who would see us
through from start to finish. Once we were accustomed to post-positions
instead of pre-positions and minor differences in the construction of
verbs, we made good progress and within eight weeks most passed the
elementary examination. Lectures on Indian military law, the structure
of the Indian Army, customs and traditions and action in aid of the
civil power – a topical subject at that moment – introduced us to a
phrase we would live with for the next few years: 'modified for India'.
British military law, administrative procedures, calculations, clothing and
equipment – even weapons – all seemed to require some modification
to take account of the different circumstances.

In September 1942 I left Bangalore for the North West Frontier
where I was to join the 6th Battalion of the Rajputana Rifles stationed
at that time in Mir Ali, a fort in Waziristan. After several days and
nights in the train I reached Delhi, where I was able to take a week's
leave with my eldest brother, Douglas, and his family. He was a medical
officer in the military hospital and had already spent more than four years
in India. The Frontier Mail took me to Rawalpindi where I changed
to the branch line for Bannu. The adjutant met me and we drove to
the Bannu Club where, he said, we had important business to transact.
This was the selection of my bearer. The steward at the club, whose
patronage was clearly essential for out of work bearers, had selected a
tall, lean Pathan more than twice my age with an aquiline nose and a

grip of steel. Abdul Janan Khan was the kind of person of whom one thinks: "I'm glad he's on our side."

The 6th battalion had been formed only in 1940 and still had some of the characteristics of a scratch team. There were no fewer than twenty King's Commissioned Officers on the battalion's strength – at least six more than were needed, given the role in Indian regiments played by Viceroy's Commissioned Officers as deputy company commanders and platoon commanders. Mir Ali fort was a hollow square, each side about five hundred yards long, set in a partially cultivated plain which stretched three or more miles to the first range of barren mountains. These, when the rising sun cast light and shade on their steep, rugged slopes, were a magnificent if forbidding backdrop.

The main task of the battalion was to protect convoys taking supplies to Miranshah, the next fort on the road to the Afghan frontier, from attack by hostile tribesmen. This task was performed at irregular intervals two or three times a week. The battalion was notified of a 'Road Open Day' the previous evening and orders were issued soon after. The normal method was for the companies concerned to drive across the plain in armoured vehicles to the edge of tribal territory where a platoon would dismount, scale a hill in bounds and occupy sangars – round dry-stone emplacements. This would continue until the whole stretch of the road for which we were responsible was protected by a series of mutually supportive picquets. Some platoons would be accompanied by a troop of mountain artillery – easily man-handled howitzers – and occasionally a light tank. The strong points communicated with each other by hand-held flag or heliograph. For convenience, the more important topographical features had been given names – Kidney Hill, Aeroplane Hill, Qabristan Tekri (graveyard hillock), Chalis (forty) Pathan, Corunna Corner.

The Tochi Scouts were our neighbours in this part of Waziristan. The Scouts, officially known as the Frontier Corps, had been formed after the first world war to serve as the private armies of the political agents who represented the imperial presence in the tribal territories. The Tochi Scouts took their name from the Tochi river which flowed alongside the road and eventually joined the Indus. From time to time the Scouts, who were recruited locally, would reinforce our presence by sending 'gashts' – fast-moving company-strong patrols – through our positions. The male members of the local tribes all carried rifles in canvas cases, some of them rakishly embroidered, and went about their business while we were engaged in ours. Part of their business was, of course, to have a good look at what we were doing, how and with what.

On the eve of one Road Open Day, in the absence of the Colonel and the Second-in-Command, the acting commanding officer decided to change the routine and to put our picquets in position by night. This was quite contrary to frontier warfare doctrine. Some other company commanders were also absent and soon after midnight, in accordance with my orders, I set off on foot in command of two companies advancing in open order towards the hills. I felt as if I had been catapulted into the pages of the *Boys' Own Paper*. The inevitable happened. A party of tribesmen on our right front, no doubt disapproving of this change in the routine, opened fire with rifles. The leading platoon commander halted his troops. When firing died down he sent back his orderly to say nobody had been hit and to request orders. My reply was the Urdu equivalent of 'bum on'; I felt Captain Read would have been pleased. We resumed the advance and, despite further sporadic firing and increased heartbeats, the two companies, providentially unscathed, took up positions an hour before dawn.

This was not the war I had left home for and, when a request for volunteers to go to the Middle East was posted in the Mess, I responded. The youngest of my three older brothers, Ian, was already in the Western Desert with a British tank regiment and I looked forward to joining him. I spent some weeks with the training battalion at the regimental depot in Delhi Cantonment, where Abdul Janan Khan ensured that I was served breakfast before any of my contemporaries. When my posting came it was not to either of the battalions in the desert, but to Persia and Iraq Force, where I was to await further orders.

❖

Christmas in a reinforcement camp at Zubair in southern Iraq was not what anyone would choose. The cold at night was intense and I was relieved when I received orders to join the 2nd Battalion of the Rajputana Rifles. This entailed a journey by night train to Baghdad, a few days there in a transit camp, and then by train and truck across the Persian border to the battalion's encampment near Qasr-i-Shirin.

In the wartime army friendships were important. Based on mutual dependence and nourished by common experience, they provided reassurance and encouragement. For those still young enough to be susceptible to influence, they hastened progress towards maturity. These friendships were invariably rewarding and I was about to experience the first of three wartime encounters which made an especially deep impression.

I was posted to the headquarters company and given command of the signal platoon which worked closely with the intelligence section. This was commanded by another lieutenant, Lewis Penny.[1] Rapport was instant. He had been commissioned directly into the regiment with which he had a family connection. He looked forward to returning in due course to Trinity Hall to complete his geology course. He had a flute and gave me one of his recorders; our attempts to make music amused and puzzled our orderlies.

The role of our division was to deceive the Germans in the Caucasus about the real strength of allied forces in Persia and Iraq. To do this large-scale set-piece exercises and long route marches were arranged and brigades and battalions frequently moved to new encampments. When the winter rains stopped we moved to Kermanshah, where Lewis Penny and I took an opportunity to climb Kuh-i-Parau; later to Kifri near Kirkuk in Iraq where heat-stroke became a problem, then to Sultanabad, Qum and Hamadan in Persia. We acquired some expertise; an order to move received one evening could be executed by early morning – all six hundred troops, tents and other equipment already on the road to the next site. Documents captured after the war showed that this elaborate deception was on the whole effective.

The composition of both the signal platoon and the intelligence section reflected the battalion mix – one quarter Hindu Rajputs, one quarter Muslims from the Punjab or North West Frontier, and one half Hindu Jats. My second in command was a Jat, Havildar Badri Ram. When new wireless sets arrived we had to teach the platoon how to operate them and in particular how to ensure that all the sets were on the same frequency. Badri told them that they had to practise 'netting' until they could do it by instinct. "What's instinct, Badri?" they asked. "Well," he replied, "when you're eating, you pick up your food like this and you put it in your mouth. You don't put it in your ear" – this accompanied, of course, with appropriate gestures. The platoon enjoyed this and thereafter, at tedious moments, someone would say: "Badri, do instinct again."

When we were encamped near Qum my orderly was transferred to another company. His replacement, who had only recently joined the battalion, was a Hindu Jat who rejoiced in the name of Rura Ram. And he really did rejoice. As he polished my boots under the flap of the tent he would chant: "Mera nam Rura Ram ("my name is Rura Ram); Rura, Rura Ram" in time to the brush strokes. When I asked him whether he had any brothers in the regiment, he said yes, he had a brother. In which battalion? This battalion. Really, in which company? This company. Which platoon? This platoon. Wonderful; I didn't know that. What's his name? You know his name; his name is Rura Ram. In his own estimation, this invented brother put Rura Ram on a par with others in the platoon and made it easier for him to regard the regiment as family.

Persia was an important route for American aid to the Russians. Russian soldiers collected ten-ton trucks at one or other of the southern ports and drove them north to the Russian-occupied zone. Many of the drivers were from Siberia or central Asia. Gangs of Persians armed with long shovels spread gravel continuously on the roads which had not been built to take such weights. The Russian drivers kept themselves to themselves, presumably on instructions. Other Russians were not above a bit of spitefulness. Three of us returning from Tehran to Hamadan were detained for some hours at a Russian checkpoint at Kazvin on the border of their zone. Neither explanation nor apology was offered.

Local banditry and rumours of German spies dropped by parachute relieved the monotony, but not the tensions in the mess. The more senior officers were regular soldiers and seemed ill at ease with the young university-educated amateurs who had been wished on them. In the nine months I spent in the battalion only two of them took the trouble to engage me in conversation in the mess. It was therefore no surprise that, when divisional orders called for applications to join a new parachute regiment, six of us sent in our names. This raised eyebrows at divisional headquarters. The major who came to interview us was sympathetic and before long we were posted elsewhere – none to the new parachute regiment. My regret was leaving Lewis Penny behind; I appreciated however, that for him family loyalty to the regiment was a factor. He had stimulated my interest in classical music, in poetry, in belles lettres, in geography as it was then understood and, of course, in geology. But this was not the end of our war-time encounter.

❖

The Intelligence School at Karachi, like the training unit at Dunbar, was highly professional. Intensive instruction over six weeks, oriented towards future operations in Burma and Malaya, provided the essential knowledge for intelligence officers in the field. The course completed, I was posted once again to Bangalore where I joined the security intelligence branch of Southern Army headquarters in November 1943. Our brief covered subversive movements, ranging from extremist religious groups to the JIFS – 'Japanese Inspired Fifth Columnists'. Given that the Japanese were at the gates of India, the definition of our target groups was comprehensive. Information flowed regularly between our office and General Headquarters in Delhi and it was from there that we obtained the material for a lecture about the Indian National Army which I was required to give to the staff of Army headquarters. I was astonished, years later, to read the same lecture as delivered by Paul Scott's Captain Merrick in *The Towers of Silence*. From time to time we received reports of Indian agents landing from Japanese submarines on the Madras coast. In almost all cases these poor souls either surrendered at once or made their way to their home villages. Liaison with the police was close and effective and I was able to see something of the Madras underworld.

Delhi also ensured that we were kept informed of developments further afield. They arranged for Major Bernard Fergusson,[2] as he then was, to talk to headquarters staff about the first Chindit expedition.

What he said about this audacious but painful experiment in long range penetration was the official account. Over lunch afterwards in our mess he was more forthcoming. "The only good thing about a campaign like that," he said, "is bullshitting about it afterwards."

My colleagues in the security intelligence branch were for the most part old India hands. I shared a desk with Ruth Fox, a tall, donnish woman with bobbed hair. A long bone cigarette holder kept the smoke out of her eyes as she wrote. She had been involved in security work during the First World War, after which she and her husband had established themselves in Assam where they had a tea estate.

Meeting Ruth Fox was the second special wartime encounter. No one I had known possessed such a powerful intellect and I felt privileged to be taken under her wing. Through her I came to know Muriel da Costa, who wore her khaki sari with the grace of a princess in a Deccani painting. Her concern was Southern Army's public relations. She shrewdly exploited the arrival in India of a different type of British officer – young, inquiring, not of the military tradition and therefore likely to be more susceptible to the notion of Indian independence after the war. Between them Ruth Fox and Muriel da Costa arranged for a few of us to penetrate Bangalore City, ostensibly out of bounds to British officers because of the civil unrest, in order to meet some of the moderate nationalist leaders – editors, writers, lawyers, teachers. These meetings were amicable and, after the evening meal, our hosts saw that we were returned to the safety of the cantonment. They had argued their case without rancour and may have been surprised that, for our part, we seemed to have already accepted a great deal of it.

On other evenings Ruth Fox's head-to-head tutorials over dinner focused on the events which accounted for my being in India at this time and how this circumstance could best be exploited. We moved on to the role of the individual in war and in the post-war society, fallibility and the fulfilment of human potential. Though she instructed me in the tenets of Hinduism and Bhuddhism, her preferred guidance was in Micah 6:8: 'and what doth the Lord require of thee, but to do justly, and to love mercy and to walk humbly with thy God'. Life was emptier when Ruth was transferred to another post. It was some compensation that I was called on to take over her work on promotion to captain.

Ruth Fox had also extended my knowledge and appreciation of classical music. As for so many others before and since, Beethoven's pastoral symphony turned the key in the lock. In the Bangalore bazaar I bought a second-hand all-metal portable gramophone, whose case was the sound-box, together with a quantity of fibre needles. The local carpenter made a stout box which would hold the collection of 12- and 10-inch records I had been buying in Bangalore in such a tight embrace that they would not break even if the box were dropped.

Meanwhile, on the Burma front our troops had been hard pressed. Imphal had been under siege and the decisive battle fought at Kohima. It seemed that the tide was at last turning. At this point I received my posting to 4 Indian Corps headquarters at Imphal.

2

Burma: The Real Test

I had time to reflect on some of these experiences as I set out on the road to the Chindwin river to face the real test. My team was compact – only four in all. Arthur de la Taste, an Anglo–Burman who had served in the police before the war, was to be my interpreter. Najindar Singh, a devout Sikh with nineteen years service in the infantry during which he had declined all offers of promotion, was my orderly. Our driver was a member of the Corps pool. At the ferry we learned that 19 Indian Division, which had recently joined 4 Corps from India and was seeing action for the first time, had made better progress than expected. We were also warned that parties of Japanese stragglers had been seen making their way south. As we drove east through the jungle we saw none of these; in fact we saw nobody for the first hour. In mid-afternoon we reached the crossroads where I had expected to join the division. The area was deserted except for a couple of vehicles and a few engineers, who said the division had moved on some hours earlier. We were short of petrol and already more than two hours' drive beyond the Chindwin. In three hours it would be dark. The choice was: try to catch up, or go back.

Earlier in the day the division had received an air drop at this cross-roads. We collected all the used and battered tins which still contained some petrol. The spirits of Philemon and Baucis must have been with us; we recovered enough petrol to half-fill the tank of our vehicle. We set off on the jungle road back towards the Chindwin. Our driver was to pessimism what Vera Lynn was to optimism. Half a tankful of petrol would not get us back to the river. In any case the ferry was already packing up when we crossed in the morning and would have gone by now. What would happen if we had a breakdown? What if we were ambushed by a Japanese patrol? And variations on these themes. Half an hour of this was enough. I told him to change places; I would drive and he would keep his mouth shut. The sun was beginning to set when we reached the crest of the river bank with a cupful of petrol to spare. Fifty yards ahead was a small unit of engineers who willingly filled our tank. The ferry was still operating, and we returned in darkness and silence to headquarters.

It was just as well that we turned back. A large-scale deception had been devised. This required the clearing of the route selected for an offensive by our corps further south. I was assigned to the Lushai Brigade, at that time preparing to assault the town of Gangaw on the Myittha river. This had to be captured so that the route to the Irrawaddy opposite the ancient capital of Pagan could be made ready for the assault forces.

The Lushai Brigade, unusual in that it contained battalions from the Indian States as well as the Indian Army, had been operating on this part of the front during the monsoon and was due to be relieved. For some months the brigade had endured the worst conditions the Burma front could offer – malarial jungle, the occasional tract of land infected with the lethal scrub typhus, torrential rain, high humidity, floods and mud. The day after my arrival I went to a village a few miles to the south west where many of the inhabitants of Gangaw had taken refuge. The 'thugyi' – the headman – distributed the longyis and needles I had brought with me to the most in need. He then asked if I could help the sick. When I offered to do my best, a queue formed. My supply of aspirins, cotton wool and sticking plaster quickly ran out. "Come back tomorrow, please, please", they said.

I told the headman that I wanted detailed information about Japanese strength, weapons and positions in Gangaw. If he could bring me people who had such knowledge and had recently left the town, I would return the following day. The commander of the field ambulance was sympathetic and gave me a fresh and more abundant supply of medicines. The headman's response exceeded my highest hopes. The following evening, after several hours interrogating in the village, I was able to send my first report containing intelligence obtained from local sources.

Two days later a messenger arrived from the village headman. Something important had happened; would I come at once? When I reached the village he directed me to a *basha* – a hut of branches and leaves – a mile or so down the slope towards Gangaw. Someone wanted to meet me there. Najindar Singh, with his rifle, and Arthur de la Taste, with his Thompson sub-machine-gun, kept the basha under observation from concealed positions nearby. I laid my own rifle on the ground beside me. Presently the slim figure of a young woman appeared. De la Taste joined me in the basha and did his best to calm her nerves. Ma Mya Twe, it transpired, was the mistress of the local commander of the Kempei Tai, the much feared Japanese military police. She had had to make a choice: to stay in Gangaw and suffer the consequences of her relationship, or withdraw with the Japanese. She had decided to stay and now wished to help us. Under interrogation Ma Mya Twe seemed to be well informed and observant; her information confirmed and, more important, complemented reports from air reconnaissance and ground patrols.

When she had gone I went back to the village. Another medical queue had formed. A young girl, escorted by her parents, hung back. She had a pain in her right side. I still remembered where our family doctor had pressed my body when I had appendicitis and how I had reacted. The girl's reactions were similar. The colonel at the field ambulance said he would try to bring her in for examination. Before he could do this I had left Gangaw and never knew if my amateur diagnosis was accurate.

On the morning of 10 January 1945 I returned to the slope overlooking Gangaw. The assault on the town was to be preceded by an 'earthquake'. This took the form of a raid by B25 bombers of the Strategic Air Force on the Japanese positions which had been pinpointed. The weight of the attack was awesome. The bombs were followed by rocket and cannon fire as the Lushai Brigade moved in to finish the job. The smoke drifted away and the dust settled. Where, I wondered, was the dainty Ma Mya Twe?

Back at brigade headquarters I found one of my colleagues from 4 Corps had arrived to relieve me. He explained that the expected offensive was to begin soon and I would forgo my annual leave unless I took it at once. Urgent telegrams to Lewis Penny in New Delhi; a ride in the bomb bay of an American Liberator to Calcutta; a fairy-tale train journey into the foothills of the Himalayas; then rendezvous with Penny at the Himalayan Hotel in Kalimpong. Here we were welcomed by a man of influence in these parts. Mr Macdonald was the son of a senior member of the Younghusband expedition to Tibet at the beginning of the century. He had married a Tibetan noblewoman and now ran the hotel with his four charming daughters. In Persia Penny and I had often discussed the possibility of a challenging journey and good fortune seemed to smile on us. Penny had applied for the necessary permits in Darjeeling. We were medically examined at the hospital in Gangtok, the capital of Sikkim, and were given letters of commendation from prominent Sikkimese on the strength of introductions from Macdonald. We engaged a guide called Topchen Chiring, who was to provide two riding mules, for use if we were injured, and three pack mules.

Early in the morning of 25 January we set off on foot from the capital, Gangtok, with not only Topchen Chiring and the five mules we were expecting, but also two extra men and two extra mules. In answer to our questions, Chiring explained that he was employing the two muleteers, that the sixth mule carried their baggage and the seventh food for all the mules.

As time was limited, we had no choice but to try to complete two stages each day. We crossed into Tibet by Nathu La, spent a day resting in Yatung, recrossed the border by Jelep La and were back in Kalimpong at noon on 31 January. We had covered 108 miles and climbed two passes of over 14,000 feet in seven days. The Macdonald girls awarded us mock 'Tibet medals' and we sang and danced until their father sounded lights out. As the saying goes, this was the experience of a lifetime.

❖

I rejoined corps headquarters on the eve of the offensive. The objective was Meiktila, a vital communications centre on the road to Rangoon. Its capture would cut off a substantial part of the Japanese army on the Mandalay front to the north. My orders were to operate in close collaboration with the staff of General Drummond Cowan, who commanded the 17th Indian Division.

On 20 February together with the headquarters of the 17th Division, my team crossed the Irrawaddy which at this point was some 2,000 yards wide. As our rafts propelled by outboard motors approached the east bank we had a full view of the pagodas of Pagan. When we reached Nyaungu we opened what we called a 'Civil Report Centre' in the former offices of the Japanese-sponsored 'East Asia Youth League'. Powell, the new driver, who unlike his predecessor took a rosy view of life, set up a canteen no doubt inspired by his local grocery at Mobberley in Cheshire where he drove buses before the war. It took us six hours to interrogate all those attracted to Powell's seat of custom. By then we had a longer list of contacts along the route ahead than we could hope to exploit.

While we were at Nyaungu Major Toby Fforde joined our party. He had been in the Burma Police and was to be district superintendent at Meiktila once it was captured. Later two other former Burma government servants joined us – Colonel Edgerly and Captain Barrington, who later served as Burma's ambassador in London.

The 17th Division advanced rapidly towards Meiktila – eighty miles ahead. Drawing on the experience of the Chindit expedition, we had cut our physical links with the rest of the corps and were self-contained. The air force supplied us and a 'cab-rank' protected us from air attack; this consisted of Hurricane and Thunderbolt fighter bombers, two of which were constantly in the air in daylight hours. I discovered long after that Mohsin Ali, for many years Reuters' diplomatic correspondent, piloted one of these aircraft.

We had left jungle behind. The great central plain was ideal country for the Sherman tanks of the two Indian armoured brigades which accompanied us. Japanese patrols probed the perimeter we formed at night to little effect. Within seventy-two hours the first airstrip serving Meiktila had been captured. But the makeshift force of defenders resisted stubbornly and it was not until 3 March that the main parts of the city had been cleared. As we moved in, we were warned that small pockets of resistance and some snipers had still not been dealt with.

In a warehouse we found hundreds of sacks of rice commandeered from nearby villages, a light machine-gun, still in its packing case, which de la Taste quickly made ready for use, and a wooden crate full of condoms. I was searching the office of the Indian Independence League – another Japanese sponsored organisation – when an Indian soldier rushed in to say there was a Japanese in the cellar with a grenade in his hand. The pent-up rage of years overwhelmed me. I checked that there was a round in the breech of my rifle and went down into the cellar. When I climbed out I spent the next ten minutes looking for others and finding none. When I met up later in the day with Edgerley and his two companions, he said: "We hear you have blood on your hands." I did not have much of an appetite that evening.

For the next month Meiktila was under siege. The Japanese sustained their attacks on the airport on which we depended for supplies and shelled our positions at irregular intervals. During each bombardment we waited in our slit trenches until we heard the comforting bark of the 'Priests', our self-propelled 105 millimetre guns, which were never fired until the Japanese batteries had been located.

At my request my colleagues in the intelligence branch at 4 Corps had sent me a general questionnaire listing the types of information they wanted me to obtain. This included not only intelligence about the enemy's order of battle, intentions, positions and movements, but also topographical details – the condition of roads, tracks and bridges, fords, gradients and defiles as well as sources of water. This proved an invaluable check-list.

On 11 March I set up office in the village of Kyauktaing some miles to the west of our perimeter along the road to Kyaukpadaung. I had arranged for some of the rice we had found in the warehouse to be returned to Kyauktaing for distribution to other villages. The headman recruited half a dozen young men to work on my behalf. They provided a screen in the surrounding villages which served two purposes: first, to warn me of the approach of any Japanese and, secondly, to collect information about Japanese movements. This system provided a steady flow of news and informants. All that Colonel Keely had told me about Burmans was confirmed. They seemed to know at any given time in what direction they were walking and they calculated distances by the time it took to smoke one of their cigarettes. When I tried to explain an air photograph of Toungoo, one of our next objectives, to one informant, he was at a loss until I asked him what a pagoda would look like from above. He paused for a moment and then said: "A circle". He took another look at the photograph and cried out: "There it is; but you've got the picture the wrong way round." He immediately turned it until north on the photograph faced north on the ground. I learned my lesson and was careful in future to set photographs correctly.

Early in the morning of 25 March I received a message to go urgently to Kyauktaing. There I was introduced to a thick-set young man called Thakin Tha Hnin. He needed my help. The Anti Fascist League, consisting of the Burma National Army, under Aung San, and its civilian counterparts, under Thakin Soe, which had been supporting the Japanese hitherto, were to begin operations against the Japanese at 7 o'clock that evening. Tha Hnin gave me a copy of the orders issued to all units of the BNA and the civilian cells, together with the names of the leaders in upper, central and lower Burma. These orders included instructions to arrange recognition signals with British forces, to ask them for medical supplies, to arrange communications between guerilla bands with British help, and to spread the news among the population that the rising had begun.

I hurried back to report to General Cowan's staff who passed the news at once to corps headquarters. The general agreed that until the position was clarified I should maintain contact with Tha Hnin. The following day the general sent a personal message to corps headquarters noting the apparent determination of the Anti Fascist League and suggesting that they could be useful in disrupting Japanese communications. He said his intention was to wait for the League to prove itself and then offer help. He also asked that a liaison officer with background knowledge from Force 136 – the equivalent of the European Strategic Operations Executive – be attached to the division to help to coordinate the rising.

After several days of silence Major Boyt of Force 136 arrived. As a senior executive in Steel Brothers before the war, he had acquired an intimate knowledge of Burma. He disclosed that contact had been established some months earlier with Aung San with a view to persuading him to defect, but he could not enlighten us about policy towards the rising. We were not of course aware that this was the subject of bitter dispute at the highest political level, some arguing that Aung San was a traitor who should stand trial, others that we should exploit the opportunity and so hasten the defeat of the Japanese in Burma.

A few days later General Cowan decided to put the League to the test. This took the form of a night operation sweeping the territory between Meiktila and Thazi on the railway line to the east and destroying any enemy encountered. I was appointed examiner. The following morning I was able to report that the Burmese troops had carried out their orders to the letter, efficiently and in a disciplined manner. And we suffered no casualties. When General Cowan reported this success, the corps commander was moved to intervene with army headquarters. He pointed out that the addition of up to 10,000 Burman soldiers to our strength would give us the means to disrupt the Japanese effort on a greater scale than had been expected. He asked for a command and staff to organise the BNA to be attached at once to his headquarters. There was no reaction and Boyt and I continued to be the sole contact with the Burmans on this front.

One afternoon, while I was busy with interrogations, the villagers reported a large number of British troops approaching Kyauktaing from the direction of Meiktila. A British captain appeared. He had noticed our vehicle and had come to investigate. The air force had seen a detachment of Japanese entering a village a mile or so beyond Kyauktaing and his company of Gurkhas was due to attack them in about an hour. At this moment one of my young intelligence screen arrived with the same news. On a map he showed the captain where the Japanese were preparing a meal. I was invited to join the assault. At the appointed time a single shell landed short of the occupied village. The captain signalled a correction. Then the entire divisional artillery opened up for half a minute. As we moved forward we discovered that none of the Japanese had survived the bombardment.

A few days later, on our way back from Kyauktaing we found that the causeway beside Meiktila Lake, which we had to cross to reach our perimeter, was being shelled. The driver of another truck had pulled off the road and had taken cover behind the embankment. He signalled to Powell to do the same. The shells either landed on the near side of the causeway or passed over our heads. I decided to wait for a few minutes for a response from our own artillery. None came. So I applied the Read principle – 'bum on'. I told the driver of the other vehicle to follow one hundred yards behind us. Powell needed no encouragement to break the Fourteenth Army speed record. As we raced along the causeway, the shelling stopped. I have often wondered why.

❖

On 11 April the 5th Indian Division took over the lead from the 17th and my team operated with them in the same way as before. Before we set off from Meiktila, I went out to Kyauktaing to take leave of the people who had helped me, protected me and become my friends. In an impromptu ceremony the headman presented me with a silver-handled 'dah'; I use it to this day to keep down nettles and brambles.

The 5th Division made good ground. When from time to time the convoy was held up, Driver Powell displayed his special talent. He could smell a brew-up at a range of five hundred yards. One day, as we sipped hot tea, he asked if we had reached Japan yet. This was carrying optimism to the extreme.

As before, the fighter bombers of the 'cab-rank' provided air cover during the daylight hours. When the division halted for the night, the usual perimeter was formed. We would seek out a convenient place within it and immediately dig a slit trench long enough to accommodate the four of us. I had noticed that an education corps lieutenant was in the habit of parking his vehicle near ours and that, instead of digging a slit trench, he would lie on the ground reading. One morning, soon after first light, I went down to the road to get the latest news from division headquarters. A Japanese Zero fighter aircraft suddenly appeared, flying low and firing its machine-guns. Another followed immediately. I dived for the nearest cover – a burnt-out Japanese truck. The raid lasted no more than three or four minutes. Several of the division's trucks were destroyed and casualties inflicted. The 'cab-rank' appeared and I hurried back to see if our team was intact. It was, but I also found the education officer in the bottom of our slit-trench. I gave him an explicit account of what would happen to him if he did not dig his own slit trench in future. We never saw him again.

Information continued to flow in wherever we set up office. In one village inhabited largely by Indians, I learned that Subhas Chandra Bose, the inspiration of the pro-Japanese movement, had left only half an hour earlier. It was too late to give chase and, in retrospect, it was just as well he was not captured and that fate dealt with him otherwise. Not long afterwards his death in an air crash deprived him of martyrdom.

On 25 April the 17th Division resumed the lead. Pegu was the next objective. Three days later the third of my special wartime encounters took place. We had left the main road and were approaching a village on foot when I saw several figures in khaki emerge from trees at the other end of a paddy field. Japanese uniforms were khaki, ours were olive green. We took cover. As the figures came closer we realised they were British prisoners still wearing the uniforms in which they had been captured three years earlier. We ran forward to greet them. At this point some British signallers arrived in a truck with three Japanese prisoners in the back. One of the signallers gave a young Scottish private a cigarette, pointed to the Japanese prisoners and said: "I suppose you would like half an hour alone with one of those." "No" was the reply; "I wouldn't treat anyone the way they treated us."

❖

The monsoon broke early and we were still some way from Pegu. When we did move in, we prepared for the last lap – the drive to Rangoon. I visited corps headquarters to seek fresh instructions and ran into Colonel Holbrook who, months earlier, had disputed Ken Boome's assessment of the value of intelligence from civilian sources. "Well, Maitland" he said, "and what have you been doing with yourself?" How's that for man management, I thought.

General Cowan sent his aide-de-camp to Calcutta to fetch cases of gin for the celebrations when we entered the capital. No one was more dismayed than the general when we learned that Rangoon had been taken by a combined paratroop drop and sea-borne landing and that we had to remain in Pegu, where we disconsolately consumed the gin. His division had been in continuous action since 1942 and General Slim had intended that he would have the honour of leading the Fourteenth Army into Rangoon. Slim would also have had it in mind that, at the height of the battle for Meiktila, Cowan had learned of the death of his son, an officer, as he himself had been, with his beloved Gurkhas.

Our corps was transferred to the newly created Twelfth Army. The remaining problem was the remnants of the Japanese army in the Pegu Yomas to the west. These were doomed men. Beri-beri was rife, they were being harried by the BNA guerillas and the paddy fields between their positions in the hills and the line of the river and railway which we held were flooded. Worse, in June a Japanese operation order was captured. When the Japanese broke out, the scale of the slaughter appalled even one hardened sergeant. He came down in tears from his position on a bank from which he had been firing his Bren gun, desperate for a moment's relief from the carnage. Stragglers were shown no mercy. A local villager, one of many thousands who had suffered at the hands of the Japanese military police, came to my office in Pegu with a small cloth bundle. When he opened this four severed right hands fell to the floor. "Kempei Tai", he said. He wanted blood money. When the battle was over twelve thousand Japanese had been killed; our losses were ninety-five dead and some three hundred wounded.

We were still in Pegu when the war ended. My team was disbanded. Ken Boome, who throughout had been an understanding and supportive chief, sent me for a week of rest and recuperation in the former hill station of Maymyo, where we were welcomed by recently arrived members of the Women's Voluntary Service. Swimming, tennis, dances and forgotten delicacies were the order of the day. On my return I was posted to the headquarters of Allied Land Forces at Kandy in Ceylon to await my turn for repatriation. On 24 October 1945, with a group of others, I left Kandy for Colombo. Our kit – mine including the portable gramophone and my still intact box of records – was loaded on to a lighter which was to take us out to the *Athlone Castle* anchored in the bay. As we drew near we were puzzled by a white line along the main deck. Then someone shouted: "My God. It's Wrens." We cheered our heads off.

On board the *Athlone Castle* homecoming was uppermost in our thoughts. And after that, what?

As the weather stayed fair, I slept on deck every night until we reached Southampton on Armistice Day, 1945. Some ludicrous regulation required all officers to report to their regimental depot before going on leave. The adjutant of the Royal Scots at Glencorse Barracks outside Edinburgh gave me a drink and sent me straight back to Waverley Station to catch the night train south, my parents having moved to Berkshire some months earlier. My father met me at Camberley station and took me to our new home. My mother, who had devoted herself to her work at the Scottish headquarters of the Women's Voluntary Service, looked tired. Over the next few days I learned something of the hardships neither she nor my father had mentioned in their letters. She began to tell me about my school and university friends. I had no idea so many had been lost or maimed. This caused me great distress. I said to her: "What I did was nothing. They gave their lives." "Yes," she said, "they gave their lives. You offered yours."

3

Rock, Domes and Desert

Three and a half years' absence had left me unprepared for conditions, attitudes and expectations in immediate post-war Britain. Physically and psychologically exhausted, the nation seemed to face three enormous tasks – rebuilding the economy; carrying through a social revolution; and assuming a major role, alongside the United States, in fashioning a new world order. It was in this context that I had to lay plans for the future.

So much had happened since I left university that any ambition I might have had to become a searcher for truth in the groves of academe had long since been extinguished. Colonel Shaw in AG 23 – the branch which looked after military intelligence at the War Office – wanted me to make a career in the army. My second brother, Alastair, and Robert Dundas, our favourite older cousin, both of whom were already well established in the Foreign Service, wanted me to join them. I was in two minds, but there was no need for an early decision. My age group – I was twenty-two when Japan surrendered – was required to remain in the army for the best part of another year, so the immediate issue was how best to occupy the interval.

Colonel Shaw suggested that, since I had read Spanish as well as French at university, I could usefully head the intelligence section at the rather grandly named Fortress Headquarters at Gibraltar. This was a military establishment separate from the office of the Governor in The Convent. There I would join the compact staff of Brigadier Vale, the Fortress Commander, and work under his chief of staff, Colonel Douglas. Another embarkation on the Clyde, followed by another storm. The sea was so rough that one night in the Bay of Biscay the *Nea Hellas*, known to its crew with a mixture of affection and contempt as the 'Nellie Wallace', had to heave to. The piano rolling backwards and forwards across the saloon kept us all awake.

Gibraltar in 1946 seemed largely untouched by the war. Food was abundant, social life active and Spain and Morocco were within easy reach. My ostensible task was to keep an eye on what the Spanish armed forces were doing in the Campo de Gibraltar – the territory facing the Rock. But, since there was no evidence that anything in particular was happening or was likely to happen in the Campo, Colonel Douglas filled my time with a miscellany of other tasks – arranging programmes of entertainment for visiting ships of foreign navies, an inter-service shooting match, or taking the diplomatic bag to the British consular offices in Málaga or Tangier.

When I studied Spanish at school and university, the civil war and then the second world war had ruled out any visit to Spain. Now I had the chance to test my long-distance perceptions against reality. In Andalucía there was, of course, no problem in finding castanets, 'zapateado' and flamenco. Nor olives and cork trees, nylon-stockinged 'penitentes' in Holy Week; nor bull-fights at the climax of the fiesta. The beauty of the landscape was as striking as the modest life-style of the country folk and the elegance of the local aristocracy. Further north, on the 'meseta', the miles and miles of sweeping 'horizontal plains' were exactly as Pérez Galdos had decribed them.

Colonel Douglas had business with the British Embassy in Madrid and asked me to accompany him. Over breakfast at the Gran Vía Hotel he said he wanted to visit some shops before going to the Embassy and would be grateful if I could interpret for him. I knew that he was a keen yachtsman but had not expected that his shopping list would begin with 'bull-nosed pliers' and 'waterproof gold-leaf'. While he was at the Embassy I visited the Prado. In the Velasquez gallery *Las Meninas* was placed in a special compartment in such a way that one saw it first in a mirror. As I was looking at it, a captain in the Spanish Army joined me. After a few minutes he said: "I come here every week. It is said that if you watch for long enough they will move." By good luck I left the Goya section to the end; I found his war etchings more disturbing than I had imagined.

One of my colleagues in headquarters was married to a Spaniard and had long-standing connections with the sherry producers and other entrepreneurs in Andalucía. He suggested that I call on friends of his on one of the bag-carrying trips to Málaga. These were a recently retired RAF squadron leader and his wife who had bought a small hotel on the coast; and they would like to offer me lunch. I followed the careful directions I had been given and found the hotel on the approach to the village I had been told to look out for. The hotel buildings and swimming pool seemed to have been cut out of the cliffs overlooking a sparkling white beach. The situation was breathtaking. During lunch the squadron leader asked about my future plans; would I consider working in Spain? He was convinced that this particular region, which had been neglected in the past, offered good prospects and he could do with a partner. I agreed to think this over. But, as I left the hotel and continued through the village of Torremolinos on my way to Málaga, I was sure my answer would be no. I suppose reaching that conclusion cost me a fortune.

With colleagues I visited Ceuta, Tetuan and Tangier, where the favourite cousin Robert was acting Consul-General. An accomplished linguist, he encouraged me to learn Arabic, given Britain's important economic interests in the Middle East and the fact that we had deeper knowledge of the region than the Americans. His parish, the city of Tangier, did its best to live up to its reputation as an international centre for café society, stimulated by the occasional presence of Barbara Hutton. In the souks the traders did their bit. The proprietor of a leather goods stall dismissed the lurking urchins with a shout of 'imshi' and then turned to the tourists: "C'est bien fabriqué, y además no es expensive."

On the return voyage by ferry from one of my official trips to Tangier, I was standing by the rail with the diplomatic bag between my legs when I smelt burning. Looking down I saw that the bag was smouldering. Someone further along the deck had thrown away a cigarette which the wind had blown back. I stamped out the fire and took the bag to the captain who gave me another container in which I was able to seal the diplomatic bag. But not before I had noticed that what had been smouldering was a wad of Spanish banknotes. That evening I delivered the bag to the Governor's office in The Convent, together with a report on the fire, and returned to Fortress Headquarters to await the reaction. There was none.

My brother Alastair in the Foreign Office told me that applications were being invited for a one-year course at the Middle East Centre for Arab Studies in Jerusalem. This was due to begin in September 1946. This centre had been established two years earlier by the Foreign Office who foresaw a greatly increased need for Arabic speakers in a variety of fields after the war. The ever-solicitous Colonel Shaw, who still wanted me to remain in the army, also encouraged me to take advantage of this opportunity and sent in an application on my behalf. This was accepted and I arranged for my release from the army to be deferred for a year so that I could complete the course at the Middle East Centre. A few weeks later I received a signal from Shaw saying that my application had now been rejected on the grounds that there were 'better qualified applicants'. A little research on his part established that no other applicant had read modern languages at university. He never told me precisely what use he made of this intelligence, but the consequence was a further signal after some anxious weeks to the effect that circumstances had changed and room could after all be found for one more student. By now time was short. Shaw managed to find a replacement for me at Fortress

Headquarters and I sailed for the Middle East at the end of August, one week before the course was due to begin.

The Austrian Hospice, which housed the Centre, was a substantial building in the Old City of Jerusalem at the junction of the Via Dolorosa and the Damascus Road. On the opposite side of the Via was a small coffee house from which, for eighteen out of the twenty-four hours, arose an aroma of arabica and a steady murmur of conversation. Nearby was the Sixth Station of the Cross, where Veronica wiped the face of Jesus. At regular intervals groups of tourists would stop there while their guide pointed them in the right direction and said: "Kodachrome; a fiftieth at f eleven." My room looked on to a cluster of small houses where mothers with small children seemed interminably engaged in washing and drying clothes. The Austrian nuns were still in residence and looked after us with quiet efficiency and loving concern for our well-being. I was elected mess secretary for the first term of the course and had daily dealings with Sister Liliosor, a latter-day angel who was in charge of the kitchen. What could have been a chore was unalloyed pleasure.

By the time everyone had reached Jerusalem we totalled twenty-three students, of whom the majority were still in the armed services. Four had recently joined the Sudan Political Service, one was a new entrant to the Foreign Service and others came from the British Council, the Colonial Service and BOAC. The Director of the Centre was Colonel Bertram Thomas, who had made his name in 1930 by completing a courageous journey across the Empty Quarter of Arabia – the first European to do so. He had subsequently served as Wazir to the Sultan of Oman. During the first two courses at the Centre the Principal Instructor had been Major Aubrey Eban, who later achieved international distinction as Abba Eban, the immensely articulate foreign minister of Israel. His successor was an academic historian, George Kirk, an authority on recent Middle Eastern history, who however did not know Arabic.

Responsibility for language instruction was delegated to a handful of Palestinian Christians, some of them with experience as schoolteachers. They were in their element teaching us the Arabic script and the fundamentals of grammar. But some of them found it hard to respond to our demand at a later stage for instruction in the kind of Arabic we expected to use in our future work. Story books for young Arab children were of limited appeal and even less use. 'Would that I Were a Cat!' was not an ambition I was ever called upon to express in several years living and working with Arabs.

While we felt reasonably secure in the Old City, we had to be on our guard when we wanted to penetrate the New City. A few weeks before our arrival in Jerusalem the Irgun Zwai Leumi had bombed the

King David Hotel, killing over ninety of the occupants. Public buildings and military posts were protected with barbed wire and sandbags. We were required to move about in civilian clothes and in pairs and, later, at least one of us had to carry a concealed pistol. Nonetheless social life continued. With a fellow student I called by invitation on Mrs Vester, described by Sir Ronald Storrs as 'that charming and great-hearted leader of the American Colony'. She had lived for over sixty years in Jerusalem. Jemal Pasha, Allenby and Storrs himself had been among her friends and she had been hostess to almost all of those who had left their mark on the Near East. We did not discover what had brought her father to Jerusalem in the first place, whether it was a proselytising or commercial mission. The ungenerous said that the Vesters came to Jerusalem to do good and did very well. Whatever the facts, we spent an agreeable and instructive hour or so at her feet.

A notice was posted in the Centre advertising a Voigtländer camera for five pounds. The name of the advertiser was Petrie. I responded and was invited to tea. My hostess was Lady Flinders Petrie, widow of the archaeologist. She explained that she was in the middle of packing up to return to England and had been sorting out her late husband's belongings. She did not need the camera herself and would be pleased if it could be put to good use somewhere in the Middle East. I was privileged to be shown a selection of archaeological photographs dating back many years. Among these was a picture of a lunch party at a dig. I thought I recognised the face of T. E. Lawrence. "Quite right," she said, "the best-read and most interesting young man I have ever met."

Bertram Thomas, who took little interest in our studies, called on members of his wide circle of contacts to come to the Centre to lecture. In this way our horizons were undoubtedly widened and, over drinks and dinner, we were able to talk with a number of personalities who had hitherto been no more than names. The Patriarch of the Armenian Orthodox Church explained the roles of the various churches in protecting Christian holy places; we were glad to have an authoritative guide to help us through this particular maze. We had expected a panegyric about the Arabs from Glubb Pasha and were surprised not only by his objectivity, but also by his well-researched assessment of the prospects for the entire region. This unassuming man, held in high esteem in many parts of the Arab world, invited us to call on him should we ever need assistance or advice.

My good fortune lay in the friends I made. John Rae[1] was at that time a recruit to the British Council. Peter Tripp[2] had joined the Sudan Political Service. Both had served in the Royal Marines during the war. What brought us together was a common desire to take full advantage of the opportunities the Centre offered. In the late afternoon one or other would knock on the door: "Up and down the Mount

of Olives before tea?" "Of course". And we went further afield – to
Bethlehem, Hebron, Haifa and Acre, Nazareth, the Dead Sea – and
spent an unforgettable weekend in a monastery overlooking the north
western shore of Lake Tiberias. It was not difficult to imagine those
muscular Galilean fishermen unloading their drafts of fish on that same
shore many centuries earlier. All these were rewarding experiences; the
dictum was proving to be true that no one can leave the Holy Land
unaffected.

❖

Over the Christmas holiday spent skiing in Lebanon, I reached a
conclusion. By this time I had learned enough about the Middle
East to know that there were important interests in the region to
protect and further. Earlier I had seen deprivation and disease and the
consequences of hatred and war in several parts of the world. These and
other considerations persuaded me to apply to join the Foreign Service.
Correspondence with London suggested that I would be called upon to
sit the entrance examination in the autumn when the present course at
the Middle East Centre ended. Events were to alter this timetable.

Nineteen forty-seven began with the news that my mother's work
for the Women's Voluntary Service in Scotland during the war had been
recognised in the New Year's honours. Good news on the home front at
least. Later in January, after a brief lull, the terrorist campaign in Palestine
resumed. The Stern Gang sought to emulate the Irgun's bombing of
the King David Hotel by attacking a police compound at Haifa. They
inflicted severe casualties. Later in the month two British civilians were
kidnapped as hostages for a terrorist who had been condemned to death.
Although the hostages were set free after an ultimatum from the High
Commissioner, the authorities felt obliged to heed a warning from the
terrorists of a 'bloodbath' if the condemned man were executed. On 31
January the High Commissioner ordered the evacuation of all British
women, children and other non-essential personnel. The British staff
and students at the Centre fell into the third category.

We faced a crisis. In normal circumstances the Centre would have
closed in the Spring for six weeks while the students went to different
parts of the Middle East on a 'language break' before returning for the
final term. It was decided to bring the break forward, send all students
out of Palestine immediately and meanwhile try to find an alternative
location. Each of us had to draw up a plan. We were told to send our
destination addresses and any subsequent addresses to the administration
office which would remain in Jerusalem in the charge of a Palestinian
member of the staff. Together with two others I opted for the familiar
ground of Iraq. We had to wait a few days in Haifa for army transport
to Mafraq, in what was then Transjordan. There we boarded a bus
belonging to the Nairn company which ran a cross-desert service. This

was one of the coldest and most uncomfortable overland journeys I have ever undertaken. After eighteen hours we reached the outskirts of Baghdad where we left the bus to freshen up to the extent possible at a rest camp. We then made our way to the British Embassy where we were to call on Stewart Perowne, the Oriental Counsellor. He was on the telephone when we entered his office. He looked up, put his hand over the microphone and asked: "Hunt on Sunday?" Two of us indicated dissent. I left a request with his secretary to forward my mail to an address which I would send as soon as I was settled. Then my non-hunting companion and I retreated to the RAF station at Habbaniya to recover from the journey across the desert and take stock.

The following night I returned to Baghdad and took the night train to Basra, where I called at the Consulate-General to explain my problem and my plan. The vice-consul thought that the Director of the British Institute was best placed to help. This was a sound judgment. Reginald Keight offered me token employment as a teacher of matriculation students to begin with and said he would consult his friend the chief of police about my idea of staying with an Arab family. The chief of police was adamant. No respectable family would take a British man into their household. Gossip would be vicious. If there were daughters in the house it would be said I had my eye on them; if not, that I had my eye on the wife. I found a room at the YMCA instead.

Thanks to Reg and Enid Keight my prospects improved rapidly. Opportunities for speaking Arabic multiplied and their friends among the members of the British community were generous with their hospitality. One morning Harry Fletcher, the information officer at the Consulate-General, had a brain wave. Every few days his cinema truck would visit villages in the Basra district to show Arabic newsreels and documentaries about Britain. The truck was due to visit the village of Hamdan, some ten miles south of Basra, that evening; would I like to accompany the team? Badri Yusuf, one of his locally engaged staff, would be delighted to introduce me to some of the village notables. Would I be willing to make a short speech in Arabic about the work of the Middle East Centre?

This was too serious a challenge to decline. I spent part of the afternoon drafting my speech and memorising it. Badri Yusuf suggested a few changes and then made me rehearse it twice. Within a few minutes of our arrival at Hamdan the screen had been erected and the truck parked with the projector facing it. Half a dozen villagers watched the preparations with growing interest. When the operator began to play gramophone records, the palm groves suddenly seethed with life. People appeared from all directions – by boat along the creek, by taxi, by bus and on foot – until there must have been one hundred and fifty folk clustered in the clearing. Badri commented with assumed nonchalance that this was about normal for one of his shows. A microphone appeared magically from inside the truck and Badri introduced me. As I finished my speech with the customary 'peace upon you', a great shout went up from one hundred and fifty throats: 'and on you peace'. It was dark and nobody saw how moved I was.

Harry Fletcher had another idea. It was time, he said, for another visit with the cinema van to his Reading Room in Nasiriya, the capital of the Muntafiq province. Nasiriya is situated on the Euphrates ninety miles north west of Basra. I welcomed Harry's suggestion that I join the party. We made an early start in the biting cold and, after leaving the date gardens and tamarisk groves behind, followed the railway line across the desert. We arrived in Nasiriya shortly before one o'clock and immediately called on the 'mutasarrif' (provincial governor), Abdul Rahman Jaudat, a distinguished looking man of wide interests. The afternoon was spent paying innumerable calls, each of which required us to consume at least one cup of coffee and one glass of sweet tea. In the early evening Badri set up the screen and, before the film show began, I delivered a fuller version of my Hamdan speech, this time to an audience of some fifteen hundred townsfolk. We spent the night in the municipal guest house and left after breakfast for Suq al-Shuyukh, a market town and district headquarters an hour's drive downstream from Nasiriya and on the edge of the Hor al Hammar, the great marsh area which extends eastwards to the Tigris south of Amara.

Another round of calls. This time I stopped counting after fourteen glasses of tea and nineteen of coffee. After lunch with the district commissioner we boarded a motor launch which was to take us to the house of Risan al Gasad, the sheikh of the Hacham tribe. As we left the Euphrates we travelled along shallow, palm-lined creeks with rapids here and there until we reached the marshes proper. These consisted of a vast expanse of water broken by dense clumps of reeds and occasional narrow tongues of land on which were perched the reed huts that were the homes of the tribesmen and their families. We passed several skiffs from which young men and boys were fishing with spears, and groups of water buffalo knee-deep in the mud-red water. Spring flowers sprouted from the banks only an inch or two above the water and herons and kingfishers showed off their skills. After an hour we reached a brick-built house – the only one in the area and, accordingly, a source of great pride to the sheikh. Here we were to spend the night. The sheikh had arranged an hour's shooting. This was not a success; we saw no birds and were bitten by the insects which swarmed a foot or two above water level. A skiff took us to pay our respects to Sheikh Risan's brother at his guest-house, a remarkable structure of near-cathedral dimensions made entirely of reeds, the curved matting roof being supported by elegant arches. After tea and coffee we sat on the water's edge and talked as the sun set.

On returning to the brick house we found our host in a drunken stupor. The evening meal was served in a large hall. In the light of the oil-lamps I could just distinguish up to fifty men of the Hacham tribe sitting cross-legged with their backs to the walls. On the floor in the centre of the hall was a tray fully four feet in diameter heaped with rice at the angle of repose on top of which lay a whole sheep – a *quzi*. Two smaller dishes flanked the centrepiece and around these were scores of plates heaped with chicken, mutton, vegetables, rice, spices and various sweetmeats. This display was surrounded by cushions on which we were invited to sit. As we did so, twenty-five of the shadowy figures stepped forward and began to eat in silence. One by one and then in groups these withdrew when they had finished eating and were replaced by others from among the remaining twenty-five.

Chatter went on into the night. I was wakened by the clinking of tea glasses at six o'clock and we left the brick house soon after to return to Suq al-Shuyukh.

The rest of that day was the most enjoyable part of our excursion to the Muntafiq. The commander of the infantry battalion stationed at Nasiriya had invited us to spend the afternoon and evening with him. Colonel Afram Hindu, a fair-haired Christian, was noted for his efficiency. In a dressing room in his barracks we found riding clothes and boots laid out for us. Horses were waiting outside, together with an escort of a dozen or so of his men, mounted and carrying shotguns across their shoulders. We rode for an hour and a half along the bank of the Euphrates, through palm groves and vegetable gardens, until the bank widened and we could let our horses gallop. Further on two soldiers were waiting for us with a skiff. We handed over our horses to the escort in exchange for the shotguns. After the duck shoot, tea in the mess, another cinema show and dinner with Afram Hindu and his charming Syrian wife, also a Christian, and her sister.

Another surprise awaited us the following day. We visited the district of Shatra, forty minutes' drive north of Nasiriya and, after calling on two sheikhs who seemed none too pleased to see us, we lunched with the commissioner. Doctor Hussain Kubba had travelled widely in Europe. He studied psychology for five years in Germany and spoke English and French in addition to Arabic and German. Over lunch he quoted Lamartine. I wondered what on earth he could have done to deserve his posting to Shatra.

For some weeks I had received no mail from home. The Embassy in Baghdad claimed that none had arrived. Having exchanged telegrams with my parents, I asked the Embassy to make another search. This produced an abject apology and the following day a package of letters arrived at the YMCA. I went early to bed to read them. First, I learned about power cuts and the unusual severity of the winter. Then my mother's letters were written in pencil from hospital in Reading. I read on with growing alarm. The bravery of her words could not disguise the pain the cancer was causing her. Two days later the Consulate-General at Basra received a telegram from my brother Alastair in the Foreign Office asking me to return home at once. Reg Keight and other friends set about raising funds to enable me to buy a ticket on a KLM flight leaving Basra that night. Then another telegram reached me at the YMCA. This said that the War Office had authorised my immediate return home because my mother was dangerously ill. Soon after this the RAF at Habbaniya telephoned to say that, if I could get there by noon the following day, the Commander-in-Chief Far East, who would be staging there, would gladly offer me a place on his aircraft.

Two days later the C-in-C deposited me at Lyneham. I had arrived in time; the family were together at the end. My mother exhausted herself in the service of others. Under the rules of the Colonial Service my father had had to spend eighteen months out of every two years in Africa. For them both this was sacrifice enough. But this also meant that my mother was left to bring up the four sons virtually single-handed. So long as she felt we needed her, she allowed herself no other life, and nothing she taught us was without its worth. Now my father faced yet another separation and his well-being became a major preoccupation for all four sons.

The Civil Service Commission took advantage of my presence in England to arrange for me to take the entrance examination for the Foreign Service. One of the essay subjects was: "Do you believe in immortality?"

❖

Meanwhile, Bertram Thomas had re-established the Middle East Centre in a corner of the camp of the Transjordan Frontier Force at Zerqa, north of Amman. Each student had a ridge tent of the type known in India as EPIP – Eight Person Indian Pattern. Two of these were erected side by side to serve as mess. The teaching routine was the same as in Jerusalem, except that a degree of specialisation was introduced to cater for our different future requirements.

I arrived about a week late for the start of the new term to a sympathetic welcome from John Rae and Peter Tripp. They had incidentally been pressing their suits and were both on the point of becoming engaged. At our encampment at Zerqa there was of course no 'up and down the Mount of Olives before tea'. Instead the three of us met each evening after completing our studies to talk over cups of Turkish coffee. The final examinations were on our mind as well as our future prospects.

The desert landscape in which we were encamped stimulated interest in T. E. Lawrence's account of the Arab Revolt and a group of us decided to visit Wadi Rum during the next break in our studies. On midsummer's day five of us set off from Zerqa. We had taken Glubb Pasha at his word. He arranged for our travel to Aqaba and had also provided camels and a guide for the trip to Wadi Rum. At Amman the train reversed out of the station for half a mile to give itself room for a run at the steep incline which carried the line from the valley on to the surrounding plateau. The carriages of the Hejaz Railway proved unexpectedly cool and dust-free. Hours dragged by, reminding us of the vastness of the desert. Since the service operated only once a week the infrequent stops at isolated villages created a carnival atmosphere.

After over eight hours we reached Ma'an where we inspected the fort and the remains of the trenches the Turks had dug in their effort to check the Arab advance in 1918. The following morning a truck of the Arab Legion arrived to take us to Quweira and on to Aqaba. For some time we continued on the desert plain. Then we turned a corner where the plateau fell away into a wide valley of white and pink scrub-covered sand, broken on all sides by mountains of extraordinary shape and colour. Two of our party unloaded their kit at Quweira. They intended to penetrate Wadi Rum from the north while the remaining three of us drove on to Aqaba, where we camped on the shore in a hut of grass and palm leaves.

Two days later Edward Henderson,[3] who was an officer in the Arab Legion, and I rose early to pack the kit, food and water we were to take with us to Wadi Rum. At five o'clock 'Auda bin Howeitat, who was to be our guide, arrived with three camels as promised by Glubb Pasha, and by half past we were on our way. The going uphill was easy. After four hours we reached the junction of the tracks from Quweira and Rum and turned east along a narrow valley. At noon the heat of the sun and the need to rest our camels obliged us to halt. 'Auda hobbled the camels, prepared a brushwood fire and in a few minutes served us hot, sweet tea from a pot which seemed never to empty.

We had our midday meal here and started off again at three o'clock. By now my legs where they crossed in front of the hump were becoming bruised and the backs of my hands, which I could not easily protect as I held the rein, were beginning to blister in the sun. At five o'clock we entered the mountain fantasy we had seen three days earlier from the road to Quweira. Sheer cliffs rose seven, eight hundred feet to reach a gnarled, knotted summit. As the sun began to set we turned into Wadi Rum. The floor of the valley was about a mile wide and on either side two long parallel lines of mountains rose steeply, their faces split into slabs of red and brown and white. In Lawrence's words we were dwarfed by the 'whelming greatness of Rum'. Without a word we put our camels into a trot and raced the last long miles to the police post. By now the moon was high and bright, the sky blue velvet.

We dismounted at a quarter to eight, unloaded the camels and joined our hosts inside the post. We had been over fourteen hours on the way and eleven in the saddle. My body ached so that I could hardly move and my hands were severely burnt. But our hosts wanted to talk and nearly two hours passed before eggs and bread appeared. Edward and I rose at half past four and were ready to move off on our return journey within an hour. Sleep had proved a wonderful restorative; the aches had almost all gone. But our hosts were in no hurry to let us go and it was not until eight o'clock, when the sun was already high that we were able to leave.

As we wanted to be well on our way before noon we decided to trot. I had not reckoned on the discomfort of trotting downhill. The camel saddle consisted of a rigid V-shaped wooden frame, covered by a mat, with a short wooden pillar at front and back. Although we had padded the saddles with blankets and pillows, the jolting revived all the aches and pains of the previous day and induced others. At noon we stopped for two hours under the sheer face of Jebel Kara at the exit from Wadi Rum. Then the agony began again. When we reached the track junction at five o'clock we stopped once more. We found some shade and rested our aching bodies and our patient camels. As we drank 'Auda's sweet tea, we decided to press on to Aqaba that evening. Half an hour later we began to feel the sea air from the Gulf of Aqaba on our cheeks. Our spirits rose.

At the seventy-fifth mile I began to sing. I sang all the songs that came to mind. I dropped behind my two companions. Then I sang the Twenty-third Psalm, much loved by my mother. I felt disembodied; the pain seemed to drain away. Some weeks after my mother died I had told my father that the days of mortal separation were ended and that she would be with us wherever we might be. I believed then that this was true; now I was convinced.

I watched the sun set behind Sinai. In the moonlight we saw the corner of the Gulf. Another half hour and then, after eighty-four miles and twenty hours in the saddle, we sat on the beach sipping delicious tea and exchanging experiences with our three companions until the moon had set.

❖

In the middle of July I received a curious request to go to Cairo for an interview with a representative of the Civil Service Commission. Ronald Searight of Anglo-Egyptian Oilfields, who happened to be in Transjordan at the time, offered to fly me to Egypt. Breakfasting on the terrace of the Continental Savoy Hotel in Cairo, I recognised St John Philby at another table. In 1930 he had crossed the Empty Quarter a few months after Bertram Thomas, and in the opposite direction. I introduced myself. He was most interested in the Middle East Centre of which he was only vaguely aware. But what impressed me was that he spoke charitably about all his fellow orientalists and modestly about his own achievements.

John Rae had asked me to deliver a letter to his beloved Nonie, who worked in the British Embassy. There I was introduced to Mary Grepe in the ambassador's office – an encounter which was to prove of great significance. We arranged to dine together. After cocktails on the terrace of the Continental Savoy, I called a taxi. At this point a policeman on duty at the hotel stepped forward and insisted on travelling with us to the restaurant. Throughout dinner he remained in view and again sat in the front seat of the taxi as I delivered Mary to the House of the Palm and then returned to the hotel. When I asked for an explanation he said, with what he no doubt intended to be a knowing look, that it was the duty of the police to protect Colonel Lawrence whenever he visited Egypt.

The Civil Service interview was equally enigmatic. I was asked a number of questions about my papers in the written examination and about the Arabic course. Two weeks later I received a summons to appear before the Civil Service Selection Board immediately after my return from Zerqa. The final examinations at the Centre took place late in August, I sailed from Port Said a week later and arrived in England in the first week of September.

The so-called 'country house weekend' at Stoke d'Abernon in Surrey, part of the civil service selection process, was less of an ordeal than I had feared. This was due entirely to the personalities and skill of the examining staff. The final selection board was more intimidating. Alone on one side of a long, wide table facing a dozen or so of one's distinguished elders and instructed by a discreet card to 'speak up', was not the most comfortable situation. Questioning was insistent, much of it inspired by what one had written in the examination, or said at the country house weekend. When the interview was finished I was asked to wait outside. Presently an elderly figure emerged. He had not spoken throughout the interview, but I was conscious that he had never taken his eyes off me. I recognised him as Sir David Scott, who had formerly held a senior administrative post in the Foreign Office. He said he had been upset to hear of my mother's death; she had done wonderful work during the war. He had read my essay on immortality with close interest. Then, with a gesture towards the interview room, he said: "Oh yes, and that went all right."

The day after I was demobilised in October 1947, I began work in the Egyptian Department of the Foreign Office. The six years spent in the army were for me a critical part of what the French felicitously call one's 'formation'. I benefited in different ways. Despite its size, the wartime army was a remarkably well-run organisation. I was taught ordered processes of thought which have proved their worth time and again, and I still find it awkward to discuss a problem when the objective to be achieved has not been defined. I learned much from experience, and from my elders, about the structure of our society and the place of the individual in it. Early on I discovered responsibility for others. I made numerous friendships, many of which have endured. And I met in their own environment and on their own terms peoples of different races, religions and traditions. I saw that what could be achieved through national unity, magnificent though it was, did not compare with the possibilities of international action. If I was exalted by these revelations, how much more was I humbled by what I had seen of human wretchedness. Altogether these experiences yielded a dividend to be prized – and one to be set against the tragedy, horror and anger of war.

4

Nile Waters

I had not expected to be assigned to a desk in Cubicle D on the third floor. During the war temporary accommodation had been installed in various parts of the Foreign Office to house extra staff. This was still in use in 1947 and some of it was occupied by junior members of the Egyptian Department. My immediate superior was some distance away. Exchanging papers took time and there was little opportunity for education through osmosis in the ways of the Foreign Office.

At five o'clock each afternoon the eight members of the department assembled to exchange news and views in the office of the head, Dan Lascelles.[1] Tea was prepared by the two personal assistants, known in those days as departmental ladies. Lascelles was a reserved man with a reputation for devouring foreign languages in the same way as the aardvark devours ants; he was already competent in fourteen.

The filing system was quite different from that used by the army. Each paper, whether it originated in the Foreign Office or came from elsewhere, was 'entered' into its own file cover, known as a jacket. Minutes could be written on the front and inside of the jacket and, if necessary, extra sheets could be inserted for additional minutes. Copies of any letters or telegrams issued in response to the original paper would be put into the same jacket. The virtue of this system was its flexibility; files could be made up of as many or as few papers as were relevant and held together by red tape. The department's papers were kept by the corresponding registry, known as division. All of our papers in the Egyptian department bore the initial letter J. Our registry was J division and many of its members felt as closely committed to the success of the department's efforts as we did.

My area of responsibility was Egypt and the Sudan. Others in the department covered Ethiopia and what were then the former Italian colonies in north and éast Africa. When the department's portfolio was extended in 1948 to include the countries of the Maghreb, its name was changed to African Department. The context in which we worked was the world-wide process of decolonisation stimulated by the grant of independence to India and Pakistan in 1947. So far as Egypt was concerned, our relations were influenced by Egyptian impatience to achieve complete independence. Under the treaty signed in 1936 Britain retained the right to station troops on Egyptian territory; this rankled. The Egyptians also claimed, but with little justification, that the people of the Sudan, which had been an Anglo-Egyptian Condominium since 1899 and administered in practice by the British since 1924, wanted union with Egypt. Egypt's ambitions were sharpened by the growth of Arab nationalism. Relations were placed under further stress by the war that followed the creation of Israel in 1948, in which a young colonel, Gamal Abdul Nasser, distinguished himself during the siege of Falluja. Attempts by London and Cairo to renegotiate the terms of the treaty and to give the Sudanese people a greater share in the government of their country made slow and painful progress.

❖

During my first few months in London I stayed in a bed-sitting room in Notting Hill Gate. My landlord, former captain Jurczinski, had been an officer in General Sikorski's army and was married to a Canadian. On returning in the evenings I occasionally found him haranguing a group of other Polish exiles, presumably former officers like himself. I admired the dignity with which these victims of Yalta faced their uncertain future. The accommodation in Ladbroke Grove was spartan and life during the week was not diverting. I was at my desk about nine o'clock in the morning and it was usually after seven before we had cleared our desks. The five-day week had not yet been invented and we worked on Saturdays until lunch-time.

My fortunes changed when Ian Bell[2] and his wife Ruth made a useful discovery. Ian's main responsibility in the department was Ethiopia. He had spent a number of adventurous years in South America, had published a book of poems and he painted. He and Ruth lived with their young family in Hampstead and they heard of a woman with a theatrical background who ran a guest house for young people in the early years of their careers in nearby Kidderpore Avenue. I took the first available vacancy. This intervention by Ian and Ruth began a life-long friendship. Ruth's mother lived in Devon and I spent a delightful summer holiday with the Bell family in Chudleigh. We hired horses and rode along the lanes in the morning and in the afternoon Ian instructed me in the use of pastels.

Meanwhile, the department had been rehoused. The cubicles were abandoned and all of us except Dan Lascelles and his deputy, known as the assistant, who had their own offices, moved into a large room overlooking Downing Street. This was a reversion to the traditional Foreign Office arrangement whereby the junior secretaries who have been known, since American terminology was adopted, as desk officers, occupied the Third Room.

One of my tasks was to coordinate instructions for the British Government representative on the board of the Suez Canal Company. He owed his influential position to the Government's large shareholding. Ronald Fraser, the minister in charge of economic affairs in the British embassy in Paris, kept us regularly informed about company business and was adept at anticipating problems, whether over adjustments to transit dues or Egyptian representation on the company board. Several departments in Whitehall had an interest in the affairs of the company and I had to consult them on forthcoming company business. For this reason our correspondence was invariably copied to a string of colleagues whom we knew intimately on the telephone but rarely, if ever, met. The last paragraph of countless letters would read: 'I am copying this to Miss Loughnane (Treasury), Dodds (Admiralty), General Money (Ministry of Transport) . . . " and so on. Recipients copied their replies likewise. On one occasion Geoffrey McDermott,[3] my sometimes impish immediate superior, added to this list '. . . and Scroggins (Ministry of Town and Country Planning)'. A week or so later, Geoffrey received a telephone call from the mail room at the ministry. A pained voice said: "Mr McDermott, I've got a lot of letters here for a Mr Scroggins and there's no Mr Scroggins on my list." "P J Scroggins, ISO ?" Geoffrey suggested. "No, not any Mr Scroggins." "Funny", said Geoffrey, "he was at the meeting."

One afternoon in the spring of 1948 Moya McGinn, who looked after documents on Egypt and the Sudan in J division, brought me a thick bundle of papers, some obviously old, which she had been told to give to me as the junior member of the department. She added that she was keeping another bundle upstairs until I had finished studying these. The bundle bore the romantic title *Nile Waters*. I began reading from the bottom of the pile. From the outset my attention was closely engaged and I stayed late in the office until I had read all the papers. The following morning Moya brought me the second, slightly smaller, bundle. This had an equally alluring title – *Congo Basin Treaties*. What emerged from these papers was that where rivers flowed from one sovereign territory into another, no action should be taken upstream which could affect the flow of water without the consent of the authorities downstream. The Congo basin was geographically complicated. When H. M. Stanley, who had penetrated central Africa in 1870 in search of David Livingstone, led his third expedition to central Africa in 1883 on behalf of the International Association of the Congo, he explored four of the rivers in the basin and concluded a thousand treaties on behalf of the Association. Of course, only a few of these related to the Congo and the other rivers, but the parallel with the Nile was clear. The issue had come alive because of a plan to exploit and develop the resources of the Nile for the benefit of all the riparian states.

This plan was based on a study by Hurst, Black and Simaika, three eminent irrigation engineers with profound knowledge of the river from its sources in Uganda and Ethiopia, through the Sudan and Egypt to the Delta. The potential benefits were enormous. Egypt would be protected from flooding and an extra 7 million acres of new land would become cultivable. Given the rate at which Egypt's population was growing, this was not merely desirable but essential. The Sudan would also benefit in two ways. The swamp in the Sudd region in the south of the country would be drained and, in addition, 2 million more acres would be irrigated. Through the construction of dams where the White Nile flowed out of Lake Victoria and where the Blue Nile left Lake Tana, Uganda and Ethiopia would acquire great quantities of hydroelectric power.

The full development of the plan called for a number of major new works. The first of these, a reservoir on the main Nile in the region of Wadi Halfa on the Sudanese side of the border with Egypt, would be used for flood protection and to store water for the dry season. The second would convert Lake Victoria into a reservoir for what was called 'century storage'. This entailed building a dam at Owen Falls which would enable the level of the lake to be raised by up to three metres and, at the same time, provide Uganda with the hydroelectric power it needed for its planned industrial development. A similar dam could also be built at Mutir in the Sudan to control the waters of Lake Albert for the same purpose, and a regulator might be needed to control the discharge from Lake Kyoga in Uganda. The most ambitious element in the plan was the Jonglei Canal; the waters of the White Nile, which would otherwise be dissipated in the swamps, would be diverted into a channel, five metres deep and over a hundred wide, which would be cut through the Sudd. It was also intended that Lake Tana would be used for century storage and that the dam built for this purpose, like the Owen Falls dam, would generate hydroelectric power.

It was obvious that such a comprehensive development could trans-form the economic and social prospects for the peoples of central Africa and the Nile valley and that the cooperation among the states concerned, which was needed if the full benefits were to be secured, could be a model for other regions of the developing world. The more I read the more my imagination was stirred. The question was: would the will and the funds be available to execute such a grandiose and complex scheme?

In 1929 Britain and Egypt had agreed on the conditions under which the waters of the Nile might be exploited. In an exchange of notes, the two governments acknowledged the right of the Sudan to more water than it had been using hitherto. For its part, the Egyptian government undertook that local interests would be safeguarded if any works were constructed on Sudanese territory for the benefit of Egypt. The most important provision was that no work would be undertaken in the Sudan, or in territory under British administration, which would either reduce the amount of water reaching Egypt, or change the time of its arrival.

The Nile Waters Agreement of 1929 echoed certain principles contained in a grandly named 'International Convention and Protocol relative to Development of Hydraulic Power affecting more than one State' concluded in Geneva in 1923 and still in force. Britain, on behalf of Uganda and Kenya, and Egypt had signed that Convention. It was clear that the agreement of Egypt had to be secured if Uganda was to obtain the power it wanted from the dam at Owen Falls and if the Sudan was to reclaim two million acres. It was also desirable that the approach to Ethiopia about the dam at Lake Tana should be undertaken jointly by the British and Egyptian governments. Since part of Lake Albert was in the Belgian Congo, where some flooding could be caused, the Belgian government had to be kept informed.

Sir John Hall, the Governor of Uganda, was impatient to begin work at Owen Falls. While Egyptian irrigation experts were cooperative, at political level no progress could be made, primarily because of the situation in Palestine, and there was resistance in Cairo to the idea of a joint approach to the Ethiopians. In any case the Ethiopian government was unlikely to cooperate until the future of the former Italian colonies – Eritrea and Somaliland – had been settled by the United Nations. The Governor-General of the Sudan, Sir Robert Howe, insisted that no action be taken in Uganda without the consent of Egypt.

In July 1948 this complex of issues was submitted to Ernest Bevin, the foreign secretary. His interest in economic development was well known and it was no surprise when, at a meeting in his office the following month, he instructed that this great project be given high priority. He felt that the right course was to press the Egyptians to agree or otherwise be seen as the obstacle to a scheme of immense benefit to their own people and the region as a whole.

Meanwhile, the department had acquired a new head. Dan Lascelles had been appointed ambassador to Ethiopia. During his final few weeks in the office he was visited each evening by his Amharic teacher, whose accounts of his pupil's progress suggested that Lascelles's capacity to absorb languages was undiminished. Dan complained to us over tea about the irrelevance of the phrase book he was using. Its author, it seemed, aspired to membership of the 'Ho, postilion, your coach has been struck by lightning' school of language training. Lascelles quoted certain phrases which he hoped would prove misleading: "Question: where, please, is the toilet?" "Answer: on the fourth floor." This was not the only example of his mischievous humour. In the late 1920s he had studied Persian with a colleague called Terry Brenan, who loathed being importuned by beggars in the bazaar. Some years later Lascelles, clad in black jacket and striped trousers, was waiting in Sloane Square for a bus to take him to the Foreign Office, when he saw a familiar figure in the queue in front of him. He stepped down into the gutter, shuffled forward and tugged the man's sleeve, muttering: "Bakhsheesh, sahib." The owner of the sleeve turned out to be a complete stranger.

Our new head, George Clutton,[4] felt that our embassy in Cairo were not arguing our case on the Nile waters with sufficient vigour. He therefore asked me to try to enlist the support of the Egyptian embassy in London. My principal contact was the urbane counsellor, Fuad Youssef. He was a Copt and a popular member of the London diplomatic corps. Over numerous lunches I rehearsed our arguments. In the first place we and the other governments concerned had scrupulously honoured our obligations under the Nile Waters Agreement of 1929. Agreement on the technical aspects of the project had already been reached. All concerned, and not least Egypt, stood to gain. Yet, despite this, the Egyptian government were holding up African economic development as a whole for what appeared to be purely political reasons. Finally, as Youssef would know, this was a project in which the foreign secretary took a personal interest. This last point seemed to impress Youssef; when he next invited me to lunch at the Egyptian embassy, I found on arrival that the two of us were to be joined by his ambassador. Amr Pasha, a former world squash champion and something of an Egyptian hero, was known to enjoy the confidence of King Farouk and was therefore an important potential ally. He questioned me closely about the extent of Ernest Bevin's commitment to the scheme, which I had no need to exaggerate.

In December 1948 we increased the tempo. The Egyptians were told that the Uganda government had decided to place orders for the construction of a hydroelectric power station at Owen Falls which would operate at the outset only on the natural flow of the river. This was coupled with an offer by the Uganda government to allow an Egyptian irrigation engineer to inspect the completed works in order to satisfy himself that the 1929 Agreement had not been breached. The Egyptians pleaded for more time.

The best we could hope for at this stage was Egyptian agreement to the construction of the dam at Owen Falls. This limited objective would not prejudice the prospects for subsequent agreement on the other elements in the project. In April 1949 it was decided that I should go to Cairo to assist the embassy with their representations. The head of chancery, who was to achieve international notoriety two years later, offered to accommodate me at his house in Sharia Ibn Zanki on the Gezira. Donald Maclean and his wife, Melinda, were generous and considerate hosts. They included me in their social engagements. This enabled me to meet numerous prominent Egyptians, but also caused me some embarrassment. Donald Maclean had a poor sense of time; hardly ever, during the six weeks I spent as his guest, did we arrive on time for a social engagement. It was also obvious to everyone that he drank too much. Before I left Cairo I asked what I could send him as a token of appreciation for his hospitality. He wondered if I might find him a set of the novels of Turgenev in a second-hand bookshop in Charing Cross Road.

The critical meeting with the Egyptians took place on 5 May. With Lees Mayall, the Embassy first secretary, I called on Samy Bey Abdul Fettouh, the head of the political section of the Egyptian foreign ministry to discuss the draft exchange of notes and announcement about the Owen Falls dam. I returned to London on 12 May. On the morning of 18 May 1949 I received a telephone call from Amr Pasha: "I want you to be the first to know. His Majesty has today authorised me to convey Egypt's agreement to the Owen Falls scheme." Amr went on to say that he would be calling on Mr Bevin later that day. George Clutton passed on this news at once to the Secretary of State's private office. In the middle of the afternoon I was told that the Secretary of State wanted to see me. He and Amr Pasha were alone in his room. Ernest Bevin turned to me and said : "We did it." I was then swept up into a three-man bear hug. For the rest of that day I walked on air. In his statement to the House of Commons the following afternoon, Ernest Bevin referred to the great material benefits both Egypt and the Sudan would in due course derive from the scheme, while hydroelectric power would become available for the develoment of Uganda and the increase of its prosperity. It was this aspect of the project which had always appealed to him.

I rose early the following morning and went to Charing Cross Road where I found a set of Turgenev's novels in excellent condition. Later in the day I posted them to Donald Maclean in Cairo. He was grateful.

❖

Early in 1949 I had replaced one of the three resident clerks. These were junior secretaries who took it in turns to deal with urgent business outside office hours. The tour of duty was from Monday to Monday with two interruptions; each of the other two resident clerks would be on duty for one night during the week. These duties were additional to work in our departments during the day. For this extra labour we received a modest allowance and accommodation on the third floor of the Foreign Office, overlooking either Horse Guards parade or St James's

Park. We each had a study and a bedroom. We shared a dining room and employed a housekeeper, Miss Curtis, and her cat, Tiger, who got stuck in a chimney one night but fortunately did not burn bright. Our rooms were well furnished. I had the bed of William Pitt the Younger; someone else had Shaftesbury's desk.

During our week on duty we dealt with whatever was the current crisis. Time differences, notably between London and New York where the United Nations Security Council might be in session, often meant sleepless nights. The compensation was participating in major decision-making and working with the foreign secretary and his ministerial colleagues, ambassadors and other senior members of the service.

There was another compensation – my two colleagues. Gordon Campbell[5] had been wounded towards the end of the war in Europe and he bore his disability with remarkable courage. Anthony Montague Browne,[6] who had been a pilot in the RAF, liked to tease. Our fellow resident clerks in the Commonwealth Relations Office were not as comfortably installed as we were and frequently found some excuse to walk along the corridor to 'consult' us. In this they were merely following the example of their permanent under secretary, a frequent visitor whom we dubbed Sir Gilbert 'not-so-much-pink-please' Laithwaite. One evening Anthony determined to end the practice. When the expected call came from the Commonwealth Relations Office he said: "Very well then. But come along straightaway. I have a tart coming up in half an hour." The startled visitor was in and out of Anthony's study in two minutes.

I was wakened at about three o'clock one morning by an operator on the international exchange who asked if I would take a call from a Mr Palmer in New York; he wanted to speak to me about British exports to the United States. I said that exports were a matter for the Board of Trade, but in the end I agreed to take the call. When he came on the line, Mr Palmer – he pronounced the 'l' – said that he was in a bar in Manhattan and was unable to buy Scotch on the rocks. He wanted to know what the British government were doing to ensure that American citizens were not deprived of Scotch whisky. I expressed sympathy and explained the efforts we were making to increase our exports. Mr Palmer was not satisfied. Could he speak to Mr Bevin? I said that Mr Bevin was asleep and in any case responsibility lay with Sir Stafford Cripps, the President of the Board of Trade. Mr Palmer wanted to be put through to him. I said that he too was asleep. What about the King, Mr Palmer asked. I asked him to wait while I looked out of my window to see if the lights were still on in Buckingham Palace. I reported to Mr Palmer that the lights were out and suggested that he write to the King. Mr Palmer was enthusiastic. "You mean I could write to the King?" "Of course," I said. "You should address your letter to His Majesty King George the Sixth, Buckingham Palace, London SW1." The call must

have cost Mr Palmer as much as a case of Scotch whisky – if he had
been able to find one.

During all these months in London I was able to resume contact with
former colleagues. John Rae had resigned from the British Council
and was with the BBC. I visited Lewis, and now Mary, Penny in
Cambridge, where he was completing his geology course before taking
up an academic post in Hull. We resumed where we had left off. With
others I tasted what the theatre had to offer. In October 1948 with
a group of friends I attended one of the Beethoven Cycle concerts
at the Albert Hall. The great Wilhelm Fürtwangler conducted the
Vienna Philharmonic Orchestra. I had never heard a live performance
of Beethoven and I will not forget the thrill of the first chord of the
Ninth Symphony.

I had also kept in touch with Mary Grepe with whom I had dined
in Cairo in 1947. She was due to take up a post as social secretary to
the United States ambassador in London. In the spring of 1949 I gladly
accepted her invitation to a cocktail party. As I was about to leave the
Foreign Office for Mary's house in Chelsea, a telegram arrived from
our embassy in Cairo which needed urgent attention. I had to consult
George Clutton about the reply and, by the time I had drafted this and
delivered it to the communications branch for despatch, I was afraid that
I would arrive too late at Mary's party. Fortunately the taxi made good
time and the party was not over. I had no idea, of course, that the next
few moments would be the most important of my life. When I entered
Mary's drawing room I saw a beautiful young woman with wide eyes
and long fair hair standing near the fireplace and immediately fell in
love. During the next several months, over dinner at the Boulogne,
Manetta's, Casa Pepe, or the resident clerks' flat, Jean Young and I
got to know each other. Miss Curtis and the messengers who let her
into the Foreign Office by the park door expressed their approval of my
visitor.

In December 1948 the possibility of my being posted to the consulate in
Amara in southern Iraq had been raised, but this was not pursued until
the summer of 1949. The personnel department sought to persuade me
that Amara was important as a listening post in a sensitive tribal region.
They said that, although I was only of third secretary grade, I would carry
the title of consul. My predecessor, Colonel Berkeley, had held this rank
and downgrading the post could be misunderstood by the Iraqis. When
I suggested modestly that it would be useful to know what I might hear
in this listening post, I was assured that I would be fully briefed by our
embassy in Baghdad.

Meanwhile, it was my turn to take a summer break. Michael Stewart,[7] the assistant in the department, offered me the use of his house in Berkshire for two weeks, my only obligation being to exercise his horse, Ginger. On our first outing either Ginger was startled by some creature or he decided that he disliked my company. He reared up and over backwards. I saw the sky passing between his ears before we hit the ground. My right leg, left wrist and a bone in my right hand seemed to be broken. I crawled through a hedge to reach a farm track and waited. After about twenty minutes a tractor towing a trailer appeared. Back at the Stewarts' house I telephoned for a taxi to take me to the hospital in Newbury. There I waited on a bunk for five hours until I was seen by a doctor wearing a mackintosh and smoking a cigarette. After X-rays and plaster casts, I was given a pair of crutches and told I could go. Later that evening my eldest brother Douglas, the army doctor, took me to his house at the other end of Berkshire.

As soon as I was mobile I returned to the department and my flat in the Foreign Office. Jean and I became engaged in the middle of December 1949 and parted ten days later, when I sailed from London Docks in the *Cyprian Prince*, bound for Beirut. We planned to marry as soon as I was installed in Amara. Until then, sweet sorrow.

5

Rivers and Tribes

The *Cyprian Prince* was a cargo ship with accommodation for twelve passengers – an ideal setting for Agatha Christie. She would no doubt have recalled the martyrdom in the year 258 of St Cyprian, the bishop of Carthage, when we spent Christmas Day across the bay at Tunis while the ship unloaded and loaded. For the same purpose we spent three more days at Malta and two at Alexandria, where my brother Alastair and his wife, Betty, were waiting on the quayside when the *Cyprian Prince* arrived. Alastair at that time was in the British Middle East Office in Cairo. From Beirut, our destination, I was driven to Damascus where I boarded a more luxurious Nairn bus than the one in which I nearly froze two years earlier. I arrived in Baghdad on 7 January 1950 to be welcomed by the counsellor at the embassy, Humphrey Trevelyan,[1] who had been among those I had consulted in the Foreign Office on the Nile Waters problem. For the next week I stayed with Geoffrey Arthur,[2] the oriental secretary. He had learned Arabic at university and had spent several years during and after the war in southern Iraq. Geoffrey and others in the embassy offered helpful advice on practical matters, but neither he nor anyone else gave me a clear definition of my responsibilities at Amara. I was left wondering whether they knew something I did not know. I had to wait some months for the answer.

Amara was subordinate to the consulate-general at Basra, my next stop. Frank Cook, the consul-general, was a rather pathetic figure. Unlike Doctor Pangloss, he believed that everything – or nearly everything – was for the worst in the worst of all possible worlds. He suffered from hypochondria and disapproved of the younger members of the service who had no idea how difficult things were in former times; he and his contemporaries had had to learn the hard way. His wife, Phyllis, on the other hand, shed a warm glow wherever she went.

Cook's original idea was that I would spend one month in every three in Basra. It emerged later that the files in the consulate archives had not been weeded for several decades and before long the inspectors would descend on Basra. Cook wanted me to sort them out. He accepted however that how I divided my time would depend on the situation at Amara. He had no clearer idea of what I was meant to do there than the embassy in Baghdad. So I felt I was stepping into the unknown when I left Basra on the morning of 31 January on the hundred mile journey to Amara. Hadi Muhsin, the Amara consulate driver, had brought the station wagon to Basra a day or two earlier. The third member of the party was Abbas, who had been recruited for me in Basra as a general purpose servant.

As we travelled north we passed through several miles of date gardens. These gave way to tall eucalyptus trees lining the road and then groves of tamarisk before we entered the desert. We crossed the bridge at al-Qurna ('the horn'), the legendary site of the Garden of Eden, where the Tigris and Euphrates meet to form the Shatt al-Arab. We ate Phyllis Cook's picnic lunch on the bank of the Tigris. As we continued north, the road deviated from the river bank from time to time and I was intrigued by the sight of sailing boats and steamers apparently ploughing their way through fields of rice and barley, date plantations and flocks of round, brown sheep grazing on the alluvial plain.

Four hours after leaving Basra, Hadi pointed to a group of tall chimneys standing out against the deep blue of the Persian mountains, forty miles to the east. These marked the site of the brick kilns in Amara. A few minutes later we saw a line of villas separated by dark green trees on the waterfront. Hadi pointed out the consulate – the 'father of the tower' he called it. We crossed a bridge into the town and drove along the corniche to the consulate where the staff were waiting in the garden to greet us. All was hustle and bustle. After tea I went up to the roof and looked across the farmland to the desert beyond. Hadi climbed the tower and raised the Union Jack. He turned to me and said: 'mubarak' – 'may you be blessed here'. I knew I would be when Jean had joined me.

At that time Amara, which was a major agricultural centre, had a population of about twenty thousand, most of them Shia Muslims. There were small communities of Jews, Christians and Sabians, also known as Mandaeans, who venerated John the Baptist and made exquisite objects in silver. Farming depended on irrigation and Amara was fortunate in this respect. The town was surrounded on three sides by rivers: the Tigris – the only real river – to the west, the Musharrah to the north and the Chahalla to the east. The latter two existed only to distribute the waters of the Tigris, which eventually disappeared into the marshes. The flow of water once it left the Tigris was controlled by sluice-gates on regulators. The system was well conceived and efficiently operated. But the potential for disputes among the tenant farmers was obvious.

The consular building and its contents needed a lot of attention – repainting here, sewing there and plenty of soap and water almost everywhere. No wonder. The consulate had been unoccupied since my predecessor, Colonel Berkeley, left ten months earlier. Throughout this period the consul's office had been locked. After dinner the clerk, Gurji Salman Shubbath, gave me the key and I unlocked the door. I felt like Howard Carter approaching the tomb of Tutankhamen. Unlike the ancient tomb, the place was in disarray. A packet with four cigarettes in it lay on a table. On the desk were private letters Berkeley must have received the day he left. On a pad beside the telephone were the notes he had been making. It was as though, in the middle of his work, Berkeley had left the room and not come back. Then I noticed some movement on the wall opposite the desk. Closer inspection identified an active hornets' nest. I retreated quickly and locked the door after me. I was told the following morning that Hadi knew how to deal with hornets; the remedy was kerosene. He found a small round tin, half filled it with kerosene which he then directed from a safe distance at the nest. At the second attempt he succeeded. The effect on the hornets was instantaneous.

During the next two days I paid my formal calls. Amara was one of the fourteen provinces, or *liwas*, of Iraq. The two senior officials, whom I visited first, were the governor, or *mutasarrif*, and the commandant of police, both of whom were responsible to the minister of the interior in Baghdad. Musa Kadhim, the governor, expressed surprise when I addressed him in Arabic. The British embassy had told him that a young man was being posted to Amara to learn Arabic. He wondered aloud why I had been sent to this place; that makes two of us, I thought. The director of health had married an English girl he had met when working at the Brompton hospital in London. Though she had dual nationality, she was the nearest thing to a British community in my consular district. In this provincial capital she felt it prudent to keep a low profile. The commander of the river force had four British-built gunboats under his command; the gunboat he showed me was immaculately maintained. The mayor, an engineer trained in Germany, suffered severely from outpost syndrome; Baghdad showed no support for his carefully prepared and costed development plans.

The only foreigners were members of an American mission based in Minnesota. Dr Heusinkveld operated a medical practice. My landlord, Louis Burjony, and his wife, Daisy, were thoroughly westernised Christians who hoped my arrival might revive social life. They spoke of tennis parties, supper on a river boat, picnics in the desert. But not until the spring. The winter of 1950 was exceptionally severe; snow had fallen for the first time in living memory on the road between Damascus and Baghdad and reports of heavy snowfalls in Turkey suggested high water levels in the Tigris in the spring.

The news that I had called on the mutasarrif and other officials opened the flood gates. For the next several weeks visitors streamed into the consulate, ostensibly to pay their respects. Some of these were merely curious to meet the newcomer, but many seemed under the impression that the days of British administration in Iraq had not ended. A number offered their services as informers, others wanted me to intervene with the provincial or central government to settle some dispute. And others, I suspected, came for the coffee and the chance to gossip.

The most intriguing of these early visitors was Taga bint Maula, the only woman head of a tribe I met. She was hunchbacked, her eyes were sad and her smile radiant. She had a lot to say and stayed for three cups of coffee and six cigarettes. She rode and shot with the best of the men in her tribe. She had not married because she considered herself a man and, in any case, her tribe was her family. She was the first of my visitors to talk in practical terms about improving agricultural methods. The previous year she had bought a water pump and wanted another. She had other ideas for the general improvement of her land, but needed a loan of six hundred dinars – the same sum in pounds. For once I was able to respond to a request from a visitor. When she returned two days later I told her that I had discovered that the Agricultural Bank would give her a low-interest loan if she mortgaged her pump. She said that if she obtained the loan she and her tribe would be my children.

❖

On 7 March there was an interesting development. I had returned to Basra to support the Cooks during the visit of the ambassador, Sir Henry Mack, and Lady Mack. A full, if not hectic, programme had been arranged. As we were leaving a large tea party given by one of the Basra notables, Lady Mack said to me: "You're coming to Baghdad, aren't you?" When I expressed surprise, the ambassador intervened to say: "Yes, but it's not fixed up yet." It emerged that Geoffrey Arthur, the oriental secretary, was due to leave in the summer and it was intended that I should replace him. This indiscretion on Lady Mack's part seemed at long last to explain the purpose of my posting to Amara. My spirits and hopes rose, only to be dashed a few days later. Jean wrote to say that she had to go into hospital for an operation. Even on the most optimistic assessment she would not be fit to travel until the late summer.

I counted the days. Some were worth counting. The irrigation engineer for the area invited me to accompany him on an inspection of the regulator on the Butaira – a tributary of the Tigris an hour and forty minutes by motor boat upstream from Amara. Ibrahim had his own personal plans for the development of agriculture in Iraq. What was the point of all this water flowing into the marshes when it could be used to reclaim the desert? He could imagine great fields of barley and rice where now there was marsh and flat wilderness. Wide tractors such as he had seen in the United States would till the ground and reap the harvest.

We enjoyed the warm sun as we talked; then we noticed simultaneously that in its light the heavily silted waves falling away behind us looked like liquid gold. Ibrahim suggested half seriously that this might be an omen. He got out the map and we began marking on it where dams and regulators might be built, where drainage canals might be dug. On the basis of recent experience elsewhere, Ibrahim estimated the possible costs and the time needed for completion. He made a rough calculation of the savings and other benefits. Then he struck the balance – money back in fifteen years and a substantial political dividend. As events were to show within a few years, neither Ibrahim's ideas nor his estimates were all that fanciful.

Another day worth counting was 19 April. The two great tribes in the region were the Beni Lam and the Albu Muhammad. The head of the latter, Sheikh Muhammad al-Araibi, was a member of the Iraqi Senate. When he had called on me soon after my arrival, he had invited me to visit him at his home. Hadi and I drove for half an hour through the barley fields and along the banks of the Chahalla river until we reached the small town which served the Albu Muhammad as market and inland port. A smart police guard presented arms in front of the local administrator's house when I arrived to pay my call. Coffee and sherbet were served before we boarded a 'mashhuf', a gondola-like skiff, which was to take us to the sheikh's house a quarter of an hour's paddling and poling downstream from the town. This was a mashhuf unlike any other. Midships was covered by a palanquin of heavy embroidery. We sat on an arrangement of spotlessly white cushions, our feet resting on a Persian rug.

Sheikh Muhammad had known many of the British who had worked in Iraq since the kingdom came into existence in the early 1920s. He had a speech impediment but I was just able to decipher his rendering of their names. Sir Percy Cox became 'Cowcuss', Sir Henry Dobbs became 'Dobbis', Freya Stark became 'istarak', Sir Kinahan Cornwallis 'colonel Wallis' and Gertrude Bell 'mazbal', one vowel short of the word for dung-heap. Turning to the present he expressed some concern about the prospects for Iraq. Baghdad, he said, was too remote from the people; the new generation, better educated than any of their predecessors, was impatient to see real social reform and to play a role. From one who had had hardly any formal education himself, this was a remarkable comment and it figured prominently in my next monthly report to the embassy. As I took my leave, the sheikh said that all I had to do was telephone when I wanted to visit him again. Why not come in the evening and stay overnight? And when you and your lady are married, he said, this house will be yours for as long as you wish.

❖

The news from home was good. Jean's operation had been successful and the long process of recovery and convalescence had begun. Whether in sympathy or not, my own health had not been of the best. For some weeks my stomach had been upset. After examining me, Dr Heusinkveld said that everyone in Amara suffered from dysentery from time to time. There was nothing to worry about; but I should be careful about food. I was not wholly reassured, but decided to proceed with a planned journey to the Muntafiq, the other province in my consular district. I had visited the provincial capital, Nasiriya, on the Euphrates north west of Basra three years earlier with Harry Fletcher, the information officer in the consulate-general at Basra, and on that occasion we had penetrated the Hor al Hammar – the great tract of marshland – as guests of one of the tribal sheikhs.

We left Basra after breakfast on 2 May for the five-hour journey. This time there was a new member of our party. Abbas found life in Amara uncongenial and had been replaced by Ruhaiyim. Despite a thunderstorm three days earlier, the road was dry and the sun warm. We headed first for Zubair, the original site of Basra and home port of the mythical Sindbad, in whose honour a tower had been erected at the southern end of the town. There was no sign of the reinforcement camp in which I had spent a cold Christmas in 1942 before joining the Rajputana Rifles across the border in Persia. Zubair was a walled town and most of the houses were below ground – the best way of tolerating the extreme heat of the summer.

As on my previous trip, we followed a line of tamarisks which led out into the desert. From then on the road was where other vehicles had been – sometimes a narrow track, at others a vast causeway. The surface was sand and grit with here and there clumps of camel thorn. We waved to groups of Bedouin resting their sheep and watering their camels. Some had erected their black goat-hair tents and were enjoying the shade. We passed the half eaten carcase of a camel and then another, now a disordered heap of bones whitening in the sun. Out of the mirage we had been pursuing for some time, the remnants of the biblical Ur of the Chaldees suddenly emerged. I paid my respects to the stationmaster, a handsome Assyrian who wanted to prepare a meal for us. We shared tea and bread with him and then drove the remaining nine miles on a good road to Nasiriya. To reach the centre of the town we had to drive over a bridge of boats.

Ahmad Zaki al-Mudarris, the mutasarrif of Nasiriya, was only thirty-seven years old. The commander of the local garrison was also of the younger generation. They proved congenial companions and over the next few days we established a warm relationship. No doubt because of their leadership and example, morale among all the officials, officers and notables I met was far higher than in Amara. I spent the next two days absorbing the life of Nasiriya. The third was spent in Suq al-Shuyukh, from where Harry Fletcher and I had embarked on our visit to the marshes. The district commissioner's lunch accorded fully with the town's reputation for producing the best fish in Iraq. Our plan for the following day was to visit three towns on the Gharraf river. We left Nasiriya at seven on a dull, strangely warm morning. As we left Nasiriya we found ourselves in a sea of swirling dust no more than three or four feet from the ground. We passed long camel trains and flocks of sheep and goats and groups of Bedouin horsemen moving north on their return from winter grazing in the southern desert. We reached cultivated land on the outskirts of Shatra, where, three years earlier, the polyglot district commissioner, Hussain Kubba, had quoted Lamartine over lunch. His successor refreshed us with a glass of sweet tea and we pressed on to Rifa'i, where his colleague was well known to me as he had only recently been transferred from Amara. We had been on the road two hours, and it took us only twenty minutes to travel the distance between Rifa'i and our final objective, Qala'at Salih, where I was entertained briefly in the officials' club by the commandant of police and the township officer.

Back in Rifa'i I had a splendid lunch with my Amara friend, after which we began our return journey to Nasiriya. We had almost reached a village half-way between Shatra and Nasiriya when a large dark cloud appeared from the west. The sky above our heads was pink and the air still full of dust. Rain storms are grey, sandstorms are yellowy brown; I had never seen any cloud quite so dark. It now spread over the whole horizon to the east and seemed darkest near the ground. I opened the window to see more clearly and heard a loud rushing noise. I shut the window at once and told Hadi to drive on as fast as he could. Two minutes later the storm struck us. One moment it was light, the next we were in pitch darkness.

Hadi stopped the station wagon and put on the headlights. They merely lit up the whirling mass around us – a combined sand and rain storm. The air was full of flying mud and the wind was hurricane force. I opened the sunshine roof and stood on the back of Hadi's seat. I could just see the line of the road and told Hadi I would guide him with my knees; when I pushed his left shoulder he was to drive more to the left and the opposite on the other side. I tried to shield my eyes from the rain and sand with one hand while hanging on with the other. The surface of the road was rapidly becoming slime. In forty minutes we covered three miles. Suddenly it was light again and we could see where we were going. The road was by now pure slime and another car in front of us seemed to be making most progress sideways on.

We now had our first sight of the havoc the storm had wrought. Most of the Bedouin tents were down, horses and foals had broken loose and were rushing about aimless and terrified. As we approached Nasiriya, we saw the first of the trees that had been uprooted, the first of

the roofs torn off. We heard that evening that railway wagons in Basra
had been blown over, long stretches of telegraph poles broken or bent,
and that three ships in the port had broken their moorings. The steady
wind was measured at 85 miles an hour with gusts up to 110. Incredibly
and wonderfully, there had been no loss of life. When I looked in the
mirror in the guest house at Nasiriya, I saw that I was splattered with
mud from head to waist and that my face was covered with cuts from
the flying grit.

On the journey to Basra the following morning we found that the
prehistoric course of the Euphrates, which had been dry for years, had
become a torrent two and a half feet deep. This was too deep to risk
driving across; the fan would have blown water into the distributor. So
we stripped and pushed the vehicle over to the other side. Then on again
to the tamarisk groves, Sindbad's tower at Zubair and a warm welcome
from concerned colleagues in Basra.

I spent some days in Basra sorting files before returning to Amara. I
was notified formally that I would be replacing Geoffrey Arthur at the
embassy and received a questionnaire from the wife of Dugald Stewart,
who was to take my place at Amara. I sent a dart board and darts which
I found in the Basra souk to Ahmad Zaki, the mutasarrif at Nasiriya, for
use in the officials' club. This crossed in the post with a leather-bound
volume from him about Syrian resistance to the French at the end of
the first world war. This remains a prized possession. Our friendship was
being cemented.

I had lost weight and was still suffering from dysentery when I left
Amara for good on 29 June for Basra. And I was frustrated. I felt that
over the previous six months there had been no way in which I could
have advanced Britain's interests. Frank Cook called in Dr Maclean, the
medical officer at the Port Directorate. He thought at first that I had a
stomach ulcer, but Cook wanted a fuller examination. This led Maclean
to recommend that I be invalided home. Cook informed Baghdad at
once. Humphrey Trevelyan, who was in charge of the embassy at the
time, wanted me to go immediately to Baghdad where the senior British
physician in Iraq, Professor Robert Drew,[3] would see me. I stayed with
Humphrey and Peggie Trevelyan while further tests were undertaken.
The results left no doubt. I had had amoebic dysentery for some time
and this had caused ulceration. I was despatched without delay to
London and admitted to the Westminster hospital. Drew's diagnosis
was confirmed and a course of treatment was prescribed which I was
to follow on my return to Iraq.

Jean and I were married in the chapel of the Royal Agricultural
College at Cirencester and flew to Baghdad on 27 August 1950. Sweet
sorrow had yielded to a brave new world.

6

Oriental Secretary

As our aircraft taxied towards the passenger terminal, the purser welcomed us to Baghdad. "Local time is 16:25 hours," he announced, "and the outside temperature is 114 degrees Fahrenheit, 45 degrees centigrade." When the cabin door was opened we were hit by a blast as from an oven. An embassy car took us to the house of Humphrey and Peggie Trevelyan, where we were to stay for our first week. The consideration we received could not have been more timely because, on the day after our arrival, Jean succumbed to heatstroke. Her temperature rose alarmingly and she developed a severe headache. One aspect of the treatment – applying ice to her body until her temperature was under control – was, as she said later, more unpleasant than the condition, but it was effective. Within two days she had recovered and we were able to begin the process of absorbing our new surroundings.

The Trevelyans' house was as comfortable as any in the city. In the early 1950s air-conditioning in Iraq was rare and, where they were installed, the machines were bulky and noisy. Water-fed air coolers and ceiling and desk fans were the usual means of providing relief from the heat and working practices were adapted to the conditions. Office hours in Baghdad during the summer months were usually from seven-thirty in the morning until half past one. In the afternoon shutters were closed and curtains drawn and Baghdad slept for four hours. Some houses dating from Ottoman times had special cellars, known by the Persian word 'sirdab', to which the whole family would retreat during these oppressive hours. Normal life would resume when the temperature began to fall with the setting of the sun.

The commercial counsellor, Herbert Gamble,[1] had offered us the use of his house while he and his wife Janine and their family were away on summer leave so that we could house-hunt from an established base. The search did not take long and we were soon installed in a well-built and well-insulated house in the Karradat Miriam quarter about a mile south of the embassy compound. Our neighbour on one side was the

first secretary in the Spanish legation, who regarded the welfare of the
several Spanish dancers in the Baghdad night-clubs as one of his special
responsibilities. In the early hours of the morning we were frequently
wakened as he summoned his servant with his car horn to open the
garage door. On the other side was an Iraqi family who kept themselves
and their assorted livestock to themselves. Karradat Miriam was almost
a rural village. When we slept in an insect-proof cage on our roof on
summer nights, we were lulled by the cooing of doves and wakened,
when Pedro was already safely home, not by our other neighbours'
cockerel but by 'crow-crow'. The cooing of doves – a familiar Baghdad
sound – was celebrated in a children's song one of our friends taught us;
he explained that *bajilla* was a rather tasteless vegetable which happily
rhymed with Hilla:

kuku úkhti, ya bítti	coo coo, my sister
wain ráiha, lil–Hílla	whither are you going, to Hilla.
wa shtákilin? Bajílla	and what will you eat? Bajilla.
wa shut shíribin? mai úllah	and what will you drink? The water of God.
ya kúku	oh, coo coo.

Meanwhile, under Robert Drew's direction I had begun the amoebic
dysentery treatment. This was my first experience of antibiotics. My diet
was severely restricted and it was even suggested that I might not be able
to eat roughage of any kind in future. Robert also said that if I really
wanted to give the treatment a fair chance I should stop smoking. I acted
at once on this wise and true advice. Within a few weeks I felt better
than I had done for many months or even years, and within six months,
to Robert Drew's satisfaction, I was eating a normal Baghdad diet. This
diet did not include lettuce or water melons, which all expatriates were
advised not to eat because, it was said, their cellular structure made them
prone to infection by polluted water in the irrigation channels.

❖

With the advent of cooler weather in October, political life in Baghdad
resumed. My immediate chief, the oriental counsellor, was John Richmond,[2] who had taken part in a number of archeological expeditions in
the 1930s and served with the army in the Middle East during the second
war. He left the department of antiquities in the Palestine government to
join the Foreign Service in 1947. Baghdad was his first diplomatic post.
He was succeeded in 1951 by Morgan Man,[3] who in turn was succeeded
by Richard Beaumont[4] in 1953.

The main tasks of the oriental counsellor and secretary were to
monitor and advise on the domestic political scene in Iraq in the
light of British interests, to draft the ambassador's political despatches
and to keep the staff of the Air Officer Commanding RAF Habbaniya

abreast of political developments. Gertrude Bell had been the first to occupy the post of oriental secretary. This was in 1920 when Sir Percy Cox, the Civil Commissioner, tried to devise a new status for the territory which the British had somewhat inadvertently acquired with the collapse of the Ottoman Empire. Captain Vivian Holt had held the post more recently and had won the admiration of Mr Jacob, the embassy's translator, who lost no opportunity to compare him favourably with his successors. Others in the political section of the embassy – the chancery – were occupied with a variety of tasks, including the provision of technical assistance to Iraqi government departments and services; they worked closely with the commercial and consular sections. The information section, the military attaché, the administration, registry, communications section and typists completed the British staff of the embassy.

Sir Henry Mack returned from home leave in October and resumed charge of the embassy. His insistence on strict observance of protocol was well known. One rule to which he attached importance was intended to demonstrate the cordiality of his relations with his staff. The reasoning behind this injunction was plain. Even if the ambassador had been discussing some problem with members of his staff at six o'clock, none of the other guests at a reception at seven o'clock was likely to know that. Therefore, the argument went, if members of the staff were seen by others present to ignore the ambassador or his wife, a false and unfortunate impression could be given. Accordingly, each member of the staff invited to a reception which the ambassador and his wife were to attend had to make a point of wishing them a good evening. This posed no particular problem, but Henry Mack added a refinement. He also insisted that all members of the staff should arrive at receptions before him and leave after him. Easy enough when there was only one reception in one evening, but frequently there were two. On such occasions this requirement taxed our ingenuity, and we spent some time finding alternative entrances to and exits from our hosts' house or garden as well as traffic-free short cuts from one reception to another. We had a useful ally in the ambassador's driver who drove the ambassadorial Rolls between receptions at a suitably serious speed, gave way to all other traffic and spurned short cuts.

Every morning Henry Mack toured the extensive embassy grounds with the Khan Sahib, an émigré from the Indian subcontinent, who had performed the role of major-domo for longer than anyone could remember and held sway over the locally recruited messengers and domestic staff. This daily ritual had a soothing effect on the ambassador. As his private secretary would say: "Mack's in his garden, all's right with the world." But he also said, when the aide-de-camp asked what on earth the twelve new refrigerators ordered from the Ministry of Works were for: "To keep the cold shoulders in."

Iraq owed its existence as an independent state to the British. Through a series of treaties in the 1920s, its boundaries had been fixed to include three former provinces of the Ottoman empire – Basra at the head of the Persian Gulf, Baghdad in the centre and Mosul, which included the great Kirkuk oilfield, in the north. The fledgling state had established reasonable relations with Turkey and Iran, its neighbours to the east and north. Ever since the Hashemites, the traditional guardians of the holy places in Arabia, had been driven from the Hejaz by the Saudis and had found alternative roles in Iraq and Transjordan, relations between the two dynasties had been strained. In 1930 the British promoted a meeting between King Faisal of Iraq and King Abdul Aziz ibn Saud when they resolved outstanding problems. Iraq was thus secure within her borders. The Anglo-Iraqi treaty was signed in the same year but did not come into force until Iraq was admitted to the League of Nations as an independent state in 1932. This treaty created an alliance between Britain and Iraq under which Britain was allowed to establish air-bases at Habbaniya in the desert west of Baghdad and at Shu'aiba near Basra and had the right to move troops and supplies across Iraqi territory. This right was invoked in 1941, at a moment of great danger to the British presence in the Middle East, when a revolt under the pro-Nazi Iraqi Rashid Ali al-Gailani was crushed. Succeeding governments in Baghdad had supported the alliance.

By any standards the treaty of 1930 was a remarkable achievement. The Ottomans had found their three south-eastern provinces more than usually troublesome; the facts that the population was predominantly tribal, that a high proportion especially in the south were Shia and that communications were minimal, made effective administration virtually impossible. Ottoman policy had been one of not particularly benign neglect. In his study of the early years of Arab nationalism, 'The Arab Awakening', George Antonius attributed the success of British efforts to build up a viable state in Iraq to two circumstances. First, the British as mandatory power soon discovered that they had acquired a hornet's nest rather than the garden of Eden and had to choose between abandoning the country to its fate or enabling it to stand on its own feet. But, just as important in George Antonius' view was the calibre of the British officials to whom it fell to reconstruct the country after the first world war. These were the revered figures of whom Sheikh Muhammad al Araibi had spoken with such warmth when I visited him in the spring – Percy Cox, Henry Dobbs, Kinahan Cornwallis and Gertrude Bell.

Iraq's problems twenty years later stemmed from the opportunities which had been missed since those days. Once the Ottomans had left, the Shia, who were a majority of the population of some five million, were no longer second class citizens. Higher education and the most senior posts in the administration were open to all and the younger generation took full advantage of these opportunities. However, while a new educated class was being created, the membership of successive governments continued to be drawn from a narrow band of professional politicians, merchants and landowners, and the majority of the members of the Chamber of Deputies belonged to the same clique. This meant that, with rare exceptions, members of the new generation were effectively excluded from political power.

At the time of our arrival in Baghdad in 1950, three figures dominated the political scene. Nuri Said had been one of the leaders of 'al-Ahd' (the Covenant), a group of dissident Arab officers in the Ottoman army. With other young Iraqis he had defected to the British in the first world war and played a prominent role in the Arab Revolt in which T. E. Lawrence found fame. He had already served as prime or foreign minister in several post-independence governments and acquired the stature which enabled him from time to time to play an international role as mediator. Among British politicians he was rightly regarded as a loyal friend of Britain, but not in the sense conveyed by Stewart Perowne, John Richmond's predecessor, in his witty glossary of diplomatic terms. In this he defined 'loyal' as 'one who puts the interests of Great Britain before those of his own country'. Saleh Jabr, who was Shia, was equally attached to the principle of the alliance with Britain, but he suffered a setback when the revised treaty he had negotiated with Ernest Bevin at Portsmouth in 1948 was rejected in Iraq by an alliance of left- and right-wing extremists. Nonetheless, his wisdom and moderation were widely admired and he remained the most plausible alternative to Nuri Said. The third of the key figures was Prince Abdulillah. Ghazi, the son of the first King Faisal, had been killed in a motor accident in 1939, and his son, also called Faisal and still only a child, became king. Young Faisal's uncle, Prince Abdulillah, had acted as Regent since then, but he lacked the strength of personality to play the role of impresario in which the first King Faisal had distinguished himself.

Before long I found my days were full. I had calls to pay on officials in the foreign ministry and other government departments, including the ministry of the interior where I met the remarkable Major Ditchburn, the last survivor of the team of officers who had created the administrative structure in Iraq under the direction of Percy Cox and Henry Dobbs. 'Ditch' carried the title of adviser in the ministry and this exactly described what he did. He had a deeper knowledge of personalities in the south than any Iraqi and successive directors-general and ministers knew that his judgments would be impartial and his discretion absolute. He was due to retire within a year of our arrival and was already withdrawing from social life. When we met he said enough to confirm my supposition that he had been kept fully informed about my activities in Amara and the Muntafiq.

The senior official in the foreign ministry was Yusuf al-Gailani, the head of the leading family of Sunni notables in Baghdad. The modesty and courtesy of Sayid Yusuf and his wife and cousin, Mas'uda, belied their position in the aristocracy of Iraq. He arranged for me to see the treasures in the splendid Gailani mosque, of which his family were custodians. And later, Mas'uda presented us with our first cat, a magnificent Persian whom we named Almas, after the white diamond-shaped patch on her breast.

The facts that the title of my post in the embassy was oriental secretary, that, thanks to the six uncomfortable months I had spent in Amara, I was familiar with the spoken Arabic of Iraq, and that Jean and I were newly married, made us objects of some curiosity. Jean was able to experience at first hand the Iraqi hospitality of which I had told her and both of us were introduced to the camaraderie characteristic of expatriate communities in capitals where living conditions can be harsh. Unfortunately, she contracted infective hepatitis – commonly known as jaundice – shortly before our first Christmas and was confined to bed for several weeks. It was nearly a year before she regained her strength. Her spirits were raised by an unexpected visit. The stationmaster at Ur junction, whom I had met on my way to Nasiriya a year earlier, called with a wedding present – a four thousand year-old brick. Barbara Parker who spent part of the winter in Baghdad with Professor Max Mallowan and his wife, Agatha Christie, at the School of Archeology, read the inscription for us. This proclaimed the achievements of Bur-Sin, one of the kings of the third Sumerian dynasty who ruled Ur between 2210 and 2100 BC.

Our Iraqi friends were solicitous. For the most part they were either in politics, government, or the professions. But they also included tribal leaders, one or two of whom were members of the Iraqi parliament. I soon realised that the dissatisfaction with the government expressed by the educated Iraqis I had met in Amara and Nasiriya was shared by many of my new contacts. Extreme opposition to the government of Nuri Said came from the Istiqlal (Independence) party, whose newspaper sustained a daily barrage against the alliance with Britain. However, its impact was deadened by its predictability. More serious opposition came from those within the political establishment who, while unhappy that they were for the time being out of office, genuinely wanted a wider distribution of political responsibility. While the ambassador had fairly frequent opportunities to meet the Regent and Nuri Said, it was with these members of the parliamentary opposition and the supporters of Saleh Jabr that John Richmond and I sought to maintain contact.

At that time the stability of Iraq was an important British interest. The Soviet threat and resentment over the establishment of Israel put this stability at risk. Wealth was unequally divided and ordinary people had seen no benefit from the immense royalties the country earned from the activities of the Iraq Petroleum Company in the north and its sister company, the Basra Petroleum Company, in the south. Maintaining the RAF presence at Habbaniya and the flow of oil were particular concerns, especially following Dr Mossadegh's dismissal of British technicians from the great Anglo-Iranian refinery at Abadan in October 1951.

There was desultory talk about revision of the Anglo-Iraqi treaty but little more. Kuwait, however, was a troublesome issue. Britain in 1950 was still responsible for Kuwait's external relations and any incident affecting Iraq's relations with its small but prosperous neighbour involved the embassy. I inherited two fat files. The first dealt with the problem of certain date gardens belonging to the Sheikh of Kuwait at Fao, a port at the southernmost point of Iraq. For many years these had been managed and cropped by local Iraqis and, under Iraqi law, anyone who had enjoyed continuous 'usufruct' – a new word to me then – of the date palms for ten years became their owner. This problem was a lawyer's dream and a diplomat's nightmare. The same was true of the second file which concerned an encounter between a member of the Sabah family, the ruling house of Kuwait, and a member of the Iraqi Sa'adun tribe, which had ended in murder. The Iraqi government occasionally raised these two cases as pinpricks, but in 1951 they went further and revived their claim to Kuwait – the "fifteenth province of Iraq". When the ambassador, on instructions from London, protested on the grounds that this was a breach of a clear understanding, Taufiq Suwaidi, the notoriously devious foreign minister, listened carefully and then said: "That, your excellency, is precisely what I told my cabinet colleagues when we discussed this."

In our work we were at something of a disadvantage. Many ordinary Iraqis believed that the British still wielded critical influence and were therefore disposed to hold us responsible for perpetuating what they regarded as the injustices of the political system. This was a view which some of the less competent or scrupulous ministers in the government of the day found it convenient to encourage, especially when something they had been handling went wrong. Time and again over the next three and a half years I came up against ingrained scepticism about our detachment from the day-to-day processes of government.

❖

Henry Mack was succeeded early in 1951 by Sir John Troutbeck who until then had headed the British Middle East Office in Cairo. He responded at once to the friendly atmosphere he found. In social, if not climatic, terms Baghdad was indeed an agreeable place. Since, apart from the antiquities, of which few had survived in Baghdad, there was little art or culture on offer, conversation was the principal intellectual and social activity. I had learned in Amara how articulate Iraqis were and that they needed little encouragement to air their views. This characteristic was useful to the diplomat monitoring the domestic scene and hospitality exchanged between members of the diplomatic corps and other expatriates and Baghdad society provided ample opportunities. Although many politicians and senior officials had received their higher education in Europe or the United States and were thoroughly western in outlook, many others were at ease only in Arabic. But despite, or perhaps because of this, John Richmond and I found them helpfully forthcoming.

In 1951 Jean and I moved to a single storey house on the west bank of the Tigris – except in the month of May, when it was in the Tigris. A balcony ran along the river side of the house and, when the snows in Kurdistan and Turkey melted and the level of the Tigris began to rise, this provided a base for a wall of sandbags which kept out most of the flood water. When the river fell, a mud beach appeared alongside our house which some of the street folk treated as a public convenience. White Lodge had been occupied by the head of the British Council and had many advantages; it was close to the embassy and the city centre and it had an extensive garden, ideal for summer entertaining. Our domestic staff consisted of Khalaf, the butler, John Lobo, another émigré from the Indian subcontinent who was our cook, and an occasional gardener called Abbas. Khalaf was a devout Muslim. He took time off during the first ten days of the month of Muharram, when the Shia lament the death of Hussain and Abbas at the battle of Kerbala in the year 680 AD. On this occasion he would join countless others at the magnificent twin-domed mosque at Kadhimain, a few miles north west of Baghdad, where the seventh and ninth Imams are buried. When he returned to our house he was still in a state of high emotion. John Lobo was a Madrassi Christian and henpecked.

Evening receptions and dinner parties were the preferred form of hospitality. Iraqis did not like to drink after a meal and it was often as late as ten o'clock before food was served. In the late summer, when the level of the Tigris fell and mud flats appeared in the middle of the river, those expatriates who were not taking summer leave and Iraqis who had not escaped to Europe or Lebanon were able to enjoy a special pleasure. On a bright moonlit evening we would assemble in casual clothes on a jetty, board a river boat and set off downstream towing a number of so-called Tigris salmon caught earlier in the day. Eventually we would land on one of the temporary sandbanks where a brushwood fire would be lit. The belly of the fish, which were up to two feet long, would then be slit and the side without the backbone folded back until the whole fish was open and flat – what the Iraqis called 'masgouf'. Sticks placed in the ground on either side of the fire, which by this time was glowing embers, held two fish upright, their open sides towards the heat. When they were cooked the fish were placed skin downwards on the embers and oil and spices were sprinkled on the sizzling flesh. Watching this process whetted our appetites and, when the fish and their accompanying rice and vegetables were ready to be served, most of us were prepared to risk burnt fingers and tongues.

Our hosts on one of these river excursions were Fadhil al-Jamali, the foreign minister, and his American wife. Jamali was an unusual Arab politician. He had one of the largest collections of gramophone records in Baghdad and his knowledge of classical music was encyclopaedic. His defence against the frequent charge that he was anti-Jewish was to play Mendelssohn. Soon after we cast off on our trip downstream, he took me aside and asked how I saw the prospects for his country's future. Given the occasion I thought it right to speak frankly about my misgivings. He nodded and throughout the rest of the trip he held my hand in a firm grip. He expected me to understand that this was his reply.

❖

As often as we could Jean and I visited other centres in Iraq. Our purpose was not merely to deepen our knowledge of the country and its people but also to identify their aspirations and understand their anxieties.

Sheikh Abbud al-Haimus, the head of a tribe in the province of Hilla, a member of the chamber of deputies and a frequent visitor to White Lodge when he was in Baghdad, abetted us in achieving these aims. At his house at Shomali he ensured that we heard a variety of opinions about the prospects for the province and the state of the country. He was also on hand to protect Jean when, on a black partridge shoot on his estate, a family of wild boar emerged from a clump of reeds a few yards in front of her. Sheikh Ghazi Ali Kuraiyim, with whom we stayed at Samarra on the Tigris north of Baghdad, was equally keen for us to see what he called 'the real Iraq'. He showed us what he was doing to improve the standards of his own people and then, perhaps as a cautionary tale, he took us round the ruins of the ancient city of Samarra. This was built in the ninth century by Mutasim, one of the sons of the legendary Abbasid caliph, Harun al-Rashid, as a new capital to displace Baghdad. But it was occupied for just over fifty years and then abandoned. When we told Ghazi that we wanted to climb the great spiral ziggurat, he was unenthusiastic. We soon learned why. The walkway narrowed the higher we went, and vertigo obliged us to stop and turn back when we were still only two thirds of the way to the top.

These were rewarding encounters. Less enjoyable was our excursion with Iraqi friends to the holy city of Kerbala. Out of respect Jean covered herself from head to foot in an *abaya*, and I concealed myself in our car some distance from the mosque. Yet, for a reason we could not explain, we were never more conscious of our foreignness than on that day.

❖

Common interest encouraged close working and social relationships with members of other embassies. The Americans had a substantial presence in Baghdad. The ambassador, Edward Savage Crocker, had a passion – bridge. Dinner parties he and his wife attended were held up until the rubber had been completed. He travelled for three days by river boat from Baghdad to Basra 'to see the country', and never left the bridge table. His wife also had a passion. She hated cats, and claimed she knew instinctively when one entered any room she was in. This prompted E. Savage Crocker to say, quite truthfully, on one occasion: "I doubt if that's so. There's one behind your chair right now."

The staff of his embassy were of high calibre. Philip Ireland, the deputy head of mission, was a noted student of modern Iraqi history. Equally distinguished was David Newsom,[5] who was in charge of the information department in the United States embassy. David and his wife – another Jean – were lunching with us when a riot broke out in protest against a statement in Washington construed as pro-Israel. The information office in downtown Baghdad was set on fire and from our terrace we watched as hundreds of sheets of paper were carried aloft in the smoke and flames. David remained calm. "I suppose," he said, "that this is the widest distribution our material has ever achieved." Our paths were to cross again.

David Newsom also had dealings with the other second secretary in the chancery, Robert Belgrave. Robert and Susan had come to Baghdad from Belgium, their first post, and frequently claimed, when colleagues protested about the recklessness of some Iraqi drivers, that in this respect Baghdad was less hazardous than Brussels. One morning the news spread quickly that a wing of Robert's estate car was severely dented. When curious colleagues went to the car park to inspect the damage, Robert appeared. In answer to the inevitable question he said: "You'll never guess who. It was the Belgian chargé d'affaires."

Robert Belgrave was closely concerned with the work of the Development Board, the establishment of which was the Iraqi government's somewhat belated response to the need to distribute the benefits of the country's oil wealth. The board's mandate was to invest the income received from the oil companies to the nation's advantage. A veteran political figure, Arshad al-Umari, was appointed president of the board. Arshad was the wise owl of Iraqi politics and had a gift for the apt phrase. Once, when I commented on the virtual absence from the Iraqi calendar of spring and autumn, he said: "*Yaum lift, yaum dundurma*"

– "One day turnips, the next ice-cream." In the depths of winter for a few pence the people of the streets could buy enough boiled turnips to keep body and soul together from itinerant vendors in the souks.

In an astute move, the goverment invited Sir Edington Miller, a recently retired senior official in the Sudan Political Service, to be secretary general – in practice the chief executive – of the Development Board. An impartial figure of this stature would reassure the public that the highest standards would be applied to the work of the board. Robert Belgrave helped Miller find experts with appropriate qualifications and experience to draw up specifications for some of the major projects. Flood control was given high priority; the Habbaniya Lake scheme was designed to end the periodical destruction caused by the overflow of the Euphrates, and the dam at Wadi Tharthar was intended to serve a similiar purpose with the waters of the Tigris. The preparatory work on these projects brought to my mind the river trip in the spring of 1950 with the irrigation engineer at Amara when for a few moments we had shared a vision of a golden future for the country.

However, not all the news was good. Iraqi Jews, who had played a valuable role in the administration and in commerce, were having a hard time and in the end arrangements were made to deport them to Israel. They were flown out at a rate of over 13,000 each month and in all over 100,000 left. A tragic incident occurred early in 1951 when an explosion at Mashuda Shentob Synagogue, where Jews were assembling for the journey to the airport, killed two and injured another twenty. However, to judge by reports we received from other Arab posts, the Iraqis' treatment of their former fellow citizens was relatively humane, as I saw for myself on my occasional visits to the airport.

A demonstration in Baghdad in January 1952 on the anniversary of the Portsmouth Treaty signalled the beginning of an uneasy period. A serious rift opened between Nuri Said and Saleh Jabr, whose new party, the Popular Socialist Party founded in July 1951, had attracted popular support. In July 1952 Nuri Said resigned as prime minister, more out of fatigue and exasperation than as a contribution to the political process. He was replaced by another veteran, Mustafa al-Umari. Nuri had told Harold Beeley, Humphrey Trevelyan's successor as counsellor, that governing Iraq was easy: "Give this man a nut, that man a banana." Nuri may have thought this a *bon mot*, but to my mind it betrayed the extent to which he was out of touch with opinion. The message I received in conversations day after day was unchanged; popular disquiet at the extent to which power was concentrated in a few hands was widespread.

It was our turn for home leave. When we returned we found that Nuri's departure had done nothing to reduce tension. On 22 November

1952 rioting broke out in Baghdad. Police posts were overrun by the mob and their occupants brutally murdered. At this time Jean and I were sheltering Michael and Norah Errock who had been evacuated from Tehran with all the other members of the British embassy staff when diplomatic relations were broken off earlier in the month. I was in my office at the embassy and Michael happened to be in our garden when a crowd tried to break down the entrance. Jean told me later that he brandished a pistol, which neither of us knew he had with him. This act could have had either of two consequences: it could have frightened the mob, or infuriated them. On this occasion the mob opted to be frightened. Martial law was declared later in the day and, from then on, we had a police guard at our gate.

❖

Health was an important consideration for all expatriates. Fevers of the type known in the wartime army as 'NYD' – 'not yet diagnosed' – were common. So was dysentery – in one form or another – but methods of prevention and treatment were improving steadily. There were other scourges. Robert Belgrave was struck down by poliomyelitis and rushed to the RAF hospital at Habbaniya. Susan drove the hundred and ten miles to Habbaniya and back every day for several weeks encouraging Robert's fightback. Her devotion, the skill of the medical staff and Robert's determination enabled him to recover the use of almost all his muscles. This was, of course, several years before Salk developed his vaccine.

John Troutbeck's warm personality not only endeared him to his staff and the diplomatic corps in general, but also won him the regard of the Iraqis. The state of his health could have political implications. For some time Guy Clarke,[6] the consul in Kirkuk, had been pressing the ambassador to visit the north of Iraq to meet some of the Kurdish sheikhs who, having heard of other visits he had paid to centres in southern Iraq, were beginning to feel neglected. A programme was drawn up, but John Troutbeck fell ill a week before we were due to set out and he was strongly advised to postpone the visit. When this news was conveyed to his prospective hosts they were dismayed. Like others, they attributed to the British ambassador influence on Iraqi internal affairs he did not possess and assumed that their tribes had in some way caused offence.

Guy Clarke suggested that the sheikhs might be persuaded to shed their misconception if I would receive a deputation. I agreed and two days later half a dozen Kurdish sheikhs came to my office, accompanied by a young man imperfectly dressed in western clothes. He was the Kurdish interpreter. The spokesman for the sheikhs began by expressing their hopes for the ambassador's full and speedy recovery, which I acknowledged on his behalf. For the next half an hour they tried to provoke me into saying that the postponement of the visit had causes other than the ambassador's illness. Time and again I promised that the visit would be reinstated as soon as possible, but I felt they preferred their version of the facts. Eventually they gave up the struggle. When they rose to leave, I asked the interpreter to stay behind as there was something I wanted to say to him personally. He eagerly helped the sheikhs on their way out of my office. When we were alone I said: "I have something to say which, like everything else I have said, is true and you can prove it. Your buttons are undone." The ambassador's subsequent visits to the provinces of Mosul, Kirkuk and Sulaimaniya in the early summer of 1952 were highly successful. Satisfaction at his recovery was expressed and the postponement of the visit was never mentioned.

That same year – 1952 – was a landmark for Jean and me. Our son, Colin, was born at Habbaniya in December. She could hear the distant howling of jackals as she held him in her arms for the first time. We were taken aback by the pleasure his birth gave to our Iraqi friends. For the first-born to be a boy was considered a special blessing; "*ma sha' Ullah*", they said – "what God willed". Jean and I felt the same. To keep him in comfort during the following summer we installed a crude cooling system in our bedroom. This consisted of two trellisses of the same size as the window between which was sandwiched freshly-cut camel thorn, the overall width of the sandwich being about six inches. This was lodged in the open window. A hose was connected to a pipe with a line of holes from which water dropped slowly on to the camel thorn and eventually into a bath. A table fan in front of this contraption sucked air through the damp camel thorn. Evaporation did the rest. For the first two weeks the thorn gave off a delicious cool scent, but it had to be replaced when it began to rot. Fortunately, camel thorn was not scarce and Colin did not suffer unduly.

Although he did not realise it, Colin undertook his first great journey at the height of the summer of 1953. We took a week of local leave and, together with Mary Steele-Perkins, who had joined us from England to help look after Colin, a few embassy colleagues, an American visitor and Adnan al-Qadhi, an Iraqi lawyer friend who made many of the arrangements, we set off for a climb in Kurdistan. There was no metalled road to the north from Baghdad and, to reach Kirkuk and Erbil, one travelled east from Baghdad along the main road to Iran and then turned north into the desert following a line of oildrums marking the track. In places, through wind erosion, the surface of this desert track was corrugated and one had to find an optimum speed to reduce vibration. We reached Kirkuk in time for lunch and dined in Erbil, said to be the oldest continually inhabited site in the world. The following day we entered Iraqi Kurdistan, passed through the precipitous Rowanduz gorge and reached Hajji Umran on the frontier with Iran in time for dinner at the rest house. The next day was devoted to acclimatisation and lunch with the sheikh of the local tribe. The following morning we drove to a nearby village where we lunched with another Kurdish sheikh and then picked up our police escort, loaded our kit into mule packs and selected our riding mules and ponies.

Before we set out from Baghdad we had had a basketwork cot made for Colin. This was supported by two sacks attached to either side of the horse's saddle, to which the cot was securely strapped. Behind the cot sat the rider, a watchful Kurdish policeman, who crooned lullabies to Colin as we made our way towards Halgurd. His repertoire seemed inexhaustible. At just over 12,000 feet, Halgurd was the highest mountain in Iraq. The track zigzagged up the slope of a valley through mud-brick villages half-hidden under mats of vines, and groves of mulberry trees. Out in the full glare of the sun, we seemed to be heading towards a mountain wall. The ascent became steep and rough and soon too difficult for our horses and mules. When we dismounted, we found it was hard enough for us to find footholds and we had to urge the animals to greater efforts. Over the crest a grassy meadow cut in two by a narrow rushing stream fell away before us, and half a mile ahead was our camp for the night. This consisted of a bell-tent and a large goat-hair marquee with walls of rush matting and woven carpets on the ground. The water in the stream was ice-cold and as soon as the sun set the temperature plummeted. The extra clothing we had brought with us just about kept us warm, but we were all eager to slip into our sleeping bags as soon as the evening meal was over.

The following day we climbed on foot in separate parties to the summit, Colin meanwhile revelling in the cool weather in the camp. I was surprised and delighted to find a swallowtail butterfly in a hollow rock on the peak, sustained no doubt by the numerous small plants which flourished in patches where the snow had melted. After a second night in the camp we descended the way we had come, lunched in the colourful town of Galala and dined in Shaqlawa, where we stayed overnight. The next day we spent with the Khoshnau tribe before going on to Kirkuk. We left at 5.30 in the morning to avoid the worst of the heat and were back at White Lodge, hot and dusty but relaxed, within five hours. In those few cool days in Kurdistan our tiny son had developed rapidly and made up all he had lost during the previous months in the Baghdad summer.

❖

The major event in 1953 was the coming of age and accession of King Faisal. The then Duke of Gloucester represented The Queen and among the guests was one of the young king's British friends from his days at Harrow. Jean and I found it difficult to share the confidence in the country's future expressed on this special occasion. By the time we left

Baghdad to return to London at the end of that year, we had visited every district of every province in Iraq. The provincial governors, district commissioners, business men, professionals and tribal chiefs we met had given us an insight into life in one corner of the Arab world. We felt that these people, and those for whom they spoke, deserved better from their government and we left Baghdad concerned that, unless power and prosperity were more widely shared, discontent could undermine the fabric of the state the British had created a generation earlier. London, however, was preoccupied with the Soviet threat to the Middle East, and the survival of a pro-Western regime in Iraq, insensitive though it might be to popular opinion, was the more important consideration in the short and medium term.

7

A Most Honourable Marquess

The handsome round panelled room on the first floor of the old India Office, which Secretaries of State for India occupied in imperial days, overlooks Horse Guards Parade and the north-east corner of St James's Park. On the walls hang Deccani and other Indian miniature paintings from the Johnson Collection in the India Office Library. There are several identical doors and anyone contemplating a theatrical exit runs the risk of walking into a cupboard.

For the only son of one of the great viceroys and a former foreign secretary, it must have been a matter of some satisfaction to be installed in this room. In 1954 the second Marquess of Reading was the minister of state who spoke for the government on foreign affairs in the House of Lords. His particular responsibilities in the Foreign Office were international economic affairs, including overseas aid, and relations with Latin America and east Asia. On 18 January of that year I replaced Patrick O'Regan as Lord Reading's private secretary. When briefing me on my duties, Patrick painted a picture of an able, courteous minister, devoid of personal ambition, who did everything asked of him without fuss and made no unnecessary demands on his staff. This proved an accurate portrayal. Patrick might have gone on to say that Lord Reading was also a shrewd judge of people and found humour in many situations, to the surprise of his more earnest ministerial colleagues.

I was lucky in a number of respects. The assistant private secretary, Daphne Ledger, was well established in the private office and had a talent for anticipating problems. The two under-secretaries primarily reponsible for submissions to the minister of state presented issues in a way which appealed to his legal mind. John Coulson,[1] who supervised the economic departments in the Office, regularly extracted from even the most complex submissions the essential issue, or issues, which he then summarised in one or two sentences. The far eastern and south east Asia departments reported to Denis Allen,[2] who was to play an important international role later in the year. Denis's talent lay in devising solutions to seemingly intractable problems. Seldom did Reading find it necessary to seek clarification of a brief from either of these senior advisers.

The Readings had a flat in Cadogan Square and Jean and I were invited to dine there two weeks after I had taken up my new post. This gesture was characteristic of Lord Reading; from this point on he treated Jean and me as family; together with our son we were invited to watch Trooping the Colour from his office. The Marchioness, who was a significant public figure in her own right and a leading member of the world Zionist movement, was more inclined to regard me as household. Throughout my three years as her husband's private secretary she addressed me by my surname.

On the other side of the hole in the wall which divided the old India Office from the Foreign Office proper were the offices of the other minister of state, Anthony Nutting. The mutual respect on which their relationship was based was to be tested at the moment of crisis. Lord Reading held Anthony Eden, then foreign secretary, in high regard, if not affection.

Since the Foreign Office is only rarely a legislating department of state, its ministers appear before parliament almost exclusively to make statements, answer questions and participate in debates on foreign affairs. Although procedures in the House of Lords differ in some respects from the Commons, the task of ministers is the same. Reading prepared his appearances in parliament with special care and wrote his own speeches on the basis of drafts submitted by the departments concerned. In the 1950s members of the House of Lords other than those on the front benches were supposed to speak only from notes rather than prepared texts and this convention was generally observed. The debates I attended were enlightening not only because many peers spoke from deep knowledge and extensive experience, but also because the level of debate was high. I was especially impressed by a ten-minute speech by Lord Vansittart delivered from the cross benches without a note. His language was elegant, his argument clear, the content erudite and his delivery worthy of a Shakespearean actor. As we walked back to the office after the debate, I told Reading I thought this had been the high point of the debate. He agreed that it was a good speech, but assumed I had noticed Van's mistake. When I confessed that I had not, Reading said that, when using the words of Palmerston in aid, Van should have made a show of reading the quotation; that he did not betrayed the fact that he had learned the whole speech by heart. This was only one of many pieces of worldly wisdom Reading was to share with me.

Lord Reading represented the United Kingdom at the annual ministerial meetings of the United Nations Economic Commission for Europe in

Geneva. This Commission was intended to provide a forum for east–west discussion of economic and trade issues. Gunnar Myrdal, the Swedish economist and former minister, had been executive secretary for seven years and every spring made diligent and persistent efforts when ministers congregated in Geneva to breathe life into the Commission. Instinctively neutral in the cold war, he became impatient when his attempts to build bridges proved fruitless. He stubbornly refused to accept that there was no meeting of minds and no prospect of any.

For the most part plenary sessions consisted of set-piece speeches, those by the east Europeans being catalogues of the so-called achievements of the state system. The Commission came to life only rarely, but almost always when André Philip, the French representative, intervened. A large man with a large voice and a moustache of the kind French soldiers wore in the first world war, he geared himself up like a ship preparing for sea. He would fill the bowl of his pipe with ample gestures and, when he had created a sufficient cloud of smoke, he would begin. His technique varied. The most successful was his demythologisation of the claims of the east Europeans. At one session the Romanian had unwisely bored the Commission with abundant statistics about increases in shoe production – all expressed in percentage terms. André Philip went through the motions of consulting a number of files and making calculations. Then he spoke. He congratulated the Romanian on the striking success of the footwear sector in increasing production. But he had a question. If this year's percentage increase was added to last year's percentage increase and the sum added to the numerical total we had been told about two years earlier, it appeared from the calculations he had made that Romania could shoe the entire population of eastern Europe and still have plenty of shoes to spare. Could the distinguished delegate say where and how this impressive quantity of footwear was stored?

❖

More serious business lay ahead. At the end of 1953 French forces in the Tonking delta in the north of Indo-China were being hard pressed by the Vietminh. The Americans were convinced that if the French were defeated the whole of south east Asia would come under Chinese threat. In discussion with the French and British governments, they had raised the possibility of military intervention in support of the French. However, British ministers had been unable to establish exactly what the Americans had in mind and feared that they had not fully considered the implications of military involvement. For their part, the Americans professed themselves disappointed at the lukewarm response of the British and French. The Russians were also concerned at the turn of events. In January 1954, Molotov, the Soviet foreign minister, proposed that the United States, the Soviet Union, Britain, France and China convene a conference to find a way of reducing tension in the region.

The purpose of the Geneva Conference, which lasted from late April 1954 until the end of July, was not merely to stabilise the situation in Indo-China but also to consolidate peace in Korea. Except for a weekend break in early June, Lord Reading and I remained in Geneva throughout. Apart from his advisory role, Reading acted as head of the United Kingdom delegation in the foreign secretary's absence; with Number 10 already in his sights, Eden attended cabinet meetings in London whenever possible.

In the event, the conference was convened by only four of those originally suggested by Molotov; the People's Republic of China declined to act as co-host, preferring freedom of action for their first appearance on the international scene. Nineteen delegations assembled in the Council Chamber of the Palais des Nations for the formal opening on 26 April. The first moment of drama was the entry of the Chinese delegation led by Chou en-Lai, the foreign minister, who was greeted by the heads of delegations in turn. John Foster Dulles, the American secretary of state, pointedly turned his back and, during the days he spent in Geneva, did not exchange even a glance with Chou. The conference agreed that chairmanship should rotate between Prince Wan of Thailand, Anthony Eden and Molotov. On the following day the two Koreas, north and south, presented their case and surprised everyone with their comparative moderation. Dulles, Chou en-Lai, Richard Casey, the Australian minister for external affairs, and Molotov spoke on 28 April. Molotov addressed himself not so much to his fellow delegates as to the absent leaders of non-communist Asia, and it seemed to me that his disingenuous interpretation of events in Asia since the end of the second world war must have appealed to Indians, Burmans and Indonesians.

Our difficulties in aligning our views with the Americans were appreciated by the three old Commonwealth delegations – the Australians, New Zealanders and Canadians. The Japanese threat during the war had brought home to everyone how vulnerable Australia and New Zealand were to any untoward event in south east Asia or the Far East, and our delegation was reassured by the thinking of our Commonwealth colleagues. Their assessment of the problems and ideas about possible solutions marched closely with our own.

Members of our delegation, including Reading himself, stayed at the Beau-Rivage hotel, close to the corniche. Eden had accepted the offer of the use of a villa – 'Le Reposoir' – at a modest distance from Geneva for the duration of the conference. His private secretaries, Evelyn Shuckburgh[3] (later succeeded by Anthony Rumbold) and John Priestman, operated from this villa. The conference department of the

Foreign Office had secured another property for the delegation's use as offices. 'Villa les Ormeaux' stood in spacious, immaculately maintained grounds; Reading and I dubbed it 'Elm Park Gardens'.

The strain in our relations with the United States delegation distressed us all. Dulles seemed over-influenced by Walter Robertson, the Assistant Secretary for Far Eastern Affairs in the State Department, whose undisguised hatred of the Chinese communists made him unreasonable in discussion. And we were also conscious of the long shadow of Admiral Radford, the chairman of the American Joint Chiefs of Staff Committee, noted for his hawkish views. These difficulties might have been easier to manage if the personalities of Eden and Dulles had been more compatible. Fortunately, after one week, Dulles had had enough. Neither of his private secretaries being available at the time, Eden asked me to accompany him to the airport to say goodbye to Dulles. On the way Eden railed against Dulles. I had no idea that he was capable of such venom and I hoped that ridding himself of the bile in his system in this innocuous way would ease his frustration. General Bedell Smith, the Under Secretary of State, replaced Dulles. He had learned a lot about the British in the latter years of the war and his arrival quickly restored harmony to the relationship.

Eden had meanwhile been cultivating Chou en-Lai with a view to establishing what outcome might be acceptable to the Chinese. He had cleverly brought Humphrey Trevelyan back from Peking, where he had been the head of the British office since 1953 without being recognised as chargé d'affaires by the Chinese. Humphrey became a member of the British delegation and Eden made a point of showing Chou that Humphrey enjoyed his full confidence and that he would be a trusted and authoritative channel of communication. Humphrey was included in a dinner Chou gave to the heads of our delegation and was later to have a separate meeting with Chou. Reading told me after the dinner that the pink sparkling wine the Chinese served was better than expected, that discussion had been serious, friendly and occasionally humorous, and that, as Eden and he took their leave, Chou told them that he now understood what divided the British and the Chinese. "You think you are right," said Chou, "whereas we know we are right." Reading thought Chou said that to all the boys.

Soon after the departure of Dulles, the delegations from the Republic of Vietnam, Cambodia, Laos and the Democratic Republic of Vietnam – the Vietminh – arrived in Geneva, bringing the total number of participating delegations to twenty-four. We presumed that the Vietminh had delayed their arrival until after the fall of Dien Bien Phu, the French stronghold in the Tonking delta which had been under siege for several months.

The advent of these delegations enabled the conference to turn to the

Indochina item on its agenda. Discussion opened on 8 May. Georges Bidault, the French foreign minister, looked grey with fatigue. While the photographers were busy exploiting the ten minutes allowed to them before the debate began, he sat still with his eyes closed. All members of his delegation wore black ties out of respect for the lost garrison of Dien Bien Phu. It was Eden's turn to take the chair. Bidault was the first to speak. He was quiet, calm and moving. When he tabled his proposals it seemed that, in one moment, we were far ahead of the stage we had reached on Korea. Predictably the thoroughly obnoxious Pham-van-Dong, the acting foreign minister of the Democratic Republic of Vietnam, broke the spell. A thin man with hollow cheeks – Ho Chi Minh without the beard, someone said – he ruthlessly exploited the fall of Dien Bien Phu, as no doubt he felt entitled to do. However, his truculence and sarcasm won him no friends – not even the Chinese delegation enjoyed his intervention. The Vice-President of the Philippines unwittingly provided some relief. He gave what he intended to be a spirited defence of American policy towards Asia. However, most of us detected in his script the hand of the American who had 'ghosted' the opening speech of the foreign minister of South Korea, which was full of floral tributes to the United States. Three times Carlos Garcia assured us: "That is the rock of conviction upon which I take my stand." Had he uttered these words again, the conference would have collapsed in laughter.

On 12 May, for the first time since our arrival in Geneva, Reading and I were fully occupied. Eden was to make a major statement on Korea the following day and had asked Reading to coordinate preparation of the text. At 'Elm Park Gardens' members of the delegation produced draft paragraphs on points Reading wanted included and he then built these into a speech. When we saw the final text at lunch time next day we were gratified to discover how few changes Eden had made, and even more so when the speech was warmly received.

The opening positions of the main parties having been exposed, the conference entered the phase of probing for compromise. This process was helped by agreement to Eden's suggestion that discussion be continued in restricted sessions with only three or four members of the relevant delegations present. Nonetheless the conference remained in deadlock over the terms of the armistice agreements for each of the three Indochina states. Towards the end of May Denis Allen devised a formula which proved generally acceptable and raised hopes of an eventual settlement. But the going was still heavy.

❖

Although Geneva was unseasonably cold and wet, a few of us took advantage of a lull in the negotiations to spend a day walking in the French Alps. The same interval provided Lady Reading with an opportunity to join her husband. She saw at once that there was not enough room in Geneva for two ministers and she was anxious, on general grounds, that Lord Reading should not be left too long without real work to do. The problem was to find a sound reason for him to return to London, where ministers were at that time thin on the ground. The eventual compromise was no better than a weekend in London. When I returned to our small flat in Kensington, I found Jean in good heart and health – our second child was expected later in the year – and was able to see for myself the progress our eighteen month-old son had been making during my absence. We decided that unless the conference came to a quick conclusion, Jean and Colin would join me in Geneva and that I would at once start looking for a suitable apartment.

On our return to Geneva Reading assumed charge of our delegation in the absence of the foreign secretary. Questions about the chairmanship of the conference required Reading to call on Molotov at his villa. I was curious to see at close quarters the man who had negotiated and signed one of the more infamous documents of the century – the Soviet–German Pact of August 1939, which had cleared the way for the Nazi invasion of Poland and thereby precipitated the second world war. We were struck, on entering the villa, by the sombre, somewhat oriental atmosphere. Molotov was accompanied only by Oleg Troyanovsky, the gifted Russian interpreter. Molotov had a high brow and restless, deep-set eyes. His complexion was of a curious grey and Reading and I agreed later that we had seen that colour before only on lampshades. The discussion was genial and business-like and I wondered how Troyanovsky, who looked like everyone's idea of an American college boy, could bring himself on formal occasions to translate paragraph after paragraph of communist diatribe against the west not only fluently but also with apparent sincerity.

When the conference debated Indochina on 1 June we saw the other Molotov. He lambasted Bidault without pity, exposing the weaknesses in the French position. Of course Molotov had one eye on the debate about to take place in the French Assembly which would determine the fate of the French Government. Despite this onslaught and the precariousness of his position, Bidault retained his composure and even his dry sense of humour. A few days later, first Molotov and then Chou en-Lai delivered abusive and uncompromising speeches on Indochina. It seemed that after weeks of skating around our differences, the deep crevasse that divided the west from the communists, had been brutally revealed. Eden reacted strongly; unless there was some move towards our point of view on the cardinal issues, the conference had to face the possibility of failure.

This response was warmly endorsed by our colleagues in the Commonwealth delegations. They shared our concern that nothing agreed at Geneva should be unacceptable to the non-aligned Common-wealth countries in south and south east Asia, and India in particular. Krishna Menon, the architect of Indian foreign policy, had appeared in Geneva to monitor developments at the conference. He asked to see Reading 'for a few minutes' and harangued him non-stop on the inadequacies of western policies for half an hour, in the course of which he said little we had not heard before. When Menon left, Reading said: "Interesting exchange of views."

Meanwhile, the conference had disposed of the first part of its business. Late in the evening of 15 June the Korean problem was settled. The western position at the end would have been worse but for the polemical skill of Paul-Henri Spaak, the Belgian foreign minister. A large, jolly-looking man, he spoke mostly without notes, his language full of imagery and metaphor and at all times unmistakably clear. Some of the communist delegations suffered from his sharp wit. Eden, who was in the chair, handled the session brilliantly and was commended at the end by both Chou en-Lai and Molotov for his spirit of conciliation. They could afford to be generous.

The French government was defeated on a vote of confidence in the Palais Bourbon on 18 June. On 20 June Pierre Mendès-France, the new prime minister, gave a pledge to the Assembly that he would settle the Indochina problem within a month. For those of us in Geneva depressed by the obduracy of the communists and with no immediate end in sight, this seemed a foolhardy undertaking.

On that same day Eden left Geneva and did not return until 12 July for what proved to be the final phase. The intervening weeks were trying for Lord Reading. While talks at technical level about armistice arrangements continued, the rest of our delegation had little to do. By this time we had patronised almost every restaurant in Geneva and the surrounding villages and across the border in France and tasted such culture as Geneva had to offer. Reading's spirits remained surprisingly high. One morning, as we were leaving the Beau-Rivage, a white Rolls Royce drew up on the corniche. Out stepped two swarthy men dressed in white from head to toe, except for their shirts which were black. I expected Reading to say: "Mafiosi"; instead he said: "Look, negatives."

Pressure on the Chinese eventually produced results. On 18 July Chou en-Lai tabled agreed proposals for the composition of the Commission which was to supervise the armistice arrangements in the three Indochina states. Two days later, at the end of the month Mendès-France had allowed himself, the French and the Vietminh agreed on a demarcation line just south of the 17th parallel. In the afternoon of 21 July Eden chaired the final plenary session. In his summing-up he pointed out that, while the results of the conference were less than might have been hoped for, an eight-year war had been ended. What remained was for the agreements to be implemented in good faith. For Eden this was achievement enough. Following the success of his diplomacy over Trieste and the Austrian state treaty, the Korean settlement and the ending – for the time being at least – of the Indochina war undoubtedly enhanced his international standing. None of us knew then how this might affect his own ambitions and his judgment.

The Geneva Conference of 1954 was my first experience of multilateral diplomacy at top level and my first exposure to communist leaders. I learned that plenary sessions were necessary to let the public know at the outset what was at stake and, at the end of the process, to commit all concerned publicly to what had been agreed. However, quiet diplomacy in the corridors and uninhibited bargaining in restricted session were the only effective means of achieving consensus. I also saw and heard confirmation of the verdict of those who had dealt with the communists in the past. The communists could be liberal with their public abuse, and in private they would remain intransigent until persuaded that they had nothing more to gain, at which point compromise became possible. I did not realise how useful this lesson was to prove, nor how soon. Yet, what had struck me most was the personal animosity between Eden and Dulles which surely did not bode well for Anglo-American relations.

❖

It had been understood from the beginning that, in the event of a reasonable outcome at Geneva, steps would be taken without delay to establish a system of collective defence for south east Asia. As soon as delegations had dispersed from Geneva, plans were made for a conference in the Philippines in September to agree on the membership and objectives of a south east Asian equivalent of NATO.

When Jean and I returned with Colin from a holiday in Scotland in the last week of August, I learned that there was some uncertainty about the leadership of the United Kingdom delegation to this conference. Soundings in the foreign secretary's private office suggested that Eden would decide in the end not to go to Manila. He was still on holiday in Austria, but his attention was focused on the final efforts of the supporters of a European defence treaty to prevent its being rejected by the French Assembly. The final decision about Manila was taken two days before the delegation had to leave: Eden would not go and Reading was to take his place. In anticipation I had arranged inoculations at the Queen Alexandra hospital at Millbank and for a Full Power authorising Reading to sign the treaty we were to negotiate to be sent to Balmoral for The Queen's signature.

In the course of the next day and a half the Cabinet approved the delegation's brief, Reading discussed potentially troublesome points with members of the delegation, and authorised instructions to our representatives on the working party already in Manila. The contentious issues were the area to be covered by the treaty and the characterisation of 'communist aggression' as the type of action against which the parties to the treaty were uniting. To satisfy Congress, the Americans wanted to include the adjective 'communist'. We argued that this was not only a departure from past practice but also certain to arouse the suspicions of the non-aligned countries in the region. As regards the territories to be covered, we wanted both east and west Pakistan (as they then were) to be included.

We left London in a special aircraft on 3 September. Our delegation included General Brownjohn, the Chief Staff Officer at the Ministry of Defence, the Foreign Office legal adviser, Sir Gerald Fitzmaurice, and Denis Allen. We stopped at Rome and Beirut, sweltered for an hour at Bahrain, and recovered somewhat at Karachi after a shower and a change of clothes.

In the early hours of the following day we stopped to refuel at Calcutta. Senior members of the delegation were asleep. Wing-Commander Disney, General Brownjohn's staff officer, and I were the only members of the delegation to leave the aircraft. On the tarmac we were met by the Counsellor in the High Commission office in Calcutta, a representative of the Government of West Bengal, and a group of photographers and journalists, all of whom had been waiting to greet Lord Reading. I went back on board to consult. Reading was adamant; he intended to stay on board. I was not surprised when senior members of the delegation unanimously and enthusiastically proposed that I should respond to the government representative's welcome and brief the press on Lord Reading's behalf. I returned to the tarmac. In speaking to the press I repeated the points Reading had made when interviewed by Godfrey Talbot of the BBC at London Airport the previous day. I explained why the foreign secretary had felt unable to travel to Manila himself and emphasised that the purpose of the eight countries in negotiating this agreement was purely defensive. I was heard in silence. I asked if there were any questions. Still silence. Then one of the journalists – a role model for Peter Sellers – stepped forward. He said: "It is too bad Lard Ridding would not come down. Our all-night wiggle has been in wain."

Another stop at Bangkok and then across Indochina to the South China Sea which was calm and blue. As we approached the Philippines we flew into high banks of cloud and landed at Manila in a violent storm. A salute of guns added to the thunder while the ambassador, Sir Frank Gibbs, helped Reading into his raincoat before he left the shelter of the aircraft's wing to inspect the guard of honour and stand to attention while the national anthem was played at an unfamiliar tempo. Reading and I were accommodated at the ambassador's house. Frank Gibbs told us that immediately after the war the owner had offered to sell it for a modest sum. The Treasury had vetoed the deal and we were now paying more each year to rent the property.

In the meantime the working party had made good progress and few points were left for decision by ministers. These were soon settled. This meant that the proceedings of the conference had more symbolism than substance. Our Philippine hosts had planned the programme in great detail and revelled in the ceremonial – formal calls on President Magsaysay at Malacañang, flag-raising outside the Congress of the Philippines where the conference was held, and wreath-laying at the monument to José Rizal, the national hero. Vice-President Garcia chaired the conference without referring even once to the rock of conviction on which he took his stand. But this was John Foster Dulles's occasion. The South East Asia Collective Defence Treaty, signed on 8 September 1954, achieved what he had been seeking throughout the year – the drawing of a line which the Chinese would not dare to cross. The other signatories – Australia, New Zealand, Pakistan, Thailand, France and the United Kingdom – were also reasonably satisfied. Our aim had been to secure a result which would not alarm the Indians and the other non-aligned states in the region. This had been achieved. Before we flew home Reading and I visited the museum in which some of the relics of José Rizal are displayed. These included books, papers, personal possessions and, incongruously, an undergarment. We also had time to see something of the countryside and the farming communities. We drove through cultivated fields, woods and villages to Lake Tagaytay, which filled an ancient crater. On the way back from the hills to Manila, we had a clear view of some of the prestigious American military presence. It was right that Dulles should have held centre stage – and just as well that Eden stayed at home.

❖

Later that month I sailed from Liverpool to Montreal and went on by air to Ottawa to join the Readings who had been staying with friends in Canada. In line with his responsibility for overseas aid, it fell to Reading to represent the United Kingdom at the annual meetings of the Colombo Plan Consultative Committee. It was the Canadians' turn to host the meeting and they had appropriately fixed a date when the fall colours were at their best. This was my first visit to the north American continent and my expectations were more than fulfilled by the beauty of the Gatineau River valley. From Ottawa we travelled by train to New York to pay calls at the United Nations headquarters, where we attended a session of the General Assembly and inspected the Security Council chamber. The Readings dined that evening with a movie magnate known to Lady Reading through her work with the world Zionist movement. Reading told me the following day that Gina

Lollobrigida had been among the guests. When Lady Reading asked her: "And you, my dear, what do you do?" Gina said: "Oh, I paint a little."

We arrived at Southampton aboard the *Queen Elizabeth* on 18 October. I was in good time for the birth the following month of our daughter, Alison, and the move to our new home on Kingston Hill.

Singapore hosted the 1955 Colombo Plan meeting and Reading took the opportunity to visit Jakarta for talks with the Indonesian government. Our relations needed nourishment. Architecturally, Jakarta was at that time a fine Dutch colonial city, but in October it was hot and humid. For some relief we drove up to Bogor, the former Buitenzorg, set on a river in beautiful hills. There we saw the orchid collection in the botanic gardens – one of the living monuments to the remarkable Stamford Raffles, Singapore being another – and were told by one of the curators, perhaps with his tongue in his cheek, that the sirens of the President's escort when he visited his mistress in Bogor were known locally as Sukarno's mating call.

During the East–West summit meeting in Geneva in July 1955, Eden who, on becoming Prime Minister in the spring of 1955, had been succeeded at the Foreign Office by Harold Macmillan, raised the possibility of a visit to Britain by the Soviet leaders. This had been welcomed. Six months later, during a tour of India and Burma and again when addressing the Supreme Soviet in Moscow, Khrushchev had spoken in abusive terms about the West. It was decided nonetheless to proceed with plans for the visit to Britain. Lord Reading was asked to assume responsibility for the programme for the visit.

From January 1956 until April, when the Soviet leaders arrived, arranging the programme was my major preoccupation. The vexations, which I shared with Murray Simons of the Northern Department, were caused, simply because he was the messenger, by Ivan Ippolitov of the Soviet Embassy. While the aim of the visit and the agenda for the talks between the leaders were agreed in principle, it seemed to be the Soviet intention to shape the programme to suit their own purposes and to disregard ours. I decided to apply the lesson I had absorbed during the Geneva conference two years earlier. Murray and I refused to accept the more outrageous of Ippolitov's proposals however many times he reiterated them, until he either abandoned or amended them. Likewise we repeated those to which we attached importance until he eventually acquiesced. After some weeks Ippolitov appreciated that this way of proceeding was becoming ridiculous. A twinkle entered his eye and he began to share with us the difficulties his instructions caused him. On our side we had no wish to make his life harder and from then on we made good progress. Marshal Bulganin had the courtesy in his first conversation with Reading to apologise for the problems we had been caused over the arrangements.

The programme as eventually agreed included plenty of time for talks both at Number 10 and at Chequers, a call on The Queen at Windsor, and visits to Birmingham and Edinburgh, Harwell and Calder Hall and the RAF station at Marham. The Soviet cruiser *Ordzhonikidze* arrived at Portsmouth shortly before noon on 18 April. The Soviet party was met by the First Lord of the Admiralty and Lord Reading. We all travelled by train to Victoria where the main party was assembling. Girls in an office block overlooking the railway station at Portsmouth waved cheerily at Khrushchev, who seemed pleased. One of the Special Branch officers was scornful. "No accounting for taste," he said, "some women will wave at anything in trousers." On the journey to London I enjoyed sharing a table with Tupolev, the aircraft designer, and Kurchatov, the nuclear scientist, and was impressed by their affability and the pertinence of their questions.

The visit was judged a success and on 27 April the Soviet party returned in good humour to their cruiser in Portsmouth. Eden expressed himself satisfied with the handling of the visit and, as an exception to the general rule, authorised those involved to keep the presents they had received from the two Soviet leaders. Through this gesture I acquired an east German camera ostensibly made in Kiev.

❖

During the summer of 1956 ministers' attention was directed increasingly towards the Middle East. Although his responsibilities lay elsewhere, Reading followed developments with some anxiety. Tony Nutting, who was directly involved, came through the hole in the wall at regular intervals to keep Reading informed and to seek his views. In the early autumn, when it seemed that Eden was leading the country into a major crisis over Suez, Reading sent the foreign secretary a personal memorandum in which he warned of the risks to the Commonwealth, and our relations with the developing world in general, if we were to resort to force. His immediate reward was to be removed from the list of those in the Office to whom papers on the Suez crisis were circulated. His ultimate reward was to lose his post when Harold Macmillan succeeded Eden as prime minister in January 1957. By then, Jean and I and our young family were elsewhere.

❖

8

Centre for Arab Studies

One day in the summer of 1956, as I was crossing St James's Park on my way back to the Foreign Office after lunch, I heard the familiar voice of John Henniker[1] behind me: "I have been looking for you", he said. John Henniker was at that time the head of the personnel department. He went on: "What would you say to going back to the Middle East Centre?" "To do what?" I asked. "To be Director," he replied. I was astounded.

John Henniker-Major had joined the diplomatic service in 1938. While serving in the army during the war he had been wounded in the western desert. Later he joined Fitzroy Maclean's mission to Tito's partisans in Yugoslavia. His ambition as head of the personnel department – a post he held from 1953 to 1960 – was to modernise the service and make it professional. He recognised that the post-war environment in which the service had to operate was quite different from that to which the old-style diplomats had been accustomed. He had the advantage that senior members of the service regarded him as one of their own and were therefore more likely to go along with the reforms he had in mind.

So far as British interests in the Middle East were concerned, John took the view that, if these were to be adequately protected and fostered, training in the Arabic language had to be taken more seriously. While there were notable exceptions, many members of the pre-war Levant service had got by with a superficial knowledge of Arabic. Apart from this, they were regarded by the rest of the service as a somewhat exotic breed apart. John Henniker had two objectives in this regard: first, to raise the standard of Arabic training and, secondly, to 'normalise' Arabic by persuading members of the service as a whole that specialisation in Arab affairs was no different from other specialisms, and did not close the door to other types of work, or the most senior posts.

From previous conversations John Henniker was aware that I agreed with his approach and that I felt that the potential of the Middle East

Centre had not been realised. My experience in Amara and Baghdad, where I had to speak and read Arabic for many hours every day, had persuaded me that Arabic tuition at the Centre could be improved in several ways. The teaching texts ought to deal with contemporary subjects and the situations students would encounter in their everyday business. More opportunities had to be created to practise speaking. But there was a more serious problem. The Arab concept of language differed from the European and the Asian. For religious reasons the Arabic language had for centuries been the principal medium of artistic expression. Moreover, the Koran was a revealed scripture – the words of God made known to the prophet Muhammad in the Arabic language – and this gave all books a certain sacrosanctity. For Arabs therefore their language was the core of their culture and the richness of its vocabulary one of its esteemed features. This presented the foreigner who had to live and work with Arabs and for whom a knowledge of the language would be uniquely valuable, with a formidable challenge: how best to assimilate a working vocabulary three times as extensive as would be needed in almost every other part of the world. The solution probably lay in a systematic approach over several months.

As we approached Downing Street that summer afternoon, John explained that he had decided that the Middle East Centre had to be re-launched and that he wanted me to do this. It took me only as long as it takes to draw breath to agree. I was excited and honoured.

❖

Jean and I had adequate time to prepare for our move to Lebanon. Through the friend of a friend, we met a charming young woman called Celia Pridham, who agreed to come with us and help to look after Colin, then nearly four, and Alison, who was nearly two. In agreeing to join our household on this exciting venture, Celia can have had little idea of the effect it was to have on her destiny.

The nationalisation of the Suez Canal Company in July 1956 and the crisis this precipitated cast a cloud over our preparations. Although the situation deteriorated over the following months, there was no suggestion that our posting would be affected. On 14 October we crossed the Channel with our car by air ferry from Lydd in Kent, drove in stages to Venice and sailed from there on 17 October. The ship called at Alexandria on the way to Beirut, where we arrived on 25 October.

After the enforced camping out at Zerqa in 1947 as guests of the Transjordan Frontier Force, Bertram Thomas had found a new site for the Centre in the village of Shemlan, situated in the hills some twenty miles by road to the east of Beirut. As Alan Trott, the retiring director, and his wife Hester were not due to leave Shemlan for a few days, we stayed at the local hotel. Alan Trott had retired from his last post as ambassador at Jedda some years earlier. The Trotts' farewell to the staff of the Centre coincided with Israel's invasion of Sinai. On the following day, 30 October, while we were moving into the director's house, the British and French governments issued their ultimatum to Egypt and Israel, threatening to intervene militarily if hostilities had not ceased within twenty-four hours. Egyptian airfields were bombed on 31 October and 1 November. On 4 November I was instructed by the Foreign Office to go immediately to Cyprus to take over a radio station. I would be briefed on arrival by John Shattock, the political representative with Middle East forces and Brigadier Bernard Fergusson, who was in charge of the armed forces' public relations – the same Bernard Fergusson I had met in Bangalore when he gave an account of the Chindit expedition in Burma in 1944. While I flew to Nicosia on 5 November, British paratroops were consolidating their positions at Port Said, in preparation for the seaborne assault.

The story I was told in Nicosia was barely credible. Because it was dissatisfied with the way the BBC Arabic service had been reporting the Suez crisis, the British government had decided to requisition 'Sharq al Adna', the Near East Broadcasting station. This station had been established in Palestine in 1941 and removed to Cyprus in 1948 when the British mandate was coming to an end. Its programmes – news and comment as well as entertainment – were highly regarded in the Arab world. On 30 October 1956, the day the British and French governments issued their ultimatum, the director, Ralph Poston, was informed that the name of the station and its nature would be changed as from 3 p.m. on that day. 'Sharq al Adna' became 'The Voice of Britain' and on its wavelength messages were broadcast warning the people of Egypt to expect bombing raids. Poston had sought to persuade both the British and the Arab staff to accept the change but, at the request of the Arabs, most of whom were Palestinian Christians, he broadcast a message explaining that they were operating under duress. As soon as news of this broadcast reached allied headquarters, Bernard Fergusson ordered Poston and his wife to be placed under house arrest. At this point the entire editorial staff, British and Arab, and the announcers walked out. This meant that the British government had acquired an Arabic radio station, but had no one to operate it. My job was to take it over.

I was joined in Cyprus by three Arabic-speaking members of the foreign service from other Middle East posts. On the morning of the following day, 6 November, we were flown to the south of the island where we were met by a squadron-leader. He drove us to the broadcasting station situated beside a military camp on a slope overlooking the bay of Limassol.

Our situation had an unreal quality. The station had been kept on the air by an engineer, the output consisting of endless gramophone records. My appeal to Beirut to recruit Arabs who could act as announcers produced rapid results. Two brave men, a Lebanese and a Palestinian, joined us within a few days.

On 9 November I received a telephone call from the political representative's office in Nicosia. Having identified me correctly, the voice said: "I am afraid I have bad news for you. We have just heard that there was a bomb attack on the Centre in Shemlan last night. The building has been damaged. Some of your students were injured. Your family are safe." I was still feeling numb when the telephone rang again. This time it was the British Embassy at Beirut. "I have bad news for you," the voice said. The anxiety that swept over me was soon allayed when this turned out to be the same story and not a sequel. Later in the day I managed to telephone to Jean in Shemlan. She demonstrated, not for the first nor the last time, her remarkable composure in moments of crisis or distress.

When I eventually returned to Shemlan, Jean told me what had happened. She had arranged a dinner party for that evening in our house, which was about a hundred yards from the Centre. Those invited included James Craig,[2] the principal instructor, and his wife, Margaret. The bomb exploded during dinner. The verandah windows along one entire wall of the dining room bulged inwards under the force of the blast, then shattered. No one in the dining room was cut. The children, safe in their room on the other side of the house, slept throughout. James Craig went across at once to the Centre to discover what injuries and damage had been caused. The wall of his own office had been blown in; had he been working late rather than dining at our house, he could not have survived. In one of the upper rooms Terry Clark,[3] one of the foreign service students, had been sitting in his armchair with his back to the window. That part of his head which was above the back of his chair was severely cut and the chair itself was riddled with shards of glass. Whatever the intention of the terrorist, said to be from a neighbouring village and in the pay of the Egyptian embassy in Beirut, it was only by good fortune that no one was killed.

The news of the bomb attack did nothing to improve the morale of the team at Limassol. By this time we had established a routine. London sent us broadcasting material by two methods; the less urgent came daily by air and the immediate by wireless. We recorded the latter and transferred it to tapes suitable for transmission. We even contrived to compile our own entertainment programmes by drawing on the large quantity of recorded material accumulated by the station over the years.

For the first several days we were ostracised by the British staff of the station who had walked out when Ralph Poston was arrested. No doubt they saw us as instruments of a policy with which they disagreed and resented our taking over their functions, however inexpert we were. It seemed not to have occurred to them that we might share their view about the government's handling of the Suez affair, nor did they appreciate that we were in duty bound to carry out the instructions of the government we served to the best of our ability, however disagreeable we might find this. One of them, with more imagination and charity in his heart than his colleagues, did eventually visit us and, when he realised our situation, offered helpful advice on the understanding that this did not compromise his position. Later on others followed his lead.

We were not yet aware that the obnoxious nature of the bombing broadcasts at the time of the Anglo-French intervention had gravely damaged the credibility of the station in the Arab world. However, the futility of our endeavours was evident to us all. After two weeks I asked London how long it was intended that I remain in Cyprus; I was anxious to get on with the job I had come out to do. A few days later I was asked to return to London to report. My recommendation that the station and its transmitter be handed over at the earliest opportunity to the BBC was received more stoically than I had expected. I was released and allowed to return to my new job and my family in Shemlan.

❖

On my return to Shemlan on 27 November I faced an immediate problem. One of the foreign service students, Peter Mansfield, asked to see me on a personal matter. He said he found it impossible to continue in the service of a government capable of such actions as we had seen over the past several weeks. He therefore wanted me to know that he was submitting his resignation from the foreign service. I said that if this was indeed his considered view, then I had to respect it. He should not assume, however, that he had a monopoly of indignation over the Suez affair. Moreover, there was an alternative to resignation. This was to remain in the service, contribute to the great effort which would be needed over coming years to repair the damage done to British interests in the Arab world, and use one's influence from within to prevent such folly in the future. This was what I intended to do. He agreed to reflect further, but in the end did not alter his decision. This enhanced my regard for him. Peter left the service and went on to make a successful career commenting authoritatively over many years on Middle East affairs.

I was at last able to focus on the affairs of the Centre. A pleasant surprise was in store. James Craig, a considerable Arabic scholar, had been lecturing in Arabic at Durham University when he was seconded to the foreign service in 1955 to become principal instructor at Shemlan. He and I discovered that our views on the teaching of Arabic had much in common; indeed he had already been planning a number of reforms.

So there began a creative and enjoyable partnership. We worked late into the evenings compiling a list of some three thousand Arabic words which we arranged in broad order of the frequency of their use in modern literary and spoken Arabic. These three thousand words were then grouped into ten sections each of three hundred words – the commonest words in the first sections, the less common in the later sections. The Arab instructors, some of whom were the same Palestinian Christians who had taught me ten years earlier, were rather bemused but treated our efforts with benign tolerance. We then prepared new teaching texts each of which was related to a particular section of the word list. In this way students would learn from the beginning to use the commonest words which would become instinctive as they progressed steadily through the ten sections. We intended that the vocabulary would be mastered in from six to ten months. Subsequent experience justified this expectation. The word list and its companion teaching texts were only the first of our innovations.

I also had an opportunity to absorb our new surroundings. Shemlan was a mixed village. Most of the inhabitants were Maronites – Christians in communion with Rome – and they belonged to four families of which the Hitti family were dominant. The two substantial buildings which housed the Centre at the lower end of the village belonged to a Druze sheikh, Fuad Muqaddim. These had formerly been used for the manufacture of silk. The ground floor of our residence on the other side of a small stream was occupied by our landlord, Sheikh Fuad's cousin, and his two spinster sisters. Fuad's younger brother owned a hotel in the village; 'Mulberry Lodge', as it was called, evoked the Muqaddim history of cultivating silk-worms.

Married students rented houses in the village from Hittis, Tabibs, Jabbours and Farajullahs. The grocers, bakers and butchers had a captive market which they served to mutual satisfaction. In his restaurant, Cliff House, from which his customers enjoyed a view over terraces planted with olive trees, down to the shore and out across the Mediterranean towards Cyprus, the village headman, another Hitti, offered a splendid Arab meal accompanied by one of the delectable wines of Lebanon – the white Ksara, the Tourelles rosé, or the majestic red Musar – all at a reasonable price.

At weekends we took Celia Pridham and the children on visits to other parts of Lebanon. Celia's rapport with Colin and Alison ensured that they enjoyed the snow at the Cedars, the fountains in the courtyard at Beiteddine, the ravine through which the Dog River flowed, the waterfall at Jezzine and the columns and lions' heads at Baalbeck. A special pleasure in these early days was resuming contact with John Rae. He had left the British Council to join the BBC and, at the time of the Suez affair, he was the Corporation's representative in

Cairo. When hostilities began he was expelled, together with others. The BBC posted him to Beirut and he became a frequent visitor to Shemlan. One weekend we planned a joint trip to the ancient port of Byblos, twenty-five miles north of Beirut. We welcomed John's suggestion that he bring with him a colleague from Cairo, Michael Adams, the Middle East correspondent of *The Guardian*. We met on the great stone jetty of the old harbour. Michael and Celia exchanged looks. A few months later, in July 1957, I had the honour, *in loco parentis*, of giving her away to Michael at a joyful marriage service at the Church of All Saints in Beirut.

James Craig and I continued our reform of the methods of Arabic instruction. In the absence of a practical alternative, we based instruction in colloquial Arabic on a purified version of the language spoken locally. Instead of sending students off to fend for themselves during a six-week 'language break' as had been the practice, we kept them in Shemlan for the first two weeks, during which they were gradually introduced to the situations they would encounter. What we called the 'colloquial fortnight' began with a lunch party in the shade of the pine trees which surrounded the terrace in front of the Centre. Jean and I offered an Arab meal to staff and students, colleagues from the Embassy in Beirut and notables from Shemlan and neighbouring villages. The centre-piece of the meal was a *quzi* – whole roast lamb stuffed with rice, dried fruit, nuts and pine kernels – but ours was a modest version of the dish I had seen when I dined with the Hacham tribe in the marshes of Iraq in 1947. The domestic staff of the Centre came into their own; Nasib and Jadullah, Druzes from adjacent villages, and Karim Hitti performed a sword dance to the accompaniment of pipe and drum. Our neighbours returned the compliment by entertaining our students to tea parties in their villages when they enjoyed playing their role as surrogate instructors in the spoken language.

Visitors to the Centre came from further afield and were a welcome interruption to our routine. One morning Freya Stark and St John Philby, whom I had met briefly in Cairo ten years earlier, who happened to be visiting Lebanon at the same time, drove up from Beirut to lunch with us. Rather unfairly perhaps I suggested that they sit in on some of our classes. The advanced students happened to be reading and discussing *Hayati* (My Life), by the notable Egyptian writer, Ahmad Amin. Both our distinguished guests confessed to me afterwards that they were quite out of their depth. I saw St John Philby's son, Kim, only once but was unable to speak to him; the occasion was a cocktail party in Beirut and he was incapable.

The 're-launch' intended by John Henniker required more than reform of the teaching methods. The Centre itself, our dedicated Arab instructors, our teaching materials and the range of contacts we had developed with academics and others in public life in Beirut – all these were important assets which had to be better exploited. The previous annual intake of just over twenty students from the foreign service, the armed forces, oil companies and other commercial enterprises did not constitute adequate use of our resources in Shemlan. The remedy was to reshape the existing courses. Students who obtained their intermediate standard qualification at the end of the ten-month long course were encouraged to continue their studies for another five months. Those who passed the higher standard examination at the end of this additional course qualified for a modest language allowance when serving in Arabic speaking posts. The response of the students to the more intensive advanced course could not have been more positive. All eight who stayed on were successful in their final examination.

This examination consisted of a written and an oral test, each worth 50 per cent. The written papers were returned to London for marking and the oral test was conducted by an outside examiner. The embassy in Beirut made their head translator available for this purpose. Mr Akhal was a precise and courteous man. To put candidates at their ease, he would begin by asking about their family, their interests and so on. One of the foreign service students, noted for his eloquence in English, responded enthusiastically to Mr Akhal's routine enquiry about his health. "I am glad you ask," he said. "Health, I believe, is more important than many people think. After all, without good health . . . " and so on in fluent and grammatically correct Arabic. Mr Akhal's subsequent questions were despatched to the boundary in similar fashion. When the interview was over it was Mr Akhal who felt drained. "Fifty out of fifty," he said. I demurred; I was anxious about the reaction in London. "I agree that he made no errors. But was his performance perfect? What about his accent? Would you have taken him for an Arab?" Mr Akhal relented and settled for forty-eight out of fifty.

By increasing the number of students attending courses during the year we were of course contributing more in fees to the exchequer. But any extra expenditure we incurred, whether to engage an additional Arab instructor, or to buy new brake linings for the Land Rover, required London's approval. Throughout the process of change our recommendations were strongly supported not only by the Foreign Office, but also by the oil companies and banks who regularly sent members of their staff to our courses. With their combined help we were able to accept applications from private individuals and we began to receive more foreign students working both in government and in business.

❖

It became increasingly clear that we could not expand our activities further on our existing site. No other suitable accommodation was available in the village. There were other considerations. Fuad Muqaddim was proving an awkward landlord and was vaguely threatening some undefined legal action against the Centre. Living conditions in winter were barely acceptable; indeed one generation of students renamed the Centre 'Stalag Muqaddim'. There were occasional problems over the supply of water. This had to be pumped manually from underground cisterns by an immensely strong Druze named Nimr, who lived in another village three miles away. The supply of electricity was even less reliable. One evening we were expecting George Middleton, the ambassador in Beirut, and his wife for dinner. A severe storm half an hour before they were due to arrive fused the electricity in our residence. We sent for Mulhim, the village electrician. He refused to come. We sent him an even more urgent message: "The British ambassador is coming to dinner. You must come and mend the fuse." Mulhim's reply was emphatic: "I'm not going out in a storm like this – not even for Queen Victoria." Our cook, Mikhail, fetched a step ladder and replaced the burnt out wire in the fuse with a three-inch nail. We dined in well-lit comfort.

Jean and I toured areas of Lebanon within easy reach of Beirut in search of suitable premises for an expanded Centre. At first the people of Shemlan treated these trips with scorn. They became concerned however when an American quaker school in the hills north of the Beirut river showed interest in offering us space. At this point, I received an approach from Eddie Hitti which began a friendship between our families that has endured ever since.

Eddie had graduated in the United States and was effectively running the travel business in Beirut called Hitti Frères. Eddie and his wife, Janet, offered to provide·a site for a new Centre on land they owned above the main road that ran through the village. Eddie's motive was clear. The livelihood of many of his relatives depended on our presence in the village. He said half seriously: "You know my relatives; I'd rather you provided for them." His original proposal was that he and Janet would provide the site on a long lease and that the British government would build the new centre. However, after a few encounters with representatives of the British Ministry of Works, Eddie changed his mind. He offered to build to our specifications and to lease the building and the land to the British government. His only condition was that the building should be adaptable for use either as a hotel or a clinic in the event of the Centre's closing, or moving elsewhere. Eddie's price was reasonable and London endorsed the deal.

Work began immediately on clearing the site. This gave welcome employment to the inhabitants not only of Shemlan but of other villages in the neighbourhood. However, there was an early setback. Excavation uncovered an ancient landslide and digging had to begin again further up the slope. Bedrock was eventually struck at sixteen metres. Thereafter work made rapid progress and the industrious and practical Jeffrey Greaves, who had taken over the post of administrative officer at the Centre in August 1957, ensured compliance with the agreed plans.

At the beginning of March 1958 John Henniker visited Shemlan to see for himself the effect of the changes we had made. James Craig, to whom the service had wisely offered permanent establishment, left the Centre to take up a post in the Foreign Office later that month. His unique contribution to the work of the Centre commanded the admiration of our staff and successive generations of students. I was especially grateful for the patience with which he had persuaded our Arab instructors to accept the new teaching programme, of which they soon became enthusiastic advocates. James was replaced on a temporary basis by Denis Michell, one of the foreign service students who had successfully completed the advanced course. Denis was a gentle giant. During the war his aircraft had been shot down over Germany. He baled out and landed beside a detachment of German soldiers. Elated by his survival he told his captors, apart from his name, rank and number, what a remarkable experience it was to float down in silence through the darkness of the night. His captors listened patiently. One said: "We know. You have landed in the middle of a parachute regiment." Denis spent the rest of the war in prison camps.

❖

The Suez affair had greatly enhanced Nasser's prestige throughout the Arab world and given fresh encouragement to Arab nationalists. It was inevitable that this would create new tensions in Lebanon. The Lebanese constitution was based on a balance of interests which favoured the Maronites; it stipulated that the president of the republic would invariably be Maronite, the prime minister Sunni Muslim, and the speaker of the parliament a Shia Muslim. Even though the demography was changing, this division of power was acceptable so long as the country pursued policies which were balanced with similar sensitivity. This meant in practice that Lebanon's long-standing connections with western Europe and the United States, which were well understood throughout the Middle East, should not be seen to conflict with the nationalist aspirations of the rest of the Arab world. Camille Chamoun, the President of Lebanon, saw a threat to the position of Lebanese Christians in the growth of Nasser's influence. In the spring of 1958 relationships within the political community in Lebanon deteriorated sharply and fighting broke out. Although the hostilities which continued for the next few months did not match in ferocity the two subsequent civil wars, they interfered with everyday life.

The Druze leader, Kamal Jumblatt, whose so-called 'forces of popular resistance' were based at Mukhtara, some twelve miles by twisting mountain road to the south east of Shemlan, supported the nationalist cause. This caused some anxiety among the Maronites in our village, but the predominant feeling was that the people of Shemlan should keep their heads down and get on with their work. Some may have calculated that the presence of a British government establishment and some eighty British and other foreign nationals in Shemlan would ensure that they were left undisturbed. They might well have been right. However, one of the four families in the village, the Farajullahs, who had links with the PPS, the Parti Populaire Syrien, a militant right-wing Christian organisation which supported Chamoun, upset this calculation. The Farajullahs brought a number of armed members of the PPS into the village who, on most nights, took to firing at imaginary infiltrators.

Discreetly we drew up contingency plans. The owner of the Hajjar hotel in the neighbouring village of Suq al-Gharb, where Denis and Gillian Michell lived, agreed to accommodate our families in the event of our having to leave Shemlan and we prepared a provisional allocation of accommodation according to the size of the families. Students with their own cars were advised to keep their petrol tanks filled and everyone was asked to have one suitcase ready containing essentials for a few days. One of the Royal Air Force students, 'Danny' Daniel, who was knowledgeable in such matters, prepared a portable short-wave radio link with the embassy for use if the telephone line was cut. By this time Danny was in any case becoming an honorary member of our household, as he and Kathleen Worsley, who had taken Celia Pridham's place in August 1957, were forming a close attachment.

Early one afternoon one of the PPS gunmen was stricken with panic. He fired at Jeffrey Greaves' car, wounding Jeffrey in the back. Fortunately, the upholstery reduced the velocity of the bullet and Jeffrey was soon able to resume his duties. The culprit was immediately sent away from Shemlan, but my efforts to persuade the Farajullahs to remove the PPS detachment altogether were of no avail. The embassy in Beirut, whom I kept regularly informed and from whom I occasionally sought guidance, were inclined to suggest that I keep in touch with the local authorities. Since the cause of our difficulties was the complete absence of anyone in authority, this was of little help. But on the occasion of the wounding of Jeffrey Greaves my appeal had slightly more impact. On our behalf the embassy asked President Chamoun to have the PPS replaced. This appeal proved equally ineffective but, no doubt as a sop, the gendarmerie detachment in the village was reinforced by the arrival of two elderly reservists charged specifically with protecting the Centre.

Nightly alarms continued. On the afternoon of Sunday, 29 June,

Colin Keith, one of the Royal Navy students, was detained by a party of armed Druzes while out walking his dog a few miles to the south of Shemlan. While under guard he counted up to thirty trucks full of armed men heading north in the direction of Shemlan. Colin was released after a few hours and immediately reported to me what had happened. Everyone was put on the alert. Under an arrangement with All Saints Church in Beirut, the intrepid rector, John Grinstead, who travelled everywhere on a Vespa scooter, visited Shemlan once a month to conduct evensong in the drawing room of our residence. It so happened that he was due that evening. The Third Collect perfectly expressed what was in our hearts and minds: 'Lighten our darkness, we beseech thee, O Lord; and by thy great mercy defend us from all perils and dangers of this night'.

Jean and I were wakened in the early hours of Monday morning by the sound of small arms fire. Unlike the night-time shooting over the previous two months, this seemed to have a purpose. From our verandah we saw a number of villagers and some of our Arab instructors making their way down the slope away from the village. At 8 o'clock Denis Michell telephoned from his house in Suq al-Gharb to pass on a message from Kamal Jumblatt, which had just been conveyed to him by one of his Druze neighbours. According to this message, the attack about to be mounted was not directed at the British residents of Shemlan but at the paramilitary group belonging to the PPS. Jumblatt advised me to evacuate our people. This message had obviously been seriously delayed. The firing which had wakened us must have been the start of the assault. I asked Denis to get his neighbour to explain the situation to Kamal Jumblatt and to request a brief cease-fire to enable us to move our people out to Suq al-Gharb. We would fly white flags from our vehicles.

Our own suitcases were ready. Jean began tearing up sheets to make white flags. As far as I could see, Jumblatt's men had occupied the old Turkish trenches dating from the first world war on the hill to the east from which they could observe all movement in the village. Except that there was none; the village seemed deserted. At deliberate pace I walked the hundred yards to the Centre. I asked two of the students, Bill Norton and Andrew Johnstone, to call on all our families in the village and tell them to assemble with their luggage and cars on the track below our residence. We telephoned the same message to the two other families in the village of Ainab, a mile to the south. As the vehicles arrived we formed them into small convoys and gave each a white flag. The two elderly gendarmerie reservists came over to our house from their billet in the Centre. They had in their eyes the same look as family pets when they see luggage by the front door and wonder if they are going too. I told them to take off their caps and jackets, put their rifles and packs on the floor of the Land Rover and keep their heads down. They called on the Almighty to lengthen my life. I recounted this incident several years later when accompanying the foreign secretary on a visit to Yugoslavia. One of our hosts said accusingly: "You interfered in the internal affairs of Lebanon."

By 11 o'clock the evacuation was complete and we spent the rest of the morning settling into the Hajjar hotel. Colin Keith and his wife, supported by other willing hands, organised activities for the children. News from Shemlan in the late afternoon suggested that Jumblatt's forces had withdrawn to the south. We resumed language instruction the following day in the hotel. When I visited the pharmacist in Suq al-Gharb, who had proved a good source of local information in the past, he said several wounded from both sides in the fighting had been brought in the previous day. He objected strongly to having to treat those who had received their wounds after they were captured.

A day too late armoured cars and mortar units of the Lebanese army arrived on the scene. To our disappointment they did not replace the PPS irregulars, who were claiming victory. This claim was premature. On the morning of 3 July Druze elements were reported to have returned to the high ground and to be pushing north. Vampire aircraft of the Lebanese air force flew low over the hotel before releasing rockets at positions alleged to be occupied by the Druzes. In the absence of decisive and effective action by government forces to stabilise the situation in this area, I felt we had no choice but to suspend our activities. After discussion with senior members of the staff I ordered the evacuation of all British personnel to Beirut. The Arab teachers elected to remain with their families. I promised to keep them informed of developments.

John Rae generously offered our family hospitality. On 5 July, accompanied by Charles Wheen, the naval attaché at the embassy, I returned to Shemlan to collect more of our belongings. We had to negotiate our way through a PPS road block. They insisted on showing us what they claimed was evidence of Egyptian involvement in the attack on Shemlan. This turned out to be the corpse of a large man of African origin clad in combat uniform, lying on the roadside at the southern entrance to the village. I could not imagine how he had come to be involved. The PPS seemed surprised when I asked when they intended burying the corpse.

Charles Wheen and I went on to the largely Druze village of Ainab to recover certain personal effects for one of our young couples. We found their house occupied by half a dozen armed PPS. It had been systematically ransacked. Clothing had been torn to shreds and gramophone records smashed. While Charles and I were inside retrieving what was retrievable, a hand grenade exploded outside. When I went out to investigate one of the PPS said rather sheepishly, "It's only training."

I called out their leader and told him, among other things, that I had never seen a squad of so-called soldiers more in need of training or discipline.

The students were dispersed from Lebanon for the time being. Jean and I paid two more visits to Shemlan before she and the children left for home in the middle of July. Soon after the US marines landed in Beirut, I followed. In discussion with the Foreign Office it was agreed without difficulty that there could be no question of a return to Lebanon until the situation was stabilised. Meanwhile, I should look for temporary premises for the Centre in England. The search took us to Oxford to inspect surplus accommodation at one of the colleges and to a redundant military establishment at Husbands Bosworth, which looked like a real-life 'Stalag Muqaddim'.

Early in September the embassy in Beirut reported that the situation in Lebanon had stabilised. Camille Chamoun had been succeeded as president by the highly regarded General Fuad Chehab. The Lebanese government were keen for the Centre to return. I flew to Beirut on 9 September and drove up to Shemlan the following day. There were few villagers about, and most of the familiar faces were absent. Our buildings seemed not to have been damaged. Armed PPS were much in evidence, behaving as if they owned the place, which at that moment was probably true.

That evening Ian Scott, the chargé d'affaires at the embassy, took me to General Chehab's residence on the outskirts of the capital. The president pressed for the early return of the Centre to Shemlan. "Your presence," he said, "can bring more stability to that area than anything I can do." I said that I would gladly contribute to a return to stable conditions, but I could not recommend that families be allowed to return so long as the village was effectively under the control of undisciplined irregulars. Within a couple of days a unit of the Lebanese army arrived in Shemlan and instituted what were termed 'joint patrols', consisting of equal numbers of soldiers and irregulars. This device saved the face of the Army's allies in this area. Within a week the PPS irregulars had vanished. Calm returned to our mountainside. One evening I joined a group of villagers and their friends on the terrace of Cliff House. They were reviewing the tragic events of the past few months. They could not understand why the compromise which ended hostilities could not have been worked out months earlier. A young woman said: "Perhaps conflict was necessary. Now we can say we have won our independence." There was a murmur of approval. But, of course, they were all mistaken.

Jean returned with Colin and Alison on 20 September. Other families followed and we prepared to resume the work we had been doing when we had been so rudely interrupted. Kathleen Worsley stayed behind in England; she and the resourceful Danny were to be married six weeks later. Betty Fripp joined us within a few weeks; she too was to marry one of the students, Vivian Thomas.

William Kensdale, the new principal instructor, supervised the engagement of the extra teachers we needed to cope with the increased number of students. I was concerned that the language instruction still did not relate sufficiently to contemporary affairs. Reading the Lebanese press, which was of high quality by any standards, and listening to the radio provided a basis. But we needed to build on that. Discussion with the embassy pointed the way to a solution. They were prepared to second Talaat Dajani to the Centre. Talaat was a British subject of Palestinian origin who worked in the information department. He monitored political developments not only in Lebanon but in the Middle East generally and was personally acquainted with many politicians, academics and editors. He enjoyed the title of Arab Adviser which we gave him when he and his handsome Egyptian wife joined us. He added an important dimension to the advanced course and to the life of the Centre. We had another success. London agreed to a scholarship scheme under which each year two school-leavers who intended subsequently to read Arabic at university could attend the long course.

Work on the new building resumed with vigour. Colin and Alison were fascinated by the cutting of stone, the pouring of cement, the plastering of walls. Piped water reached the village for the first time. At night some canny villagers unscrewed the pipe, diverted water into their own cisterns and then rejoined the pipe. New power lines were installed. Jean and I had wondered for some time whether the former protestant church could be brought back into use. This was a small, neglected building in the middle of the village surrounded by trees. We asked Karim Hitti how he thought the village would react. His response was to bring us the keys and ask what he could do to help. The building seemed to be in good order. Karim helped us whitewash the walls. We accepted John Grinstead's offer of some surplus railings and wrought iron he had found in the church at Beirut. The blacksmith, the only Muslim in the village, made a lectern out of the wrought iron and refused payment. Jean made cloths for use at communion services out of brocade from Damascus. And on the Sundays between John Grinstead's monthly excursions on his Vespa, we held lay services, students taking it in turn to lead.

Before hostilities broke out in the summer of 1958 we had been able to hold the first of a planned programme of background courses. These were designed to give foreigners working in the Middle East a concise introduction to the history of the region, the economic situation in each country, religions, customs and traditions and the main issues of the day.

These proved popular. Up to thirty people with different interests and backgrounds from as far afield as Iraq and the Gulf spent five days at the Centre hearing presentations on these subjects from a range of experts, several of them from the American University of Beirut.

David Cowan joined us from the School of Oriental and African Studies in London in September 1959 at the end of Bill Kensdale's term as principal instructor. David, or Daud as he preferred, was a Scottish Muslim married to an Egyptian. He was a scholar not only of the language, written and spoken, but also of Islam. He was also a modest man. He arrived in time for the opening, in some minor discomfort, on 1 October 1959 of the first course in Eddie Hitti's magnificent new building. A day or two before Christmas we moved into the new director's house adjacent to the main building. Once the teething troubles had been dealt with, we all enjoyed and benefited from the splendid amenities.

For Colin and Alison, and for the children of our students, life in Shemlan was idyllic. The climate on the mountain knew no extremes. The countryside was beautiful and in many places spectacular. We were privileged to witness a way of life which must have endured in the hills and mountains of Lebanon for centuries. The people of Shemlan were straightforward, unsophisticated folk with the same characteristics of warmth, passion, and violence just below the surface as other peoples along the shores of the Mediterranean. As for the children's education, the PNEU system which Jean used in our do-it-yourself school provided a sound basis for the future. Jean and I were impressed by the methods and materials, for example, those which encouraged early appreciation of the visual arts.

My father spent many months with us in Shemlan. As he acknowledged later, this was for him an especially happy time. On behalf of Kew Gardens he accumulated a large collection of plants and, in the process, caused us anxiety from time to time. Our favourite activity at weekends was to drive into the countryside, visit a few places of interest and then select a spot for a picnic lunch. No sooner did we stop the car than my father would disappear from view over the hill, round the corner, or down into the valley in search of a new botanical specimen. How he detected these we never knew. It may have been his sense of smell. We knew this was acute because, when we had laid out the cloth and Jean had opened the thermos jars and begun to serve his favourite mutton curry, he would soon reappear. On other occasions he took great delight in introducing Colin and Alison to the mysteries of nature, whether at their favourite 'grassy sward', or 'lizard point', or on 'crystal mountain', so named by a previous resident of Shemlan, fascinated by the glinting of the quartz. It seemed to me that the magical hours the three of them spent together were some compensation for his having missed my childhood through his long absences in Africa.

Soon after we returned to London at the end of 1960, Norman Reddaway, a friend of long standing, suggested that I would look back on these four years at the Middle East Centre as the most rewarding in my life. This may have been intended as a compliment but, as a forecast, I wondered if it would prove accurate. Graduates of the Centre were certainly better qualified than before. And the position of Arabic speakers in the foreign service had been 'normalised'; since 1982 three former students have been appointed permanent under-secretary at the Foreign Office. Therefore in this sense the ambitions which John Henniker shared with me as we crossed St James's Park in the summer of 1956 had been fulfilled. But I was uneasy about the future.

A member of the British business community in Beirut had offered me a partnership if I would stay on in Lebanon. I declined, not simply because I wanted to remain in the foreign service, but because I believed that the calm which had descended on Lebanon after General Chehab became president in 1958 was illusory. My business friend said, and I agreed with him, that not too much notice should be taken of the charge, occasionally regurgitated by the nationalist press, that the Centre was a training ground for spies. Lebanese who followed public affairs found this notion somewhat comical and were even more amused when, in 1961, George Blake, then a student at the Centre, was identified as a Soviet agent. My anxiety was different. I felt that trends in the Arab world would continue to threaten, and might before long upset, the delicate balance on which the Lebanese constitution was based. In 1978, at the height of the atrocious civil war, the Centre had to close and I have sometimes wished that I had pressed harder in the early 1970s for an alternative site to be considered.

When James Craig and I had completed the word list in 1957 and were preparing the final text for printing, we asked our Arab instructors to suggest a motto which we could inscribe on the title page. The flamboyant Constantine Theodory, one of the Palestinians who had taught me in 1946, suggested a phrase which, while apposite, had the disadvantage that it contained two rather recherché words which we had not included in the list. This needed further work. Our final version was: "To increase understanding among nations." Needless to say, this sounds better in Arabic than in English. All of us at the Middle East Centre intended what this motto said, even though we knew that the task would be never-ending and that other forces, either by design or through inadvertence, would promote the opposite.

9

A French Love Affair

I was assured that working with John Russell,[1] whom I had not met, would be an interesting experience. As the assistant in the News Department of the Foreign Office, I was to be his deputy and was expected to cover the whole range of topics, as he did. Briefing the press required me to learn new skills and new rules and I was carefully and patiently tutored by a long-serving member of the department, John Bourgoin, who seemed to know everyone and to have seen everything at least once before. His guidance stood me in good stead over the following years.

In January 1961, a week or two after I joined the department, John Russell received a minute from the Lord Privy Seal's private office. Since the foreign secretary, Lord Home, sat in the House of Lords, the prime minister had appointed another member of the cabinet to represent the Foreign Office in the Commons. This was Edward Heath. Harold Macmillan had invited him to explore the prospects for an application to join the European Community and Heath was forming a team for this purpose. He wanted John Russell to nominate a member of the news department to join this team to act as spokesman. At the departmental briefing meeting that morning, Russell made it clear that he found this request tiresome. He had been unable to find out from Charles Wiggin, Edward Heath's private secretary, exactly what this would entail, for example, in absences from the department. In any case Russell doubted whether anything would come of the intended soundings of the Community. However, he had to respond to the request; were there any volunteers? Silence followed for ten seconds. Then I said I would take the job. In the twelve years I had spent in the service I had seen little of Europe. Here was an opportunity to redress the balance and, perhaps, to be part of an important enterprise from the beginning. It was also a chance to revive one of the dominant enthusiasms of my youth.

❖

I grew up at a time when children were discouraged from asking questions about the Great War of 1914 to 1918 – the War to End All Wars, as it was optimistically called. Almost every family had known bereavement and the scar tissue was still tender. I had to imagine what such words as 'shell-shock' meant; and I wondered why my mother became sad and silent when a young cripple, the Military Cross pinned to the lapel of his fraying jacket, came to our front door selling boxes of matches for a few pence. This adult reticence merely intensified my curiosity and I read everything I could about the tragedy and heroism of those awful years. The cupboard under the stairs was a treasure house. My mother had kept scores of issues of *War Illustrated*, a weekly publication which described various aspects of the war from military operations and acts of individual bravery to rationing, the U-boat menace and the manufacture of munitions. There were countless photographs – of Tommies drinking tea, or dancing to a phonograph, British subalterns trying to look older than their eighteen years, French 'poilus' with the bottom corners of their greatcoats buttoned back so that they could march the more easily, and sad-eyed, hollow-cheeked German prisoners of war.

In our household, from the moment Hitler came to power in Germany in January 1933, we followed events with mounting apprehension – the liquidation of the parliamentary system in Germany; the suppression of all political parties except the Nazi party; the persecution of Jews and intellectuals; Germany's withdrawal from the disarmament conference and the League of Nations; the decision in 1935 to rearm; the re-occupation of the Rhineland in 1936; the invasion and annexation of Austria in March 1938.

To us another war with Germany seemed inevitable and we found it hard to understand why influential sections of opinion in Britain should choose to ignore evidence apparent to the majority and to vilify their opponents. Many of our friends shared our puzzlement and our concern. We gave sanctuary in our home to two of the hundreds of Jewish children who had been allowed to leave Germany. For two years Peter and Wolfgang Ziegel were members of our family.

I divided my energies between my favourite school subjects – history and French language, literature and civilisation – and the Officers Training Corps. In the long summer evenings I joined with like-minded boys in carrying out mock reconnaissance patrols in the neighbouring countryside. In other ways we sought to sharpen our skills as potential platoon commanders. We were determined, when the time came, to survive rather longer than the six weeks' average life of subalterns on the western front in the Great War.

Our family's affection for France was aroused in the first instance by the French reading book used at school, and, secondly, by our teachers. I was the fourth son my mother had helped tread a path through *Le Beau Pays de France*, the seductively entitled reading book which was our basic initial text. The modern languages department was led by R. T. Currall, a towering figure, both physically and intellectually, whose beetling brow and heavy jowls earned him the inevitable nickname 'Piggy'. Ethel Davidson, one of his ablest lieutenants, was generous to the point of prodigality with her perfume. She swept along the corridors enwrapped in her own personal aura of fragrance. In her classroom successive generations were drilled in French irregular verbs, their accents were honed, and they ate out of her hand. If sex raised its head in 'Stinky' Davidson's classroom, it was not ugly.

Our favourite older cousin, Robert Dundas, was another strong influence. He spoke French fluently and brought us exciting accounts of life in Bordeaux where he had spent a year as a student. My second brother, Alastair, followed in his footsteps. In 1936 he was assistant at the Lycée Champollion in Grenoble and my parents decided that this provided an opportunity for the family to visit the country whose language and customs we had been studying so assiduously. So we made the journey from Edinburgh to Paris, where Alastair joined us. He had found rooms at the Grand Hôtel du Lion d'Argent, whose elevator should have been consigned to a museum of the industrial revolution, and devised a programme which enabled us to see the essential Paris in seven days.

This was a different Paris from today's. Virtually all the buses were open-backed and, from the rear platforms, as from a seat in the orchestra stalls, one could take in the movement, the sounds and smells of the city scene — the scores of forty year-old cripples from the Great War, the black-shawled widows selling evening papers at the street corners, their voices rising above the noise of the traffic: "*L'Intransigeant! Paris-Soir!*" Of course the architectural glories that took our breath away have survived. So has preoccupation with food. It was this which took us, on our first evening, to a restaurant in a corner of the Place de la Madeleine. We were enticed by the word *merlan* on the menu. The waiter assured us that the whiting was excellent; in this he was mistaken. The *merlan* was like wet blotting paper, with bones.

When we had finished the following morning's sightseeing, we found a more modest restaurant in the rue Boissy d'Anglas, not far from the Place de la Concorde. The mimeographed menu in the window of La Croisette seemed to offer exactly what we wanted, and at the right price. Lunch was a success, so was dinner, and lunch the following day.

The waitress clearly thought three consecutive visits merited recognition. Could we stay a few minutes? The patron would soon be finished and would like to meet us. Gladly, we replied.

The patron emerged from below stairs wiping his hands. No one could have looked less like the bustling Parisian we had expected. Orville Cunningham was tall and heavily-built, with close-cut red hair. He had served as a cook in the United States Navy. The Great War had brought him to France where he had met the girl who was now his wife. He had decided to settle in Paris doing what he most enjoyed – cooking.

For my brothers and me this was the beginning of a rewarding friendship. Our meals at La Croisette were unalloyed pleasure. Madame Cunningham made a fuss of us – which we did not in the least mind. Their teenage daughter, who had inherited her father's red hair, helped her mother at the seat of custom. The waitress carried out her duties with military, or perhaps naval, precision: "Deux haricots – deux!" and "Trois potages – trois!" she would shout down the hatch to the boss below.

In the summer of the following year – 1937 – I visited Paris again with two of my brothers. This was the year of the International Exposition and Paris was unbearably hot. Orville Cunningham found us lodgings in the Cité du Retiro, two minutes' walk from La Croisette, and told us what to see and what to miss at the Expo. Of course no one could miss the physical confrontation between the Soviet and German pavilions. Symbolising the armed confrontation between fascism and communism already taking place beyond the Pyrenees, this contained more than a hint of menace.

One Sunday Cunningham took us to the races at Auteuil. He said I was too young to place a bet. He rejected my protest, but agreed that I could at least mark my card. When I picked the winners of the first two races, he relented and let me bet on the third. I lost. "I told you it was a fool's game", he said and, as consolation, out of his own winnings he bought me a *bock* – my first taste of beer.

From Cunningham we learned not only how to find our way around Paris but also something of the subtleties of French life. We admired the skill with which this archetypal middle American had established himself in such a competitive city and won the respect of his friends and clientele.

❖

From Paris Alastair and I took the train to Lyon and then on to Grenoble. We were making for the village of Uriage-les-Bains in the foothills some twelve kilometres from Grenoble. During his year at the Lycée Champollion, Alastair had been given an introduction to a couple called Lucy. Arthur Lucy, who was English, was the managing director of a glove manufacturing concern in Grenoble – Gants Fownes. Madame Lucy was very French. They lived in a charming house – Eden Villa – in Uriage and were leading members of the golf club. Alastair and I had reserved a room in the Pension Sans Souci run by Madame

Prost. The other guests were for the most part families on summer holiday. For three sunny weeks we were immersed in a thoroughly French environment. The golf club was more cosmopolitan. Three Greek entrepreneurs – messieurs Zaffiri, Tamvaco and Rigopoulo, with accompanying womenfolk – were regular summer visitors. They spent more time on the terrace of the club house than on the course, drinking tisane and conversing in accents warmed by the hot, Aegean sun. There were outings to other golf clubs and neighbouring villages, and bridge with the Lucys in the evening.

In the summer of 1939, this time alone, I stopped in Paris on my way to Uriage-les-Bains. Once again Orville Cunningham found me lodgings. After dinner at La Croisette, we exchanged news and discussed the threat of another war. Cunningham was pessimistic and, despite the glorious summer weather, it was with some unease that I set off south the following day. At Uriage-les-Bains I was glad to find that Madame Prost had a full house. Among the families there were several young folk of my own age. I accompanied the Berthaud family on excursions to the resort of La Grave, dominated by the magnificent peak of La Meije, to the Galibier and Lautaret passes and to the massive seventeenth century monastery, the Grande Chartreuse. With Monsieur Eisseron and his son, Louis, I climbed to the Cascade de l'Oursière and joined Monsieur Delnomdedieu at *pétanque*. I played golf with Lally Vagliano, a talented French girl, who was to achieve fame in later years as a champion under her married name, the Vicomtesse de Saint-Sauveur. Bridge on most evenings as before with the Lucys, who prescribed a brutal but effective paregoric when I succumbed to a stomach infection.

Madame Lucy did not share my worries over political developments. She placed her trust in the Maginot Line, which she was convinced would deter German aggression. Not even when the German–Soviet Non-Aggression Pact was signed on 23 August was she moved. I consulted my parents in Edinburgh by telegram. They agreed that I should return home at once. When I went to Eden Villa to tell Madame Lucy that I was leaving, she met me with a warm embrace and I had no need to say my piece. She had at length appreciated the danger. Her daughter, who was on holiday with her children nearby, was as alarmed as I was by the news from Moscow, and had decided to curtail the family holiday and return to Paris. Arthur Lucy drove us all to the station at Grenoble and arranged a seat for me on the train north.

In Paris, on my way from the Gare de Lyon to Gare Saint-Lazare, I called at La Croisette to see Orville Cunningham and wish him well. He was out on business and I could not spare the time to await his return. The railway station was crowded with reservists in new uniforms and with new kitbags, taking leave of loved ones before moving off to join their regiments. The cross-channel steamer from Dieppe was crowded, but I found a perch on top of a hatch. One of my more chatty fellow travellers said he supposed we would all be coming back in uniform in a few months' time. Most of us were either too tired or too preoccupied for conversation. At that same time, perhaps even on the same ship, a young woman called Jean Young was also going home after cutting short her French holiday.

❖

Clutching my Certificate A from the Officers Training Corps, I presented myself at the headquarters of Scottish Command on 1 September 1939. A sergeant-major with the Mons Star and a waxed moustache told me politely to "go home, sonny, we may need you in a couple of years." When the time did come for my age-group to be called on to test our nerve and military skills, Europe had been overrun; so most of us went to war in other continents. When in due course those who survived came home, our horizons had widened and we placed Europe in a global rather than a continental context.

In the post-war world I found the prospects for our continent obscure. In 1946 Churchill had declared at Zurich that "the first step in the re-creation of the European family must be partnership between France and Germany". A bold statement so soon after the defeat and occupation of Germany; but what role did Churchill envisage for Britain? Meanwhile, at that very time General de Gaulle, of all people, was expressing the view that one of the conditions for a European settlement was "a real and sincere agreement between Britain and France". These differing prescriptions were as disconcerting as the attitudes towards continental Europe which I found on joining the Foreign Office in 1947.

Senior members of the foreign service had been intimately involved in creating the war-time alliance and implementing the strategy which not only brought victory, but also designed the political and economic framework for the post-war world. They had worked in close partnership with Washington – and with the State Department, the US Treasury and the Department of Defense in particular. It was understandable then that a number of key figures in the Foreign Office, including the two most senior, should place a higher value on Britain's connection with the United States which, they felt, would be endangered by too close an association with continental Europe. Some in the Office believed that moves towards European unity were a device by France to persuade other countries, and especially Britain, to shoulder a disproportionate share of the economic burden. Others took the view that an organic connection with the continent would undermine valuable links, both political and economic, with the Commonwealth. The obscurantism of the time was vividly illustrated by Robert Belgrave soon after he arrived in Baghdad. He told me that, when serving in his previous post at Brussels, he had been summoned to London to be upbraided by the under-secretary for European affairs. The complaint was that in their telegrams and letters to the department he and his ambassador had supported Belgian appeals to the British government to join, and indeed, to lead, the burgeoning European movement. This practice, he was told, must stop.

The Foreign Office was not alone in suffering from myopia. In other Whitehall departments – the Treasury, the Board of Trade and, especially, the Ministry of Agriculture – opinions were even more hostile to the idea that Britain might become involved. What was still more confusing was that, when he returned to office as prime minister in 1951, Winston Churchill showed little enthusiasm for the ideal he had himself expounded on several occasions as leader of the opposition. Of course, the same was true of Eden, his foreign secretary, who became absorbed in his self-selected role as peacemaker in Trieste, Austria, Indo-China and finally, and disastrously, the Middle East. So we had stood aside as the European Community was conceived, born and thrived. Perhaps the mandate Harold Macmillan had given to Edward Heath might enable us to join in the enterprise on reasonable terms before it was too late.

❖

Before serious discussions with the Community leaders could begin, the British government had to explain its intentions. A meeting of ministers of the Western European Union in Paris at the end of February 1961 provided a suitable opportunity. I was invited to accompany Edward Heath to this meeting. In Paris I took time off to visit rue Boissy d'Anglas. La Croisette had disappeared. Where it had been, at number 23, there was a plaque on the wall. This recorded the arrest of Orville Cunningham in September 1942 and his death in December 1943.

I learned later through the courtesy of the Secrétariat aux Anciens Combattants and of Henri René Ribière, a distinguished resistance leader, that from his base at La Croisette Orville Cunningham acted as paymaster to members of the resistance network in the centre of Paris known as les Cloches des Halles. This group, which was part of the North Liberation Movement, suffered severe losses. Of 130 volunteers, 33 were deported and of these 23 did not return alive; 17 were killed in fighting at the barricades and 11 were shot by firing squads. Following his arrest by the French militia, Cunningham was arraigned before a military court which sat at number 11 rue Boissy d'Anglas. More than a year later he was shot without having been tried. In the summer of 1944 many Americans lost their lives in the liberation of Paris. None of them knew about their fellow American who had died the previous year in the same cause. It is impossible to measure Cunningham's courage, or to imagine the torment of his months in captivity. The laconic inscription on the plaque where La Croisette once stood disguises the esteem in which he was held: "From the Cloches des Halles resistance group to the memory of their lamented comrade, Orville J. Cunningham, American citizen, arrested 24 September 1942, died 4 December 1943."

I was still in Burma when I received news of the Lucys, who had been so generous with their hospitality. Arthur Lucy continued at his work after the German occupation. In 1942 he was denounced to the Gestapo and sent to a concentration camp in Paris. When he was released he was a broken man. He returned to work but, a week later, they picked up his body where it had fallen from his office window. I wrote at once to Madame Lucy. I heard later from her daughter that she died two days before my letter arrived. Le Beau Pays de France had much grief to bury.

10

Frustration in Europe

On the morning of 28 February 1961 *The Times* carried a report from its Paris correspondent on the main news page under the headline:

'BRITISH OFFER ON COMMON MARKET
HARMONISED TARIFF AS BASIS
FUNDAMENTAL CHANGE'.

This was a product of the press briefing I had given the previous evening in the hotel suite in the rue du Faubourg St Honoré which had been reserved for this purpose.

When the meeting of the Council of the Western European Union ended, Edward Heath asked if I needed any more guidance before seeing the press. I replied that his statement, the responses round the table and the briefs we had brought with us from London gave me enough material. "Good," he said, "so you can go and tell them the story."

I had in mind, as he had, that there were a number of interested constituencies: public and parliamentary opinion at home; the governments of the Six; the Commonwealth; and our partners in EFTA – the European Free Trade Association. The correspondents I briefed on that occasion were of various nationalities and most were based in Paris. They realised at once that what Edward Heath had said to his WEU colleagues marked a significant step forward. They noted in particular the passage in his statement in which he said: "if the Common Market countries can meet our Commonwealth and agricultural difficulties, the United Kingdom can then consider a system based on a common or harmonised tariff on raw materials and manufactured goods imported from countries other than the Seven, or the Commonwealth." It was evident from their questions that the journalists recognised that any subsequent negotiations would have to concentrate on these two areas of difficulty – agriculture and Commonwealth trade. Needless to say, they wanted to know how the Lord Privy Seal's statement had been received. I was able to tell them that the other members of the Council had understood the importance of the occasion and that there would be an opportunity for a more detailed exchange of views before the Assembly of the Union met in the summer.

When he saw the press reports the following morning, Edward Heath seemed well satisfied. The reaction was different in the news department. My chief, John Russell, was disconcerted; he found it difficult to understand why *The Times* should have given such prominence to this story. He remained of the view that nothing would come of this initiative and suggested that I might be leading the press up the garden path.

❖

Over the next several months, apart from brief excursions as a member of Edward Heath's entourage to Bonn and Paris to discuss the Common Market initiative with the two governments, I was heavily involved in the work of the news department, including regular periods of night duty. Unlike press offices in other ministries which were staffed by members of the information service, the Foreign Office news department was composed for the most part of regular members of the service who had worked in diplomatic or consular posts abroad and in either geographical or functional departments in the Office. One or two, such as the encyclopaedic John Bourgoin, brought to bear their years of experience in journalism, or the more general information field.

The daily routine was dictated by the press conference held each weekday in Room 25 at 12.30 p.m., and the various briefing sessions with groups of correspondents each afternoon. Preparation for these events began with careful scrutiny of the telegrams exchanged overnight between the Foreign Office and our diplomatic posts abroad, as well as the morning's press cuttings. There followed a period of urgent consultation by telephone or face to face with the relevant departments in the Foreign Office or elsewhere in Whitehall – most frequently the press offices at Number 10, the Treasury and the Ministry of Defence. The latter were known to have what we euphemistically called a 'close working relationship' with Chapman Pincher of the Daily Express and it was important to avoid any crossing of wires. This consultation had to be finished in time for the departmental meeting chaired by John Russell at which each member of the department reported the guidance he or she had received on the topics of the day. In the light of this the line we would take on each topic was decided. On the more important issues either John Russell or I would consult at higher level, including ministers' private secretaries. Russell regarded himself as the secretary of state's spokesman and, in addition to keeping Lord Home informed of the current of press opinion, he would consult him on any controversial issue.

The 'twelve-thirty' press conference provided the opportunity for the 'Foreign Office spokesman' of the day to make any announcements and answer questions 'on the record'. The regular audience included representatives of those organisations which had either early or rolling deadlines, such as the evening papers and news agencies, radio and television. Mohsin Ali of Reuters and Arthur Gavshon of the Associated Press could be relied upon to open the question and answer session. As we became better acquainted, Mohsin and I discovered a special bond. He had piloted one of the Hurricanes in the 'cab-rank' which provided air cover in daylight hours for the ground troops advancing south from the Irrawaddy during the Burma campaign. Mohsin was a persistent seeker after truth; Reuters' reputation rested on the accuracy of its correspondents' reports and he set the highest standard. The pensive Arthur Gavshon was no less conscientious, and it was almost always he who asked the question no one else had thought of.

More often than not it fell to me at the end of the 'twelve-thirty' to take the correspondents of the two surviving London evening papers along the corridor to my office to discuss the stories of the day on a non-attributable basis. This was an important test; Robert Carvel of the *Evening Standard* and John Dickinson of the *Evening News* were among the most experienced observers of the political and diplomatic scene. Because their editors allowed them only a few column inches for their daily story, they had little patience with nuances. However, the influence they exercised on radio and television news bulletins later in the day and on the following morning's papers increased their importance as messengers.

Each afternoon groups of up to eight or ten journalists came to the department at appointed times for non-attributable briefings. This arrangement had been established over the years largely on the initiative of the correspondents themselves and it took account of community of interest as well as personalities. For reasons for which I received differing explanations, the diplomatic correspondents of *The Times* and *The Daily Telegraph* were briefed alone. The four or five other heavyweights came in a group at three o'clock and were usually briefed by the head of department. This group included Thomas Barman and Elizabeth Barker, respectively the BBC's home and overseas diplomatic correspondents, Brian Horton of Reuters, as well as Richard Scott, a descendant of the great editor, C. P. Scott, who in a leading article in the *Manchester Guardian* in May 1926 coined the magnificent truism: "Comment is free but facts are sacred." French, German, Italian and other European and Commonwealth correspondents also had their set times in the weekly briefing programme. The Americans formed the biggest group and John

Russell himself normally conducted their Wednesday morning briefing. I attended when topics were likely to arise which I had been handling.

All these groups practised self-discipline. Any correspondent guilty of serious disregard of the ground rules would be excluded by his colleagues for a period. This happened rarely. I was briefing one of the groups named for convenience, if not illumination, 'the Circus', when an equally rare event occurred. In answer to a question about negotiations which were at a particularly delicate stage, I said that I would be prepared to comment on a 'not-for-writing' basis if that were agreeable to the group. At this point Douglas Clark of the *Daily Express* asked to be excused. He explained that he had received information on this subject earlier in the afternoon which he was in a position to use and wished it to be clear that he had not obtained this from me.

While these group briefings were taking place other members of the department were answering telephone enquiries. Unless there was a late crisis the number of calls to the department began to decline in the early evening, at which point whoever was to take calls overnight became the sole point of contact. Experience on night duty varied. On what we regarded as a 'good night', most calls came from the agencies or broadcasters checking details, or assuring themselves that they had not missed any late development. But now and then a story broke, frequently across the Atlantic, which meant a sleepless night. I happened to be on duty when Lord Caradon, then the United Kingdom's representative at the United Nations, resigned over government policy on Rhodesia and I dealt with telephone calls throughout the night.

❖

The time I spent as assistant in the news department added a valuable dimension to my experience. In a sense this was an answer to the petition of Robert Burns in his Ode to a Louse: "O wad some Pow'r the giftie gie us to see oursels as others see us." Actions and policies may be intrinsically meritorious, but if they are to achieve the intended result, they must be seen to be so. It was salutary to be required day after day not only to explain what the Foreign Office was or was not doing, but also to justify its actions to sceptics, critics and opponents. Gaining the confidence of the corps of diplomatic correspondents was essential and any newcomer to the department was on probation for the first few months. If one passed the test the relationship could be mutually beneficial. Michael King, the foreign editor of the *Daily Mirror* and, until his tragically early death, one of the great exponents of lucid modern English, took me to lunch when he felt I had passed the confidence test. The time had come, he said, for a good talk. He assured me that he and his colleagues understood that there would always be times when we were not at liberty to say everything we knew, for example, when an ambassador had been unable, for one reason or another, to convey a message from the foreign secretary to the head of a foreign government. He also accepted that we never wilfully misled the press, for the good reason that any deception would soon be revealed. What he and his colleagues looked for when they came to the Office was a story – with at least a beginning and a middle, if not an end. In other words, we should leave as few questions unanswered as possible. Michael believed that such a policy would serve our ends as much as those of the press.

The members of the American group were a different breed. What struck me at once was their self-confidence which I presumed reflected the status they enjoyed in the United States. Many were bureau chiefs and an assignment to London was not only congenial, but also welcome from the point of view of their careers. As they covered every aspect of life in the United Kingdom, their range of interests and their knowledge were wide. Briefing this group was more like a seminar than a cross-examination and I could well understand why, for successive heads of the news department, this was one of the more popular events of the week. From time to time individual briefings were continued over lunch at the Connaught Hotel, where Joseph Fromm of the *US News* and *World Report*, the leading light in the American correspondents' group, introduced me to Campari on crushed ice and disclosed that he had served with the Gurkhas during the Second World War. Through him, Joseph Harsch of NBC, Bob Estabrook of the *Washington Post*, Rod MacLeish of Westinghouse and Bill Stoneman of the *Chicago Daily News*, I was kept well informed about attitudes in the United States towards our approach to Europe and other major issues.

❖

In August 1961 the appointment of Edward Heath to conduct our negotiations with the six Common Market countries was announced. The team assembled to support him was finely balanced. The brilliance and ebullience of Eric Roll[1] complemented the wisdom and reserve of Pierson Dixon, who continued in his post as ambassador in Paris while heading the official delegation. Eric Roll's varied career and his knowledge of agriculture equipped him to master the detail with ease; and there was plenty of that. Other senior members of the delegation included Herbert Andrew,[2] Roderick Barclay[3] and William Gorell-Barnes, who represented respectively the point of view of the Board of Trade, the Foreign Office and the Commonwealth Relations Office. Contemporaries of mine occupied a number of important positions in the delegation. A sensible decision had been taken to introduce a Treasury official into Edward Heath's private office for the duration of the negotiations. The attribute of a highly developed sense of humour which Roger Lavelle shared with the private secretary, Charles Wiggin, cemented their relationship; Edward Heath was well served. Two members of the Foreign Service were appointed to act as secretaries to the delegation; this entailed, among other things, coordinating the preparation of briefs, maintaining records and drafting progress reports. Christopher Audland[4] and John Robinson[5] were selected for these tasks.

Formal negotiations opened when Edward Heath presented the United Kingdom's case to the Six and the European Commission in Paris on 10 October 1961. For the next fifteen months Jean and I found our family life dominated by the endeavour to secure Britain's accession to the European Community. Our time together was precious.

Unlike the Geneva Conference in 1954, our negotiations with the Six were bilateral, not multilateral. The Six addressed us through the president for the time being of the Council of Ministers although, by agreement among them, other ministers occasionally added to the president's statement. On the other hand, what took place behind the doors that were closed to us when the Six argued among themselves was a multilateral negotiation. And that required us to spend long hours waiting in the offices allocated to us by the Six in their headquarters while they concerted their response to our latest proposals.

During these visits to Brussels our delegation was accommodated at the Metropole Hotel, which overlooked the Place de Brouckère – at that time in the heart of Brussels. The elegant Grand-Place was only a few minutes' walk away. Edward Heath occupied a suite with a drawing room large enough to enable all of us to sit in reasonable comfort at the end of each working day, when we reviewed events and planned for the morrow. On these occasions news and views gleaned from the delegations of the Six were reported and I gave an account of press reactions to my briefings. Within the first few days Edward Heath managed to create an almost tangible team spirit among members of the delegation. He was relaxed yet totally in control, he let others speak, including the most junior, and he ensured that by the end of the evening we each knew what was expected of us. For my own satisfaction I tried to identify the qualities which constituted his talent as a leader. I failed and was content to count myself lucky that I was a member of the team. There was no question, so far as this delegation was concerned, but that these qualities, whatever they were, inspired not only respect but also warm regard.

❖

It was my responsibility, as spokesman for the delegation, to ensure at every stage that, through the press, the case Edward Heath was presenting was understood by opinion at home, in the Six, the Commonwealth, the EFTA countries and further afield. As the negotiations proceeded and interest rose, more and more London-based correspondents accompanied us on our trips to Brussels. Those who were quickest off the mark reserved rooms at the Metropole Hotel, rightly assuming that

that would be the source of the less prosaic stories. When negotiations were in progress titbits were leaked to the press by various delegations and, when we were asked to comment on these, I held impromptu press conferences in the front lobby of the Council headquarters and, if necessary, set the record straight. More formal briefings took place at the end of each session when I explained the rationale for whatever proposals we had tabled.

In discharging my responsibilities I was handicapped by the fact that the political intent, namely to secure the accession of the United Kingdom to the European Community, was not obviously reflected in the subject-matter of the negotiations. The reason for this was historical. The first step towards a new Europe was the creation by the Six of the European Coal and Steel Community in 1952. This bound the heavy industries, which had fuelled the war machines in the past, so closely together that they could never again serve conflicting ends. The opportunity to take the next step arose from the need to strengthen the western alliance by re-arming Germany. Between 1952 and 1954 plans were drawn up, largely on French initiative, to create a European Defence Community and a complementary Political Community. For reasons which remain mysterious to this day, Pierre Mendès-France, the French prime minister at the time, failed to argue in support of his own proposal when it came to be debated in the French national assembly. In consequence, the debate which could have opened the way to a Defence Community was closed by a procedural manoeuvre. However, the advocates of closer European integration were not to be deterred. When they met at Messina in Sicily in June 1955 leaders of the Six decided to establish a robust basis for European Union by creating a common market. The discussions begun there culminated in the signature of the Treaty of Rome in March 1957. Jean Monnet, who had provided so much of the inspiration for the movement towards closer European integration, expressed his ambition in terms everyone could understand: "The real change we are after is not the free flow of goods. It is a change in the relationship between people." However, the method chosen did not reflect this. As Paul-Henri Spaak, the Belgian foreign minister, confessed to Edward Heath: "We set out to build a new Europe and ended up arguing over the tariff on bananas."

The United Kingdom's effort to join the European enterprise had to take account of this reality. And so, as the months passed, a generation of correspondents was initiated into the relative merits of soft and hard wheat, the unit costs of New Zealand and European lamb, the significance of the hides of young animals, known as *kips*, for sectors of the Indian economy, the doctrine of comparable outlets and the visionary ambition of zero tariffs – and all this not long after the spokesman himself was similarly initiated. While these issues were important, and in some cases vital, to those directly concerned, they could hardly be expected to arouse the enthusiasm of the public as a whole. Many of the correspondents appreciated the difficulty and did their best to remind their readers of the high political stakes for which we were playing.

Late in the evening Edward Heath would join correspondents in the basement bar of the Metropole. On these occasions too he was thoroughly relaxed and totally in control. His mastery of detail was complete and his confidence infectious. These evening exchanges prepared him well for the radio, television and press interviews which he gave on his return to London. The BBC television programme 'Gallery' frequently offered him an opportunity to explain the serious issues which lay behind the unfamiliar detail.

Most members of the British press contingent shared the delegation's commitment to the success of the enterprise in which we were engaged. There was an honourable exception. Alexander Kenworthy of *Express Newspapers*, whose proprietor, Lord Beaverbrook, was relentless in his opposition to any link with continental Europe, loyally and courageously sustained his hostility and regularly accused Heath of putting Commonwealth ties at risk.

My relations with the journalists reporting our progress in Brussels were not limited to formal briefings. Over breakfast I was able to fill in some of the detail and learn what line other delegatons had been taking with the press. At the end of each round of negotiations, when our work was done and we prepared to return home, I dined with Tom Barman and Willie Forrest of the *Daily Mail* in a small restaurant at the north end of Boulevard Adolphe Max. We ordered jambon d'Ardennes, salad, cheese and a pichet of red wine. We talked of anything except the European Community. They reminisced about the events which led to the war in Europe, they analysed the character of the French, recalled life in wartime Moscow and deplored the opportunities the British had missed to exercise decisive influence in post-war Europe.

In the course of several sessions between the formal opening in October 1961 and the summer of 1962, steady progress was made on Commonwealth trade, tariffs and agricultural issues. One complication early on was that the Six were still formulating their response to proposals from Dr Sicco Mansholt, the member of the European Commission responsible for devising a common agricultural policy. Dr Mansholt attended one of the negotiating sessions to explain the Commission's approach. Inasmuch as his exposition shed light on the possible structure of the policy, it merely complicated the process in which we were engaged; it was clear that we were negotiating against a volatile background. In January 1962 the Six adopted the outline of an agricultural policy and over the next few months we and they negotiated deals product by product, country by country. Eugène Schaus, the foreign minister of Luxembourg, chaired the sessions in the early stages and was succeeded by Joseph Luns, the foreign minister of the Netherlands. The attitude of both was positive. Our case was also strongly supported by the Germans, Gerhard Schröder and Rolf Lahr, and by Paul-Henri Spaak and his deputy, Henri Fayat. Edward Heath established a close rapport with Jean François Deniau, the brilliant French diplomatist who headed the Commission's official delegation to these negotiations. His advice on procedures, presentation and tactics was of great value.

The enigma was Maurice Couve de Murville, the French foreign minister. At first he was not obviously obstructive. He appeared to go along with the consensus, but from time to time he would intervene at the last moment with words with which we soon became familiar: "Monsieur le président, il y a une petite équivoque . . . " The little misunderstanding usually turned out to be more apparent than real and we concluded that his purpose was to slow the pace and to remind us and his colleagues among the Six that France was not to be taken for granted. His personal advice to Heath was that the United Kingdom should accept the Community's rules and then negotiate its requirements from within. In theory this could have been an effective way of proceeding; and it might well have made sense for the French if they had been in our position. But our need to satisfy opinion at home and in the Commonwealth ruled this out. We had no alternative but to grind away at the problems.

We also had to exercise patience. Each time Edward Heath presented fresh proposals we were obliged to wait for a summons to the council chamber to hear the reaction of the Six. In the dark winter months Joseph Luns would walk along the corridor to our offices, his body wrapped in a tartan rug, to convey interim reports on the Six's discussions. During these vigils members of our delegation occupied themselves in different ways – reading, writing, speculating, day-dreaming:

> This is the house that Schaus built.
> And this is the Couve
> That made the move
> That lit the Spaak
> That started the Fayat
> That burned the house that Schaus built.

In July 1962 a serious problem arose. Reports from our embassy in Paris suggested that the French government were becoming concerned at the rapid progress being made in Brussels; the British were showing more flexibility than had been supposed. At the end of the month the French delegation in Brussels tabled new proposals on temperate agricultural products, thereby virtually ruling out the possibility of settling the agricultural issues before the summer break. The mood was sombre when members of our delegation assembled that evening in Edward Heath's suite at the Metropole. Pierson Dixon was uncertain about the attitude of the French. Unusually, he was accompanied this time by his private secretary, Michael Butler.[6] Even more unusual, Michael, perched on a despatch box in a corner, intervened in the debate. At meetings of this sort, private secretaries, even private secretaries of members of the cabinet, obeyed the Victorian rule, were seen and not heard, and spoke only when spoken to. Michael clearly felt that his ambassador had understated French unease at the situation we had reached. The question now being raised was whether we should accept the latest French proposals of which, through skilful negotiation, only a handful now caused us difficulty, or resume the argument after the summer recess. After consulting his two cabinet colleagues directly concerned – Christopher Soames, the minister of agriculture, and Duncan Sandys, the Commonwealth secretary – Heath sought instructions from the prime minister. Opinion among members of the delegation was divided. Roderick Barclay and the two delegation secretaries, Christopher Audland and John Robinson, thought we should settle there and then for what was on offer and deal quickly with the remaining trade issues when negotiations resumed after the holiday. I shared this view. However, in the event caution prevailed and whether the bold stroke would have produced a different outcome will remain one of the ifs of history. We suffered another minor blow; Couve de Murville insisted that the resumption of negotiations be postponed until October. We left Brussels early in August with stiff upper lips. A few days after my return home Jean received a bouquet of flowers with a card from Edward Heath expressing his apologies for having so often kept us apart.

The next challenge was confrontation with the Commonwealth at the London conference in September. On the eve of this conference, Edward Heath discussed tactics with his principal advisers. We were joined by Harold Evans,[7] the press secretary at Number 10, in a state of high anxiety. In vivid terms he expressed the prime minister's apprehension about the impending onslaught by his Commonwealth colleagues. I was astonished. The delegation led by the Lord Privy Seal had spent a good deal of the past year in Brussels accommodating the trade concerns of our Commonwealth partners, even to the point of risking jeopardy to our own interests. I pointed out that we had known all along that this would be a difficult conference and we had a good case to make. We knew precisely the concerns of each

Commonwealth country; they knew full well from the comprehensive reports they had received throughout the negotiations that the Lord Privy Seal had secured the best possible arrangements for their trade in a wider market than had been available to them hitherto; and, as a member of the Community, the United Kingdom would be better placed to serve Commonwealth interests. Edward Heath seemed well satisfied with the outcome of this briefing meeting and, ten days later, Commonwealth heads of government left London moderately reassured.

❖

When the grinding down process resumed in the autumn, differences continued to be narrowed. Spirits began to rise. In December 1962 Harold Macmillan discussed collaboration over defence with President de Gaulle at Rambouillet and, later the same month, concluded a deal with President Kennedy at Nassau for the supply to Britain of Polaris missiles.

I returned home from the last session in Brussels before Christmas late on 20 December 1962. The next two days were spent preparing for a brief family holiday in France with friends dating from our days together in the Egyptian department in the Foreign Office – Ian and Ruth Bell. Ian at this time was consul-general in Lyon. Our eight-year-old daughter Alison, who was recovering from measles, was declared fit to travel. The warmth of the Bells' welcome when we stepped off the Mistral at the railway station compensated for the intense cold in and around Lyon. The unusually severe weather did not rule out excursions to the recently restored town of Pérouges and the Beaujolais country, nor conversations with local editors, all of whom looked forward to the successful conclusion of our negotiations early in the new year.

All our expectations were confounded. On 14 January 1963, at a press conference in the Salon des Fêtes in the Elysée Palace, President de Gaulle pronounced his veto on British membership of the European Community. A dark cloud formed over Brussels as negotiations limped on for another two weeks.

On the morning of 30 January 1963 *The Times* led the main news page with a report from its Common Market correspondent in Brussels under the headline:

COLLAPSE OF BRUSSELS NEGOTIATIONS
MINISTERS OF THE FIVE FAIL TO MOVE FRANCE
BRITISH ENTRY "THWARTED BY ONE MAN"

This was a product of my last press briefing in Brussels. It was twenty-three months – almost to the day – since I told the press in Paris about Edward Heath's presentation to the Western European Union which started the process.

The report in *The Times* recounted the events of one of the black days in Europe's post-war history. At 4.15 p.m. on 29 January Henri Fayat, who had succeeded Joseph Luns as chairman of the conference, invited Edward Heath, Christopher Soames, Duncan Sandys and Eric Roll to see him in his office. Fayat said that he regretted that the member states were prevented from continuing the negotiations. He was convinced that this regret would be shared throughout the free world, as with anxiety and fear people considered the unhappy consequences which would follow. Back in the council chamber Couve de Murville argued that British unwillingness to accept Community policies and disciplines was the cause of the breakdown. Had his allegations not been so outrageous I might have felt sorry for him. In their turn each of the Five expressed their regret at the turn of events. Edward Heath rebutted Couve's accusations point by point. He added that he was deeply moved by the remarks made by five delegations round the table. In a statement issued to the press he said: "We entered sixteen months ago into negotiations in good faith. The high hopes of many have been thwarted for political reasons and the will of one man."

The international press gathered in Brussels shared the indignation felt by the Five. And, like the Five, they admired Edward Heath's calm reaction and his determination to sustain Britain's commitment to Europe. Michael King, dismayed that the story now had not only a beginning and a middle but also this particular end, aptly recalled Churchill's phrase: "In defeat, defiance . . . "

On my return to London I found Michael Hadow,[8] who had served as counsellor in the embassy in Paris before replacing John Russell as head of the news department, in a sympathetic mood. A few weeks later he told me that Edward Heath had asked the head of the personnel department to ensure that the prospects of the members of the delegation should not suffer because the negotiations had failed; none of them was to blame. Not long afterwards it was suggested that I go to Mali as ambassador. Then, Berne as commercial counsellor was mentioned – "You are fluent in German, aren't you?" "No". And, finally, counsellor in Cairo. On 26 March 1963, at a reception in the Henry VIII cellar below the Department of Trade, Jean and I took leave of our colleagues in the news department and of the many correspondents who had shared the hopes and disappointments of the past two years. None of us knew that evening how soon we were to meet again.

11

Nasser's Egypt

We were warned before leaving London that Nasser's Egypt in 1963 had many of the characteristics of a police state. None of these was evident when Jean and I disembarked at Alexandria on the morning of 7 May for yet another felicitous encounter with my cousin, Robert Dundas, at that time the consul-general. That same evening, soon after our arrival in Cairo, I reported to the ambassador, Harold Beeley, with whom I had served in Baghdad in the early 1950s.

The house we were to occupy in the Zamalek quarter was on the opposite side of the street from the Tunisian ambassador's residence and barely a minute's walk from where I had stayed for some six weeks with Donald and Melinda Maclean in 1949 when negotiating the Nile Waters agreement. Number Twenty Ibn Zanki had a fair-sized garden approached from a well-shaded balcony. This adjoined the garden of our neighbours, Michael and Sybil Hannam;[1] Michael was the first secretary in the commercial section of the embassy. Between the two gardens stood a hut in which the gardener we employed jointly – a man of ox-like proportions named Abboud – kept his tools and himself to himself. From Abboud's point of view this arrangement had several advantages, not the least being that, when not obviously at work in our garden, he could claim to be fully occupied on behalf of the Hannams – and vice versa. Not everything in the garden was lovely. Since my previous visit in 1949 a large block of flats had been built immediately to the west. This denied us a view of the Little Nile, and enabled any curious residents to observe what went on in our garden below. One neighbour who was especially discreet was Fatin Hamama, a leading actress married to Michael Chalhoub, better known as Omar Sharif.

The household staff had been recruited by Amin, who performed in Cairo the same major-domo role as the Khan Sahib in the Baghdad embassy. It was generally accepted that the best domestic staff came from Nubia in the south, or from the northern Sudan, and ours were no exception. They shared with us their concern about the fate of their families once the high dam at Aswan was completed; this would flood vast tracts of land to the south. This anxiety did not dampen the early morning spirits of the 'bawwabs' – the watchmen on Ibn Zanki street, who were also willing exiles from Nubia. As they swept the pavement outside the house or block of flats for which they were responsible, they would test each other's ingenuity with competitive morning greetings. 'Morning of goodness' would receive the standard reply 'morning of light'. 'Morning of Gamal' would provoke the obvious 'morning of Abdel Nasser'. 'Morning of Jackie' – 'morning of Kennedy'; 'Morning of Coca' – 'morning of Bebsi', there being no letter 'P' in Arabic. And so on, but steadily more abstruse as the contest proceeded.

❖

Relations between Britain and Egypt had been partially restored after the Suez débâcle when a British Property Commission was set up in Cairo in 1959, largely to deal with financial claims and counter-claims. The head of this commission was Colin Crowe,[2] who was soon recognised by the Egyptians as British chargé d'affaires. However, relations were not fully established until the appointment of Harold Beeley as ambassador in March 1961.

The Suez affair in 1956 had greatly enhanced Nasser's prestige. Two years later this seemed to have reached its zenith when the United Arab Republic was proclaimed on 1 February 1958. Under pressure from a group of young Syrian army officers Nasser had somewhat reluctantly agreed to an Egyptian-Syrian union. This union lasted less than four years. Another attempt a year after this reverse led to the declaration of a union between Egypt, Syria and Iraq in January 1963. Coups d'état in Baghdad in February and Damascus in March of that year put this union at risk and, despite Nasser's efforts at a special conference in April to salvage the union by giving it a federal character, this initiative lost momentum and never recovered.

These events harmed Nasser's reputation, but he already faced a more serious problem. In September 1962 an army coup led by General Abdullah Sallal had overthrown the Imam al-Badr of the Yemen only a week after he had succeeded his father. Within two days Nasser had recognised the new regime in the Yemen and, a few weeks later, Egyptian troops were sent across the Red Sea to support the republican movement. Alarmed by these developments, Saudi Arabia gave moral and material support to the royalist cause. Relations between Saudi Arabia and Egypt, or the United Arab Republic – the UAR – as it continued to call itself, came under severe strain.

This was the situation I found when I took up my work as political counsellor and deputy to the ambassador. Apart from observing and reporting on political developments which might affect the stability of the Middle East, the embassy's efforts were directed towards sustaining the slow and sometimes painful recovery from the damage British interests in Egypt had suffered at the time of Suez. At the political level this was uphill work. Her Majesty's government had not recognised Sallal's regime in Yemen; Nasser regarded the South Arabian Federation as a cloak for continued British military presence on Arab soil. By the same token he objected to British bases in Libya and regarded our presence in Cyprus as menacing.

There was little to be done in the short term to resolve this conflict on matters of policy. For our part we had legitimate questions to ask and a strong case to make, but we faced another difficulty. The attitude of the Nasser regime towards the Egyptian people at the time of our arrival in 1963 was as autocratic as at any time since the revolution in 1952. The activities of the intelligence and security services discouraged nonconformism and contacts with foreigners, and seemed to be based on the assumption that it was best to stifle discontent at birth. The government information machine exercised rigorous control over all means of communication. From time to time criticism, whether by inference or implication, was tolerated, but the principal function of the information machine was to disseminate a mass of optimistic, eulogistic and otherwise misleading accounts of the government's achievements in both the domestic and international spheres.

Through prejudice, and perhaps fear, members of the former capitalist class and many intellectuals, who were no less anxious than the regime to use their talents in the service of their country, were denied any share in the effort to confront its problems. In addition, the Free Officers who had led the revolution in 1952 and now constituted the regime, seemed unwilling or unable to delegate responsibility. This had two effects: they and their personal staffs suffered avoidable stress and fatigue; and many of the civilian ministers in charge of specialist departments, who were drawn from the professions or the pre-revolutionary public service, lacked authority and confidence.

The chronic problem for the diplomat was how to gain access to those who took the decisions. This did not affect the British alone. The entire diplomatic corps, including the Soviet embassy, was kept at arm's length. This circumstance induced a strong sense of fraternity among members of the corps, who devoted much of their time to exchanging news and views. Despite having only partially emerged from the dog-house, the British were regarded as a source of good information and advice and the staff of the embassy enjoyed a high rating on the popularity scale. The heads of the Commonwealth missions consulted on a regular and systematic basis. This Commonwealth solidarity extended beyond the ambassadors; Jean and the wife of the Indian minister found a variety of outlets for the enthusiasm and ingenuity of the Commonwealth wives and their families.

Like others before us, Jean and I found that many Egyptians were only too anxious to compensate for the reluctance of the members of the regime to mingle. Journalists, academics, artists, intellectuals and other public-spirited but politically neutral individuals were quick to make us welcome. For them exposure to the views of others and, in particular, the opinions of disinterested observers was important and we were glad to share our impressions with them. In return, while loyally and advisedly refraining from specific criticism of the regime, they were candid about developments in Egypt. The worldly wise Ali Amin, the chairman of the newspaper group 'Akhbar al-Yom', the astute Ahmed Bahaeddin, editor of the magazine *Musawwar*, the cosmopolitan Mursi Saadeddin who doubled as editor of *The Observer* and as secretary of the Afro-Asian People's Solidarity Organisation, a body set up on Nasser's initiative at the Bandung Conference in 1955 – these three we found to be well-informed and reliable interpreters of the political scene. The statuesque Maha Abdul Fattah of the magazine *Akher Sa'a* was a dedicated admirer of Gamal Abdel Nasser, a vigorous critic of what she called imperialism and an effective opponent in debate. Through these and other contacts with the press we kept ourselves reasonably informed about major developments.

Every Friday Mohammed Hassanein Heikal, a leading personality of the day, published a signed article in *Al Ahram*. This was widely regarded as one of the significant political events of the week and anyone claiming to be anyone had to read it. Before Colin Crowe as head of the British Property Commission was given diplomatic status, it was not possible for Egyptian officials to deal with him except in the matter of claims. During this period Heikal was authorised to act as informal and unacknowledged link between the presidency and Crowe. This was clear evidence that Heikal enjoyed the confidence of Nasser. But this did not mean that on every occasion he was Nasser's mouthpiece. Heikal himself did nothing to dispel the impression that his Friday articles reflected Nasser's thinking. I had reason to take a different view. One of his articles contained what I knew to be a factual error. It may not have been a coincidence that I received an invitation a few days later to call on Hassan Sabri al Kholi, one of President Nasser's advisers, in his office at Heliopolis, a suburb of Cairo.

Hassan Sabri was Nasser's main link with the Palestinians. But, as he had explained to me not long after my arrival, the president had given him another task. This was to maintain informal contact with the British and United States embassies to ensure that misunderstandings on either side were avoided. The only condition was that what transpired between us would not be mentioned in any formal communication between the governments, nor divulged to those concerned in the Egyptian foreign ministry or any other ministry. I was to feel free to visit him from time to time to maintain our dialogue and, apart from this, I was to contact him at once if ever any particular development caused us concern, or if we had a special message to convey. As I took my leave on this occasion Hassan Sabri said: "I am sure you do not believe everything you read in the papers. When the president has something important to say, he will say it himself."

Over the next two years I made frequent use of this privileged channel of communication. I looked forward to my six-weekly visits to Heliopolis not only because of Hassan Sabri's admirable personal qualities; he was a valuable interlocutor and our dialogue provided a unique chance of influencing events. Donald Bergus, my American opposite number, felt the same.

❖

The Cairo routine offered us an opportunity to enjoy rather more family life than had been possible over the previous three years. Our daughter, Alison, who had travelled out to Cairo with us, attended a local school and was learning to play the piano. Colin, now ten years old, was at school in England, but when he came out for the holidays we enjoyed what Egypt and its great capital city had to offer. Our young folk were suitably impressed by the immense scale of the Sphinx and the pyramids of Giza and, despite the August heat, they enjoyed the pungent smell of fenugreek and cumin, the brightly decorated leather goods and the array of brass candleholders in the Mouski, the lush panorama of the Delta lying to the north of the Nile Barrage, and the visit to the farm where the milkman, who brought us two cans of milk on his bicycle every evening, kept his water buffaloes.

The high point of our first summer holiday was to be our trip to the Mediterranean. We welcomed a suggestion by one of our Egyptian friends that we camp at Sidi Abdul Rahman on the coast west of Alexandria. We had brought with us from home the frame tent we had used when camping in Scotland. In the souk Jean found a length of stout blue material suitable for the extension we thought we would need to protect us from the heat of the afternoon sun. A tent-maker cut it to the right size and inserted eyelets at appropriate places to take the extra poles. Jean also made mosquito nets for Colin and Alison.

Our first sight of the sea surpassed expectation – a restless mix of emerald and turquoise. We stopped for a cold drink at El Alamein and went on to the next town to fill up with petrol. As we were doing so the local policeman approached us. He gave us precise directions to a suitable camping place at Sidi Abdul Rahman. We had to stick to a track going straight towards the sea. "If you leave it to right or left," he said, "you will get into difficulties." We followed his advice and a group of engineers installing piped water along the coast helped us park our car on a dune only a few yards from the sea. The merit of this particular site was that the rocks between us and the water deterred the Friday visitors from Alexandria who preferred the unbroken stretch of sand to our west. But not all of them. Despite our warning a party of young people insisted on parking their car on the sand beside our tent. The following day this had to be pulled, pushed and bounced on to the track by a crowd attracted by the noise of the engine racing, the wheels spinning and the sight of the car slowly disappearing into the soft sand.

Between ten o'clock in the morning and five in the afternoon the sun was too strong for bathing and we occupied ourselves otherwise. The restaurant at El Alamein was cool and the lunch simple and wholesome. The cloistered building at the entrance to the war cemetery bears the names of nearly twelve thousand servicemen from the Commonwealth who died 'where two continents meet' and have no known grave. Two Arab gardeners were at work planting and tidying among the lines of gravestones which sloped towards the desert, as was most fitting. Except for the birds the silence was complete.

Not long after leaving El Alamein to return to our camp we passed a ruined building on the wall of which was painted a poignant message to the passer-by:

MANCO –
LA FORTUNA
NON IL VALORE
1–7–1942
ALESSANDRIA 111

This was the furthest the Italian army penetrated before the tide turned.

A few miles further to the west two large stones, two hundred yards apart, marked the positions of the forward allied and axis minefields on October 23, 1942. Further on we passed the German war cemetery, a solid and rather forbidding fortress facing north. The nearby Italian cemetery, which looks towards the sea, contains a church built in the shape of a mosque and a memorial which stands out, white and brilliant, against dark green trees – a distinctly Italian corner of a foreign field.

Two days later we set off for Mersa Matruh, half way to the Libyan frontier. For two and a half hours we drove through undulating desert, crossing and re-crossing the railway line which follows the coast and disturbing countless larks and hawks. Here and there windmills lifted the underground water. The women in the Bedouin encampments wore gaily coloured clothes – red, yellow and turquoise. Our passage was obviously an event, for everyone who saw us waved and smiled. Mersa Matruh was not what we had expected. We found a mini-Alexandria – hotels, food stalls, beach umbrellas, bikinis and, instead of fenugreek and cumin, a pervasive smell of *Ambre Solaire*.

Two young Germans visited our camp. Over coffee they told us they were preparing a study of the Sahara, much of it photographic. They had been travelling in the desert for over seven months in a Volkswagen which, they said, had two advantages: it was air-cooled and it travelled a long way on a gallon of petrol. However, since its carrying capacity was limited, the two Germans had been living off the country. Most of what they ate they had hunted and they had moved, like the Bedouin, from one desolate water hole to the next. When they reached one of these they had lain down to rest beside the wall of the well. They were aroused from their sleep by the sound of Arab music. Mystified, they scanned the horizon and could not see where it was coming from. Then a young Arab stood up on the other side of the well and placed his transistor radio on top of the wall so that they too could listen.

❖

Over the New Year holiday we undertook another family excursion. This time our party included my father who had joined us in the autumn from Jerusalem, where he had been staying with my brother Alastair and his wife Betty; Alastair was the consul-general there. Our destination was Luxor and we intended to travel south by the Red Sea route and return down the Nile valley. At the marine biology station on the approach to Hurghada on the Red Sea coast, which was our first stop, we were able to inspect tanks containing exotic fish of unimagined shapes and colours, huge turtles and a stuffed dugong, a mammal with an ape-like head, a thick neck and a cigar-shaped body. This creature, which stood some ten feet tall, was said to have contributed to the legend of the mermaid. Another of nature's wonders.

Our journey the following morning was of the kind which requires all concerned to keep their fingers crossed. We travelled south to the port of Safaga where we turned away from the coast and headed due west towards the jagged range of red and sandy mountains. The highest of the Red Sea hills was over 7,000 feet; those nearest to the road rose from ground level to about 4,000 feet without any foothills to soften their steep slopes. The road, which was magnificently engineered, ascended gradually through the steep-sided mountains. After an hour's drive we reached the highest point and for another hour descended steadily towards the plain. The terrain we had passed through was spectacular, but also forbidding. Throughout the two hours' drive we had seen no other vehicle nor any other human being. The only life we saw was one raven and two smaller birds we could not identify. We saw not even a blade of grass. I resolved that when we returned to Cairo I would warn our colleagues and friends not to undertake this journey without an accompanying vehicle. When we reached the plain we saw two or three groups of Bedouin with their camels and, further off, a range of flat-topped mountains rising from the valley floor just as steeply as those we had left behind. Shortly after this we had our first glimpse of the distant green strip of the Nile valley and uncrossed our fingers.

We arrived in Luxor in time for lunch and spent the next day and a half saturating ourselves in the glories of Karnak and Thebes and, in the evening, appreciating the view of the river and the mountains beyond from the terrace of our hotel. The first few hours of our return journey took us along a dust road as far as the great barrage at Nag' Hammadi, where we crossed to the west bank of the Nile. From this point on we travelled on an asphalt road. However, anyone who had any cause to move, whether on foot, donkey, mule, horse, bicycle, or motor vehicle, used this road. We passed through numerous towns linked by villages, all teeming with people. In the afternoon we reached Asyut, once a town of wealth and beauty. The gracious old family houses stood empty, their extensive gardens no longer tended. We hoped that the new university might attract people who would restore dignity to the city. We stayed overnight in Minya in a replica of an English provincial station hotel and, after negotiating many more crowded towns and villages, reached Cairo before noon. We had covered over a thousand miles and formed a vivid impression of the contrast between the splendours of ancient Egypt and the problems Nasser faced in the 1960s, in particular, over-population.

The High Dam at Aswan was Nasser's solution to this problem. The first stage of the work was due to be completed in May 1964. This great project had not been included in the comprehensive scheme for the development of the Nile Waters that had been the subject of the negotiations in which I had been involved in the late 1940s. That scheme, only parts of which had in the end been endorsed, envisaged that the flow of the White Nile would be controlled by works upstream beyond the borders of Egypt. The High Dam on the other hand placed control over the flow of the White Nile in the hands of the Egyptians, but at the expense of depriving Egypt's neighbours to the south of the benefits of the international scheme and of flooding large areas in the south of the country as well as northern Sudan. Some of the staff of our household had returned to Nubia to help resettle their families whose homes would be flooded when the dam came into operation.

Jean and I were anxious to see the site of the dam before it was flooded when the Nile was diverted. This time we travelled by air. Aswan was surprisingly cool for the month of April. Hassan Talaat, the public relations officer for the High Dam, drove us out of Aswan for twenty minutes through desolate country – hills of red and grey stone stretching as far as the eye could see. When we reached the bank of the Nile we were unable to see the dam itself. This was being built with stones tipped into the river bed day after day, night after night. This process was to continue until a ridge of stones with a core of sand

and cement appeared above the surface and reached a height greater than the intended level of the lake which would form behind it. What we were able to see, however, was the man-made valley from which these stones had been excavated. This was the channel into which the waters of the Nile were to be diverted. Work was still in progress in the tunnels which were to house the turbines. These would provide enough electricity to meet all Egypt's actual and potential needs at low cost.

The scale of the work was staggering. Hundreds of feet below where we stood, the floor of the excavation crawled with ant-like figures. Scores of trucks moved rocks of various sizes from one place to another. Vast machines mixed cement. Giant cranes twisted and turned, raising and lowering heavy loads. Welders sent sparks in all directions. Men shouted, engines roared and, above everything, stood huge towers with floodlights ready for the night shift. We were deafened by the constant clamour and every now and then had to move sharply to one side to avoid the huge trucks which were driven everywhere at high speed. These vehicles were British exports, the Russian trucks having proved insufficiently robust and mechanically unreliable. We were struck by the complete absence of animals on the site; mules and donkeys were indispensable components of all the work forces we had seen in Egypt hitherto. Hassan Talaat explained that this was the result of a deliberate decision; any animals would be at constant risk from the trucks and the cranes. In view of what we had seen, this seemed a wise and humane ruling.

A large grading machine stood on the bank of the river. This received rocks of all sizes from the trucks and distributed them to barges which took them to the site of the dam. At this point, by means of a device we could not see, the bottoms of the barges were opened and the stones discharged into the river. Those loaded with sand were deliberately capsized and righted themselves when empty. At each end of what was to be the Diversion Canal a man-made sand dam had been holding back the waters of the Nile while the excavation was carried out. These were to be blown up four weeks later when Nasser and Khrushchev performed the official opening of the Diversion Canal. I walked along the crest of one of these to photograph the tunnels.

The accommodation built for those who worked on the site included a hospital and social centre. The thirty thousand Egyptians lived close to where the dam was being built and the eighteen thousand Russians were housed some distance away. The costs of this tremendous project were as impressive as the size of the work force. The estimate for constructing the dam was over 85 million Egyptian pounds – virtually the same amount in sterling. Twenty million had to be set aside for compensation for those affected by the flooding in Nubia and the Wadi Halfa area in northern Sudan. The power station would cost over 57 million and the transmission lines another 50, bringing the grand total to 213 million Egyptian pounds.

That afternoon we hired a felucca and took my father and the children to the arboretum on Kitchener's Island, the Aga Khan's mausoleum on the west bank and the site of the ancient Nilometer on Elephantine Island. Before flying back to Cairo the following day, we visited the quarries from which the granite obelisks which now stand on the bank of the River Thames and in the Place de la Concorde had been excavated.

At the end of 1963 Nasser invited leaders of the Arab states to a conference to discuss a threat by Israel to divert water from the Jordan valley for irrigation and industrial use in Israel. This event turned out to have more significance than expected. Nasser's motive was not merely to co-ordinate the Arab response to this challenge. His difficulties in the Yemen had shown that, while reactionary regimes could easily be overthrown, the resultant situation could not be readily controlled. Egyptian efforts to subvert the monarchies in Jordan and Saudi Arabia could in certain circumstances prove harmful to Egypt's interests. This did not mean, however, that Nasser would abandon his opposition to regimes he regarded as reactionary, including Morocco and Tunisia, but rather that the tactics might be modified. There was another factor. The failure of his attempts to effect organic union with Syria in 1958, and with Syria and Iraq early in 1963, could have led Nasser to conclude that the foundations of Arab unity had to be laid in the economic, social, military and other fields before the keystone of political unity could rest securely in its proper place. When Arab leaders assembled in Cairo in January 1964 Nasser reverted to the principle on which the League of Arab States operated, namely 'unity of rank'. Since in practice this meant no more than that Arab states would stand side by side in the face of common danger, it seemed plain that the Cairo summit signalled a change of emphasis in Egypt's Arab policy. Hassan Sabri al Kholi did not demur when I shared this interpretation with him.

In May 1964, when the jacarandas were in bloom, Nasser prepared to welcome his Soviet benefactor. Khrushchev, accompanied by his foreign minister, Andrei Gromyko, arrived in Alexandria on 9 May 1964 to be greeted by headlines in the Egyptian press wishing 'Welcome to Khrushchev – our friend in need'. During the first few days of his visit which he spent in Cairo, Khrushchev went out of this way to identify the Soviet Union with the objectives of the Nasser regime – the creation of a socialist state and the removal of the imperialists from their remaining footholds in the Middle East and Africa. Harold Beeley and his fellow ambassadors were invited to attend the opening of the High Dam on 14 May in the presence of Nasser and Khrushchev and three other 'progressive' presidents – Ben Bella of Algeria, Aref of Iraq and Sallal of the Yemen. When breaches were blown in the two retaining sand dams, water from the Nile rushed down into the Diversion Canal and the old course of the river was blocked by the rock dam which broke the surface as the level of the river fell. The noise of the cascading waters did nothing to raise the spirits of the attendant diplomatic corps who had been left without any refreshment – not even a glass of water – for over six hours.

In the summer of 1964 Harold Beeley left Cairo and I assumed charge of the embassy. During his three years as the first British ambassador to Egypt since the Suez war, Harold Beeley had acquired a wide and influential circle of friends. I felt that if Nasser had been willing to talk to him and to Doctor John Badeau, the scholarly American ambassador, more often, some of his sillier actions might have been avoided.

In July 1964 Cairo staged a prestigious event. Thirty-four African heads of state were invited to a conference. The invitation to his African colleagues was an expression of the leading role Nasser wished to play in the affairs of the continent and of his support for other progressive regimes. The authorities took advantage of the occasion to indulge their passion for security. The Nile Hilton hotel, where it was decided to hold the conference, was commandeered and the tourists were required to leave or put up with inferior accommodation elsewhere. The diplomatic corps was excluded from the conference area. Journalists were confined to the top floor of the Cairo Governorate building, where they could watch the proceedings on television and read agency tapes. They had no means of meeting the heads of state. Nor were they the only ones to be diasadvantaged. Lance Mallalieu, the Labour member of parliament and secretary general of the World Association of World Federalists, had been invited by President Senghor of Senegal to attend the conference as an observer. He was refused a pass and Senghor's intervention on his behalf was fruitless. Lance Mallalieu spent the next three days at our house. During this time he was able to make contact outside the conference with some members of other delegations who shared his interests, and he felt his journey had not been entirely in vain.

Some delegations from the poorer countries were of appropriately modest size. To no one's surprise, given the personality of their president, these did not include the delegation of Ghana which numbered one hundred and twenty-five. At a lavish reception on the eve of the conference, the foreign minister distributed bundles of propaganda material about Ghana and copies of two books by Kwame Nkrumah, one mysteriously entitled *Consciencism*. On 18 July Jean and I attended a banquet hosted by Nasser at the Koubbeh palace and another a week later given in Nasser's honour by President Nyerere of what was then Tanganyika and Zanzibar. On both occasions the heads of the diplomatic missions were separated physically from all delegates to the conference. However, these precautions did not prevent us finding out what took place. Jean and I entertained several of the journalists who had come to cover the conference. Many of them we already knew. Several of these had succeeded in making useful contact with heads of state for whom publicity in the international press could do nothing but good with their own people. At receptions given by our African diplomatic colleagues we met their heads of state and foreign ministers, who recounted willingly and vividly what had occurred behind the closed doors. When they had all gone home, when the dust had settled and the expelled tourists had returned to their rooms in the Nile Hilton, the truth emerged that, apart from rhetoric about the plight of the Palestinians, nothing of any significance had happened. But the Ghanaians had enjoyed themselves.

Revolution Day – 23 July – fell in the middle of the African conference and Jean and Alison accompanied me to the military parade. This was most efficiently organised and the marching of the troops, including commandos and paratroops, was faultless. Alison preferred the cavalry and the camel corps to the rockets. As soon as the parade was over and Nasser and his fellow heads of state had left, the great crowds broke loose and swarmed all over the parade area. Because of this we had to wait for our cars. While we remained in our seats the military police began dismantling the stand in which we were sitting. As they did so they revealed the microphones which had been concealed in the awning above us to record our comments. I pitied the scores of young officers in some steamy barracks who would have to listen to hours of tapes in pursuit of significance in the banalities of the diplomatic corps.

Not long after this London announced that the territories comprising the South Arabian Federation, including Aden, would become independent within four years. In this connection I asked for an appointment with Mahmoud Riad, the Egyptian foreign minister. When I arrived at the ministry I was informed by an embarrassed chef de cabinet that the minister was in a meeting dealing with something urgent; I would not be kept waiting long. Quarter of an hour or so later commotion in the next room indicated that the meeting was over. Mahmoud Riad apologised. He said that a Palestinian delegation had arrived in Cairo without warning to talk to the government. He put his hands to his head: "You have no idea," he said, "how difficult this is for us. These people want us to do so much and there is nothing we can do. How can we explain that to them?"

In the summer months we entertained our dinner guests either on the balcony or the lawn, which we were keen to extend. When we could prise him out of his hut and persuade him to apply his strength to the task in hand, Abboud was a good gardener, as he demonstrated on this occasion. He brought us tufts of grass, planted these in lines a hand's width apart and watered them every evening. In a matter of days, or so it seemed, we had the larger lawn we needed. Among those we were glad to welcome were several women who had risen to the top of their professions. Amina al-Said was one of the most influential editors, Tomader Taufiq was controller of the second channel on Cairo television, Hikmet Abu Zeid was minister of social affairs. Jean had joined the Cairo Women's Club and from time to time accepted invitations to meetings with a group of women dedicated to spreading knowledge about birth control in villages in the Delta. Although Hikmet Abu Zeid seemed personally sympathetic, this group of women received no practical support from the government even though over-population was universally recognised as the major challenge. Even if the High Dam at Aswan fulfilled all expectations, the extra acreage and electric power would merely sustain the estimated future population at the existing standard of living. I asked Ali Amin, the chairman of *Akhbar al Yom*, why Nasser could not advocate birth control in one of his periodical radio broadcasts when, through his brilliant populist rhetoric, he held the nation in the hollow of his hand. His reply surprised me: "The president will not tell the people to do something they are not prepared to do. And he knows they are not yet ready for this message."

❖

When the school year ended in England we were joined once again by Colin and this time by Elizabeth and Laura Scarlett, the daughters of friends and neighbours at home. Laura was a contemporary of Alison's. Political activity declined in August as many Cairenes made for the Mediterranean. We did the same and drove in two vehicles to a rest house at Agami near Alexandria which the embassy staff rented for the summer. The undertow at this beach was unusually strong and swimming was strictly controlled by lifeguards. On the last day of our stay we were invited by Egyptian friends to their house and farm at Aboukir, to the east of Alexandria. Hassan Nashat had been Egyptian ambassador in London before the revolution, his wife, Patricia, was English and their daughters matched our young in age. My father was in his element collecting wild plants while the children rode donkeys on the estate. We returned in the evening to Agami and during the night one after another was violently ill, except for Colin. What we had eaten, and he had not, immediately identified the source of the food poisoning – crab. We fared better than our hosts. When Patricia telephoned the next day to find out how we were, we learned that all the Nashats had been afflicted and that Hassan had been taken by ambulance to hospital in Alexandria for emergency treatment. By the morning Jean and I, though delicate, felt sufficiently restored to drive the two vehicles home.

We wanted the Scarlett girls to take back with them an unusual impression of Cairo. With our neighbours, the Hannams, we arranged a picnic in the Mokattam Hills to the south east of the city. We chose a night when the moon was nearly full and found a spot near a ruined mosque from where we could see across Cairo to the Pyramids in the distance. The first performances of *Son et Lumière* were in progress at both the Pyramids and the Citadel below us. I was somewhat concerned about our proximity to the mosque and asked the man in charge if there was any objection to our having a picnic there. He reassured me. I then asked whether we would be disturbed. He smiled: "By my eyes you shall not be disturbed." So it proved. As we prepared our picnic, lights came on all over the city and we were bathed in moonlight.

Early in September George and Tina Middleton, whom we had known in Lebanon, replaced the Beeleys. Thanks to the British announcement on independence for the constituents of the South Arabian Federation, at the moment of their arrival there was less strain than before in our relations. However, Nasser still had a major preoccupation. His hopes of extracting his forces from Yemen were disappointed and this unnecessary, cruel and unpopular war continued to cause distress to the many Egyptian families with loved ones in the battle zone.

Jean and I accompanied the Middletons to the annual service of remembrance at the Commonwealth war cemetery at El Alamein at the end of October. A number of Commonwealth ambassadors sympathised with our view that the time had come to invite our German and Italian colleagues to take part in this service. The word from London was that this was out of the question so long as Field Marshal Montgomery was alive. We did the next best thing. As agreed in advance with the two other embassies, in company with our military attaché I signed the visitors' book at the German and Italian cemeteries.

A few days later, following the practice among parents of young children, Jean and I flew on separate flights to Beirut. John Wilton,[3] my successor at the Middle East Centre for Arab Studies at Shemlan, had invited me to talk on Egypt to one of the background courses. We were delighted to renew acquaintance with so many friends and counted ourselves lucky that our visit coincided with the monthly evensong service in the tiny church we had been able to bring into use during our last year at the Centre. When we dined out in Beirut with Eddie and Janet Hitti, who had played a critical part in facilitating the expansion of the Centre and its activities, Jean and I were so conditioned

by our eighteen months of constrained social life in Cairo that we were
shocked by the freedom with which those at neighbouring tables aired
their views.

At the end of January 1965 a memorial service for Sir Winston
Churchill was held in the Anglican Cathedral. On this occasion, as
on each Sunday throughout the year, the provost, Donald Blackburn,
found the words to move and encourage those present. The provost
was a saintly man highly respected by the congregation, which regularly
included a substantial proportion of Egyptian Anglicans in addition to
expatriates and visitors. When asked one evening if he did not object
to an elderly Egyptian praying on the Cathedral lawn in the direction
of Mecca, he replied: "How wonderful that he should say his prayer in
the shadow of the Cross."

When opportunity offered we sought to widen our knowledge of
the art and architecture of both Islamic and ancient Egypt in and
around Cairo. So far as the former was concerned, we were more
fortunate in our choice of guide than Harold Beeley had been. Claudine
Shawarby, a French architectural historian, had the capacity to explain
the essentials in plain yet vivid terms. She also appreciated that the
capacity of the non-expert to absorb information was limited. For this
reason her services as a guide were much in demand. Harold Beeley
had been visited soon after his arrival by the venerable and revered
Professor Creswell, a world authority on Islamic art. So pleased was
the professor to see a British ambassador re-installed in Cairo that he
offered his services as a guide to the Islamic monuments, beginning
with al Azhar mosque. This was an offer Harold Beeley could hardly
refuse. Each time they went to the mosque Creswell was intercepted
by old students, or by officials of the mosque who either wanted to
pass on news of their families or ask his opinion on some controversy
that had arisen. When he had dealt with these importunities Creswell
would begin his instruction. However, so detailed was his knowledge
of the mosque that after two years Harold Beeley had been initiated
into the significance of the main features of the first ten yards of the
entrance.

A particular pleasure for our family was our friendship with Professor
Bryan Emery and his wife. As a member of the Egyptian department of
antiquities in the 1930s, Bryan had set himself the aim of discovering the
tomb of Imhotep, the grand vizier of the Pharoah Zoser who flourished
in the middle of the third millenium BC. Imhotep, whom the Greeks
identify with Aesculapius, their own father of medicine, was a man with
an extraordinary range of talents. He was not merely a physician but,
among many other things, an architect. He designed the 200-foot step
pyramid at Saqqara, the oldest large-scale stone structure in the world.

The Emerys had returned to Egypt from the Sudan where they had been retrieving treasures which would otherwise have been lost in the flood when the first stage of the High Dam at Aswan was completed. Bryan was now able to resume his search for the tomb, which he was convinced was to be found at Saqqara. We paid several visits to the site he and his team were excavating and became infected by his enthusiasm. The magazine where everything removed from the excavations was stored – from fragments of cooking utensils to votive offerings – contained hundreds of ibis mummies removed from their earthenware jars. Each had been wrapped in fine linen strips which crisscrossed at the front from head to tail. Some had a 'badge' in the shape of a baboon outlined in black. Many were in poor condition. Before being placed in their jars they had been dipped in pitch to preserve them, but over the millenia this had in some cases eaten away the body. A particular hazard at Saqqara was posed by the maze of subterranean trenches. A roof fall could occur at any time and, since the trenches frequently divided and diverged, the team followed the precedent of Theseus to whom Ariadne gave a clew of thread to enable him to find his way out of the Maze after slaying the Minotaur.

At the end of each season the site was sealed with barbed wire. On our last visit we found Bryan in a state of some excitement. A wall with rock carvings of gods had just been discovered; this was further, but not yet conclusive, evidence that he was following the right trail.

❖

The early months of 1965 brought numerous visitors to Cairo. We entertained a number of the journalists whom I had met in the Foreign Office news department – David Webster of the BBC, Bob Estabrook of the *Washington Post*, Joe Alex Morris of *Newsweek* and Katharine Graham, the doyenne of the *Washington Post*. When Robin Day lunched with us he tried out the questions he wanted to put to Nasser during a television interview he was hoping to record a few days later. "How will he react if I ask why he condones terrorism in Aden, which is the sort of thing that makes the British public angry?" "How will he reply if I ask so-and-so?" "What if he says so-and-so?" Robin Day appreciated the briefing and we looked forward to the result. The presidency may have been daunted by Robin Day's reputation; his request for an interview was refused.

In the meantime, while Nasser's difficulties in the Yemen persisted, he achieved a success in his dealings with the Palestinians. Opposition to the establishment of the Palestine Liberation Organisation, which he had been promoting, was eventually overcome at another Arab summit conference. However, Habib Bourguiba, the president of Tunisia, when visiting Jordan in March 1965, criticised Arab attitudes to Israel which, he said, owed too much to emotion. This brought down on his head the wrath of the Egyptian propaganda machine. Our neighbour, the Tunisian ambassador, had prudently absented himself from Cairo. At this moment unexpected news reached us from London. It had been decided to set up an Oil Department in the Foreign Office and I was to return to London to be its first head. Another round of packing up and farewells. With the agreement of the Hannams, we decided to leave a note for our successors recommending the replacement of our ox-like, but often invisible, gardener.

While I was at the foreign ministry taking leave of the chief of protocol he received a telephone call. He became agitated; a mob was attacking our house; police were being rushed to the scene. My thoughts raced as I hurried home. Jean and I had been congratulating ourselves only the previous day that we had at last survived one Middle East posting without being exposed to civil or military strife. As the car approached Ibn Zanki, I heard the clamour of the mob. Stones littered the street. But by then the demonstrators were not at our house. They were swarming over the Tunisian ambassador's residence and seemed to be sacking it systematically. I found Jean, Alison and my father shaken, but safe. They told the story. It seemed that a large group of students had been instructed to attack the Tunisian embassy, which had been identified to them as a two-storey house with blue shutters in Ibn Zanki. Ours was the first building they came to which fitted that description. The first stones broke a window sending fragments of glass over our packing cases. Abboud ran to the front gate shouting "Not here" and pointing to the Tunisian house, which also had blue shutters. He was struck on the leg by a stone. Jean dressed and bound his wound. Abboud was the hero of the hour; and he knew it. At a stroke he had saved our house, its inhabitants and his job.

Our two years in Egypt were culturally and intellectually satisfying, but professionally frustrating. The aims of the Free Officers, who still constituted the government of Egypt despite the various changes of nomenclature – from Council of the Revolutionary Command to Presidential Council to Executive Council – were unexceptionable. They held that the unequal distribution of wealth, the incompetence of the armed forces, the corruption and nepotism characteristic of Egypt in 1952 could be attributed to an alliance between the monarchy, the capitalist landowning class and the imperialists; by imperialists they meant, of course, the British, whose troops were still stationed in the Canal Zone, and the French, whose interests dominated the Suez Canal Company. Their ambition was to wrest control from this unholy trinity. They did not use the absolute power they seized in July 1952 to sweep away everything they detested at once; they chose their moments.

Naturally the monarchy had to be removed immediately, but other processes were more gradual. The agrarian law limiting the size of holdings broke the backbone of the landowners; the influence of the mercantile class was destroyed by the nationalisation of major enterprises; foreign undertakings were sequestrated or nationalised out of existence; and the British base, already under notice, was removed in the wake of the Suez war.

The aspirations of the Free Officers were not wholly negative. They wanted to regenerate their country within the framework of the re-awakening Arab world, the liberation of the African continent and the solidarity of the Muslim peoples – the three concentric circles of Nasser's *Philosophy of the Revolution*. Their chosen instruments were agrarian reform, increasing the cultivable area and the availability of electric power through the High Dam at Aswan, industrialisation and socialism. Some agricultural projects, such as the the irrigation of Liberation Province on the western edge of the Delta, were impressive; there the desert bloomed, not with the rose, but with cotton, maize and millet. The effect of the High Dam was still to be felt. The industrialisation programme, originally regarded as the passport to prosperity, had absorbed a large proportion of investment funds and had not yet produced a dividend. The aims of the Free Officers' social programme were not vouchsafed until ten years after the revolution when the *National Charter* was published. Though this document had been accorded the reverence normally reserved for holy writ, Nasser's own expectation was clear: "You can build a village in a day, but how long does it take to build a man?"

The question I found hard to answer was why the Free Officers thought they could carry through such a fundamental programme of reform while insulating themselves from their people and the outside world. Equally enigmatic was Nasser's attachment to his international role. In his early years he had restored pride to the Arabs; that was an historic achievement. Yet I saw little evidence that Egyptians as a whole were anxious to perform on the world stage – foreign adventures in the nineteenth century had been unrewarding and the current Yemen imbroglio was detested. Some of my colleagues argued that the role of leader of the Arab and Afro-Asian worlds had been thrust upon Nasser's reluctant shoulders, others that it was the consequence of his lust for power. I felt the explanation lay in a combination of over-confidence and a mistaken conviction that Egypt's Arab and African neighbours shared his preoccupations and aspirations. Clearly a potent influence had been the experience of 1956, when the disaster which had faced the Free Officers turned into a kind of victory. Nasser himself said that the success of the revolution would depend on its comprehension of the real conditions facing it. When I left Egypt in the spring of 1965 I had formed the view that, splendid though his contribution to his country had been, in his later years Nasser had misread the challenges he had to face and that this led him to commit the same errors as his arch enemy, Anthony Eden.

12

Michael and George

In the high summer of 1965 I took my empty briefcase to the Foreign Office expecting to fill it with essential reading material about the current state of the petroleum industry. In the office assigned to us I met the two colleagues who were to form the nucleus of the new Oil Department. By mid-afternoon we had drafted a plan for discussion with our superintending under-secretary and others concerned, both in the Foreign Office and elsewhere in Whitehall. At this point my telephone rang. David Muirhead, the head of the personnel department, asked nervously where I was, what I was doing and how far I had got. He seemed relieved when I told him. His next words startled me: "Stop what you are doing. Go home and wait till you hear from me". I obeyed all three instructions and in due course I received a telephone call from the secretary of state's private office: "Would it be convenient for me to call on Mr Stewart the following afternoon?" Needless to say, it was. Michael Stewart asked a number of questions about Egypt and the Middle East generally, about my previous jobs in the Foreign Office and my family, and then thanked me for coming to see him. A few days later I was told that my posting had been changed. Further thought was being given to the setting up of the oil department and I was to succeed Michael Hadow as head of the News Department.

In the two years since I had left the news department there had been a number of staff changes, but most of the correspondents with whom I had worked previously were still in place. This circumstance facilitated my re-entry into Foreign Office spokesmanship. Having had an opportunity while in Egypt to reflect on my previous experience in the department, I introduced a number of procedural changes designed to make life easier both for the staff and the correspondents. There was a significant new factor. Michael Stewart had brought with him a political adviser, John Harris,[1] who was particularly interested in the presentation of policy and was knowledgeable in the field of television. While there was in theory a risk that he and I might cross wires, this did not happen;

John took special pains to keep me informed about his contacts with the press and we, for our part, ensured that he knew what we were saying on all important issues. Some months after I joined the department, John left to work with Roy Jenkins, then chancellor of the exchequer. One member of the department suggested that we should regard his departure as a compliment; if he had thought we were incompetent, he would surely have stayed.

Over the next two years Jean and I and our children became accustomed to the long hours I had to spend at the Foreign Office, the interrupted weekends and the occasional sleepless night when the news agencies and the broadcasters required to be briefed about a major international development, or a newsworthy case involving a British subject in some sort of difficulty abroad. As the secretary of state's spokesman I had to brief the press on all the issues which he himself was handling. This meant not only acquiring sufficient knowledge to speak authoritatively on these issues, but also access to the secretary of state at any time of day or night to ensure that I could reflect his views faithfully. Foreign affairs were rarely out of the headlines. The Vietnam war, Rhodesia, President de Gaulle's attitude to NATO, efforts to encourage East–West détente, nuclear disarmament, our relations with the European Community, the Spanish claim to Gibraltar, the Argentine claim to the Falklands, confrontation with Sukarno's Indonesia, civil war in Nigeria – all these at one time or another gave rise to major press stories.

❖

Although I had shuttled between London, Brussels and other European capitals with Edward Heath during the abortive Common Market negotiations between 1961 and 1963, I had not appreciated how much of the secretary of state's time was spent on travel. His journeys abroad had a variety, and sometimes a combination, of purposes; attending conferences of organisations to which the United Kingdom belonged, influencing opinion, discussing bilateral problems, promoting trade and projecting Britain were among the more frequent objectives. Together with his principal private secretary, as his spokesman I was a permanent member of the foreign secretary's travelling team.

In September 1965 Michael Stewart visited Poland. Detente between East and West, which was a major British and NATO concern, depended among other things on persuading the countries of eastern Europe of Germany's good intentions. It was evident as soon as we arrived that the Poles still carried the burden of their recent past. We were shown a film taken by the Nazis themselves of their systematic destruction of Warsaw after the rising had been crushed in October 1944. The plan to rebuild the city on the opposite bank of the Vistula had been abandoned when surveyors reported that, despite the Nazis' efforts, the underground sewerage and cabling were intact; they had therefore recommended that it would be more sensible to reconstruct the city on its original site. This had been done, even to the extent of reproducing a superfluous wriggle in the main street. Over dinner our hosts told us how the Soviet army had stood idle across the Vistula while the resistance of the people of Warsaw was crushed. A few days later we ourselves saw tragic evidence of this Soviet policy when we visited the graves of RAF aircrew who flew supplies to the besieged city and were denied permission to land behind Soviet lines and refuel for the return flight to Italy. When they turned back after releasing their loads these aircraft were sitting ducks for German fighter aircraft.

Cracow was more graceful than we had imagined. Virginia creeper covered many of the public buildings which glowed in the autumn sunshine. We were shown scientific instruments designed by Copernicus as well as his original drawings – all works of art. In the thirteenth century Wawel castle, which dominates part of the city from the crest of a rocky hill, we learned how the tapestries were smuggled out to Canada when Poland was overrun – another heroic story in the annals of this most courageous of peoples. Within NATO German sensitivities were judged still to need attention and for this reason Michael Stewart resisted the Poles' pressure for us to visit Auschwitz – a gesture appreciated by our German allies, but not easily understood by our Polish hosts.

The weeks preceding the political party conferences were regarded as a suitable time for foreign travel, especially since the General Assembly of the United Nations convened in the middle of September. As the opening debate attracted foreign ministers to New York from a large number of countries, it was the best opportunity in the year for bilateral discussions at top level. Appointments with the secretary of state's fellow foreign ministers were made well in advance and, when we set off for New York at the beginning of October 1965, Michael Stewart knew he faced a heavy schedule in New York. Because I had been involved in the preparations for the journey and was present when the secretary of state met his opposite numbers either in his suite at the Carlyle Hotel or at United Nations Headquarters, briefing the press on what transpired was for the most part a matter of routine.

When we went on to Washington I had to exercise more discretion. In his talks with Dean Rusk, the secretary of state, and later with President Johnson, Michael Stewart sought their agreement to re-convening the Geneva Conference on Indochina as a means of promoting an end to hostilities in Vietnam. At Geneva in 1954 the Conference had been chaired in turn by the United Kingdom, the Soviet Union and Thailand. Since that time we and the Russians had retained a nominal responsibility for supervising implementation of the conclusions of the Conference. In the course of his discussions in Washington, Michael Stewart's proposal was not rejected, but the Americans still hankered after our support for the effort they were making in Vietnam. Not for the first time did Dean Rusk appeal for "even one platoon of the Black Watch". But Michael Stewart was adamant that for us to intervene militarily would undermine the mediatory role we could play as co-chairman of the Conference, which, he felt, carried more value at that stage. The war in Vietnam was to preoccupy him for months and years to come.

In brilliant sunshine we flew from Washington over the prairies of the middle west and the Rocky Mountains to San Francisco which had been neglected by senior ministers for too long. Here the task was trade promotion and the projection of Britain. We took time off to enjoy the Golden Gate, which fog had concealed from Francis Drake nearly four centuries earlier, and understood why Alcatraz was considered escape-proof when we saw the strength of the current in the narrow channel between the island and the shore. After a night-stop in Hawaii, we crossed the date-line on our way to Tokyo where our party was accommodated in the British embassy compound. This miniature estate opposite the royal palace was a legacy of the close relations Britain and Japan had enjoyed in the earlier part of the century. The compound contained not only the ambassador's residence and the embassy offices, but also the houses of senior members of the staff. I had been invited to stay with the information counsellor who, with excessive zeal, had arranged a working dinner on the evening of our arrival so that I could meet the three senior British correspondents resident in Tokyo. However, he had failed to allow for the effect of the time difference between the opposite coasts of the Pacific, or the length of the flight from Hawaii, or the loquacity of his guests. Seldom have I so longed for sleep.

The Japanese press rated Michael Stewart's visit a success. He received an even warmer reception when we made a two-day excursion to Seoul; visits by western leaders to the Republic of Korea were comparatively rare. The entertainment we were offered one evening included traditional dancing and a Korean version of a No play. One of the protocol officers quietly suggested that, if any male members of the delegation wanted to go on elsewhere, this could be discreetly arranged – an offer which was politely declined.

On our return to Tokyo one of the young women in the delegation had a surprise. Murray Maclehose,[2] the private secretary, had found out that her twenty-first birthday coincided with our last day in Japan. The embassy helped us to celebrate this event. On our flight home that evening we recrossed the date-line. This meant that when we reached Alaska we had yesterday over again. No one objected when Murray Maclehose proposed a second celebration. The ground hostess at 'Ink

Ridge' – as she pronounced 'Anchorage' – was nonplussed, but did not decline the champagne.

Although tension in Rhodesia had been rising for many months, the timing of Ian Smith's Unilateral Declaration of Independence caught everyone off guard. In the first instance Rhodesia was the responsibility of the Commonwealth Relations Office, but the Foreign Office had been involved because of the implications for our interests elsewhere in Africa and in the non-aligned world. When news of Smith's declaration reached London on the morning of 11 November 1965, it was decided that the foreign secretary should occupy the United Kingdom's seat when the United Nations Security Council met later that day in New York. Within two hours of the decision to go to New York all of our party had assembled at London airport and, with the five-hour difference in our favour, we arrived in good time to be briefed by Hugh Caradon, the United Kingdom permanent representative, on the state of opinion in the Council and to decide our tactics before the debate began. The French disapproved of recourse to the Security Council on the grounds that Rhodesia was a domestic British problem and no concern of the international community; no doubt they feared that a precedent would be set which could embarrass them in the future. The non-aligned states were of course outraged by the action of the Smith regime and looked for a decisive response.

Michael Stewart had to perform a balancing act. By the following day he had persuaded the Security Council to condemn the unilateral declaration of independence, and to refrain from recognising or rendering any assistance to the illegal regime. He rejected a vehement demand by the delegate of the Ivory Coast on behalf of the African group of states for the rebellion to be crushed by force and majority rule established by one man one vote, arguing that the use of force would merely cause misery for millions of people and thrust the prospect of freedom into the more distant future. In this way the battle lines were drawn and, until Zimbabwe eventually came into existence, this dispute infected our relations with much of the developing world, and especially the African members of the Commonwealth.

The idea of reconvening the Conference on Vietnam had not been abandoned and this was on the agenda for the foreign secretary's talks with Andrei Gromyko in Moscow at the end of November 1965. Although fitted out with fur hats, overshoes and heavy gloves, most of our party were uncomfortable in the intense cold outdoors and the excessive heat indoors, this latter generated by the hyper-efficient city central heating system. To our surprise the Russians agreed to our request that Michael Stewart be allowed to broadcast a message on Moscow radio. In this he stressed NATO's peaceful intentions and the strong desire in the west to pursue detente. He went on to list some of the achievements of British policies since the war, and notably de-colonisation. We deduced from the reaction of the Soviet authorities that this broadcast had made a greater impact on Russian listeners than they had allowed for; the newspaper *Izvestia* argued the following day that Britain was still governed by imperialists and oppressors. We judged the score two–nil to our side.

❖

Michael Stewart took advantage of the Christmas and New Year parliamentary recess to visit South America. He had two aims: to learn at first hand the views of our heads of mission in the region and to establish closer relations with certain of the more influential Latin American governments.

From time to time the Foreign Office arranged regional conferences when ambassadors could discuss their preoccupations with one or more ministers. No such conference had been held in Latin America for some years. The meeting Michael Stewart was to chair was held in Lima, the capital of Peru, in January 1966. The message conveyed to the secretary of state was clear: opportunities for trade with the countries of the continent and for exercising influence, especially on United Nations matters, were not fully appreciated at home; more effort and a higher profile were needed. This was a view I had heard expressed ever since joining the service. The problem of course was one of priorities and limited resources in our post-imperial state and the heads of mission, who were enthusiastic but also realistic, did not expect significant shifts in policy.

I was impressed by the elegance of Lima, the grandeur of the churches and public buildings and the high proportion of people of Indian stock among the inhabitants. The foreign secretary's talks with the refreshingly moderate and progressive members of the government required me for the first time to brief the local press in Spanish. It was fortunate that the tour should begin in one of the countries where the spoken language is comparatively unadulterated. Our next stop was Santiago. Here again Michael Stewart found it easy to establish a rapport with our hosts. I had a more difficult passage when I met the Chilean press. It was of some comfort to be told by British residents that I was not the first visitor to be disconcerted by Chilean diction.

At the weekend we flew south, parallel to the snow-capped Andes range, to Puerto Montt in an area farmed by people of German origin. The Chilean govenment had arranged for us to stay in a hotel at Villa Rica favoured, to judge from autographed photographs in the bar, by the aristocracy of Hollywood and other rich north Americans. The service in this hotel was superb; if one wanted to ride, fish, swim, or play golf, one had merely to ask and one's wish would be immediately accommodated. And the location was exceptional. The snow-covered volcano reflected in the waters of the lake beneath our windows emitted a plume of steam, yet seemed benign.

For the first stage of our journey to Buenos Aires, our next destination, we took the surface route. We traversed the Andes range by station wagon along grit tracks, by motor launch or steamer across lakes the colour of copper sulphate. We skirted the base of El Tronador ('The Thunderer'), the dominant mountain in this region and in the late afternoon reached the town of Bariloche in Argentina. Despite the fact that we had with us half a dozen red boxes containing the private office papers and had to manhandle these as well as our personal luggage from station wagon to launch or steamer and vice versa, the whole party felt privileged to have been able to make this most spectacular of journeys.

On the following day we flew over Patagonia to Buenos Aires where Michael Stewart did not allow either the unattractive character of the regime or the dispute over the Falklands to interfere with the general review of international questions he was anxious to have with this influential member of the developing world. So far as my dealings with the press were concerned, I was pleasantly surprised to find that Argentine Spanish was not at all the hybrid some of my interlocutors in Lima and Santiago had claimed. One of the correspondents I briefed was a rather cynical north American who was looking forward to his next assignment elsewhere. He was highly critical of the policies and actions of the regime. "Argentines" he said, "are what happens to Italians when they eat beef instead of pasta."

The atmosphere in Buenos Aires belied its name; by mid-morning the cuffs on my white shirt were already dark grey. At a lunch in Michael Stewart's honour at a well-appointed country club patronised by the polo-playing set, the Anglo-Argentine chairman pleaded for extra efforts to resolve the political differences between Britain and Argentina. His remarks tactfully concealed the divided loyalties which were to cause distress to the Anglo-Argentine community during the Falklands war in the early 1980s.

While this tour deepened Michael Stewart's appreciation of the attitude of the Latin American leaders he met and raised his own profile, it did not lead him to amend our policies or to raise the level of resources the Foreign Office devoted to the region.

❖

Australia was to host the next annual meeting of the Council of the South East Asia Treaty Organisation and it was decided to take advantage of this to arrange bilateral talks with a number of governments on the way. In the summer of 1966 Bangkok was still a riverine city, Kuala Lumpur was still surrounded by dark green forests, and the centre of Singapore had been transformed since my visit with Lord Reading in 1954. In

Indonesia Sukarno had disappeared from the scene and Michael Stewart found Adam Malik, the foreign minister, more than anxious to repair the damage done to our relations by the disgraced former president's policy of confrontation.

On our arrival in Canberra I was warned by the staff of our High Commission to expect some pommie-bashing from the Australian press. In the event their conduct at my press briefings was no more robust than what I was accustomed to in London. When I had finished my briefing at the end of the second day of the conference, Jack Fingleton, the former test cricketer and now the doyen of the Australian diplomatic correspondents, called for silence. He said that he wanted me to know how much he and his colleagues appreciated my comprehensive briefings. The pommie spokesman was then carried off to have a few jars. A day or two later an article appeared in a comparatively new journal which was already making inroads into the readership of the *Sydney Morning Herald* and the *Melbourne Age*. The editorial in *The Australian*, owned by an up-and-coming entrepreneur called Rupert Murdoch, criticised Australian ministers for their reticence about important matters of state. An example illustrated the point: it was unacceptable that the press were learning more about what Australian ministers were saying at the SEATO conference from Michael Stewart's press secretary than from any Australian source.

The High Commissioner, Charles Johnston, and his wife Natasha gave a dinner party for delegates to the conference. Dean Rusk was the guest of honour. That both Rusk and Michael Stewart were alumni of St John's College, Oxford, was one reason for the close relationship they enjoyed. Their temperaments too were similar – moderate in the way they expressed their views and calm under stress. Dean Rusk had occasion to display these qualities towards the end of dinner. Charles and Natasha had met during the war in Cairo. There they had acquired the services of a Nubian butler called Mo, who had ruled their household ever since. When Rusk helped himself to two baked apples, Mo nudged his shoulder and said: "One each. Put the other back."

❖

Late on 10 August 1966, halfway through our family holiday at St Fillans on the shore of Loch Earn, we heard the announcement that George Brown was to replace Michael Stewart as foreign secretary. The following morning I telephoned to Murray Maclehose in the private office to ask whether I should return to the Office. He thought this would be advisable and I flew to London later that day. During the next two days I had my first talks with George Brown and dealt with numerous press enquiries. He had no objection to anyone resuming their holidays. Jean and the children met me at Turnhouse on Sunday morning, 14 August. As we drove back to St Fillans, the sun came out for the first time since we had left home. We hoped this might be an omen.

George Brown inherited not only Michael Stewart's responsibilities but also many of his commitments. The first of these were the annual visit to the United Nations General Assembly at the beginning of October and delayed visits to Bonn and Berlin. However, George Brown already had his eyes on Moscow, which he was due to visit in the latter part of November. Fog delayed our departure and, two days later than intended, we flew to Copenhagen to await weather reports. These were mildly encouraging and, much to George Brown's relief, we took off for Moscow. Soon after we had crossed the Soviet frontier, air traffic control instructed the pilot to divert to Leningrad because of fog at Sheremetievo, the main airport at Moscow. This news greatly disturbed George Brown, but after some time Murray Maclehose and I managed to persuade him that he could not take charge of the flight. The authorities at Leningrad airport had little warning of our arrival, but reacted promptly and efficiently. Cars soon appeared to take us into the city, but we had some difficulty identifying our luggage as the only form of illumination in the airport seemed to be 20-watt bulbs. While we were refreshing ourselves in rooms put at our disposal in one of the central hotels, we were invited to attend a performance by the Kirov ballet before boarding our overnight train for Moscow. The contrast between the opulence of the theatre, the stage furnishings and costumes on the one hand and, on the other, the drab dress of the audience was striking. But their enthusiasm was unbounded. Before we boarded the train I walked along the platform to inspect the engine, the ballet music still ringing in my ears. As I looked along the track, I half expected Vivien Leigh, in the guise of Anna Karenina, to emerge from the mist which swirled around the lamps.

In Moscow, George Brown pressed Gromyko, as Michael Stewart had done, to join in reconvening the Geneva conference as a way of resolving the Vietnam crisis. He had no more success than his predecessor, but he was encouraged by talks he had outside Moscow with Abdul Hakim Amer, the Egyptian vice-president, who happened to be in Moscow at the same time. On the return flight to London our RAF aircrew told us of an incident in which, so they claimed, another crew had been involved on an earlier visit to Moscow. Having been warned that their hotel room was likely to be bugged, they carried out a careful inspection in silence. One of the crew noticed a small lump under the carpet. When he rolled this back a round metal knob was revealed. While the others looked on he began to unscrew it. Suddenly there was a loud crash as the chandelier in the room below hit the floor.

❖

Much thought had been given in Whitehall to the possibility of a renewed application to join the European Community. Opinion in the Labour Party required the government to adopt a cautious approach. And there remained serious doubt about the attitude of the French. To test the ground it was decided that the prime minister and the foreign secretary should visit each of the capitals of the Six in turn. George Brown had hoped to undertake this task on his own, but Harold Wilson felt that the soundings would carry more weight if he added his authority.

The order in which the capitals were visited was carefully considered. The first stop was Rome, where we spent two days in the middle of January 1967. The Italians, like the other Five, wanted us to join the Community and they offered good advice about the next critical stage of the tour – Paris. This was followed by Brussels, Bonn, The Hague and finally Luxembourg in the first week of March. In each capital George Brown's emotional attachment to Europe was evident and, through repetition when the prime minister's press secretary, Trevor Lloyd-Hughes, and I jointly briefed the press, I soon learned his contributions by heart. Harold Wilson on the other hand learned the lessons which we drew from each succeeding encounter, and adapted, sharpened and enriched his arguments accordingly. By the end of the tour I felt that he was intellectually convinced that our national interest required that we link our future with that of the Community. The sequel to the tour of the capitals of the Six was not long delayed. When he attended a meeting of the Council of the Western European Union on 4 July 1967, George Brown submitted a second application on behalf of the United Kingdom to join the European Community.

❖

In the spring of 1967 Murray Maclehose was appointed ambassador to Vietnam and I was told I was one of two candidates to succeed him as the principal private secretary. The other was Teddy Youde,[3] at that time the head of a department in the Foreign Office. One afternoon we were interviewed in sequence by George Brown and I was selected. When Teddy congratulated me, I said that it might be more appropriate for me to congratulate him. From what I had seen as the foreign secretary's spokesman and deduced from the silences of the ever-discreet Murray Maclehose, I thought I knew what was in store. I was wrong; my expectations were to prove wide of the mark.

My deputy in the private office was Derek Day,[4] who was later succeeded by Nicholas Barrington.[5] The other two members of the office were David Morphet and Jean Elliott. We became a close-knit band. When George Brown pressed his buzzer for attention, we never knew which persona we would find seated at his desk – Dr Jekyll or Mr Hyde. On social occasions the compulsive show-off took over. In the small hours, when he had returned from the House of Commons to his flat in Carlton Gardens and began to go through the box of papers we had sent him earlier, he would telephone me with instructions to tell the author of one or other of the submissions in his box to do this or that at once. When I refused on the grounds that, at that time of night, this was both unnecessary and unreasonable, I was told that the consequences of my disobedience would be visited upon me the following morning. In the event what happened in the morning was not what had been threatened. At that time of day the persona in the foreign secretary's chair was anxious to be assured that there were "no hard feelings". All of us in the private office learned the importance of forgiveness and/or selective amnesia. And, with that essential cleaning of the slate, a fresh cycle of moods would begin.

❖

The Six Day War in June 1967 precipitated a major international crisis. George Brown believed that he enjoyed a special relationship with President Nasser and that this qualified him to play a leading role in resolving it. Any mutual regard that might have existed did not prevent Nasser from stimulating malicious broadcasts by 'The Voice of the Arabs' to the effect that British and American aircraft had taken part in the air raids on Egyptian and other Arab airfields. However, George Brown saw that the military disaster which had befallen Egypt and the other Arab states offered the possibility of a fresh approach to peace in the Middle East. When he attended the special debate on the crisis in the General Assembly of the United Nations later that month, he took with him a simple message: 'Arab recognition of Israel in exchange for return of territory seized by Israel'. With great determination and eloquence he pressed scores of his fellow foreign ministers to accept this proposition. In due course this provided the kernel of Resolution 242 which the Security Council adopted that autumn and which has remained the basis for progress towards peace in the Middle East. Hugh Caradon was rightly praised for his part in negotiating this result, but credit for the initial concept belonged to George Brown.

During our preparations for the foreign secretary's attendance at the regular session of the General Assembly in September 1967, we learned that the *Queen Mary* would be paying a farewell visit to New York during the same week and that a large reception was planned. Knowing the risks, I decided that it would be best if we were to conceal this piece of intelligence from the foreign secretary. In New York attention was still focussed on the Middle East and George Brown continued his advocacy of the formula 'recognition for territory'. On Saturday, 23 September, I accompanied him and Hugh Caradon to a lunch with the Danish foreign minister at the Danish ambassador's house north of Manhattan. When he left George Brown and me at our hotel after the lunch Caradon asked: "Shall I pick you up and take you to the reception tonight?" I felt momentarily homicidal.

On board *Queen Mary*, George Brown apparently enjoyed himself as only he could. Early the following morning he telephoned to ask me to join him urgently. He sounded distressed. As soon as I saw him I realised something serious had happened. He said that he was going to resign; he could not take any more. It transpired that earlier that morning he had received an emotional telephone call from London. His family had been upset by a photograph in that morning's press which appeared to show him dancing intimately with a woman at the *Queen Mary* reception. When we eventually saw the offending photograph, it was clear that it had been taken with a telescopic lens and from an angle which gave the impression that George Brown was looking down the woman's dress. Clever journalism, perhaps. However, the damage had been done and much of Sunday morning was spent in restoring a sense of proportion to the Brown household on both sides of the Atlantic.

The following few months were hectic – visits to Brussels for a NATO Council meeting, talks with Signor Fanfani in Rome, another meeting of the Western European Union in Brussels and visits to Washington and Tokyo. George Brown's temper was not improved by speculation in the press in November 1967 that he was to be replaced by James Callaghan. I asked the prime minister's private office if they could shed any light on these stories, which were beginning to undermine the foreign secretary's credibility. They were adamant that Number 10 was not the source and added that, on the prime minister's instructions, his press secretary was making it clear that no changes in the government were planned at that stage. Despite this, speculation continued for a few more days, for reasons which were never satisfactorily explained.

Disagreement between the prime minister and George Brown over arms for South Africa added to the strain in relations between them. The fourteenth of March 1968 began as a normal day, but within thirty-six hours the prime minister had accepted George Brown's resignation as foreign secretary. George Brown spent most of the afternoon of that day in the House of Commons. In the evening Derek Day took him some papers and left him in his office in the House. At about 8 p.m. George Brown telephoned to the private office to say that his last visitor had gone and to ask Jean Elliott to join him at the House. When she went across she could not find him. Nor could the prime minister's private office who were also looking for him. Not long after this they asked us to call off the search. I learned later that George Brown and Harold Wilson eventually met in the prime minister's office in the House shortly after midnight.

At five o'clock the following morning, 15 March, William Rodgers,

Preparing to cross the
Irrawaddy, 19
February 1945.

Edward Henderson and 'Auda bin Howeitat in Wadi Rum, June 1947.

Jean and our son Colin, Baghdad, 1953.

Welcoming students and guests at the 'Quzi' party, Shemlan, April 1958.

With Lady Middleton, wife of the new ambassador, Cairo, September 1964.

Private pilot, September 1969.

Presenting credentials to Colonel Qaddafi, Tripoli, October 1969.

With Edward Heath at Springfield Road, Belfast, 23 December 1971.

Edward Heath and BBC 'Panorama' team in the bar of the Metropole Hotel, Brussels. In background DM, Nancy-Joan and Madron Seligman, and Dr Brian Warren, 22 January 1972.

With Edward Heath at Battersea Heliport on return from Chequers talks on incomes policy, 26 September 1972.

With Jean and Alison in our New York apartment, August 1973.

With Ambassador Edouard Ghorra of Lebanon, UN Security Council, August 1973.

Consulting non-aligned representatives during UN Security Council debate on the Yom Kippur War, October 1973.

Briefing European Community colleagues on the Security Council debate, October 1973.

Vote in the Security Council, 21 October 1973.

Jean, Colin and Alison at our Berkshire weekend retreat, 1975.

Twentieth anniversary lunch of the Committee of Permanent Representatives, Brussels. Guest of Honour, Roy Jenkins, President of the European Commission, 26 January 1978.

With David Owen, President of the Council of Ministers, Luxembourg, April 1977.

With David Howell at meeting of European Community Energy Council, September 1979.

With Sir Derek Ezra, Chairman of the Coal Board, at Thoresby Colliery, Nottinghamshire, August 1980.

Monitoring service calls from customers at North Thames Gas, October 1980.

At Mobil's Coryton refinery, December 1980.

Tea ceremony with John Harper, Kyoto, July 1984.

With Jean in the Aberdares during the World Telecommunications Conference in Kenya, September 1986.

Visit of Esther Rantzen and family to plan the BBC Health Show, June 1991.

one of the ministers in the Foreign Office, telephoned to tell me that George Brown had resigned after a row with the prime minister. An hour later Number 10 rang me to say that the cabinet would meet at 10.30 a.m. I waited until after eight o'clock before passing on this news to George Brown. My telephone call wakened him. His mood persuaded me to go to his flat at Carlton Gardens. When he appeared soon after nine o'clock it was evident that he was determined to leave the government. Later in the morning William Rodgers arrived at Carlton Gardens and tried to dissuade him, but without success. I crossed the park to Downing Street to test the atmosphere and deduced from what the private secretaries in Number 10 told me that on this occasion there would be no relenting; George Brown's resignation would be accepted. Back at Carlton Gardens George Brown occupied himself drafting and re-drafting his letter of resignation.

Ten days later, together with the rest of the staff of the private office, I was invited to take leave of George Brown at Carlton Gardens. It fell to me to propose his health. I had to weigh my words. I said that, for those of us who had been closely associated with him, his resignation had ended an unforgettable period in our lives. For more than eighteen months a whirlwind had blown back and forth along the corridors of the Foreign Office and in his private office we had been close to the vortex. This experience had extended methods of diplomacy. But the foreign secretary had also extended our waking hours and given us the opportunity to share in the day-to-day and night-to-night life of one of the personalities of the age. George Brown appeared appreciative and, in any case, was not in a mood to wonder how much of this was tongue in cheek.

The *Sunday Times* published an article by George Brown on 7 April 1968 under the heading: "Why I shocked the Foreign Office mandarins." Much of the material in this article was reproduced in his autobiography *In My Way*, published in 1970. These two documents shed revealing light on George Brown's own perception of his role and achievements as foreign secretary. He claimed special intimacy not only with Nasser but also with de Gaulle, but there is no evidence that this feeling was reciprocated. He regarded his instructions about the form in which issues were submitted to him as a significant innovation and was clearly unaware that most foreign secretaries ask that procedures be followed which suit their own particular thought process. He took credit for introducing informality into diplomatic exchanges, citing discussions in front of the open fire in his office and the contribution of clock golf at Dorneywood with members of a United Nations mission to the successful resolution of the problem of Aden. Informality in diplomacy is as old as human history; in her dealings with Julius Caesar, and later with Mark Antony, Cleopatra may have carried informality to the extreme, but it served her purpose. George Brown also confessed to being intimidated by the 'terrifying atmosphere' in which he had to take decisions; this, he argued, was why he felt he had to be tough even though, as he acknowledged, this led to reports – "most of them very exaggerated" – about his alleged rough treatment of officials.

The reality of life in the Foreign Office with George Brown was different. He derived much satisfaction from lively debate with a number of senior members of the service whom he regarded as Oxbridge toffs. At the same time he was prone to instant likes and dislikes. I could never understand his ritual humiliation of Paul Gore-Booth, the permanent under-secretary and a devout Christian scientist who, he knew perfectly well, would not retaliate; at times his treatment of his senior adviser bordered on the sadistic. Even more puzzling was his volatility, not always alcohol-induced. In the course of his highly successful career in the trade unions and in politics, George Brown had far outstripped those who started out with him in Peabody Buildings. This led me to wonder whether intellectual alienation from his family and their circle, which deprived him of the opportunity for intimate discussion of his problems and preoccupations, could explain his unpredictable behaviour. Perhaps his addiction to alcohol was the effect, rather than the cause – a relief from the loneliness of the long-distance runner.

The country and the diplomatic service are indebted to George Brown for Resolution 242 and for the appointments of Christopher Soames[6] as ambassador in Paris and of Denis Greenhill[7] to succeed Paul Gore-Booth as permanent under-secretary at the Foreign Office. In these three instances his instincts were right. But in many others they were wrong. When he left government for the last time, I had serious doubts as to whether such a mercurial personality was fitted for high office.

❖

I knew of no one who had any such reservations about Michael Stewart, who returned to the Foreign Office to replace George Brown. He was given a mandate to amalgamate the Foreign and Commonwealth Relations Offices – an operation which was carried out with speed and tact.

The diary Michael Stewart inherited was heavily charged. Over the next several months he attended the regular meetings of the Western European Union and the NATO Council and visited Moscow and Bonn for bilateral talks.

A visit to Yugoslavia in June, when Michael Stewart was accompanied by his wife, Mary, proved opportune. A young Briton driving a coach involved in an accident in which many students had been killed had received a long prison sentence. The proceedings at the trial suggested that he was not at fault and pressure mounted on the British government to intervene. In such cases not only must the arguments be soundly based but, if they are to succeed, any representations must take account of local sensibilities. On our arrival in Belgrade Michael Stewart engaged the attention of the foreign minister who suggested that the case be raised when we met President Tito. The fact that Nikezic himself proposed this was encouraging. On our way to meet the president we had time to admire the extensive Roman remains at Pula before taking the launch to the island of Brioni. Tito was responsive and the sentence on the young Briton was set aside.

The Yugoslavs were keen for us to see what they had achieved in Montenegro. Much of the development in the new city of Titograd was characteristic of communist architecture and in sharp contrast to the elegance of the former capital, Cetinje, where in a broad tree-lined avenue we saw the villas which used to house the diplomatic corps accredited to the former kingdom of Montenegro. It needed little effort of the imagination to envisage the gracious life of the international aristocracy in the early years of the century.

Further visits to central and eastern Europe were due to take place in August. The invasion of Czechoslovakia forced a change of plan. Since Romania alone among the countries of the eastern bloc had opposed Soviet action, arrangements to visit Czechoslovakia itself and Hungary and Bulgaria were cancelled. As our aircraft approached the port of Constanta where we were to land, a member of our party went forward to the flight deck. He said he needed to check something. He returned a few minutes later saying: "Yes, it is black after all." He was of course referring to the sea.

In the fraught circumstances of the day it was not surprising that we were warmly received. In the meetings which followed neither President Ceausescu, nor Ion Maurer, the prime minister, who had been an active communist since 1936, nor Corneliu Manescu, the foreign minister, betrayed the unease they must have been felt about Soviet intentions; at a stroke the security they thought they enjoyed had vanished. Nor, for that matter, were there any indications of the brutal characteristics which in the end led to the downfall of the regime.

On our last evening Manescu invited us to dine at a lakeside restaurant, noted for its fish dishes. By this time we had seen and heard enough of the Romanian language to have become accustomed to the addition of a final letter 'u' to the English or French version of words of Roman origin. The menu, which was printed in French, included *carpe du lac*. When we asked the head of protocol if the Romanian word was *carpu* he was evasive. We had the impression that this was not the first time he had been asked. We understood his difficulty when, under pressure, he admitted that the Romanian word was not *carpu* but 'crap'. Robin Haydon,[8] who had succeeded me as head of the news department, assured him that this was one Romanian word we would not forget.

Michael Stewart spent a lot of time preparing his 'state of the world' address to the United Nations General Assembly in October 1968; his effort was rewarded by the warm reception it received. It was the custom in the Assembly that each speaker would return to his or her seat and wait until at least one more delegate had spoken from the rostrum before leaving the chamber. Michael Stewart observed this practice. When in due course we rose from our seats Andrei Gromyko and his secretary rose from theirs. They intercepted us before we could reach the exit. Gromyko was beaming. He took Michael Stewart's hand in both of his and said: "Mr Secretary, I will study your speech terribly."

Following the decision to amalgamate the Foreign and Commonwealth services into a single Diplomatic Service, it was logical that the first Foreign and Commonwealth Secretary should visit Pakistan and India. This visit took place in November 1968. In accordance with the wisdom of the day, we were advised before leaving to protect ourselves against stomach disorders and were provided with means to do so. All those who elected to follow this advice survived the trip without discomfort; those who did not, did not.

The politics of Pakistan were still under powerful military influence; in India the anti-western prejudices of the Nehru dynasty were still in evidence; East Pakistan – not yet Bangladesh – was recovering from disastrous floods. We were not confined to the capital cities. In Agra our guide was reluctant to allow the magnificence of the Taj Mahal to speak for itself. He was determined to earn his stipend. An aspiring poet, he told us the story of the tragic love of Shah Jehan and his wife Mumtaz in language which would have warmed the heart of Peter Sellers: "Too soon his belov'd was pluckéd from his side by the icy finger of fate, thus shattering their short-lived connubial bliss." In Madras I took time off to visit Spencer's, the grocery store which had served generations of the Raj. When paying for my purchases I said to the cashier: "I used to come here during the war to buy your Madras Planter cheroots." His reaction disconcerted me: "Yes," he said, "I know."

A special event took place in the early months of 1969. Over Christmas the previous year Colonel Frank Borman and his two colleagues, James Lovell and William Anders, circumnavigated the moon in the spacecraft Apollo VIII. Frank Borman visited Britain a few weeks later. On 3 February Michael Stewart was host at a reception in his honour at Lancaster House. I was immediately struck by Frank Borman's appearance; I could not recall seeing anyone at such a peak of physical fitness and mental alertness. In paying his tribute to the colonel's achievement, Michael Stewart quoted Marlowe's *Tamburlane the Great*:

> Our souls, whose faculties can comprehend
> The wondrous architecture of the world;
> And measure every wand'ring planet's course,
> Still climbing after knowledge infinite
> And always moving as the restless Spheres,
> Will us to wear ourselves and never rest
> Until we reach the ripest fruit of all,
> That perfect bliss and sole felicity
> The sweet fruition of an earthly crown.

Frank Borman was moved. He in turn charmed us all when, asked how the moon had looked from Apollo VIII, he replied: "Not as good as it does from Hyde Park." In the general chatter that followed I was asked by many of the guests from which of Shakespeare's plays Michael Stewart had drawn this apt quotation.

My appointment as ambassador to Libya was announced in April 1969 and Michael and Mary Stewart invited Jean and me to a reception in his office to mark our departure. My tongue was not in my cheek when I recalled Michael Stewart's erudition, his courtesy, his brave persistence with the policies he believed to be right, the clarity of his expositions in the House of Commons and before the world press, and the exemplary partnership between Michael and Mary. I would remember them as good people at a time when good people were not in fashion.

It took me some days to realise that the hectic pattern of life of the previous four years had finally ended. As spokesman for two foreign secretaries and private secretary to the same two foreign secretaries, I had seen at first hand the influence of personality and politics on decision making at high level. I had learned that the seemingly endless travel undertaken by foreign ministers, which only rarely produced tangible results in the short term, had become an essential part of modern diplomacy. The number of actors on the world stage increased year on year as did the number of international organisations and, in all but a few instances, face to face encounters made quarrelling that much more difficult. I had met most of the important world leaders of the time, many in their own environment, and had been reminded that, like the rest of us, they included the good, the bad and the indifferent.

13

Qaddafi's Libya

The first item in the programme of briefings on Libya was a call on the head of the Personnel Services Department. John Leahy[1] had a file on his desk entitled 'Aircraft for HM Ambassador, Libya'. The need for such an unlikely file arose from the disposition of the government in Libya. Tripoli was the internationally recognised capital, and the principal offices of the ministries were located there, as well as foreign embassies and the headquarters of many business enterprises. Benghazi, the capital of Cyrenaica, was also a major centre. This province was the original fiefdom of King Idris, the head of the Senussi tribe, and its importance was recognised by the fact that the the embassy had a substantial office in Benghazi, whose head was the ambassador's deputy as well as consul-general. There was a further complication. King Idris intended to create a new seat of Government at Beida, close to the ancient Greek city of Cyrene. The town was being developed for this purpose and, since it was already being used by the King and his ministers, the British Embassy had acquired an office and a house which were frequently used by the ambassador, or his deputy.

Over the previous few years the ambassador had had to spend a good deal of his time, and a lot of taxpayers' money, on travel between the three centres. It had therefore been suggested that it could be both more convenient and more economical if the embassy had its own aircraft. Contrary to expectation, an approach to officials in the Treasury had not provoked a wholly negative response. However, a few days before my briefings began, the Treasury had said that, while they could see the case for an aircraft, the cost of maintaining a pilot in Tripoli for only occasional flights could not be justified. In answer to my question, John Leahy said that none of the members of the British military mission in Libya was a qualified pilot.

This quite unexpected information seemed to provide both a motive and an opportunity to fulfil a long neglected ambition. After a pause I

said: "Supposing the ambassador was the pilot?". John Leahy immediately appreciated the irony. "Why not?" he said. "At least there would
be no problem knowing where you were going; blue on the left and
yellow on the right to Benghazi, and the opposite on the way back". We
decided that it would be prudent not to reveal this ploy to the Treasury
at this stage.

Events moved quickly. After a medical examination and other
formalities I enrolled as a student pilot at the flying school at Thruxton
in Hampshire and had my first lesson in a single-engined Cessna 150
high-wing monoplane on 14 June 1969. This lesson had three elements
– learning the layout of the cockpit, preparation for the flight and
something called 'air experience'. From the start, Maurice Goor, my
instructor, made me sit in the left-hand seat. "You are under instruction,"
he said, "but you are still the pilot." He took off and after about twenty
minutes of manoeuvring he told me to hold the controls so that I could
feel the strength of movement required. Later he removed his own hands
and feet from the controls and said: "Now you have control". For the
next ten minutes or so I had the illusion of enjoying the freedom of the
skies. Maurice Goor resumed control and, as we turned on to our final
approach and prepared to land, he pointed to the racing cars practising
on the circuit below. "Have nothing to do with that sport;" he said, "far
too dangerous."

Maurice Goor was a skilled and demanding instructor and he took
me rapidly through the normal manoeuvres. His advice was invariably
clear and relevant and he paid particular stress on the need, in addition to
checking instruments at regular intervals, to keep eyes skinned for other
aircraft. Late one afternoon we flew some distance from Thruxton and
climbed in stages to 5,000 feet to practise recovering from a stall, which
I much enjoyed. At a later stage in the course we flew to the same area to
practise emergency procedures, including simulated emergency landings.
We also practised recovery from a spin. I did not at all relish seeing the
earth rotating around the propellor as the aircraft accelerated straight
down towards the ground and needed no encouragement to master the
recovery drill.

I spent day after day taking off, circling the airfield and landing in
accordance with a strict discipline. Maurice was right when he said that
the routine would soon became instinctive. This provided the cue to add
to his repertoire of anecdotes. I told him how Badri Ram had illustrated
the meaning of instinct for the edification of the young farmers from the
northern plains and hills of India in my signal platoon in Persia during
the war.

On 7 August, after we had completed yet another circuit, Maurice
switched off the engine without warning, opened his door, stepped
down and said: "You will find it's much lighter with only one person

aboard. We'll have some coffee when you come back." The warning was justified; the aircraft was airborne after only sixty or seventy yards and for the next few minutes I had serious work to do. It was only on the downwind leg of the circuit that I had a moment to appreciate the sense of ownership – even of conquest – conveyed by the first solo flight. Then I had to concentrate on getting the much lighter aircraft on to the ground and keeping it there. I parked the aircraft and feigned nonchalance as I joined Maurice for the promised coffee.

During the next several sessions I practised circuits on my own. Then the emphasis was on navigation under what were called visual flying rules – that is to say, without using instruments. The first step was to work out the compass bearing and length in nautical miles of each leg of the chosen route. These had then to be adjusted to take account of wind conditions. The control tower knew the direction and velocity of the wind at the altitude chosen for the flight – typically 2,000 feet. With the help of a hand-operated computer which worked on the slide-rule principle, one could then work out not only the compass heading one had to follow to allow for the wind, but also how many minutes it would take to get from A to B. What remained was flying straight and level and verifying one's route by map reading.

It was soon obvious that from a height of 2,000 feet the best points of reference on the ground were railway lines (and emphatically not roads), power lines (which were to be treated with respect), woods, rivers and other stretches of water. Although aeronautical maps did not show them all, one soon learned by experience or hearsay which towns had distinctive features such as a gas-holder or a prominent, isolated building.

Calculations on the computer proved reliable but, as I was soon to discover, their accuracy could be affected by a change in flying conditions. On the second of my solo cross-country flights the turning points were Chilbolton, Blandford, Frome and Marlborough. Conditions were hazy and on the leg from Chilbolton to Blandford I was flying directly into the sun and wind. Visibility ahead was negligible and I had to rely on what I could see immediately below or behind through the port window. A minute after I should have reached Blandford it had still not come into view. Over my shoulder I could see the spire of Salisbury cathedral which seemed to be where it ought to be. That at least was something familiar. Another minute passed and still no sign of Blandford. The standard advice, which was that to avoid getting lost one should not deviate from the heading, was justified in the end even though my nerve was severely tested in the process. Three minutes later than scheduled, Blandford appeared out of the mist. As I discovered when I turned north on to the next leg and had the wind at my tail, its velocity had increased by several knots since I had composed my flight plan.

As my confidence grew so did my sensitivity to experiences of flight. All air travellers become familiar with spectacular cloudscapes and the lights of cities sparkling like pins on a pincushion. But at 2,000 feet and a cruising speed of 95 knots there are other, more intimate sights to enjoy – dark caverns between the tops of trees in woods, long parallel lines across pale yellow fields at harvest time, and the spaced-out white figures on the village cricket field which seem never to move when one is watching. Deeper senses can also be touched. I found that each time the vibration ceased as the wheels left the ground on take-off the feeling of release from some earthly restraint became more marked. Similarly, at each successive landing, the forgiving embrace of mother earth as the aircraft sank on to the runway gave me greater satisfaction.

Strict though he was, Maurice was not above offering helpfully loaded advice. The next cross-country test entailed the longest leg I had yet flown, followed by a landing at Oxford airfield near Kidlington. At the end of his briefing Maurice said that there was no need to worry if my course happened to take me over any industrial plant emitting smoke or steam; there would be some turbulence, but it would do no harm. The sky was clear and as soon as I had set course and reached 2,000 feet I saw the cooling towers of Didcot power station in the far distance straight ahead. As Maurice said, the turbulence was not severe. But he had not mentioned the spectacular beauty of Blenheim Palace in the late afternoon sunshine.

Briefing for Libya continued. This entailed detailed discussions with the relevant departments in the Foreign and Commonwealth Office, the Overseas Development Ministry, the Board of Trade and the Ministry of Defence. Earlier in the year the two governments had concluded an agreement under which the British would supply Libya with military equipment, including 188 Chieftain tanks and equipment for the Public Security Forces – a type of gendarmerie. A request by the latter for a further 100 Chieftain tanks was outstanding. When I visited Stevenage, George Jefferson,[2] the chairman of the Guided Weapons Division of British Aircraft Corporation, explained the complications of the contract which his company had signed with the Libyans the previous year for the supply of Rapier air defence missile systems. The fact that I also met representatives of the Bank of England, the Chartered Bank, the British Bank of the Middle East, Shell, BP, Vickers, Vosper Thorneycroft and Hawker Siddeley among others, emphasised the wide range of interests it would be my responsibility to protect and further. Jean and I were received in audience by The Queen and I received an unexpected invitation to call on the Leader of the Opposition at his office in the House of Commons. Edward Heath congratulated me on my appointment and wished me well.

Meanwhile our family preparations continued. Our plan was to travel by surface route to Italy and sail from there to Tripoli where we were scheduled to arrive in the middle of September 1969. I still had time to qualify for my private pilot's licence. Two hurdles remained to be cleared – the qualifying cross-country flight, which entailed landings at Shoreham and Portsmouth – and the final general flying test.

On the morning of 1 September 1969 I set off early for Thruxton to prepare for the final cross-country test. Not long after I had left home Jean received a telephone call from the Foreign and Commonwealth Office. There had been a coup d'état in Libya and the department would like to know what I wanted to do. She explained where I was and said she would pass on the message. She was in two minds. Would the news hinder or help me as I set out to take the test? She opted to pass on the message. I said that the short answer to the department's question was: what I want to do is complete my test. I would contact them on my return. The test passed off without hitch and two days later I qualified as a private pilot. Although information about the situation in Libya was still sparse, one thing already seemed obvious. John Leahy could now close the file he had on his desk when I called on him.

First reports from Peter Wakefield,[3] the counsellor of the embassy, who was stationed in Benghazi, and from Marrack Goulding[4] in Tripoli indicated that the takeover had been well planned and brilliantly executed. No blood had been shed. In Cyrenaica the broadcasting station and the airfield at Benina had been immediately secured. Early in the morning of 1 September, a Libyan army captain had told Peter Wakefield that what was happening was a purely internal affair which need cause the British no alarm. In Tripoli, soon after eight o'clock, 'Mig' Goulding, together with his French, American and Soviet colleagues, was asked to meet the Revolutionary Command Council at the broadcasting station which had been seized at first light. Three young officers told them that the aims of the revolution were to abolish corruption and inequalities of wealth and to take a more positive stand on Arab and international questions. Foreigners, they said, would be protected and treaties and other agreements respected.

On the day of the takeover King Idris was in Turkey. He was reported to have asked the British to intervene in order 'to restore order and peace and to protect lives'. The Commander of the Cyrenaica Defence Force at Tobruk asked that British forces at Tobruk and the air base at El Adem help him arm the tribes and organise resistance. On 2 September, Omar Shelhi, who occupied the much resented position of Special Adviser to the King, called on the foreign secretary in London to plead for intervention on the King's behalf. All these requests were refused; the Anglo-Libyan Military Agreement of 1953 required Britain to come to Libya's aid in the event of external aggression. Nonetheless, the fact that Omar Shelhi had met Michael Stewart at the Foreign and Commonwealth Office stimulated fears that Britain might intervene militarily and on the following day – 3 September – a violently worded statement attacking the British Government for receiving him was broadcast by the Revolutionary Command Council. This naturally caused concern among members of the British community in Libya.

It was clearly important that I should take up my post as soon as possible. There were two problems. First, all Libyan ports and airports were closed. Secondly, agreement to my appointment as ambassador had been given by the King, to whom my credentials were addressed. Mig Goulding in Tripoli was instructed to establish as soon as possible whether I would nonetheless be acceptable to the new regime and to find out the name of the leader of the Revolutionary Command Council so that new credentials could be submitted to The Queen for her signature. The young officer whom Mig was able to track down saw no problem about my acceptability, but he was reluctant to disclose any names. "Could we not say simply 'the Leader of the Revolution'?" Mig insisted on a name and his interlocutor asked for time to consult. Back in London we were contemplating credentials addressed 'To Whom it may Concern'. However, within a few days Mig was given the name of Colonel Qaddafi, who was later identified as the captain who had met Peter Wakefield at the broadcasting station in Benghazi on the morning of the takeover. New credentials were prepared and sent to Balmoral for signature by The Queen. Meanwhile, in the light of the latest assessments from Tripoli and Benghazi, the British government had recognised the new regime on 6 September.

Significant developments were reported on 8 September. A captain and ten soldiers arrived at the embassy in Tripoli with orders to search for explosives. They were refused entry. Many of the 250-strong Jewish community in Tripoli, most of whom were either Libyan or Tunisian, were arrested and kept in custody for twenty-four hours. On the same day the names of the members of a mainly civilian government were announced. The prime minister, who was also minister for finance and agricultural reform, was Dr Muhammad Salim al Maghribi, who had organised strikes by dockworkers at the time of the Six Day war in 1967. Salih Bueisir, a former newspaper editor and long standing opponent of the previous regime who had spent several years in exile, became foreign minister. Two senior posts – defence and the interior – were given to army officers – a major and a lieutenant-colonel. The identity of the members of the Revolutionary Command Council other than Qaddafi remained secret.

Late in the afternoon of 11 September we learned that Tripoli airport was to open the following day. BOAC were to send an aircraft to bring back children and teachers for the beginning of the school term. Jean and I were given seats on the outward flight. This took off at 9.30 the following morning. Our fellow passengers were all Libyan. Throughout the flight they were subdued, but the moment we touched down in the early afternoon there was a spontaneous burst of applause and when we disembarked many kissed the ground. The military were of course much in evidence at the airport. We were met by Mig Goulding and his wife, Susan, other members of the embassy staff and a representative of what was now called the Ministry of Unity and Foreign Affairs. We went straight to the residence, a handsome building which, as I was unpleasantly surprised to discover later, we rented from the former Queen who was now in exile in Egypt. In the evening members of the staff came to the residence and brought us up to date.

❖

Eleven days after the revolution a twelve-hour night-time curfew was still in force, communications within the country had not been restored, ports and airports remained closed to all but returning Libyans, departing students, tourists and accredited diplomats. All government offices except for the Ministry of Unity and Foreign Affairs were still closed. Banks had been open only for one day for withdrawals and deposits. Sporadic shooting could still be heard at night, probably by bored or nervous soldiery.

The immediate tasks were to establish the nature of the new regime, its likely policies, how these would affect British interests in Libya and what our attitude should be. Who the leaders were remained a mystery, but their motives seemed clear. They were impatient for the King to pass on; they felt that his judgment was impaired and that he was unduly influenced by the Shelhi family whose extravagance he condoned. They may have thought that the Shelhis planned to take over the country. Someone had painted a slogan in red on Peter Wakefield's residence in Benghazi:

'1948 + 1956 + 1967 = 1 September'

which, being interpreted, meant that the establishment of Israel, the Suez affair and the Six Day War were the historical causes of the Libyan revolution.

Statements on behalf of the new leadership shed little light on their ultimate intentions. These proclaimed the struggle for social justice, an end to corruption and more active support for the Arab cause. A slogan was borrowed from the Baath party in Syria: 'Unity, Freedom, Socialism.' Nor were the actions of the leaders any more eloquent. After two weeks their only decisions were to double the minimum wage and to reopen government offices, but without under-secretaries, governors or mayors.

The day after our arrival Jean and I met leading members of the

British community in Tripoli and heard their first hand accounts of the difficulties British subjects were facing. A few women had been molested at the time of the military takeover, but since then personal security had improved. The immediate anxiety was difficulty in obtaining exit visas; the longer term anxiety was future prospects for British business. These concerns were repeated when we met more expatriates at morning service at the Anglican church the following day.

Over the next few days some restrictions were relaxed. However, there were also setbacks. One thoughtless British woman boasted to the press on arriving back in England that she had managed to smuggle out a quantity of foreign currency beneath her underwear. The consequence was inevitable: all foreign women leaving Libya thereafter were strip-searched at the airport. An Italian jeweller who owned a motor-boat slipped out of Tripoli harbour at night and crossed to Malta where he too boasted about his exploit. Sailing for pleasure outside the harbour was immediately banned.

On 16 September I paid my first call on Salih Bueisir to whom I handed copies of my credentials. Unlike the young military officers, Bueisir spoke English. He began by stressing the new government's desire for good relations with Britain on the basis of mutual respect. I noted this. But I went on to say that I had certain immediate concerns. When I referred to the assaults on British women Bueisir became agitated and said that such unfounded allegations were an insult to the Libyan armed forces. I told him that the women concerned had authorised me to say that they were prepared to tell him personally about their experiences. He calmed down and asked me to let him know at once of any future incident. When the conversation became more general, Bueisir surprised me by his emphasis on the Palestine question. The gross injustice the Palestinians had suffered was a humiliation for the whole Arab nation.

Jean and I flew to Benghazi the following day. Peter and Felicity Wakefield had considerable experience in Arab posts and had been in Benghazi for three years. At the time of the Six Day war in 1967 their safety and that of members of their staff had been seriously at risk when demonstrations got out of hand. They were therefore well acquainted with the background to the most recent events. They arranged opportunities for discussions with the staff and members of the British military mission and with representatives of the British community; these included not only oil company executives but also a number of academics working at the university. Back in Tripoli I had a further meeting with Bueisir to sort out some problems affecting British subjects and paid a second visit to Benghazi at the end of the month in order to visit our forces at the air base at El Adem, south of Tobruk.

On my return from the second visit to Benghazi Jean and I held a reception for a representative group of British residents in Tripoli. I told them that I believed the revolution was irreversible and that the aims of the young officers with whom authority now rested seemed clear. By socialism they meant an end to the system under which the majority of the inhabitants of this immensely rich country lived in poverty and discomfort. By freedom they meant that the actions of the government should express the popular will and that there should be no more corruption and patronage. By unity they meant that Libya should step forward into the ranks of the progressive Arab countries. But these young officers were inexperienced and they might well be overawed and frustrated by the multiplicity and complexities of the problems they faced. For this reason an unsettled period lay ahead. Until I had met Colonel Qaddafi and other members of the Revolutionary Command Council, I could not say how British interests would be affected by the revolution. It was encouraging that certain problems had already been sorted out. Others remained. The embassy was working to speed up the issue of exit visas, to have the curfew period shortened and the sale of liquor resumed. Meanwhile, we all had to exercise patience, tolerance and resolve.

When I invited questions a nervous looking young couple asked why the embassy weren't doing this and weren't doing that. I explained that none of the actions they wanted the embassy to take was within either our authority or capability. When I had finished, Tom Ashworth, the general manager of Barclays Bank, intervened. "You have told us what you and your staff are doing for us. What, sir, can we do for you?" Tom Ashworth was to prove a tower of strength in the difficult months ahead.

Salih Bueisir told me on 5 October that it had been arranged that I would present my credentials in Benghazi on 8 October. In Benghazi Peter Wakefield was told on 7 October that the ceremony had been postponed by twenty-four hours. The next day the Ministry of Unity and Foreign Affairs said that the ceremony would take place in Tripoli, not Benghazi, and promised further details. On 9 October they telephoned again to say that there would be a delay of half an hour. This was not enlightening, since we had been given no time for the ceremony. By 10 o'clock it had emerged that I was expected at 11.30. At 11 o'clock two cars and a motorcycle escort arrived at the Residence. On the way to the centre of the city the convoy was applauded, probably because the crowd thought it contained a member of the Revolutionary Command Council. As we entered Martyrs' Square, the motorcade's sirens startled a number of horses and donkeys drawing carts, shedding their loads of fruit and vegetables.

On arrival at the ministry I was hustled upstairs to the minister's anteroom. A Sterling sub-machine-gun lay on a table, its barrel pointing towards anyone entering the room. I was immediately shown into the minister's office where Qaddafi was standing with Bueisir and two ADCs. He was wearing a light khaki uniform with the insignia of a colonel on his bush jacket. He seemed more apprehensive than I was. After the formal speeches we sat at a coffee table. As though to put Qaddafi at his ease, Bueisir opened the conversation by saying that he and I had discussed the Palestine question on a number of occasions; he could assure the colonel that I fully understood the position of the Libyan Government. I said that at the time of the revolution the United Kingdom had stood back. We had noted his own statement to Mr Wakefield that the military takeover was a purely internal affair. Qaddafi said he had indeed noticed this and appreciated our attitude. He then said that Libya was a backward country; the people should have better opportunities for a fuller life, especially since Libya was blessed with such rich resources. Why should vast sums be spent on putting men on the moon while there was such poverty as existed in Libya? It was the task of the Revolutionary Command Council, on behalf of humanity, to improve conditions in Libya.

I then asked about the position of foreign experts in Libya. Qaddafi said that anyone whose presence was beneficial to Libya would be welcome. But those who had come to engage in what he called interventionism would not be welcome. When I suggested that the expatriate community would be reassured if this position were made public, he said he would consider this. He then asked about the position of Libyans in Britain. I explained the rules. Bueisir intervened to say that during the previous year the United Kingdom had stopped the immigration of coloured people. I said at once that this was not so and explained the new system of controls. This exchange prompted Qaddafi to say that he had noticed that most of those who worked on the London underground and on the buses were black. Was this not evidence of racial discrimination? I replied that racial discrimination was illegal in the United Kingdom and I described the role of the Race Relations Board. This was clearly a revelation to him. I went on to say that I had observed in many Arab countries that photographers and tailors were for the most part Armenian and that plumbers who repaired drains were almost always Christians. It had never occurred to me that these were examples of racial or religious discrimination. Qaddafi then said that there would be opportunities to discuss our future relations and I took my leave.

Qaddafi seemed older than his reputed 27 years. His face was pitted in the manner often ascribed to infantile malnutrition – not surprising since it was said he was born to a tribal couple near Sirte in 1942, when

the desert war was at its height. The most striking feature about him was
the occasional penetrating look. I recalled that Humphrey Trevelyan had
noted the same phenomenon when he first met Abdul Karim Qassim,
the brigadier who overthrew the monarchy in Iraq in 1958.

❖

By this time I felt better placed to advise London on the consequences
of recent events for our interests in Libya. What had happened on
1 September was a revolution, not a coup d'état. The new regime
intended to raise the standards of the people of Libya, to establish the
country's independent identity and to play the role in the Arab world to
which the country's wealth and potential entitled it. The leaders knew
that they were dependent on foreign expertise and would remain so for a
long time to come. But foreign enterprises, including the oil companies,
and individuals who had the specialisms they needed, would be welcome
on terms which the new Libya would determine. In the eyes of the new
leadership, the presence of foreign bases on Libyan soil was incompatible
with the new identity they sought. At the same time, they would want
to build up their armed forces; for this they would need equipment and
training. This suggested a possible basis for a new relationship between
the United Kingdom and Libya.

It was no surprise that this assessment was unwelcome to the Ministry
of Defence and to Sir Denis Smallwood in Cyprus. The air marshal,
known in the RAF as 'Splinters', was the Commander of British Forces
in the Near East, and the base at El Adem was one of the jewels in
his crown. I returned to London on 21 October for consultations
with the Foreign and Commonwealth Office and the Chiefs of Staff.
While recognising the possibility of a demand to withdraw our bases,
the chiefs of staff hoped we might be able at least to retain the right to
train army units in the desert. I returned to Tripoli on 25 October and
received a note four days later from the Libyan government requesting
that negotiations be opened immediately on the evacuation of British
forces from Libya. The note asked for an early reply.

On 2 November, the anniversary of the Balfour Declaration and the
day after Bueisir had made a speech on the subject, a mob several hundred strong attacked the embassy, damaging cars. The police detachment
outside looked the other way. The following day we were given one
week, later extended to six weeks, to close our post in Benghazi. RAF
flights in and out of El Adem were still limited to one a day and the
Libyans continued to refuse us permission to replace the army units
which had been training in Cyrenaica at the time of the revolution.
Our own movements came under close scrutiny. Wherever we went
we were followed by a khaki coloured Volkswagen 'beetle', containing
two young men with close haircuts wearing civilian suits. In downtown
Tripoli there were certain places where the superior acceleration of our

car and four quick left-hand turns enabled us to get behind them. Harmless sport, which some of the close-cropped young men were relaxed enough to find amusing.

Consultation with London and Cyprus was intense and the embassy communications staff were busy day and night. The length of telegrams was calculated in 'groups' – that is to say words, or series of numerals – and this was indicated for the convenience of the operators at the head of each telegram. One night the head of the communications section brought an unusually long telegram into the registry where I was consulting a file. In answer to my question he said: "Can't you guess? Another few hundred 'Splinter groups'". Telegrams from Cyprus were renamed from that moment.

On 11 November I was instructed to convey our reply to the Libyan note of 29 October. Bueisir was out of the country and it took us a day and a half to find anyone who could arrange for me to meet Qaddafi. Eventually an appointment was fixed for 13 November. As it was the month of Ramadan, I was asked to be at the foreign ministry at 9.20 p.m. Mig Goulding, who had been an outstanding student during my time at the Middle East Centre for Arab Studies in Shemlan, accompanied me. We were shown into a waiting room lit by a 40-watt bulb. After some twenty minutes we were served coffee which must have been intended for a previous visitor. Ambassador Khweldi, the genial chief of protocol, said with a smile: "After all, cold coffee is a speciality."

At 10 p.m. the by now familiar whine of armoured cars signalled the opening of the next act. Mig and I were shown into the minister's office. Of the six Libyans in the room I recognised only Qaddafi, who was wearing battledress and a green jerkin. He put his sub-machine-gun on the Minister's desk. The four other officers were similarly clad and three similarly armed. The fourth carried a notebook. The remaining Libyan was in civilian clothes. He turned out to be the minister of justice and, in Bueisir's absence, acting foreign minister. His sole function was to fetch tea half way through the meeting. Qaddafi took me by the arm and said: "You know the brethren." Although, as he was well aware, I did not, I shook hands with each in turn. No names were disclosed. One had heavy jowls, the youngest sharp eyes. While I introduced Mig the three armed officers stowed their sub-machine-guns on the lower shelf of a coffee table. Qaddafi said: "You know, Maitland, it's good we can do all this business in Arabic." We all then sat down round the coffee table.

I began by saying that the British government were ready to enter into detailed negotiations about terminating the Anglo-Libyan Treaty. We wanted a new relationship. As a matter of principle we would not maintain defence facilities in an independent country against its wishes. We were ready to continue training the Libyan armed forces and would wish to retain training facilities for our forces. This last remark caused a sharp intake of Libyan breath. As evidence of our intentions we were ready to send a consignment of self-propelled guns and armoured cars, if the Libyans so wanted, and we would wish to discuss the supply of Chieftain tanks as part of a review of our whole relationship. One of the Libyans immediately observed: "Your offer on Chieftains is conditional."

I then asked if British experts were indeed welcome in Libya. The contract with the British American Tobacco company had been terminated the previous day without notice. No action had been taken on my request that a Libyan customs and immigration post be established at El Adem to facilitate flights and the movement of personnel. The previous day the Cairo press had reported a statement by the Libyan minister of defence that the contract with the British Aircraft Corporation had been cancelled.

Qaddafi said the essential issue was withdrawal from our bases at El Adem and Tobruk. Everything else was conditioned by this. He ruled out training exercises by British forces in Libya, but would welcome training of Libyan defence forces by the British. He would have questions about the price and delivery dates of the Chieftains. The BAC contract had not been cancelled; the Libyans wanted missiles other than those specified in the contract.

The meeting broke up in a relaxed atmosphere. The 'brethren' were appropriately embarrassed when Mig and I helped them retrieve their sub-machine-guns from under the coffee table. Qaddafi took me aside and said that if I ever wanted to see him on an important matter I was to let him know; he knew that I would not worry him unnecessarily. He kept his word and throughout my time in Libya his attitude towards me was courteous. In other individual conversations which followed the formalities it emerged that Qaddafi and his colleagues had indeed expected the British to invade after their takeover and now realised, for the first time, that we had at no time contemplated this. They were above all relieved that during the previous two hours progress had been made. After handshakes all round, Mig and I left.

On this occasion Qaddafi himself was more confident than when I had presented my credentials. This was understandable. As a member of my staff had said at that time, if he had been brought up on the anti-imperialist propaganda broadcast from Cairo by 'The Voice of the Arabs' he probably believed that British ambassadors ate Arab leaders for breakfast. However, during these discussions he had shown that he was clever, zealous – even passionate – and humorous. If he was in fear of a counter-coup he may have calculated that an early and spectacular success, such as the removal of the British and American bases, would consolidate his position. For him this issue could be, quite literally, a matter of life or death. As for his anonymous companions, it was difficult to imagine that these eager young men in their combat dress and their sub-machine-guns were the government of Libya. Their garb and their weaponry gave the foreign minister's office the appearance of a brigands' den.

It was after midnight when Mig and I returned to the embassy to write our report and recommendations for London. Members of the staff had waited up to see if we returned in one piece and had a pot of coffee on the stove. An immediate problem was how to identify Qaddafi's anonymous companions in our report. We found inspiration in the tradition of the restoration comedies. The note-taker became Scribe, the pertinent questioner Shrewd, heavy-jowls became Prognathous and the young, sharp-eyed radical Fervent.

A team from the British Aircraft Corporation came out to Tripoli to open discussions with the Libyan ministry of defence on the missile contract. Problems arose over the British school and individuals were still having difficulty over exit visas. There was a further bout of consultation over the next phase in the treaty negotiations. On 28 November we announced that the families of British forces would leave Tobruk by the end of February 1970. On 30 November, in response to our pressure, the Libyans agreed to the rotation of 260 British troops and to an increase in the number of flights in and out of El Adem from one a day to fifty per month.

I warmly welcomed a suggestion that I be accompanied at the next round of talks by representatives of the ministry of defence and the commander in chief in Cyprus. And I was more than lucky in the selection. General John Goddard was in charge of the programme of military assistance to Libya in the Ministry of Defence; Air Commodore Trotman was the principal administrative officer at Headquarters British Forces, Near East.

John Goddard and I established an instant rapport attributable in part to Alan Bennett. After dinner at the residence we played our record of *Beyond the Fringe* with which he was not familiar. He was convulsed with laughter by *Take a Pew*. The following Sunday John accompanied us to morning service. The congregation took full advantage of *Cwm Rhondda* to fill their lungs; the *Bread of Heaven* rose to the rafters. As we sat down I whispered to John: "Wales 6, England 3". The bond was strengthened.

In addition to John Goddard and the air commodore, our team at the first round of negotiations at the Municipal Conference Hall on 8 December included David West, a principal in the ministry of defence, Michael Hannam, who had been our neighbour in Cairo and had now replaced Peter Wakefield as my deputy, Mig Goulding

and David Gore-Booth,[5] another Arabic speaker, whose task it would
be to take notes and interpret into English for the benefit of the
non-Arabic speakers. This requirement was appreciated by both sides
since it allowed a few moments of reflection between paragraphs. The
leader on the Libyan side was Abdul Salam Jallud who, it emerged,
was Qaddafi's deputy. Also present were 'Shrewd', now identified as
Captain al-Huni, Bueisir and Mansour Kekhiya, the senior diplomat
in the foreign ministry. Qaddafi turned up unexpectedly to open the
negotiations. In a high-speed monotone he read out an eleven-point
statement in which the only new element was the need to reach a speedy
conclusion. He seemed tired and preoccupied. We learned later that an
abortive coup had taken place the previous day and that the ministers of
defence and the interior – the two military members of the government
– had been arrested.

I began by reiterating the desire of the British government to
establish a relationship with Libya relevant to the new circumstances.
The arrangements for our withdrawal would depend on the degree of
cooperation we received from the Libyan authorities. Throughout the
next two and a half hours Jallud insisted that he wanted to hear only
one thing – the date for our withdrawal; everything else was irrelevant.
It was finally agreed that we would reconvene in a few days' time.

The second meeting took place on 13 December. I had in the
meantime been authorised to undertake that our forces would be
withdrawn by 31 March 1970 – that is, within three and a half months –
on the understanding that this would not be the end of the negotiations.
The further task would be the building of the new relationship.

The scenes at the Conference Hall when we arrived were disgraceful.
A crowd of several hundred young men of military age and with military
haircuts and footwear were milling around the entrance shouting 'Jalá' –
'evacuation'. We were jostled on our way into the hall, John Goddard
receiving a kick on the shin. Jallud's response to my protest was that
it was right that we should hear the voice of the people. I expressed
surprise that the voice of the people should be calling for something
which had already been agreed. When I announced that, provided no
obstacles were placed in our way by any Libyan authorities and that we
received wholehearted cooperation over flights and the movements of
ships, our forces would leave by 31 March, there was much chattering on
the Libyan side of the table. After a few minutes Bueisir asked: "Which
year?" When I told them they were astonished that we could remove
ourselves in such a short time. I said that the only thing that could
prevent us meeting this deadline would be obstruction by the Libyan
authorities. It was essential that there should be none.

We spent the next two hours drafting an agreed minute. Jallud
tried throughout to resist any mention of our future relationship. But

when the press and television cameras were brought in and we each made statements, he spoke eloquently about the basis which had been established that evening for a new era in Anglo-Libyan relations. He was not always to be so forthcoming. After the press had left both delegations stayed on for a cup of coffee. At this moment an urgent telegram from the Station Commander at El Adem was handed to me. There had been a mysterious explosion, probably caused by a grenade, in a British mess at Tobruk. By good fortune no one had been injured and the damage was slight. I read this report to Jallud, who was visibly shaken. I said he should understand that, if anything of this kind happened again, the agreement we had reached that evening would be in jeopardy. He assured me there would be no recurrence. I judged that someone in Tobruk was about to have his head scrubbed.

Gamal Abdul Nasser and Jaafar al Nimairi, the President of the Sudan, visited Libya at the end of December 1969. This confirmed the new Libya's acceptance by the progressive Arab states and, as was intended, boosted Qaddafi's reputation in the Arab world. Members of the Revolutionary Command Council told me and members of the staff that they had never dreamt that they would one day shake the hand of the man who had been their hero and their inspiration. And here they were, sitting at the same table, talking with him as if with a brother.

❖

The Americans had been told at the end of October that they would have to evacuate their base at Wheelus Field on the outskirts of Tripoli and in subsequent negotiations it was agreed that they would complete their withdrawal by 30 June 1970. Throughout we kept in close touch with our colleagues in the United States embassy. Pooling information helped us both and the warm relationships which were formed helped to sustain morale. No one who was present will forget a barbecue at the end of November hosted by Colonel Daniel "Chappie" James, who commanded the Wing of the US Air Force stationed at Wheelus Base. A tall, athletic figure and a hero of the Korean War, he had no difficulty in commanding respect and he conducted the barbecue with the panache of Toscanini.

On our own front reports by John Goddard and Trotman to the ministry of defence and to Near East headquarters on the course of our negotiations had an immediate and beneficial effect. It was recognised both in London and in Cyprus that we had achieved the best deal available. We had now to complete the evacuation within the time limit and to pursue talks on other aspects of our relationship and, in particular, the terms for the supply of defence equipment. The problems over the air defence contract could not be resolved and George Jefferson came out shortly before Christmas to wind up the negotiations. Nor was progress encouraging over the supply of motor launches for the Libyan navy. The critical issue was the supply of Chieftain tanks, which the Libyans increasingly regarded as the earnest of our good intentions.

Tobruk and El Adem were hives of activity. On the morning of 4 February Jean and I flew to Benghazi. After lunch with Keith Haskell,[6] the head of our office, we were flown in an Argosy transport plane of the RAF to El Adem where Group Captain Terry,[7] the Station Commander, told us that the current saying in Tobruk and El Adem was: "Don't stand still or you may get packed." We drove to Tobruk where we marvelled at the loading skills of the crew of the landing ship *Sir Percivale*, who seemed to leave not a square foot of deck space unoccupied. Before leaving Tobruk we visited the war cemetery and the traces of the perimeter which the South African division had gallantly attempted to defend in 1942.

Back with the Terrys at El Adem we dressed for dinner. This was to be the RAF's Libyan equivalent of the Duchess of Richmond's ball – white tie and decorations, the ladies in long dresses. Denis Smallwood had brought over the commander of British land forces from Cyprus. A splendid dinner, accompanied by the best and no doubt the last of the contents of the cellars at El Adem, marked this sad but impressive occasion. After dinner Splinters and I hatched a little plot. I reminded him that our undertaking to the Libyans was to evacuate El Adem and Tobruk by 31 March. If we could complete our withdrawal a day or two earlier, we would avoid any possible humiliation. Peter Terry was consulted and agreed to do his best. A few days later he reported that he was confident he could bring completion forward by at least two days. It was of course essential that this should not become generally known. Activity on the base intensified. At 2.50 p.m. on 28 March 1970 the RAF ensign was lowered at El Adem. The landing ships *Sir Geraint* and *Empire Gull* cast off in Tobruk harbour with the final contingent of British army and RAF personnel on board. This ended a continuous military presence over thirty years.

On the morning of 31 March the embassy received a telephone call from an agitated Libyan official in Tobruk. "Where are the British? Libyan VIPs are due to arrive any minute." "Oh, they left three days ago." "But today is 31 March." "Yes. And we honour our undertakings. We completed our withdrawal by 31 March as we had promised, and with three days to spare." We supposed that another painful shampooing was due in Tobruk.

Denis Smallwood suggested another ploy. He wanted to test the stated willingness of the Libyans to permit RAF aircraft to land at Libyan airfields, subject to normal flight clearance. He therefore proposed to send his Argosy transport plane to Tripoli to take Jean and me to Cyprus. The weekend 22 to 25 May was the chosen time. When the Libyans learned the purpose of the flight they raised no objection. Nor was there any hindrance when we arrived at Tripoli airport to board the Argosy. No sooner were we airborne than we were served champagne. At the RAF base at Akrotiri another Argosy had just landed. This had brought our predecessors in Libya, the Sarells, from the Embassy in Ankara. Peter Ramsbotham, the High Commissioner in Nicosia, and his wife Frances arrived from Nicosia by car. Over the next few days good talk about the prospects for our interests in Libya and the splendid hospitality of the Smallwoods, which included an open air performance of Noye's Flude against the backdrop of the Mediterranean, eased the tensions of the past several months. Denis, a keen gardener, gave Jean a regal pelargonium, which she planted in the garden of the residence on our return to Tripoli.

Despite restrictions on movements, Jean and I were able to make a few excursions outside Tripoli. She was able to collect botanical specimens from the edge of the escarpment south of Tripoli, which she wanted to send to Kew. The ancient cities of Sabratha and Leptis Magna were better preserved than we had imagined. The Roman emperor, Septimius Severus, who was born and served in Libya and is buried in York – at that time another outpost of the Roman Empire – played a major role in creating Leptis Magna. Part of his legacy found its way in the nineteenth century to the grounds of Windsor Great Park at Virginia Water, where a carving on an arrangement of Roman columns and arches hails the Surrey woods with the supremely irrelevant cry: 'Africa, Africa'.

❖

Reports appeared in the British press that Israel was in the market for Chieftain tanks and that those earmarked for Libya might be diverted. These provoked strong protests from the Libyans and caused alarm among the five thousand British subjects scattered all over Libya. Feelings began to run high. When I conveyed my view to London that any such decision could prejudice our efforts to establish a new relationship with Libya and put the safety of British subjects at risk, I was astonished to receive a personal message from my opposite number in the Foreign and Commonwealth Office. My representations, he said, had been ill-received by ministers and I should desist. In the end the cabinet decided not to accede to the Israelis' request and all five thousand of us in Libya slept more easily. Years later Denis Healey raised with me what he called the tendency of ambassadors in the field to send alarmist telegrams about threats to British interests. I replied that if an ambassador did not report his concerns and British subjects abroad were harmed, ministers would be the first to blame the ambassador concerned for failing in his duty, and rightly so.

About this time Jallud gave me cause for complaint. Some mischievous person, whom we never identified, made unspecified allegations to the Libyan security authorities about Basil Pitt, the chaplain of the Anglican Church. He was refused an exit visa and placed under a form of house arrest. This put him under great strain. The Libyan army then closed down our church on what they said were security grounds, citing its proximity to the principal barracks in Tripoli where Qaddafi spent much of his time. Characteristically, the Americans immediately offered us the use of their church for our services. When I reminded Jallud of the article in the new Libyan constitution on religious tolerance, he said the Libyan government would provide us with an alternative site. This proved to be an empty promise. Eventually Basil Pitt was able to leave Libya to take up another position in Cyprus. His treatment was shameful.

General Goddard came out to Tripoli again to support us in the talks on defence sales. Meanwhile the Libyans had opened up another front. During the previous decade Libyan oil production had risen from nil to 3.7 million barrels a day – comparable with production in Iran and Saudi Arabia. Moreover, Libya was supplying Europe with some 30 per cent of its requirements. After the revolution the oil companies had offered to increase the price they paid Libya by up to 10 cents a barrel over time. To the Libyans this was quite inadequate; they saw no reason why the price of oil should continue to be set unilaterally by the companies. Their reaction was to cut back production and threaten to cut off completely those companies which refused their demands. Anti-trust legislation in the United States and other factors prevented the companies from adopting a common position and it seemed inevitable that they would have to accede to Libyan demands sooner or later. The Libyan move against the oil companies was to be imitated by other oil producers and to lead eventually to the oil crisis of 1973.

John Goddard returned to London on 18 June. As he left I suggested half seriously that he would arrive just in time to see Ted Heath move into Downing Street. Two days later, on Saturday, 20 June, I was about to leave the residence to attend the parades marking the evacuation of Wheelus base, when David Gore-Booth telephoned from the embassy. A telegram had arrived from London which I was required to decypher myself. This was from Denis Greenhill, the permanent under-secretary at the Foreign and Commonwealth Office. It read as follows: "PM wants you to join his staff at No 10 as high level spokesman (cf Brandt's Ahlers). Many congratulations. You will have to drop everything and come. Will try to send your successor with very minimum of delay so that break in negotiations will be very short. I suggest that you tell Libyans that you have been summoned home but not disclose the purpose nor reveal that you are being transferred. That can all be explained later. Subject to PM's requirement, you could return to pack up later. Please telegraph expected time arrival.

"I know that you will be disappointed to interrupt a job in which you have already been sterlingly distinguished. But please see Julius Caesar Act 4 scene 3 line 217."

I arranged for senior staff to join me later in the day at the residence and then went to the parade. I told Jallud that I had to leave at once for London. He was puzzled. I returned to the residence to break the news to Jean. It was just nine months since we had arrived in Libya.

14

Number 10

I flew to London on Sunday, 21 June 1970 with mixed feelings. As Denis Greenhill had recognised, much remained to be done in Tripoli if a new relationship was to be established with revolutionary Libya. Jean and I would regret leaving behind our staff and the leaders of the British community who had given us splendid support; they had had an uneasy time since the revolution. However, to be invited to join the prime minister's office was an uncommon honour, and to be able to play a part at the centre of government a privilege. As his spokesman during the unsuccessful common market negotiations from 1961 to 1963, I had come to admire Edward Heath's talents as a leader and negotiator and to respect his personal qualities, not least his lucidity, determination and humour. I understood and sympathised with his views on relations between government and press. At the same time, the job at 10 Downing Street would be demanding and family life would once again be disrupted. Moreover, whereas the diplomatic correspondents with whom I had worked at the Foreign Office had little passion for party politics or the House of Commons, I knew from having worked with Harold Evans, when Harold Macmillan was prime minister, and Trevor Lloyd-Hughes, Harold Wilson's press secretary, that the concerns of the Lobby – as the parliamentary and political correspondents were called – were different.

Michael Wolff, one of the political aides, met me at London Airport and drove me to Edward Heath's Albany flat. The prime minister's first words and the twinkle in his eye made it clear that he intended our relationship to resume where it had been interrupted ten years earlier: "I'm so glad you've agreed to take on this job. You know what to do: get the facts out." This was the only general directive he gave me. He did not mean, of course, that 'getting the facts out' was all that had to be done. He knew that I knew that facts should be withheld from the press only if there were for the moment compelling reasons to do so, and that the background to policy decisions had to be carefully and patiently explained. Exposition had to be followed by advocacy. The prime minister's laconic instruction was intended, and accepted by me, as a compliment. He said he understood that the Foreign Office wanted to have me back in due course. I said that this was also my wish; could we regard my secondment to Number 10 as a posting for, say, three years? The prime minister noted this suggestion.

When I arrived at Number 10 the following morning I was greeted by the messengers who were to monitor my comings and goings for the next few years. Two surprises awaited me. First, I learned that Lobby correspondents were briefed each afternoon and on Friday morning at the House of Commons; on other mornings they came to Number 10. The room I was to occupy had to be cleared for these morning briefings. The correspondents made their notes perched on the arms of chairs, or leaning against the wall, or the door if it was a busy day. This arrangement seemed to carry the British cult of amateurism to absurd lengths. Secondly, I had no secretary. The outer office, I was assured, coped with everything I might need. Later that morning I learned that Michael Wolff had already told the Lobby that the prime minister wanted radical changes in the way Number 10 handled its press relations. Members of the Lobby would be curious to know what was intended.

I moved to a more convenient office closer to the cabinet room and recruited as my assistant a member of the Downing Street staff who had been reviewing archives on an upper floor. For the next few years Janet Whiting cheerfully shared a great deal of the burden. Henry James, an experienced member of the government information service, was appointed my deputy. He was more than pleased to occupy the office overlooking Downing Street which I had vacated. He wanted to be described as the prime minister's press secretary and proposed that I be designated 'chief press secretary'. It was so agreed. James was succeeded by Tom McCaffrey the following year.

From the first day I was expected to operate the Lobby system. As with many aspects of British life, tradition, convention and common sense had governed relations between Downing Street and the press. There were no formal rules, there was no statutory framework. The chief government spokesman, unlike his or her counterparts in the United States or elsewhere, operated for the most part out of public view. In 1929, George Steward, who served as press secretary to Ramsay MacDonald and his two successors as prime minister, decided arbitrarily to brief members of the Parliamentary Lobby every day. In 1932 Steward told members of the Lobby that, in addition to acting for the prime minister and the Treasury, he would thereafter act also for the government as a whole on matters of a general character. The actions of this shadowy figure inaugurated the Lobby briefing system which I inherited.

I was adjusting to the new routine and getting to know the members of the Lobby when tragedy struck the government. In the evening of Monday, 20 July, not long after a reception the prime minister had given for the Lobby correspondents at Number 10, news came from next door that Iain Macleod, the chancellor of the exchequer, had died. The prime minister was deeply affected by the unexpected loss of the one colleague of comparable stature who was to have borne a major share of responsibility. His immediate concern was the well-being of Eve Macleod and the family. He told me to let the press know in confidence that Iain Macleod's successor would not be named until after the funeral; this interval, he felt, was one way in which Eve's grief might be eased. When I conveyed this to the Lobby, they did not press me on the subject. However, as I feared, this did not prevent speculation, which began almost at once. The Lobby's failure to observe the short period of silence he asked for offended the prime minister. For their part, members of the Lobby argued, with only a small degree of exaggeration, that it was more than their jobs were worth to refrain from trying to identify the new chancellor. They missed the real story. What everyone underestimated was the political impact of Iain Macleod's death. The fortunes of the Heath government and the country could well have been different had he survived.

❖

It was understood from the beginning that, although I saw the agenda and read the relevant papers, I would not attend cabinet meetings. I was briefed on the results by either Robert Armstrong,[1] the principal private secretary, or Burke Trend, the cabinet secretary. This rule did not apply, however, to meetings of cabinet committees or ad hoc meetings of ministers, and I was frequently invited to participate in these to advise on the public presentation of the matters under discussion.

Such an issue arose soon after the prime minister's return from his summer sailing holiday. On 6 September 1970 Palestinian terrorists hijacked four airliners of different nationalities. Two were flown to the Jordan desert, one to Cairo and the fourth – an Israeli aircraft – landed at London airport after the hijackers were overpowered in flight. Leila Khalid, the sole surviving terrorist on this flight, was arrested and taken to Ealing police station. On hearing of her arrest, the other hijackers threatened to kill the passengers stranded in the Jordan desert unless she was released. The crisis these events precipitated continued until the end of the month.

Parliament was not in session and, since more than one government department as well as the attorney-general were involved, it fell to me to brief the press as events unfolded. In several respects the British government was at a disadvantage. First of all, since the hostages on board the aircraft stranded in Jordan were of different nationalities, several governments, and later the International Red Cross, were involved and had to be consulted at each stage. Secondly, the attorney general, Peter Rawlinson, was alone responsible for deciding whether or not Leila Khalid should be prosecuted. This was a legal not a governmental matter. He faced a dilemma; the precise location of the Israeli aircraft at the moment the hijack took place was unclear and a court might have concluded that the offence occurred outside the jurisdiction of the United Kingdom. If the court had taken this view, any case against Leila Khalid would have been dismissed. Only those who took part in the restricted meetings in the cabinet room were aware of this vital consideration.

With so many lives at stake, the delicacy of my task was obvious. The members of the Lobby were not as familiar as their diplomatic colleagues with the background to the crisis, nor as experienced in handling such sensitive international issues. Some of them sympathised with right wing critics of the prime minister who, at a safe distance from the seat of responsibility, demanded that there be no surrender to blackmail. Added to this was the confusing nature of some of the reports reaching London about what was happening, or going to happen, on the ground. But I had to bear in mind that, while it was important to keep the media as fully informed as possible, the hijackers would read between the lines of everything that appeared in the British press and, in their impatience and mounting frustration, might misinterpret the prime minister's intentions.

The eventual outcome was the best we could expect. The hostages were released unharmed on 29 September and on the following day, by arrangement, Leila Khalid was flown to Cairo. Only after the crisis had been resolved were we able to reveal the helpful contribution to this result which President Nasser had made at the prime minister's request.

No cause, however real the grievance, can justify blackmail which threatens the lives of completely innocent bystanders. During those tense days and nights all of us in Downing Street were conscious of the stench of evil. Yet throughout the crisis the prime minister remained composed. If he was as angry as the rest of us, this was never revealed.

One of the first acts of the government after it was formed in June 1970 was to register its intention to pursue with vigour the effort to join the European Economic Community. It had been agreed before the general election that the next round of negotiations would take place on the last day of June and Sir Alec Douglas Home, the foreign secretary, and Anthony Barber, who had been designated to lead the United Kingdom delegation, travelled to Luxembourg to express the government's determination to work for a successful outcome. When

Anthony Barber was appointed chancellor of the exchequer following the death of Iain Macleod, leadership of the United Kingdom delegation passed to Geoffrey Rippon.

As on the two previous occasions – in the early and mid-1960s – the Foreign and Commonwealth Office was responsible in the first instance for briefing the press on the progress of the negotiations, which began formally four months later. Despite the improvement in the atmosphere following the resignation of de Gaulle in the spring of 1969 and his replacement by Georges Pompidou, there were still serious obstacles in the way and the French remained determined to exact a heavy price for our entry. The prime minister's tactic was to persuade the French of our good intentions as future members of the Community and to enlist the support of the Germans. He put to effective use the good relationship he enjoyed with Willy Brandt, the German chancellor. But in the end the confidential channel of communication which had been established with the French proved decisive. Christopher Soames, whom Harold Wilson had appointed ambassador in Paris on the recommendation of George Brown, and Michel Jobert, Pompidou's right-hand man at the Elysée Palace, identified the main points of difficulty and discussed possible solutions. By the middle of May 1971 sufficient progress had been made through this channel as well as in the formal negotiations in Brussels to justify a meeting between the prime minister and the French president. Among the points likely to be in the forefront of Pompidou's mind were the international role of sterling, the trade interests of developing countries in the Commonwealth and the use of the English language in the Community.

When the prime minister's party arrived in Paris on Wednesday, 20 May, we discussed tactics with Christopher Soames at the embassy. At the Elysée Palace the following morning, Denis Baudouin, the president's press secretary, suggested that he and I discuss arrangements for briefing the press and he took me to his office for this purpose. It was evident at once that there was a new atmosphere. Baudouin knew that I had been Edward Heath's spokesman during the first unsuccessful round of negotiations and he assured me that there was no question of any political obstacle being put in our way. He was confident that he and I were about to take part in an event of great significance.

That evening Baudouin and I compared notes before briefing the press. He told me then that the president intended to hold a press conference after lunch the following day, but he gave no hint of the 'coup de théatre' which had been planned. In the event the talks continued into the afternoon. The prime minister succeeded in satisfying the president on the points to which he attached importance and, when their session was concluded, Pompidou led the prime minister into the Salon des Fêtes, where the press were already assembled. From our seats to one side of the dais, Baudouin and I could see not only the two leaders but also the serried ranks of correspondents, many of whom had been in this same salon when de Gaulle pronounced his veto ten years earlier. Pompidou reminded his audience that there were those who believed that Britain was not really European; there were others who believed that France would impose a new veto on the entry of Britain. He paused. Then he said: "You see before you two men who are convinced of the contrary." There were few dry eyes in the salon. When Denis Baudouin and I parted soon afterwards, I told him he had been right; we had lived a moment of history together.

The terms for our entry into the Community which Geoffrey Rippon secured one month later in Luxembourg were on the whole satisfatory. It remained to persuade the British public and parliament that these conditions were acceptable. I was heavily involved in this task. A group of representatives of the interested departments was formed under the chairmanship of Anthony Royle,[2] one of the parliamentary under-secretaries at the Foreign Office. This group prepared and distributed briefing papers, monitored public reactions and organised speeches and interviews with the press, radio and television. Even after 28 October 1971, when the House of Commons decided in principle by the highly satisfactory majority of 112 votes that Britain should join the Community, the work of this group was not over.

On 22 January 1972 the prime minister signed the treaty of accession along with the Irish and Danish prime ministers in Brussels. The heads of government and other dignitaries were kept waiting for an hour because a young German woman, nursing some obscure grievance over the development of Covent Garden, had the bizarre notion that her cause would be advanced if she threw ink at the prime minister as he mounted the steps of the Egmont Palace. Fresh clothes were sent for and cleaning spirit was found which gradually removed the stains from his hair, face and neck. Despite their long wait his colleagues gave the prime minister an enthusiastic reception when he eventually entered the main hall. That evening he took part in a BBC Panorama television programme conducted by Michael Charlton in the bar of the Metropole Hotel where he had spent many hours with the press in the early 1960s explaining the intricacies of the first round of negotiations.

The subsequent legislation to give effect to the treaty of accession was passed with great difficulty and sometimes dangerously slender majorities. Although this was essentially a parliamentary struggle, the coordinating group under Anthony Royle ensured that the main political arguments in favour of our membership of the Community were kept before the public. The celebration 'Fanfare for Europe', which many of the prime minister's friends in the music world helped to organise to mark our formal entry into the Community in January 1973, seemed

an appropriate finale to a major effort sustained and inspired by the
prime minister's vision and determination. This was Edward Heath's
greatest achievement. He was entitled to savour it, and he wanted as
many others as possible to savour it too.

The importance the government had attached from the beginning to
its efforts to join the European Community meant that the relationship
with the United States would be less intimate than before. While the
prime minister and President Nixon enjoyed each other's company
when they met in Washington in December 1970 and again in Bermuda
a year later, it was accepted, reluctantly on the American side, that
while there was no disagreement on the main issues and especially
the need to maintain the cohesion of the western alliance, British
priorities had undergone significant change. At Bermuda fences had
to be mended. The previous August John Connally, the United States
Treasury Secretary, had suspended the convertibility of the dollar and
imposed a surcharge on imports into the United States. This action
caused financial and economic turmoil across the world. President
Nixon announced at Bermuda that the import surcharge would be
lifted, but the prime minister insisted that the communique record
the need for closer consultation. When they met the press at the
end of the talks the president spoke of "a new America and a new
Europe". The prime minister was more explicit: the Anglo-American
relationship was as strong as ever, but it was not the same as in previous
years. The rapport between the two leaders was evident the evening the
Royal Navy took over. The arrangements when we dined aboard *HMS
Intrepid* were faultless, as were to be expected from Captain William
Staveley,[3] a future Admiral of the Fleet. The determination of the prime
minister and the president to improve consultation did not deter Henry
Kissinger the following year from unilaterally declaring 1973 'The Year
of Europe'. This patronising initiative, the purpose of which was unclear,
lacked substance and did little more than irritate the prime minister and
his French and German counterparts.

On our return from Bermuda on 22 December 1971, the prime
minister decided to visit Northern Ireland. He was keen to show his
personal concern for our troops and the people of Northern Ireland on
the eve of Christmas. In the ten hours we spent in the province on
Thursday, 23 December, we covered a lot of ground. At Aldergrove
airport, where we were greeted by the commanding general, Sir Harry
Tuzo, we transferred to helicopters for the sixty-mile flight to the
barracks in Londonderry. From there the prime minister and the general
drove into the city in a heavily escorted armoured car. I travelled with
two other members of the party and one of the prime minister's special
branch officers. As we moved off, the inspector said: "If anything

happens, I don't want any heroics from any of you. Understood?" From Londonderry we flew on to Armagh and then returned to Belfast. At each stage the prime minister was briefed by the local commanders and addressed the troops.

Over lunch with the Gloucestershire Regiment in one of the more troubled areas of Belfast, we were given an account of the regiment's most recent experiences. By now the press were aware of the prime minister's presence in the province but, for security reasons, our itinerary and timetable had not been revealed. It was intended that after lunch we should visit the combined army and police post in the Springfield Road, a frequent target of terrorist attacks. On our arrival there I was surprised to find Christopher Wain and a BBC television crew awaiting us. His presence, he confessed, was based on a technique he had used in the past: put yourself in your subject's position and ask what he or she would do. In this case Christopher's guess was inspired and he deserved his exclusive shots and quotes.

After calling on the Governor, Lord Grey, and the prime minister, Brian Faulkner, at Hillsborough, the prime minister recorded a Christmas message to the people of Northern Ireland at one of the television studios. Not for the first or last time, he appealed for the tolerance, cooperation and spirit of fairness which were essential if progress were to be made. By visiting the province at the end of a year in which Parliament had endorsed the principle of our membership of the European Community and on the morrow of his talks with the President of the United States, this broadcast was intended, among other things, to remind Protestants and Catholics alike that he was, first and foremost, prime minister of the United Kingdom of Great Britain and Northern Ireland.

This had been a good day. When he spoke to our troops and in his talks with the commanders, the prime minister was in his element. We had all noted the professionalism of those we met, from the generals who briefed us to the privates on lookout duty, and had been struck by the easy relationship between officers and men in the modern regular army. Even more impressive was their morale. On the flight back to Northolt the prime minister seemed satisfied. "Strange thing," he said. "We went over to boost their morale before Christmas and they boosted ours."

❖

From the point of view of the press office at Number 10, the creation of the Central Policy Review Staff under Lord Rothschild was excellent news. Although the work of the CPRS did not impinge directly on our day-to-day business, we and they were concerned with the work of the government across the board. As the members of the CPRS owed no allegiance to any particular department of state, the papers they prepared for cabinet were disinterested, and their analyses often alerted us to criticisms we would have to deal with when we briefed the Lobby. I drew most benefit from the occasional weekend meetings at Chequers when Victor Rothschild and members of his staff would review progress being made in achieving the government's objectives and highlight the consequences of a failure here or there. These reviews were concise and clinical. As I watched the expression on ministers' faces, I felt that some of them were being brought to understand for the first time that the work of their departments was part of a comprehensive strategy and that their performance could affect the prospects of the government as a whole.

In the end these prospects were to be linked to the domestic industrial situation, which was from the beginning a dominant concern. It was characterised in 1970 by a combination of slow growth – even stagnation – in some sectors, rapid cost inflation and the worst labour relations since the war. The government's intention to introduce legislation on industrial relations was seen by the unions as an attempt to curb their bargaining power at plant level and was strongly opposed.

On the initiative of Hugh Cudlipp,[4] the chairman of the International Publishing Corporation, the *Daily Mirror* and *The Sun* carried articles in the autumn of 1970 explaining in popular terms the causes and effects of inflation. This did not prevent further industrial action. A work to rule by electricity workers over Christmas in 1970 forced the government to intervene. An official Inquiry into this dispute by Lord Wilberforce led ministers to conclude that, in spite of High Cudlipp's initiative, there was little public understanding of the causes and effects of inflation. However, the government persisted with its policy of 'standing firm' in the public sector and this had some success in keeping down the level of wage settlements. The Confederation of British Industry – the CBI – contributed to the pressure on inflation by asking their members to avoid price increases, or limit these to no more than 5 per cent, for the following twelve months.

The situation changed in the autumn of 1971 when the National Union of Mineworkers presented a claim to the National Coal Board for an increase in wages amounting to over £100 million. When negotiations broke down strikes began. Lord Wilberforce was once again persuaded to conduct an Inquiry. His recommendations favoured the miners, who decided to end their strike. On 27 February 1972, the day before the miners returned to work, the prime minister broadcast to the nation. He referred to a double danger facing the country – price rises and the wage increases which caused them; and the determination of one group to get its way regardless of the consequences. When I lunched the following day with Michael King, the former foreign editor of the *Daily Mirror*, who had been appointed chief information officer of the CBI, I found he agreed with me that the time had come for a major publicity campaign to educate the public about the real nature of the inflation problem. I sought the views of the Treasury and the Department of Employment. From this point on the industrial situation was my principal preoccupation.

Work began on drafting a briefing paper which might form the basis of a general counter-inflation publicity campaign. By midsummer sufficient material had been prepared for a sustained campaign. The objective was to persuade the public, who were disposed to sympathise with any claim for an increase in wages, that excessive claims led inexorably to increased prices.

Meanwhile industrial unrest continued. On 18 July 1972 the leaders of the TUC and the CBI met ministers at Number 10 to initiate a series of tripartite talks aimed at working out 'sensible and constructive arrangements on a voluntary basis which would secure a steady rise in real earnings'. When the talks began in September the prime minister announced his proposals for the rate of growth and the level of price and wage rises for the following twelve months. These were discussed at subsequent meetings at Chequers, but by the beginning of November it was clear that no agreement was possible. The prime minister told the House of Commons on 6 November that there was no alternative but to bring in statutory measures to achieve the desired objective. While these were being prepared there would be a standstill for 90 days.

The standstill, known as Stage One, created a new situation so far as publicity was concerned. I formed a counter-inflation publicity group composed of representatives of the Treasury and the Departments of Employment, Trade and Industry and the Environment. With the help of William Armstrong, the head of the home civil service, who had been charged by the prime minister with heading the group of senior officials advising ministers on counter-inflation policy, I recruited an assistant secretary, John Pestell, to coordinate the day to day work of the group. Within a matter of weeks, with the support of Janet Whiting, he had fashioned this group into a most effective inter-departmental instrument.

Regardless of the time of day or night, a press conference was held after each tripartite meeting, whether this took place at Chequers or Number 10. Some of the conferences were conducted by the prime minister. At others Anthony Barber took the chair, accompanied by Campbell Adamson, the director-general of the CBI, and Vic Feather, the general secretary of the TUC. On these occasions we distributed press releases containing agreed records of the meetings.

As the end of the 90-day standstill approached, I suggested that the prime minister announce the government's proposals for Stage Two of 'The Programme for Controlling Inflation', as the eventual White Paper was called, at a press conference. There was a precedent. In the

summer of 1971 the prime minister had addressed a press conference in
Lancaster House on the United Kingdom's relations with the European
Community. On that occasion he had demonstrated his mastery of detail
and talent for extemporaneous presentation of a complex argument.

The press conference was held in the Long Gallery at Lancaster House
on 17 January 1973. In this same gallery eight years earlier George
Brown, when in charge of the Department of Economic Affairs, had
launched his ill-fated 'Declaration of Intent'. At the suggestion of the
writing press, who disliked putting their questions in front of cameras and
microphones, only the prime minister's opening statement was televised
and broadcast live. The broadcasters had their opportunity to interview
the prime minister at the end of the conference.

In his opening statement the prime minister announced that a Price
Commission and a Pay Board would be established with the aim of
keeping both prices and wages at moderate levels. The reaction of the
press was generally favourable, but industrial strife continued. At further
meetings the prime minister reminded the TUC that the government
had offered the unions what they had so often said they wanted, namely
a commitment to a high rate of growth and help for the lower paid. But,
as prices continued to rise in response to external as much as internal
pressures, agreement with the unions proved elusive.

From the beginning the atmosphere at the tripartite talks I attended
was business-like and the talking frank. Vic Feather was supported by
Jack Jones and Hugh Scanlon, representing respectively the transport
workers and electricians. Campbell Adamson was accompanied by
Richard O'Brien, who chaired the CBI's employment policy committee. On the government's side of the table sat the secretaries of
state for employment and trade and industry and their senior officials.
William Armstrong was at the prime minister's right hand. At no time
did I sense that the union leaders doubted the prime minister's sincerity
and I was sure they were attracted by the prospect of an influential role
in the formulation of policy. The obstacle was the Industrial Relations
Act which had come into operation in March 1972. This was more than
their members could accept.

❖

A serious problem had arisen on the external front within a few days
of the formation of the government in June 1970. The South African
foreign minister, Hilgard Muller, happened to be in London at the time.
South Africa wanted to buy arms; the Royal Navy enjoyed facilities at
the Simonstown base in South Africa. That the government would be
willing in principle to supply arms had been clear before the election.
Muller called at the Foreign Office as soon as Sir Alec Douglas Home,
the new foreign secretary, was installed and extracted a commitment
from him that some arms would be supplied. As soon as this news broke

there was an outcry, not only in Africa. The question was raised: would British arms be used to suppress opposition within the republic?

Commonwealth heads of government were due to meet in Singapore in January 1971. We expected a rough ride. It was decided that the prime minister would break his journey in Cyprus, where he had talks with President Makarios and Vice-President Kutchuk, and the Indian subcontinent. The High Commissioner in New Delhi had great difficulty with the Indian authorities in finalising arrangements for the prime minister's visit. The two senior Indian officials, P. N. Haksar and T. N. Kaul, who had risen to the top in the era of Krishna Menon, told Morrice James[5] that there would be no formal welcome when the prime minister arrived and no question of Mrs Gandhi's attending any function at his residence. Even as we flew into Delhi airport we had no idea how we would be received. However, the prime minister was prepared should there be an opportunity to make a statement to the press.

Our aircraft was directed to the side of the apron where Mrs Gandhi and a guard of honour and military band were waiting. After the military formalities, both prime ministers spoke from the dais. When we arrived at the prime minister's office for the first round of talks, we were again misinformed. Mrs Gandhi, we were told, would receive Mr Heath briefly alone and would then invite the two delegations to join them. We sat down to wait. After three-quarters of an hour the two prime ministers emerged. Mrs Gandhi wore an expression which suggested that she was about to say: "We have a small announcement to make." What she did say was that she looked forward to continuing her most useful conversation with Mr Heath over dinner at the High Commissioner's residence.

At the dinner Edward Heath spoke of his desire for the two countries to establish a new and more relevant relationship. When she rose to reply, Indira Gandhi took a flower from a silver vase in front of her. She held this in her hand for the next ten minutes as she identified herself with Edward Heath's ambition. She recalled visits to Commonwealth conferences in London with her father, Pandit Nehru; she listed those aspects of the British legacy which India respected, while acknowledging that there were others that India had been right to set aside. This graceful figure with the flower in her hand captivated her audience, as no doubt was her intention. What mattered was that at that dinner table, despite differences over the Soviet threat in the Indian Ocean, the basis for a better relationship was established.

Before we left New Delhi I received an invitation to take tea with the commandant of the Rajputana Rifles depot which I had not visited since I left for the Middle East in 1942. The colonel had collected some of my contemporaries, now all generals, and they told me of developments

since independence. After tea on the lawn the commandant suggested
that I might wish to visit the mess. The silver and the mementoes
of the early days of the regiment were still in place. Then I realised
what the colonel had in mind. On the wall hung photographs of all
the commandants of the depot as far back as the 1930s. "You see," he
said, "we believe continuity is important."

❖

If the arrangements made by the government of Singapore for the
Commonwealth conference were designed to impress their guests, the
effort was outstandingly successful. The United Kingdom delegation was
seated next to the Australians. On my other side was an awesome giant
from the South Seas. My Australian neighbour whispered: "And he's
only the scrum-half."

The conference itself was even more disagreeable than we had feared.
We knew of course that the African members of the Commonwealth
were strongly opposed to the supply of arms to South Africa, but
their criticism of the British decision was more virulent than had been
expected. In a debate on a document tabled by President Kaunda of
Zambia on Commonwealth principles, Presidents Nyerere of Tanzania
and Obote of Uganda not only attacked Britain's intention to supply
arms to South Africa in bitter terms but went on to cast doubt on
our commitment to the Commonwealth. We assumed that some of
this rhetoric was for domestic consumption. Prime Minister Trudeau
of Canada deplored the UN-style of oratory not normally heard at
Commonwealth meetings. West African criticism was muted. When
the debate on South Africa ended and the conference turned to the
implications of Britain's entry into the European Community, the tone
suddenly changed. After a morning of special pleading from those who
had been abusing him, the prime minister recalled the debate of the
previous few days and wondered aloud why some governments wanted
any association with Britain, let alone Britain's help in safeguarding their
interests. In the end, thanks to the conciliation of John Gorton, the
Australian prime minister, a communique was agreed endorsing the
principle of anti-racism and acknowledging Britain's right to provide
arms to South Africa for defence against aggression. I doubt if the more
vociferous African leaders realised how poorly they had served their own
interests at Singapore. If Obote had hoped to gain credit at home by his
anti-British diatribes, he was to be disappointed. As soon as he returned
he was overthrown by Idi Amin.

❖

Northern Ireland was a constant source of concern. In an effort to make
progress, the prime minister invited Jack Lynch, his Irish counterpart, to
spend a weekend at Chequers early in September 1971. The meeting
went well and it was agreed that it would be useful for Brian Faulkner,

the prime minister of Northern Ireland, to join them at a second meeting. This was arranged for the end of September. For security purposes Robert Armstrong needed to know Jack Lynch's travel plans and he could not understand why our embassy in Dublin could not find out what these were. He was enlightened when he telephoned direct to his opposite number in Dublin. I was in the private office at the time and heard the Dublin voice say: "It's all fixed. We'll fly over on the morning of the day, but in case there's fog we'll come the previous evening."

At the personal level the meeting of the three prime ministers – the first in history – also went well. But within a few months the government concluded that it had no choice but to take direct control of events. This was a painful decision painfully reached and the prime minister regretted the distress caused to Brian Faulkner and his colleagues. For his part, in entrusting the task to Willie Whitelaw, who became the first secretary of state for Northern Ireland, the prime minister deprived himself of the day by day support of one of the wisest of his colleagues.

The statement the prime minister was to broadcast about the government's decision had to strike the right balance and the right note. Various suggestions were put forward, but I was relieved when he decided he would prepare the text himself; after all, he was the best judge. The broadcast was made on 24 March 1972. After explaining the circumstances which had led the government to impose direct rule on the province, the prime minister reiterated what had been his constant theme: there was now a chance for fairness and prosperity, an opportunity to leave the past behind. He gave two undertakings: first, that so long as a majority of the people of Northern Ireland wished to remain part of the United Kingdom, that wish would be honoured; and, secondly, that all sections of the community should have their rightful opportunity to play a full part in running the affairs of Northern Ireland. It sounded straightforward and sensible. But as we watched the screen, all of us in Number 10 knew that there were many across the Irish Sea who would distort his vision and impugn his integrity.

❖

One of the last problems I had to deal with was the consequence of a ministerial indiscretion. In May 1973 Lord Lambton, the under-secretary for defence with special responsibility for the Royal Air Force, resigned from the government after allegations appeared in the press linking him with a call-girl. Given Lambton's position in the Ministry of Defence, legitimate questions were raised about the possibility of a breach of security. This affair inevitably revived memories of the Profumo scandal and the prime minister ordered an immediate investigation. He was pressed to make a statement to the House of Commons and I joined a meeting of somewhat apprehensive ministers and security chiefs called to consider the content of his statement. It seemed to me that the only way to draw a line under this affair was 'to get the facts out': inquiries had revealed no evidence of a breach of security; these were continuing and, if anything were brought to light, the security authorities would act and the House would be informed. The prime minister made a statement to the House on these lines. This was reported faithfully by the parliamentary press who then turned to other matters.

When not arranging press conferences, television and radio interviews, or ministerial broadcasts for the prime minister, I briefed the media on government policies, intentions and decisions through the Lobby. The need not to infringe the rights of Parliament was one reason for the convention under which nothing I said to the Lobby could be attributed to me. However, as time went by, I found the notion that these occasions were deemed not to have happened increasingly absurd, especially when upwards of sixty correspondents attended the afternoon sessions in the House of Commons. There was another consideration. A wide range of interests was represented in the Lobby – the national daily papers, the provincial press, evening papers, the broadcasters and news agencies. Most of these interests were in competition. The Lobby contained some comparative novices. Other correspondents had been in the business for many years and were on familiar terms with ministers, parliamentarians and senior government officials. These older hands had their own sources of authoritative information, and their accumulated knowledge and well developed antennae lent authority to their reports. The public was well served at that time, among others, by David Wood of *The Times*, Harry Boyne of the *Daily Telegraph* and Ian Aitken of the *Guardian*. If I ever had a reservation about the way they covered the range of government activities, it was minor.

Of course the traffic was not one-way. It was my responsibility to keep the prime minister informed of the manner in which the government's policies and performance were perceived by the media, and I found editors, leader-writers and commentators more than ready to share their opinions. By keeping in regular touch with Ronald Butt of the *Sunday Times*, David Watt of the *Financial Times* and Peter Jenkins of the *Guardian*, I felt I was reasonably well informed about responsible opinion from left to right of centre. This was one of the most agreeable aspects of my job.

In the early 1970s the writing press was less partisan and television had not yet become a dominant force. But even then, as in other parliamentary democracies, it was the daily task of some journalists to expose what they deemed to be the latest outrage or folly perpetrated by the government of the day, while others were on the lookout for some wise adjustment of policy to acclaim, or mistake to excuse.

From the government's point of view, a more serious disadvantage was that, because I could not be quoted, my words were open to interpretation. Even the most straightforward statement could be reproduced the following morning in a variety of forms. One correspondent of a leading provincial newspaper would spend hours on the telephone either to me or to a member of the press office seeking what he called 'an angle' on the day's story. Yet another disadvantage of the system was the scope it provided for editorialising – a habit which never failed to astonish visiting American journalists. The viewer, listener, or reader would be told what opinion to form about some development before learning what it was. How often were stories introduced with some such phrase as: "The government suffered a setback today when . . . "?

In 1972, drawing on my experience in the Foreign office news department, I suggested to the Lobby that, as far as possible, our briefings should in future be 'on the record' but that, where appropriate and by mutual agreement, part of the briefing could be on a non-attributable basis. This proposal was rejected by a majority of the Lobby. I therefore decided that those formal statements which we usually conveyed to the press through the Lobby would in future be issued as press releases from Number 10. These were carried by news agencies and broadcasters and so found their way, in the original Number 10 language, on to the desks of every news editor in the country. From then on we made extensive and successful use of this device, notably during the tripartite talks with the TUC and the CBI on curbing inflation.

In a society such as ours, the media play a number of different roles. They report current events; they articulate public attitudes and preoccupations; they comment, criticise and advocate; they shine light into the dark recesses of the state machine and society in general. Without a full flow of information from the government and as much insight as possible into the factors behind government policies, decisions and actions, the media will be handicapped in performing these tasks. Ensuring the best possible service was how the prime minister intended I interpret the cryptic instruction he gave me at Albany.

No government can expect its policies to succeed if these are neither understood nor accepted by a substantial body of public opinion and it is sensible for a government to devote as much care to the way it presents its policies as to formulating them in the first place. I tried to emphasise this point by suggesting that each cabinet paper contain a paragraph setting out how the course of action recommended was to be presented. When a paper was circulated soon afterwards with a brief note to the effect that the secretary of state proposed to announce the decision in a

statement to the House of Commons, I realised that I had a steeper hill
to climb than I had expected. However, as Douglas Hurd pointed out
in his personal account of the Heath administration: "Communication
should be the servant of policy, not the master." No amount of powerful
and sustained advocacy can persuade the public to acquiesce indefinitely
in a wrong-headed course of action. Lincoln's dictum about not fooling
all of the people all of the time is a basic truth about democratic societies.
Successful government depends, first and foremost, on wise policies and
then on the extent to which these are understood and appreciated by the
public. I believe this formulation places the role of the press secretary in
proper perspective. More often than not, the importance of this role is
exaggerated.

❖

On my return from Libya in June 1970 I had taken up flying again.
When the prime minister's new yacht *Morning Cloud III* was launched
at Cowes in April 1973, I flew in a light aircraft to the Isle of Wight to
join the celebration and on the return flight dipped the wings over the
mooring. Two years later, when his book *Sailing* was published, Edward
Heath sent me a copy inscribed 'from a sailor to a flyer'. That personal
gesture was characteristic of the man in the upstairs flat in Number 10.

For three years I was part of what seemed like a family. Robert
Armstrong, the principal private secretary, Douglas Hurd, the political
secretary, Tim Kitson, the parliamentary private secretary, Michael
Wolff, the adviser, and I enjoyed a close and effective working relationship based on mutual respect and a clear understanding of the
responsibilities of each. A line was drawn at the outset between what
the party did and what the civil servants did. My only regret was that
I failed to persuade Douglas Hurd or Michael Wolff that the speeches
they drafted for the prime minister would benefit from more references
to the 'high road' and less preoccupation with the 'high street'.

In the mornings a few of us would meet to decide who was best
placed to break that day's bad news to the prime minister. We would
then go up to his flat where he was usually still breakfasting in his dressing
gown. He would listen impassively to what the appointed spokesman
had to say. Then, after a brief pause, he would ask: "And what do you
recommend?" Hearing someone else's opinion helped him focus his own
thoughts and, knowing this, we always climbed the stairs prepared.

I had access to the prime minister whenever this was necessary. It
would take him no more than two or three minutes to approve or
amend a statement I proposed to issue on an urgent problem. There were
evenings when members of the Number 10 'family' had an opportunity
for more general discussion; these could become hilarious. On other
occasions Michael Wolff's wife Rosemary, or Sally Kitson, would offer
opinions and advice on social activities at Number 10. The personality

of the political leader, the conductor of the orchestra, the skipper of the yacht, at ease among those he had selected to carry out particular tasks because he trusted their abilities, was never revealed to the public. But, for good reasons, this private person commanded the respect and admiration of those who worked with and for him.

I left Number 10 in June 1973 to take up my new post as the United Kingdom's permanent representative to the United Nations at New York. In releasing me three years after my call on him at Albany, the prime minister was as good as his word. The view of government from Downing Street is unique; I felt privileged to have had an opportunity to enjoy it.

15

Resolution on First Avenue

As soon as *Queen Elizabeth II* docked in New York harbour on the morning of Sunday, 12 August 1973, a member of the staff of the United Kingdom Mission to the United Nations came aboard to brief me on a serious incident in the Middle East. Two days earlier a Caravelle airliner of Middle East Airlines chartered to Iraqi Airways had been intercepted in Lebanese airspace by Israeli military aircraft and forced to land in Israel. The Lebanese government had lodged a complaint with the United Nations Security Council and a meeting of the Council had been called for the following day.

The briefing continued as Jean and I were driven to our apartment overlooking Central Park. On the following morning, after meeting members of the staff who were to support me, I called on Laurence McIntyre, the Australian permanent representative and president of the Security Council for the month of August, and met the other thirteen members of the Council as well as the Lebanese and Israeli ambassadors.

The debate on the Lebanese complaint ranged far and wide. The Israeli sought to explain his government's action by arguing that abnormal times justified abnormal methods. His was a lone voice; even the United States, normally sympathetic to the Israeli point of view, expressed disapproval. From discussions in the corridors after the debate had been adjourned, it seemed likely that the Council would be prepared to endorse a resolution condemning the Israeli action. London agreed to our taking the initiative. I thought it desirable that the Council should conclude the debate as soon as possible and, in the absence from New York of Louis de Guiringaud,[1] my French opposite number, I agreed with his deputy, Jacques Lecompt, that our two delegations would sponsor such a resolution. A draft which took account of points made during the debate was quickly prepared and, after consulting the other delegations, Lecompt and I tabled this the following day, 15 August. In introducing the resolution I referred to the efforts then being made elsewhere to agree on international measures to counter terrorism. Acts which jeopardised innocent lives were inadmissible and even less excusable when committed by governments. The draft resolution, which condemned Israel's violation of Lebanon's sovereignty and called for adequate measures to safeguard international civil aviation against actions of this kind, was passed unanimously – to the satisfaction of the Lebanese and dismay of the Israelis. I deduced from the reactions of other members of the Council after the vote that it was unusual, if not unprecedented, for any delegate to secure unanimous endorsement of a resolution he had tabled within two days of his arrival. Michael Weir,[2] the head of chancery in the Mission, confirmed this. On the way back to our offices on Third Avenue, he said: "Not everyone scores a century in their first test match." However, if I hoped then that this fortuitous initial success was to prove a good omen, I had not counted on the capriciousness of the wheel of fortune.

❖

Once the Lebanese aircraft incident had been settled, Jean and I were able to find our bearings and, despite the heat, humidity and strict advice on how to avoid being mugged, begin to enjoy what the great metropolis had to offer. Labor Day at the beginning of September signalled a drop in humidity, the end of the summer holiday and the resumption of social life and we were welcomed into the bosom of the internationally-minded New Yorkers. And what stimulating and generous-hearted people they were.

The twenty-eighth General Assembly opened in the middle of the month and foreign ministers and heads of government descended on United Nations headquarters at Turtle Bay like migrant Canada geese. The Assembly's first act was to adopt the agenda. This consisted of some one hundred items each of which was allocated for purposes of detailed discussion to one of the seven main committees. Three new members were admitted to the United Nations – the Federal Republic of Germany, the German Democratic Republic and the Commonwealth of the Bahamas.

The General Debate occupied the first few weeks. When he addressed the Assembly on 26 September, Sir Alec Douglas-Home called for a return to the spirit of reconciliation and partnership which was the basis and indeed the inspiration of the United Nations Charter. He repeated this appeal when he met Andrei Gromyko. The mutual benefit to be derived from detente was the message western countries wanted to convey. Sir Alec told Gromyko that we looked for the same easy relationship with the countries of central and eastern Europe as we enjoyed with our neighbours in western Europe, the United States and elsewhere. That relationship was based on mutual trust and it would become possible with the peoples of central and eastern Europe only when artificial barriers had been dismantled. We should facilitate exchanges of information, appreciation of each other's culture, and encourage tourism. At mention of the word 'tourism' the mask of amiability fell from Gromyko's face. "We know about your tourists," he said. "In 1939 German tourists in their thousands visited my country. They came back two years later in uniform with their tanks and guns and devastated my country." This outburst was a sharp reminder that the apparently genial Soviet foreign minister, referred to affectionately by many western diplomats as 'Grom', represented a regime still convinced that the West had aggressive intentions towards the Soviet Union and as determined as ever to insulate its European empire from western influence.

❖

Sir Alec returned to London at the end of September. A week later – on 6 October, the Day of Atonement – fighting broke out when Egypt and Syria made a co-ordinated assault on Israeli forces. Soon after this news broke I received two telephone calls. The first was from Henry Kissinger, the United States Secretary of State. He asked if I had received any instructions from my government. When I said I was awaiting these, he suggested that our aim should be an immediate cease-fire and return by the combatants to the positions they had previously occupied. I noted this. The second call, later in the day, was from Anthony Parsons,[3] the under-secretary who handled Middle East questions in the Foreign and Commonwealth Office. He had just left a meeting with the secretary of state who had asked him to convey a message to me. It was straightforward: I had authority to work for a cease-fire. I could not have asked for a better instruction. The general terms of the message, confirmed soon afterwards in a telegram, gave me the discretion I felt I would need, given that the Egyptian forces who had crossed the Suez Canal and were pushing the Israelis back were not an invading force; they were re-occupying their own territory and, on these grounds, the Egyptian government would almost certainly reject the second part of Kissinger's formula.

The Security Council met on Monday, 8 October, on the initiative of John Scali, the permanent representative of the United States. He asked the Council to accept three propositions – an immediate end to the fighting, a return to previous positions, and reaffirmation of the validity of decisions the United Nations had already taken on the Middle East; he had particularly in mind Resolution 242 which George Brown had inspired and Hugh Caradon negotiated in 1967. These proposals were ill-received by a majority of delegations and the meeting ended without result. There were rumours in the corridors, which soon found their way into the press, that the Americans wanted to see the Egyptian army back on the west bank of the Suez Canal. Elsewhere in the UN building Muhammad Zayyat, the Egyptian foreign minister, and a less than usually self-confident Abba Eban, his Israeli opponent, put their respective arguments to the General Assembly.

For the next two weeks Louis de Guiringaud and I, with the full knowledge of the Americans and Kurt Waldheim, the secretary general, engaged in intense discussion with the Egyptians and their supporters among the non-aligned members of the Security Council. Our purpose was not only to establish what kind of resolution would be acceptable to them, but also to urge them to treat the renewal of hostilities as a catalyst for initiating a genuine diplomatic process which would lead inexorably to a just and lasting settlement. The Egyptians shared this ambition; they distrusted the Americans and had noted the reluctance of the Soviet Union to become too closely involved.

De Guiringaud and I met most evenings to pool our information and impressions, to coordinate our reports to Paris and London and plan the next stage. Louis exuded urbanity and disapproved of excess in any form. When I asked his opinion about what we thought were bright ideas, his usual response was: "I have no objection." As Britain and France were the only members of the European Community represented on the Security Council, we took pains to keep our Community colleagues, who now included the German, closely informed about our activities. When we suggested to the Egyptians that they might wish to put their case directly to the Nine, they agreed at once; the meetings in the weeks that followed between the Community ambassadors and our Egyptian colleague prepared the way for the subsequent more formal Euro-Arab Dialogue.

Deadlock continued in the Security Council and the press commented disparagingly on the UN's role as a bystander. Louis and I were convinced that progress was unlikely so long as each side believed it could secure a military advantage. By the middle of October the situation on the battlefields had begun to turn against the Egyptians and the Syrians. Civilians were reported to have been killed in air raids on Cairo and Damascus. The Americans had begun to supply arms to the Israelis to make good their losses and the Russians were re-arming the Arabs. Kissinger wanted the British to table a cease-fire resolution which the Americans and Russians were drafting and was annoyed when I argued that, if they thought the time was ripe, the authors should introduce it themselves. I refrained from adding that there was an inconsistency between calling for a cease-fire and continuing to supply arms to the belligerents.

By 18 October Israeli tanks had crossed the Suez Canal and on 22 October the Americans and Russians tabled their resolution. This reaffirmed Resolution 242, called for a cease-fire within twelve hours and for immediate steps to be taken towards a general negotiated settlement. After all delegations had spoken in favour of the resolution, the egregious Jamil Baroody, the Lebanese Christian who represented Saudi Arabia, asked to speak as an interested observer. Baroody never let pass an opportunity to intervene in Security Council debates especially when these were being broadcast on public service television. He was the supreme room-emptier and on this occasion his ego-trip delayed the unanimous vote by three-quarters of an hour.

Fighting continued after the twelve-hour deadline and the Americans and Russians introduced another resolution the following day calling for the cease-fire to be respected and for observers to be sent to the region. They had failed to prepare the ground with other members of the Council and the debate became acrimonious. The non-aligned members always resented being dictated to and they wondered what else the superpowers might have agreed. Louis and I did our best to calm them down.

The need for supervision of the cease-fire was urgent and the Egyptians proposed that American and Soviet troops take on this task. In the end a resolution tabled by the eight non-aligned members was approved. The Americans were determined to keep Soviet forces out of the Middle East and to achieve this they insisted on adding a clause to the non-aligned's resolution excluding troops of the five permanent members of the Security Council – the United States, Soviet Union, Britain, France and China – from the proposed supervisory force. London was unhappy and, in approving the resolution, I recorded the British view that this exclusion applied only to the force charged with supervising the cease-fire and not to any peace-keeping force which might be required at a later stage. I also stressed the need, once the cease-fire had been secured, to begin work at once on achieving a just and lasting peace.

The United Nations Secretariat worked with commendable speed to put the new resolution into effect and fighting gradually died down. A UN Emergency Force composed of contingents from Austria, Finland and Sweden was soon in place. Towards the end of October Egyptian and Israeli generals met under UN auspices in Israeli-occupied territory to discuss the disengagement of their forces. Waldheim kept me informed about the progress being made on the ground. At regular intervals I called at his office when he would read me the latest reports from General Enzio Siilasvio, the commander of the UN force. The Egyptian General Gamasy and the Israeli General Yariv met daily under UN chairmanship in a tent at kilometre 101 on the Cairo–Suez road. It was evident from Siilasvio's reports that the two generals were making more rapid progress than he had expected. Waldheim was enthusiastic; he felt the momentum generated by the intimate and effective relationship developing between these two former antagonists could well assist the more difficult peace-making process still to come.

At the end of November I received an urgent message to call on the secretary general. When I entered his office he said: "I have disappointing news. The Israeli general has just told Gamasy with much regret that he will not be coming back tomorrow. He has been ordered to discontinue the talks." Yariv had given no further explanation. Waldheim did not conceal his exasperation. Yet, neither then nor subsequently did he suggest what might have led to the suspension of the talks. His staff were less reticent; they thought it no coincidence that, almost immediately afterwards, Henry Kissinger began his diplomatic shuttling between Middle East capitals.

When the Security Council came to discuss arrangements for the projected peace conference, it appeared to the non-aligned members that the United States and the Soviet Union were using the secretary general as their messenger boy and the Council itself as a rubber stamp. These tendencies were resisted and, before the year was out, the two superpowers were obliged by the majority in the Council to permit the United Nations to play an honourable role in the peace conference.

❖

While the Security Council was searching for ways of ending the Yom Kippur war, the Assembly concluded its general debate; its work continued in the various committees. I had attended as much of the general debate as time allowed and was struck by the efforts that statesmen from all over the world made, when addressing this forum, to appear statesmanlike. For some little effort was needed. Willy Brandt of Germany, Adam Malik of Indonesia, General Romulo of the Philippines were incapable of making a dull speech. Two African heads of state impressed the Assembly. On successive days I listened to President Mobutu of Zaire and President Gowon of Nigeria; their statements differed widely in character, the one a passionate and flowery appeal to the emotions, the other a clinical analysis of the world situation. Later speakers lacked their gifts and, during the longueurs, I began to wonder how much time would be saved if participants in the debate were to refrain from addressing each other as 'the distinguished representative' of their country. Flattery as a lubricant, especially as a prelude to abuse, was understandable but, since all the delegates of over one hundred and thirty countries were in their own way distinguished, reiteration of this epithet seemed superfluous.

The Assembly settled a long-standing dispute between the two Koreas and agreed measures for the protection of diplomatic agents. But, when work began in the committees, some delegates and groups of delegates took off into Never-Never Land. They attacked forms of colonialism which had long since ceased to exist; they advocated policies on aid, trade, technical assistance and investment which, if rigidly applied, would have damaged their own economies. Some resolutions which paid scant regard to the merits of the issues at stake were passed by the built-in majority of non-aligned states as a demonstration of bloc solidarity. This kind of activity, I was told, had become the norm. But during this twenty-eighth Assembly there was an innovation – the 'wishful-thinking vote' – by which a majority sought to vote into fact a state in Africa, Guinea-Bissau, which by no objective test actually existed. One spokesman for the African group argued that a fiction that is recognised by more than seventy independent and sovereign members of the United Nations, like a reality, could no longer be considered a simple fiction. This was the fantastical technique of the Bellman in Lewis Carroll's *Hunting of the Snark*:

> "Just the place for a Snark", he said, and said it twice more.
> "I have said it thrice: What I tell you three times is true."

When the result of the vote was announced one delegate was heard to remark: "Next year it will be Disneyland". Many of the more experienced delegates told me privately of their concern at the damage this pattern of voting was doing to the standing of the United Nations and their own long-term interests.

The Chinese communists, characteristically inclined to take the long view, expected to assume leadership of what President Mobutu had referred to when addressing the Assembly as the 'barefoot section of humanity'. For their part, the east Europeans, who in their set speeches carried pursuit of the humdrum to extremes, were content to give the new nations their head. Resolutions critical of the western industrialised world took up debating time which might otherwise have been spent probing the disregard of basic human rights in the communist world. But, at Soviet instigation, the communist delegations liked to retain some initiative. They had formed the habit of inscribing on the agenda of each Assembly an item calling for the strengthening of international security. This vague formulation provided them with an opportunity to propagate their views on how the world should be organised and to seek endorsement of the status quo. Their message was simple: everything would be all right if they were left to look after eastern Europe in the way to which they wanted the rest of the world to become accustomed. All this was of no avail. Their prudish self-righteousness carried little weight and they cut a rather pathetic figure on the UN stage.

❖

Although the oil crisis precipitated by the Yom Kippur war did not figure directly on the agenda of either the General Assembly or the Security Council, it had a profound effect on attitudes.

For many years aspects of the so-called North–South relationship had been debated in various organs of the United Nations. While developing countries appreciated the technical assistance they received, the volumes of aid fell short of their expectations, and they disliked aid which was tied to imports from donor countries. Exporters of primary products sought better access to markets in the industrialised world. Since these issues, essentially economic in nature, brought into opposition people of different race, culture and historical experience, they had undertones of prejudice, resentment and fear. This added a political dimension. The central argument was clear enough. The nations of the developing world aspired to a superior quality of life and greater influence on the major political decisions. They believed that industrialised countries derived more than a fair advantage from exploitation of the earth's limited resources which, for the most part, were to be found on their territory. The sudden and immense rise in oil prices had produced new categories of states – the now even richer oil producers on the one hand and, on the other, the poor developing countries which were as dependent as the industrialised nations on imported oil, but had only limited natural resources with which to pay for it.

While beyond the precincts of the United Nations headquarters Americans sat in line in their cars waiting for whatever gasoline the filling stations were prepared to allow them, the non-aligned delegations argued over how best to handle the new situation. Abdellatif Rahal, the representative of Algeria, which stood to gain materially and politically, and the ambitious Yugoslav, Lazar Mojsov, whose motives were ideological, did their best, through relentless argument and bullying, to mobilise developing countries behind their policy of confrontation with the industrialised world in pursuit of a new international economic order. Others among developing country representatives were alive to the dangers of these tactics. Louis de Guiringaud and I concerted our response. He succeeded in persuading a number of the francophone Africans that cooperation offered a better chance of progress than confrontation. Together with Iqbal Akhund, the ambassador of Pakistan, I formed a group which met either in a corner of one of the salons in the UN building, or over lunch in our apartment, when we discussed how best to spread the same message. This group included two of the most able and conscientious members of the UN diplomatic corps – Samar Sen of India and Carlos Ortiz de Rosas of Argentina. As the weeks went by, the arguments of the moderates gained more support.

Despite the soaring rhetoric and hyperbole of many delegates and the popularity of the anti-colonial drum as an instrument, I was persuaded after my first few months in New York that the United Nations as an organisation scarcely deserved its poor reputation. No international body can play a role its members are unwilling to allow it to play and, in this and other respects, it seemed to me that the United Nations mirrored the world we lived in. The General Assembly and its committees, and the opportunities these offered for less formal dialogue, constituted a universal debating chamber – a forum in which the attitudes of the impressionable new nations could be influenced, and a Field of Cloth of Gold where developed and developing nations could choose either to confront one another or try to work in partnership.

My misgivings about the activities of the General Assembly and its committees did not alter my view of the Security Council. As the highest international body responsible for maintaining international peace and security, it was compelled to behave differently; under the terms of the Charter, its decisions are legally binding on all states. The discussions I had with my Security Council colleagues were invariably serious and relevant and, on the whole, realistic. Members take it in turns to preside over the Council for a month at a time. On my arrival in New York I learned of an admirable custom whereby the president for the month arranged a lunch to which he invited the secretary general and the fourteen other members of the Council. As I looked round the table at my colleagues, who represented every continent, numerous races and a variety of political ideologies, I was sure I was not the only one to become acutely conscious during that hour not so much of the factors which divided us as of the responsibilities we shared. I never attended one of those lunches without imagining that, for an instant, Providence had reached down to touch each one of us.

❖

Social activity continued throughout the Assembly. We had opportunities to enjoy the opera, the theatre, and – a special privilege – a poetry reading by Robert Lowell. Early in November General Romulo and Beth Day, who was to become his wife and biographer, invited Jean and me to a dinner in honour of William Rogers, the former American Secretary of State. The general and I are of similar build. As we took our leave he said: "Mr Ambassador, there is one thing I especially like about you. You are the only person in the Assembly with whom I see eye to eye." A few weeks later a dinner was held at the Metropolitan Museum to which members of a large number of delegations were invited. Tables were arranged throughout the ground floor of the museum to accommodate the many hundreds of guests. From where we and many others were sitting, the speakers, who included Henry Kissinger, were out of sight. However, the public address system worked efficiently. As we made our way in the midst of the throng towards the exit, we passed the speakers' table. A figure behind us, whom we could not identify, called out: "Great speech, Henry. But who was that with the heavy German accent who followed you?"

❖

Towards the end of the year unrest in the coal industry in the United

Kingdom became a matter of increasing comment at Turtle Bay and I was frequently called upon by the press and others to explain the government's industrial policy. A number of my colleagues as well as journalists saw a connection with the international oil crisis. I read with special interest the reports in the British press about the assurance offered by the Trades Union Congress in the second week in January 1974 that, in view of the 'distinctive and exceptional situation in the mining industry', other unions would not use any settlement as an argument in their own negotiations. It seemed to me that the actions of the oil producers the previous autumn had accentuated the 'exceptional' nature of the mining industry. That evening I stayed late in my office drafting a personal letter to the prime minister. I began by apologising for intervening from a distance, especially when I did not possess all the facts. I then wrote that, as seen from the perspective of the United Nations where the impact of the rise in oil prices was a major preoccupation, the miners in the United Kingdom could well be regarded as a special case; the industrialised world had to make maximum use of all alternative sources of energy. If the government were to satisfy the miners' demands and if any other union sought subsequently to exploit the terms of the settlement, the government, and no doubt public opinion, would require the TUC to honour their pledge. I returned to our apartment still turning over the issues in my mind. By the time I arrived at my office the following morning I had decided that the arguments in my draft must already be lodged in the minds of the prime minister and his advisers and that any intervention by me from this distance would be an impertinence. So I consigned my draft to the confidential waste.

In the first half of February I had several speaking engagements in New York and in Florida. When the general election in the United Kingdom was called, we noted in the newspaper reports of the manifestos of the main parties, that the Labour Party intended, if returned to power, once again to appoint a political figure to head the United Kingdom delegation to the United Nations. As the date of the election approached, Robert Rhodes James, who was on an assignment to the United Nations as adviser to the secretary general, told me over lunch that Hugh Caradon had been seen lurking in the vicinity of the UN building.

On 5 March, after Harold Wilson had formed his new administration, I received a personal telegram from Tom Brimelow, who had succeeded Denis Greenhill as permanent under-secretary at the Foreign and Commonwealth Office. Brimelow's purpose was to warn me, for my personal information, that the new government were looking for a political figure to head the mission. He assumed, correctly, that this would not surprise me and that, if such an appointment were made, I would wish to be transferred elsewhere. Five days later another personal telegram arrived – this time a message from the new foreign secretary, James Callaghan. In this he informed me that Ivor Richard, who had been a Labour party spokesman on foreign affairs but had been defeated at the general election, would be appointed to succeed me. James Callaghan went on to say that he knew this news would be a great disappointment and he invited me to call on him on my return to "talk over the strange turns of the wheel on which we all revolve."

When Ivor Richard's appointment was announced the staff of the Mission, who were prepared for this event, reacted stoically and my fellow ambassadors, who were not, were stupefied. Jean and I received scores of messages of sympathy and, in the hour before we sailed from New York on 26 March, our cabin on the *Michelangelo* was filled with friends, colleagues and flowers. Our most stimulating and agreeable posting had been brought to an end after seven and a half months.

16

Harold Wilson's Second Thoughts

Before leaving New York I was warned by the Foreign and Commonwealth Office that I might be required, after my return, to pay a brief visit to Iraq. In 1971 the Iraqi Government had rather petulantly broken off relations with the United Kingdom when Iran seized two small islands in the Persian Gulf, which had been until then under British protection. The Iraqis were now anxious to resume relations and had suggested that an elegant way of achieving this would be to invite the British Government to send a goodwill mission to Baghdad. This arrangement would avoid any loss of face. The Iraqis regarded my leadership of the mission as appropriate, but the date had not been settled when we sailed from New York.

By the time the *Michelangelo* reached Algeciras on 2 April 1974, the visit to Iraq had been arranged for 9 April. When we disembarked at Genoa we found we had to change our plan for the last stage of our journey home because of a rail strike. We flew to London on Saturday, 6 April, and, after being briefed at the Foreign and Commonwealth Office the following Monday, I left for Baghdad on 9 April. The flight to Baghdad on an aircraft of Iraqi Airways was not a reassuring experience. The emergency exit was jammed and I overheard one of the cabin crew say to a colleague: "Never mind. But don't tell the passengers." There was a problem with the forward toilet. On final approach at Frankfurt the pilot reversed the pitch of the engines when we were still twenty feet above the numerals at the beginning of the runway. The Iraqi newspapers I was given to read were full of the achievements of the Baath party and ideological claptrap about the struggle against imperialism. But the welcome awaiting me at Baghdad was cordial. When I called the following morning at the Iraqi foreign ministry, formal speeches completed the main business. During the exchange of hospitality which followed, I was able to thank the Swedish ambassador for housing the British Interests Section during the break in our relations with Iraq and see something of the new Baghdad. Not everything had changed in the twenty years since Jean and I had left. When I went on to the balcony outside my bedroom window before breakfast the next day, I heard a call from a nearby date-palm: 'kuku úkhti, kuku úkhti'. Then the doves saw me and flew away.

On returning to London I called on the foreign secretary as he had asked. James Callaghan began by thanking me for the work I had done in New York and for undertaking the mission to Baghdad. He repeated what he had said in his personal message: having to leave my post after such a short time must have been distressing, but he knew from experience that fortune was often unkind. Although a number of newspapers had suggested that the prime minister, Harold Wilson, had had me removed from New York because of my close association with Edward Heath, James Callaghan said nothing to suggest there was any substance to these reports; I had been removed to make way for a political appointee. As I was to learn later, this was not the whole story.

When I called on Tom Brimelow, he wasted no time expressing sympathy. He asked whether I would be willing to return to Baghdad as ambassador. I declined this suggestion. He then asked what I would like to do. I replied that, since what I wanted to do was now out of the question, my answer must be that I would consider with care any proposition he put to me. The opportunity to do this arose a few weeks later.

At the beginning of June 1974, I began my new job in the Foreign and Commonwealth Office. As one of the deputy under-secretaries, I was to supervise the economic work of the Foreign and Commonwealth Office other than that arising from our membership of the European Economic Community. For the next eighteen months, apart from visits to Bonn and Berlin for meetings of the Anglo-German Economic Committee which I co-chaired with Peter Hermes, my German counterpart, and an unsuccessful attempt during a visit to Algiers to initiate a dialogue on international economic questions, I found myself dealing with many of the issues with which I had perforce become familiar in New York, and encountering the same prejudices and ambitions. The difference was that I no longer had the opportunity to share impressions and ideas with Louis de Guiringaud.

The massive increase in oil prices in 1973 had posed a number of distinct challenges. The first was the need for security of oil supply. The second was to alleviate the burden on the balance of payments of oil-importing countries, whether in the industrialised or developing world. The third was to respond to the demand of the more radical developing countries for a wholesale reconstruction of the world economy – what they termed a 'new international economic order'.

Early in July Henry Kissinger, the United States secretary of state, visited London for talks with the foreign secretary, Denis Healey, the chancellor of the exchequer, Eric Varley, the energy secretary, and the governor of the Bank of England, Gordon Richardson. For some time Washington had been uttering warnings about a collapse of the world economy and, as I expected, Kissinger was in a more aggressive mood than were British ministers. Both sides agreed that the strain imposed by the rise in oil prices had to be eased, but no clear view emerged as to how this should be done. Meanwhile, work was in hand on establishing a forum in which the major oil importing countries could coordinate their response. The draft of a proposal for an embryo agency to perform this function was accepted by all but one of the participants at a meeting in Brussels in September. The disappointing but unsurprising exception was France, which objected to what it regarded as an 'energy NATO'.

Further evidence of the serious concern of the United States administration emerged from a domestic conference in Washington at the end of September to discuss the linked issues of inflation and unemployment. This was attended by several hundred bankers, businessmen, labour leaders and economists. In taking this early initiative, the new United States president, Gerald Ford, sought to underline the seriousness of the crisis. In his opening address he argued that inflation was an international problem for which there were no miracle cures. He also undertook to work with America's friends overseas to meet what he described as 'an international threat'.

This conference set the scene for a five-nation meeting of finance and foreign ministers which took place over the following two days. To placate those not invited, the American hosts had planned an informal gathering at Camp David. Unfortunately bad weather grounded the helicopters which were to transport the participants and the meeting was held at the State Department in Washington instead.

This meeting coincided with the general election campaign in Britain and, as he was heavily involved, James Callaghan asked me to represent him. Denis Healey led the British delegation, which also included Gordon Richardson. The other countries taking part were France, Germany and Japan. As Henry Kissinger was still in a somewhat combative mood, Denis Healey argued forcefully against any steps which would lead to confrontation. He had no objection to Kissinger's suggestion that contingency plans be drawn up to meet any new ban on exports by the oil producers in the Middle East, but was more concerned with the actual situation. To deal with the severe balance of payments difficulties oil importing countries in the industrialised world were facing, he put forward an ingenious plan devised by the Treasury for recycling oil funds through a special facility operated by the International Monetary Fund. While none of the ideas canvassed over these two days in Washington represented a 'miracle cure', they widened the area of common ground between the major western economies. Perhaps the most important dividend was that many of the differences between the French and Americans were removed. Kissinger made a special and successful effort to establish a better understanding with Jean Sauvagnargues, the French foreign minister.

In the following weeks I visited Paris, Washington and Bonn to continue the debate with my opposite numbers. This phase culminated in a real 'energy NATO'. For years it had been the custom for the foreign and defence ministers of North Atlantic Council to meet at NATO headquarters in Brussels in December. On this occasion the meeting was exceptionally dominated by the economic problems facing all members of the alliance. Without advocating confrontation with the Middle East oil producers, Kissinger called for solidarity among consumers. James Callaghan favoured dialogue with the producers and expressed strong opposition to any restrictive trade measures. Once again I felt that the most important result of this meeting was that the positions of the French and the Americans were more closely aligned.

❖

Up to this point the prime minister had played no direct part in the international debate on the crisis. He planned to remedy this when he visited Ottawa, Washington and New York in January 1975. The departments in the Foreign and Commonwealth Office which I supervised were closely involved in preparations for these visits. There then occurred an event which was to have an unexpected sequel.

On 15 January, when I saw him on another matter, Tom Brimelow told me that the prime minister had sent Robert Armstrong, his private secretary, to discuss with him the composition of the party for the forthcoming visits. Armstrong had said that the prime minister would prefer that I should not accompany him in view of my association with Edward Heath. Tom Brimelow told me he had passed on this message to the secretary of state to whom he expressed the opinion that it was quite unfair that a member of the public service should be victimised because had held a particular appointment. James Callaghan accepted this and, when he next discussed arrangements for the visits with the prime minister, he persuaded him to include me in the party.

Apart from the prime minister and Mrs Wilson, the official party included the foreign secretary and Harold Lever, the chancellor of the duchy of Lancaster, whose ingenuity and expertise in financial and economic matters were highly valued by the prime minister. In Ottawa on 28 January and in the talks over the following two days with President Ford, Henry Kissinger and other senior members of the Administration, the oil crisis and its consequences were the dominant topics. While acknowledging the strain on the balance of payments of the principal industrialised countries and the depressing effect this was having on the world economy, the prime minister expressed particular concern over the damage done to the prospects of those developing countries – and they were the majority – which depended on oil imports. What they earned from the export of their raw materials was subject to the caprice of the world market and it was hard to see how, without outside help, they could meet the greatly increased costs of their oil imports. No conclusions were reached in Washington, but both sides looked forward to a conference later in the year when energy producers and consumers might be able to reach some accommodation. As usual, American hospitality was superb and, on the flight home, I thought I could still hear the remarkable voice of Beverly Sills, who had given a recital at the president's dinner for us at the White House. When I reached home I was able to tell Jean, in answer to her question, that at no time during the entire trip did the prime minister give any indication of his initial reservations about my taking part.

❖

A few days later I received a message which was to open up unexpected possibilities. I was told that the prime minister would like me to examine the feasibility of working out some plan for stabilising commodity prices. The discussions in Ottawa and Washington had reinforced his view that help over the prices of raw materials would be one way of alleviating the balance of payments problems of oil-importing developing countries. There was another factor. The next conference of Commonwealth heads of government was due to be held in Jamaica at the end of April and the prime minister hoped it might be possible to say something on this subject on that occasion.

I welcomed this new task. One of the good friends I had made during my time at the United Nations in New York was Richard Gardner, the professor of law and international organization at Columbia University. He was a leading authority on the events surrounding the establishment at the end of the war of the two Bretton Woods institutions – the International Monetary Fund and the International Bank for Reconstruction and Development – and on the abortive attempt two years later to create an International Trade Organisation in parallel with the agreement on tariffs and trade. Richard had formed the view that one reason for the failure of the ITO was that too little attention had been paid at that time to the economic needs of developing countries; had these been addressed earlier the clamour for a new international order in the wake of the oil price rise might have been less strident, and perhaps less justified. I knew that Harold Wilson had led the British delegation to the Geneva Conference which had concluded the General Agreement on Tariffs and Trade – the GATT – in 1947 and that, as president of the board of trade, he had been involved in the International Trade Organisation negotiations. I wondered if it was in his mind that the current crisis provided an opportunity to make amends.

I discussed the message from Number 10 with the head of the Trade Relations and Exports Department of the Foreign and Commonwealth Office. Together we drew up an outline programme of work which I put to the Cabinet Office. It was my good fortune that the deputy secretary responsible for economic affairs was James Hamilton,[1] a strict but imaginative chairman of committees, who understood straightaway the political significance for our relations with developing countries, both within and outside the Commonwealth, of the task we had been given. The Treasury, the Department of Trade, the Ministry of Agriculture and the Ministry of Overseas Development were among the other departments represented on the cabinet committee charged with drafting the report to the prime minister.

For the next several weeks an intensive effort was made to collect the necessary statistics about the production of and trade in commodities. Fairly soon we identified ten commodities for which it might be possible to negotiate practicable agreements – cereals, cocoa, coffee, copper, dairy products, rubber, sisal jute, sugar, tea and tin. The prospects for workable agreements for other commodities which we examined were unpromising for one reason or another.

At the meetings of the Cabinet Office committee the representatives of the Treasury and the Department of Trade did little to disguise their lack of enthusiasm. For one thing, they doubted whether any real benefit would flow from commodity agreements, even if these proved feasible; for another, they feared that any such benefit would be at the expense of industrialised countries in general and the United Kingdom – a major importer of raw materials – in particular. With James Hamilton's support I had to emphasise repeatedly the primarily political nature of the brief we had been given. After much debate, some of it acrimonious, we agreed on four recommendations: first, there should be better exchanges of information about the forward supply of and demand for commodities; second, the circumstances under which restrictions on the import and export of commodities might be applied should be more specifically defined; third, producers and consumers should be encouraged to form associations for trade in particular commodities; and, finally, producers and consumers should be encouraged to conclude commodity agreements designed to facilitate the orderly conduct and development of trade. This last proposal would entail identifying the most suitable commodities and analysing the most appropriate mechanisms for regulating trade within the framework of such agreements. We attached to our main report notes on schemes for stabilising earnings from exports as well as trade statistics for fifteen commodities, including the ten we deemed suitable subjects for international agreements.

Not long after our paper was submitted to the prime minister I received a further message from Number 10. Our report, it seemed, had exceeded the prime minister's expectations.

The next step was to canvass the support of other industrialised nations for our approach. For this purpose I visited Washington on 18 April for talks with Tom Enders, my counterpart in the State Department, and his colleagues in the US Treasury and Department of Agriculture. I found that in Washington, as in London, opinion was divided. The economic departments doubted whether we would be able to devise specific proposals and argued that, in any case, new arrangements for pricing agricultural products were already being discussed in the GATT forum in Geneva. I was unable to counter their argument with a complete exposition of the content of our initiative, since it was the prime minister's intention to launch it himself in Kingston. On the other hand, the reaction of Tom Enders, who understood my position, was more positive. With meetings at ministerial level of both the OECD – the Organisation for Economic Cooperation and Development – and the International Energy Agency scheduled for May, which would provide opportunities to underline the solidarity of the industrialised countries, Tom was attracted by the idea of an initiative in a field of direct interest to the developing world.

❖

In the absence of any major disagreement over policy towards South Africa, it was inevitable that the vivacity and informality of our Jamaican hosts would create a different atmosphere from that in which Commonwealth Heads of Government had assembled at Singapore in 1971. From the hotel where most of the delegations were accommodated we had spectacular views over the Caribbean and towards the Blue Mountains. Breakfast on the terrace, where we could choose from a bewildering range of Caribbean and other food, provided an opportunity for bilateral and multilateral diplomacy.

Michael Manley, the prime minister of Jamaica, formally opened the conference on 29 April. The general political debate, which began immediately, occupied the first few days, during which Peter Preston[2] of the Department of Trade and I completed work on the commodities initiative. At the beginning of the economic debate on 1 May, the prime minister of Guyana, Forbes Burnham, argued on behalf of the Caribbean members of the Commonwealth in favour of a new international economic order. In launching our initiative, Harold Wilson recalled a study he had undertaken with Sir William Beveridge in the 1930s which showed that unemployment in Britain over the previous century had been associated with a collapse in the prices of primary products in countries from which the United Kingdom imported much of its food and materials. He went on to refer to his involvement in the negotiations which led to the creation of the GATT and his leadership of the British delegation to the preparatory commission of the Food and Agriculture Organisation. He then introduced our proposals; later that month these were presented to Parliament in the form of a 110-page White Paper entitled *World Economic Interdependence and Trade in Commodities*. At the end of that session the prime minister addressed a specially convened press conference. I was sitting at the back of the hall when he came in accompanied by Joe Haines and Janet Hewlett-Davies, his press secretaries. They beckoned to me and the prime minister conspicuously placed me at his right side before telling the press about the commodities initiative. His account was well received. That same evening all the delegations were invited to a spectacularly athletic and melodious performance by the national dance theatre company of Jamaica; this was my first exposure to reggae, the Jamaican belief in spirits, and the pride of Rastafari. It was quite a day.

When heads of government left Jamaica for their customary informal weekend, Peter Preston and I spent a day in a committee appointed to draft the economic section of the conference communique. We had less difficulty than we expected in securing the exclusion of the more extreme statements and we succeeded in inserting the phrase 'rational and equitable' before the reference in the draft to a new international economic order. We were released the following day and drove through mist and light rain to the Blue Mountains, where we had lunch. On our return to Kingston we penetrated some of the poorer quarters of the city; it was not difficult to understand how crime could flourish in such an environment.

The communique issued at the end of the conference recorded the decision of the Commonwealth Heads of Government to invite a group of not more than ten experts to draw up a 'comprehensive and interrelated programme of practical measures directed at closing the gap between the rich and poor countries'. It was agreed that Alister McIntyre of Grenada, the secretary of the Caribbean Community, would chair the Expert Group, as it was called, and that the other members would be appointed by the Commonwealth Secretary General after consultation wih member governments. A tight deadline was imposed on the Group. Its interim report was to be available for consideration by Commonwealth finance ministers when they met at Georgetown in late August so that governments could take this into account before the Seventh Special Session of the General Assembly of the United Nations early in September which was to consider north–south economic relations. It was clear that, after many months of agonising, the debate on the consequences of the oil crisis was at last gaining momentum.

From Jamaica the British delegation flew to Washington to compare notes with the United States administration in preparation for the ministerial meeting of the OECD later in the month. On the flight home from Washington, Kenneth Stowe,[3] who had replaced Robert Armstrong earlier in the year as the prime minister's principal private secretary, came forward and sat beside me. "I have a message from the prime minister," he said. "'Go and tell Donald he can have his medals back.'"

As it fell to the the United Kingdom to preside, our delegation to the OECD meeting in Paris on 28 and 29 May was unusually strong. James Callaghan took the chair on the first day and Denis Healey on the second. Peter Shore, the secretary of state for trade, and Edmund Dell, the Paymaster General, were also present. Under the foreign secretary's firm direction, ministers agreed that what he termed a 'sterile confrontation' with developing countries had to be avoided. Ministers unanimously adopted a declaration in which they resolved to intensify their efforts to cooperate with developing countries in order to improve conditions of life and enable these countries to play an increasing part in an 'improved and expanding world economy'. Particular emphasis was to be laid on food production, energy, commodities and development assistance for the poorest. What gave us particular satisfaction was the positive contribution of Henry Kissinger. This suggested that the State Department had prevailed in the dispute which had obviously not been resolved when I had visited Washington six weeks earlier. Kissinger went even further than we had hoped. He unveiled a 'New Deal' for developing countries. This included a proposal which he hoped the countries of the OECD would put forward to set up a $2 billion trust fund within the next year to help those most in need. He went on to announce that the United States would participate in the International Fund for Agricultural Development which had been proposed by the oil producers no doubt as one way of easing their consciences; he also suggested that producers and consumers should establish joint commissions to monitor trade in commodities in order to achieve 'reliable, long-term stability and growth in export earnings'.

Meanwhile, with the agreement of the prime minister, James Callaghan had asked me to represent the United Kingdom on the Commonwealth Group of Experts, the composition of which was announced as he and I returned to London from Paris. The group held its first formal meeting at Marlborough House, the headquarters of the Commonwealth Secretariat in London, in the second week of June. We were ten in all – four from Africa, three from Asia, and one each from the Caribbean, New Zealand and Britain – and we readily accepted an invitation from Canada to hold our first full working session in Ottawa in July, when we hoped to complete our interim report.

Our arrival in Ottawa coincided with the midge season. But they caused me less irritation than over-zealous officials in London. In accordance with usual practice, I sent a telegram to the Foreign and Commonwealth Office each evening reporting the day's discussions, partly for the record and partly to aid my own thinking. This was a mistake. The nit-pickers in London, who had made heavy weather of the drafting of the commodities initiative earlier in the year and who presumably feared that, left alone, I would pawn the crown jewels, began to bombard me with 'instructions'. Fortunately most of these reached me some time after the group had moved on from the particular point at issue.

The expert group divided along expected lines. The representatives of Tanzania and Nigeria were the most demanding; the Bangladeshi and Zambian understood that there were limits to what we could sensibly recommend. The star was Peter Lai of Malaysia whose ingenuity helped the New Zealand Professor Brownlie and me translate the aspirations of developing countries into propositions which industrialised countries could reasonably entertain.

Two days after my arrival in Ottawa it was announced in London that I was to succeed Michael Palliser as United Kingdom representative to the European Communities when he left Brussels at the end of September 1975. The prime minister wanted me to be present when he addressed his fellow heads of government on our commodities initiative at the European Council meeting in Brussels on 16 and 17 July. This entailed three days' absence from Ottawa and one of the more complicated journeys I have undertaken: flight from Ottawa to Toronto; flight from Toronto to La Guardia, New York; car from La Guardia to JFK, New York; flight from JFK to Heathrow; car from Heathrow to Northolt; flight from Northolt to Zaventem, Brussels. And that was only the outward journey. The return was simpler – only two flights, from Brussels to Paris and from Paris to Montreal and a superb drive from Montreal to Ottawa in a Chevvy station wagon. On personal grounds the effort was worthwhile as I was able during the two days in Brussels to meet my future European colleagues and members of the Commission.

In my absence from Ottawa, the Grenadian Alister McIntyre, with the assistance of Peter Lai and Professor Brownlie, had kept the experts on a sensible course. In our interim report, which contained a number of specific guidelines for action in regard to trade in commodities, we referred to a point which the new Commonwealth Secretary General, Shridath Ramphal, had stressed at the outset of our work. This was that we participated in the work of the Group in our personal capacities and not as representatives of our countries or governments.

When they saw our interim report, the nit-pickers in London accepted rather grudgingly that the crown jewels were still intact. James Callaghan expressed himself satisfied with the result of the group's work and was amused when I told him about the stream of instructions I had received. "You and I understand, of course, that this is essentially a political matter. The sentiment is as important as the content."

Commonwealth finance ministers meeting at Georgetown at the end of August endorsed the Group's report. A few days later I accompanied the foreign secretary to New York where he was to address the Special Assembly on world economic problems. This was opened on 1 September by the foreign minister of Algeria, Abdul Aziz Bouteflika, who had presided over the 29th General Assembly. His address was laden with warnings. The international community faced a choice: either the world economy could be restructured (by means which he did not specify), or industrial countries would continue to defend their privileges in what he called an 'obsolete order'. If they chose the latter course, developing countries would inevitably adopt a confrontational stance. Bouteflika's virtuoso firebrand performance had two effects: it concentrated the minds of the representatives of the moderate developing countries and made every subsequent speaker sound reasonable. James Callaghan, as he had done before, spoke of the importance of avoiding confrontation, of growing interdependence and of the need to set rhetoric aside and work for specific agreements, for example on trade in raw materials, which would bring real benefits.

For the time being this ended my preoccupation with north–south economic relations. Jean and I had only a few weeks to prepare for our new life and work. The Foreign and Commonwealth Office and the cabinet office arranged for me to be inducted by Whitehall. I met bankers, leaders of industry and commerce and many others. The tasks ahead were formidable; but I looked forward to being engaged once again in the multilateral diplomacy which I had enjoyed in New York. As I contemplated the immediate past, I thought it a pity that it had taken Harold Wilson so long to realise that at least one press secretary was capable of serving prime ministers of different political persuasions with equal loyalty.

17

One of Nine in Europe

It would have been convenient to take up my new post in August or the end-of-year recess. Circumstances dictated otherwise and, when Jean and I arrived in Brussels on 8 October 1975, we had to hit the ground not merely running, as the saying goes, but sprinting. Over the next eight days the Council of Ministers met in Luxembourg to discuss agriculture, transport, development assistance and the environment, the European Assembly convened in Strasbourg and the Community received representatives of the Soviet-dominated Council for Mutual Economic Assistance, usually known as Comecon.

At that time the European Community, which was to hold me in its embrace for the next four years, had nine members. These were the original Six – France, Germany, Italy and the three Benelux countries who had signed the Treaty of Rome in 1957 – and the United Kingdom, Ireland and Denmark, who had joined in January 1973. Over the next few years the structure and cohesion as well as the external relations of the Community were to be affected by several events. The European Monetary System was established in 1978. Greece, and later Spain and Portugal, applied to join and, after awkward negotiations, the Greek Accession Treaty was signed in 1979. A new Lomé Convention was concluded with 58 African, Caribbean and Pacific countries; this offered assistance and privileged access to the common market for the products of these countries. An overall approach to economic and commercial relations with the countries of the Mediterranean was adopted. The first direct elections to the European Parliament were held in June 1979 – the first multinational direct elections in history.

In less obvious ways the Community was to change. The European Council, composed of the heads of state and government of the member states, emerged as the dominant force in the Community. In the formative years the supreme decision-making body had been the Council of Ministers. Foreign ministers, meeting in what was sometimes called the 'General Affairs Council', determined the direction of policy.

But, when the Community entered new fields such as energy policy, the environment, transport and social affairs, the ministers directly concerned met in so-called specialist Councils. As more of the important problems fell to be discussed in these Councils, the role and prestige of the General Affairs Council declined.

Most heads of state and government enjoyed the periodical meetings of the European Council; these provided a new opportunity to exercise power. I was surprised when, in 1977, the question was raised whether meetings of the European Council should take the form of a 'fireside chat' about the major challenges facing western Europe, or a court of appeal where problems unresolved at lower level might be settled. After months of debate the startlingly obvious conclusion was reached that the European Council was bound to be both.

The General Affairs Council was not the only loser. The standing of the European Commission was also diminished, partly by the emergence of the European Council as the principal motor of progress, partly because public opinion was becoming increasingly impatient with the Commission's fussy interventionism, and partly because of adverse publicity about personal extravagance on the part of certain Commissioners.

The effect of these factors was overshadowed by the increasingly perverse operation of the Community budget. In the ten years between President de Gaulle's veto in 1963 and the eventual entry of the United Kingdom, Ireland and Denmark, the Community of the Six established the common agriculture policy, devised the 'own resources' system for funding the budget, and evolved a common fisheries policy. All three policies were appropriate to the circumstances of the Six but inimical to the interests of the United Kingdom. The fact that, largely under French influence, the Six insisted on 'deepening' the Community in this way before 'enlarging' it, betrayed their intention of presenting the three candidates with a 'fait accompli'. The train accelerated just as the United Kingdom and the two others were hoping to board it.

If the Six did not appreciate that the United Kingdom would not tolerate for long arrangements which were clearly detrimental to its national interests, they were foolish. In the late 1970s and beyond, the unjust burden of the United Kingdom's contribution to the budget was to create conditions of chronic crisis within the Community.

❖

Since a state cannot legally or logically send an embassy to an organisation to which it belongs, the missions of the nine member states were known as 'Representations'. By the same token, missions to the headquarters of the North Atlantic Treaty Organisation, also located in Brussels, were called 'Delegations'. As head of the United Kingdom Representation to the Community – known for convenience as 'UKrep' – I had two main responsibilities: first, to ensure the efficient operation of the mission and, secondly, to speak for the United Kingdom at meetings of the Committee of Permanent Representatives, known as 'Coreper'.

The composition of UKrep was unique. The staff were grouped in sections which dealt with specific community policies: agriculture; external trade; economics, finance and taxation; developing countries; industry, energy and consumer protection; social affairs, the environment, regional policy and transport. Co-ordination was the responsibility of the head of chancery – first Rodric Braithwaite[1] and later Brian Crowe.[2] The chancery included the legal adviser, the press office and a section responsible for institutional questions. The supporting staff – archivists, secretaries and communicators – were for the most part members of the Diplomatic Service, accustomed to living and working abroad. Over half of the staff were seconded from home departments, notably the Treasury, Ministry of Agriculture and Department of Trade. UKrep was Whitehall in microcosm, with one important difference; every member of the diplomatic staff of the mission was able to work in both English and French – the two working languages of the Community. At lunch and dinner parties at our house it was rewarding to hear members of our staff and our guests conversing fluently and unselfconsciously in each of these languages. The notion that the British are poor linguists was shown to be just another of our favourite national myths.

The Committee of Permanent Representatives was in two parts, composed respectively of the heads and deputy heads of the nine representations, as well as a representative of the staff of the Commission, frequently the secretary general, or his deputy. The heads met in the Charlemagne Building, the headquarters of the Council of Ministers, every Thursday and the deputies, whose agenda included the more technical subjects, on Fridays. My deputy was Bob Goldsmith, who looked forward to returning in due course to his parent department, the Board of Trade. On the basis of instructions received from the nine capitals, the two parts of Coreper prepared the dossiers for meetings of the Council of Ministers. This meant in practice that Coreper scrutinised proposals from the Commission and eventually submitted these to the Council with its recommendations. In many cases, after debate and amendment where necessary, Coreper was able to endorse Commission proposals. These were presented to Ministers at the next meeting of the Council as so-called 'A points', which were then adopted without discussion by Ministers in whom legal authority to decide rested. Matters on which Coreper had been unable to agree figured on the agenda as 'B points'. It was these which often provoked long arguments and had to be settled in the end by compromise, or trade-offs in another field.

Before papers reached Coreper they had been examined in detail by expert working groups composed of the specialist members of the nine representations and staff of the Commission. Agriculture had its own hierarchy. Alone of all Community policies, this was handled by a special committee which submitted its recommendations direct to agriculture ministers, meeting in Council. Insinuating ministers concerned with consumer affairs into the Agriculture Council had little practical effect. As time went by, my doubts grew as to whether this exclusive arrangement served the best interests of the Community.

Coreper and the Council of Ministers were well served by the Commission interpreters. Accurately and with great facility they translated simultaneously what every speaker said. Of course, it was not their function to interpret what every speaker meant and I soon realised that I had to master European Community diplomatic terms. The longer-serving members of Coreper and the Council were the principal exponents of the elegant applied hypocrisy enshrined in this language. For convenience I began to compile my own phrase book. This included the following entries:

General:
"comprehensive" = "too long"
"contains a number of points of interest" = "boring"
"detailed analysis" = "nitpicking criticism"
"may I add a minor qualification?" = "I am about to cast a major spanner into the works"
"much in this with which I can agree, but . . . " = "precious little in this with which I can agree and anyway . . . "
"in due time this idea may find wider acceptance" = "I hope that this is the last we have heard of this absurd idea"

Of Commission proposals:

"conceptual" = "vague and pretentious"
"imaginative" = "unrealistic"
"painstaking preparation" = "long overdue"
"adventurous" = "unacceptable as it stands"
"original" = "I wish I had thought of that".

In the second half of 1975 Italy held the presidency of the Council of Ministers. During these six months Italians chaired all ministerial meetings, regardless of the subject, and meetings of all other bodies acting under the aegis of the Council. These included not only the two parts of Coreper but also all working groups. As early as possible I paid my respects to my Italian colleague, a veteran diplomatist called Giorgio Bombassei. He instructed me with some care in the conventions which governed our discussions over the Coreper lunch table on Thursdays.

First, he said, no report should be sent to any capital recording what had been said. Secondly, our discussion should be neither a substitute for nor a rehearsal of what it would be appropriate for us to discuss in the Council chamber. On the contrary, he explained, our meetings over lunch afforded an opportunity to fill in the background to our official business, to discuss the difficulties this or that delegation might have, and to exchange our personal ideas as to where compromise might be found. What bound the nine of us together, he said, was the desire as far as possible to meet the legitimate interests of each member state while proceeding with the brick-upon-brick construction of the Community.

Once again I was fortunate in finding a kindred spirit in my French colleague. "You and I should go for a walk," were Jean Marie Soutou's first words. 'A vos ordres," I replied. Jean Marie assumed that I was under no illusion about the purpose of our presence in Brussels. "The Community was created," he said, "to accommodate the size and strength of Germany at the heart of the continent. You and I carry a special responsibility and have to bring our colleagues along with us." I assured Jean Marie that nothing he said surprised me. What I had not expected, however, was that this message would be repeated in different contexts by each of my new colleagues in turn. The Luxembourger, Jean Dondelinger,[3] described how his country had been incorporated into the Third Reich; every member of the present government had suffered personally in one way or another. Jan Lubbers and his wife had joined the Dutch resistance and had grubbed up daffodil bulbs when food supplies to the civilian population had been blocked. Niels Ersbøll[4] had been on his way to school in Copenhagen on a bright April morning in 1940 when he saw German paratroops advancing along the road towards him. Even Ulrich Lebsanft, my sad German colleague, who still bore the psychological scars of his long years as a prisoner of war, wanted to be certain that I understood our mission. "You know of course, that the success of the Community is of vital importance to my country and that we look to our partners for support."

❖

I had worked before with Christopher Soames, when he was ambassador in Paris, and George Thomson, when he was Commonwealth Secretary. Both were well established when we arrived and Jean and I heard on all sides complimentary remarks about the impact they had made as the first British members of the Commission. Christopher Soames held the important post of Vice-President with responsibility for external affairs. George Thomson was intent on expanding the scope of the Community's regional policy.

I had not met the Commission President before, but I found no difficulty in establishing a sound relationship with him. At a dinner that he and his wife gave in our honour soon after our arrival, I learned that in Indo-China during the war, while still in his late teens, François Xavier Ortoli had walked for hundreds of kilometres evading capture by the Japanese; he had returned after Japan surrendered to search for the sweetheart he had had to leave behind. This tale of courage, endurance and devotion had a happy ending, as anyone meeting François Xavier and his wife immediately appreciated.

The other French Commissioner was Claude Cheysson, who took pride in his role as interlocutor on behalf of the Community with the developing world. He devoted much time and effort to his task and from time to time presented himself before Coreper to give an account of his latest tour. This he did in some detail and I observed that, as he spoke, the notetaker sitting beside each of my colleagues, who collectively constituted the working party on development aid, seemed to be making a tally of some kind. My own notetaker enlightened me. He and they were recording the number of references to red carpets, guards of honour, military bands, audiences with presidents, and distinctions conferred.

For the next four years Jean and I were engaged in almost ceaseless activity – long days, late nights, interrupted weekends, a stream of house guests. In April, June and October the Council of Ministers met in Luxembourg and all participants spent a night or two in hotels there. Most meetings of the Council were held at the beginning of the week and, during the other eight months – August was avoided whenever possible – the London team would arrive in Brussels on Sunday afternoon and the minister, his private secretary and perhaps a senior adviser would stay overnight with us. The residence, in the quiet suburb of Uccle on the road to Waterloo, had been well selected by a predecessor. Outwardly modest in appearance and with a garden which was easy to maintain, it had precisely the accommodation we needed. Over dinner on Sunday the London team would be joined by those members of the UKrep staff whose subjects figured on the Council's agenda. I and members of the staff would brief the minister on the most recent developments. We would then go through the Council agenda item by item. At this stage it fell to me to forecast the course the debate on each subject was likely to take and to suggest possible outcomes. In the discussion which followed, the position the United Kingdom would adopt on each item was finalised. This advice to ministers on the eve of Council meetings was undoubtedly the heaviest responsibility I carried.

Over the years, Jean and I were host to a large number of members of the government and their advisers. James Callaghan stayed with us both as foreign secretary and as prime minister after the surprise resignation of Harold Wilson in March 1976. On 19 January of that year, while he was still foreign secretary and when the cod war with Iceland was in its most bitter phase, we arranged a working dinner at his request to enable him to meet Joseph Luns who, after fourteen years as foreign minister of the Netherlands, was now secretary general of NATO. James Callaghan wanted an opportunity to tell Luns that the British Government had decided to withdraw the Royal Navy from their task of protecting British trawlers near Iceland and to invite the Icelandic prime minister for talks in London in an effort to negotiate a settlement. At his request we had also invited the Brussels diplomatic press corps to join us after dinner to hear an important announcement. Dinner had hardly begun when a telegram arrived to the effect that the Icelandic government were threatening to break off diplomatic relations with Britain unless the Navy was withdrawn. Luns was outraged. He had returned to Brussels only a few hours earlier from Reykjavik where he had been given no indication of any such threat. Past experience had taught me that Luns, even in a genial mood, was worth treating with circumspection. To see him in a fury was an experience not easily forgotten. For the next several hours there were telephone calls to and fro. Dinner became a protracted feast – the longest fish supper in history, someone suggested – and before it was over the press had arrived. As all the main rooms were occupied by officials telephoning here and there, Jean opened up our own sitting room for the journalists who realised at once that they had a more intimate view than usual of a diplomatic crisis. In the end Luns persuaded the Icelanders to withdraw their threat, we withdrew the navy, the Icelandic prime minister did go to London for talks, and the journalists had a splendid eyewitness story to tell.

Denis Healey, the chancellor of the exchequer, had anecdotes for every occasion. He enjoyed dominating any gathering, even meetings of the Finance Council which he did not chair; however, his domination did not always result in our winning the argument. Tony Benn was one of our most appreciative guests, perhaps because Jean had a kettle and teapot put in his room. Given his hostile attitude to the European Community, it was not expected that he would be comfortable at meetings of the Energy Council. He seemed to have convinced himself that Guido Brunner, the German Commissioner responsible for research and energy, plotted continuously to extend the competence of the Community into new areas of energy policy. My eight Coreper colleagues and the Commission officials who worked to Brunner noticed, as I did, that at about four o'clock in the afternoon (Brussels time), Benn's patience would suddenly be exhausted. From then on he would oppose every proposition, regardless of its merits or what was contained in our agreed brief. For this reason, when it became known that he was to attend a Council meeting, the agenda was drawn up in such a way that the more important and urgent items were taken as early in the day as possible, leaving the dross to the end.

❖

At the beginning of January 1977 the United Kingdom assumed the presidency of the Council of Ministers for the first time. For the next six months British ministers had to chair all meetings of the Council, I had to chair one part of Coreper and Bob Goldsmith the other, and members of UKrep chaired all the working groups as well as the small team responsible for coordinating arrangements for meetings of Coreper and the Council. This indispensable team bore the name 'the Antici Group' in honour of the Italian official who perceived the need for it and, even better, invented the remedy. The new leader of this team was David Gore-Booth who, as a member of my staff in Tripoli, had acted as interpreter and notetaker during the Anglo-Libyan negotiations in 1969 and 1970.

Preparations for the first United Kingdom presidency had been in hand for several months both in London and in Brussels. The staff of UKrep had all been in Brussels long enough to know what lay in store. Their wives, who also had a part to play, were well prepared. They met our colleagues and their wives on numerous social occasions and regularly entertained them. Jean suggested that they would find it helpful to be informed about developments in the Community and especially those directly affecting British interests. I accordingly arranged regular briefing meetings for them, when I and senior members of the staff would account for ourselves. All that was needed now, I felt, was the political direction which was expected of us. In July 1975, following the decisive result of the referendum on Europe, Harold Wilson told his colleagues at a meeting of the European Council in Brussels that, from then on, Britain would play her full part in the work of the Community and its development; Britain's membership of the Community, he assured them, was now committed and total. Our partners looked forward to discovering what this meant in practice.

It was customary during meetings of the Council of Ministers for each presidency to offer some characteristic dish at lunch and dinner. During the Danish presidency, for example, we were served gravadlax. In UKrep we had given thought to this. Lancashire hotpot and haggis did not figure on our list of possibilities. In the end I asked the Secretariat, who serviced the Council of Ministers and acted as general staff to the presidency, to order English table wine from Sir Guy Salisbury-Jones' vineyard at Hambledon, to which Jean and I had been introduced by a French journalist in New York. When it arrived, the secretary general tasted it and pronounced himself impressed. I agreed with him and with Anthony Crosland, who had succeeded James Callaghan as foreign secretary, that at the first United Kingdom presidency lunch on 18 January we would not reveal the provenance of the wine until it had been tasted. When Claude Cheysson had emptied his glass without apparent distaste or curiosity, Tony Crosland asked me to say a word about the wine. When I revealed its origin Cheysson reacted immediately. With a grimace he pushed his glass away.

While Tony Crosland chaired the Council meeting the United Kingdom seat was occupied by David Owen. On 7 February we had a full house, Tony Crosland and David Owen being among our guests. A difficult day lay ahead: the Council meeting would be largely concerned with the common fisheries policy which the Community had adopted shortly before the three new members, who had important fishing industries, joined in 1973. Fishing limits had been extended in 1976 to 200 miles, but the allocation of quotas created serious economic, regional and social problems. As there was much to discuss, the working dinner at our house went on late and the Council meeting the following day was as contentious as we had foreseen. Debate continued into the night. By four o'clock in the morning, when it was clear that no agreement could be reached, Tony Crosland brought the meeting to an end. He had exercised great patience throughout and his performance at the press conference which followed was brilliant. We returned to our house at 5 a.m. and, after three or four hours' sleep, the London party left for the airport. Tony Crosland fell ill the following Sunday, 13 February, and died six days later. David Owen was appointed foreign secretary on 22 February and chaired meetings of the Council for the next four months. His transformation from minister of state to president of the Council of Ministers seemed effortless and was widely admired. He was a stimulating house guest. Over working dinners and at breakfast before we left for the Charlemagne, we discussed Council business frankly and with vigour and, on the whole, the conclusions we reached proved sound.

The fisheries policy was not our only headache. The site for the Community's experimental thermonuclear fusion project had to be selected. The United Kingdom was keen to see the project, known as the Joint European Torus, or 'JET' for short, located at Culham in Oxfordshire within easy reach of our installations at Harwell. But we had rivals. The Energy Council met on the morning of Tuesday, 29 March, under the chairmanship of Tony Benn and ended, thankfully without controversy, at 4.30 p.m. (Brussels time). This was followed after an interval of an hour and a half by the meeting of the Research Council which was to discuss the site for JET. On this occasion Gerald Kaufman, the minister of state at the Department of Industry, took the chair; Tony Benn occupied the United Kingdom seat. Both Gerald Kaufman and I thought it was understood that the case for Culham would be pressed by Tony Benn, but he remained silent for most of the meeting and indifferent to the notes Kaufman sent to him from time to time. Suspending the session for a working dinner and then again in the small hours to allow for individual consultation with other ministers – a tactic often employed when deadlock was in prospect – was of no avail and Kaufman closed the meeting without agreement at 4.15 a.m. I thought it courteous to remain out of earshot when Gerald Kaufman spoke to Tony Benn as they left the Council building.

Before our presidency began we had set ourselves limited objectives. When it ended with a meeting of the European Council in London on the last two days of June 1977, we could look back on some successes. In the end progress was made on fisheries; the debate on the next enlargement of the Community was opened; despite a difficult passage in the Council of Ministers, Portugal's application to join was endorsed; the Sixth Directive on Value Added Tax was settled. Though modest, these were achievements. But the verdict of our partners was that, in political terms, we had been insensitive to common goals and had shown overt preference for our national interests. They had not seen evidence of the total commitment Harold Wilson had spoken of two years earlier. On the other hand, no one criticised the way in which we had run the presidency. On Saturday, 2 July – a glorious summer day – Jean and I invited our staff, their wives and their husbands to a celebration in our garden. Notwithstanding our regard for Guy Salisbury-Jones, we decided that the end of the first United Kingdom presidency merited champagne. I read out a message from David Owen. "In all the mass of comment about the British presidency," he wrote, "there is one consistent factor – namely recognition of the efficiency with which our presidency has been conducted. I hope everyone in UKrep will see this as a justified tribute to your work."

For six months the entire staff of UKrep had worked long hours, long days and weeks and had demonstrated that Community business could be conducted effectively and expeditiously and with British tact and courtesy. They were, without question, the best organised, most competent and most dedicated group I had ever worked with. This was a proud day.

❖

Once the burden of the presidency had been laid aside there was time to think of other things. Not long after arriving in Brussels I learned that Terry Streeton,[5] the head of the Joint Administration Office, which serviced not only UKrep but also the UK Delegation to NATO and the British Embassy to Belgium, held a private pilot's licence and was looking for a flying partner. I had resumed flying on returning to England from New York and was delighted to have a new opportunity. Light aircraft could be hired at a well-equipped grass airfield at Grimbergen north of Brussels. Terry and I soon discovered that private flying in the Low Countries was regarded as a normal family activity, especially at weekends. We also admired the superior standard of the facilities at airfields catering for light aircraft. From Grimbergen we flew over the Dutch border to Midden Zeeland on the Walcheren peninsula, to Ghent and to Amougies across the French border. At our destination we would change places so that each of us had an opportunity to earn flying hours as pilot while the other acted as navigator. We had a problem at Amougies. Power lines straddled the countryside to the west of the runway. As the wind came from that direction I had to make a short take-off. This meant applying full throttle at the end of the runway with the brakes on and then releasing them to gain maximum speed as quickly as possible. Even so our rate of climb was inadequate and, when the stall warning sounded, I had to bank steeply to port well below recommended height for doing so. We reported this experience to the owner of the aircraft on our return. He made a cursory examination and told us that an insect had lodged in the tube which indicates airspeed and that we must have had more speed than we thought. Terry and I were doubtful. If that were true, what had activated the stall warning?

Two weeks later we flew once more to Ghent. It was again my turn to fly the return leg. After take-off it seemed we had too little airspeed. I had difficulty in maintaining height let alone gaining it. I managed without stalling to coax the aircraft up to about 500 hundred feet, but in level flight my maximum speed was only 75 knots – too little for comfort – and even at this speed I began to lose height. Terry selected a course over open country and reported our situation to Grimbergen. The control tower told us to hold to our course and to come straight in when we reached the airfield. Meanwhile, they were keeping all other aircraft away. Terry and I rehearsed our emergency landing drill and crossed our fingers. Familiar landmarks came and went, but slowly. At an altitude of about 300 feet we saw the Grimbergen runway ahead and landed a few minutes later. As soon as we had parked the aircraft, we went to the tower to express our thanks to the controllers. They required us to write a report on the incident and our earlier experience on the return flight from Amougies. We learned later that the owner of the aircraft had had his licence revoked. It emerged that he had failed to renew the aircraft's certificate of airworthiness and an inspection had shown that it was not in flying condition. How this had not been discovered before remained unclear. Terry Streeton had not relished sending our 'Mayday' message, but we did enjoy walking away after the safe landing.

During the presidency David Gore-Booth and I went to London every Friday to report to ministers and to the coordinating committee in the cabinet office on what had happened the previous day at Coreper and to discuss business for the following week. This procedure had proved so effective that it was decided to continue it after the presidency. But David's presence was no longer necessary. I took the first British

Airways flight out of Brussels every Friday morning. This was the aircraft which had made the last flight from London the previous day and was therefore ready to take off on time regardless of any previous delays. And in the latter part of 1977 there were plenty. These were caused by cracks appearing on the wings of some Trident aircraft and a baggage handlers' dispute at Heathrow. After finishing my business in London, I was often kept waiting for some hours for a flight back to Brussels.

I heard by chance that the Ministry of Defence had an arrangement with an air taxi firm at Stapleford in Essex. Certain officials from the ministry attending meetings at NATO headquarters in Brussels returned to England on Friday evenings. It was both economical and convenient for them to be picked up at Zaventem by a six-seater light aircraft belonging to Eric Thurston's air taxi and air ambulance firm. This aircraft, I discovered, travelled out empty every Friday afternoon. UKrep made a deal. Thanks to the one hour difference between the United Kingdom and the continent, I could complete my consultations in London in time to be driven from Whitehall to Stapleford to take the outward flight. Five minutes after arriving at Stapleford and showing my passport to a customs and immigration officer, I was airborne. When I told Eric Thurston that I held a private pilot's licence, he said that the time had come for me to learn to fly what he called a real aircraft. The real aircraft in question was twin-engined – either a Piper Aztec, Navajo or Apache, and I took the controls after take-off from Stapleford and relinquished control before landing at Zaventem. On arrival we taxied to the general aviation terminal. I showed my passport to a customs and immigration official and was on my way home by car within two minutes of switching off the engines.

On one of the first of these flights the pilot asked me at what height I wanted to cross the North Sea. When I hesitated he suggested 4,500 feet. We reported our route to Southend air traffic control and climbed steadily through thick cloud. I was preparing to level off as the altimeter approached the 4,500 mark when we suddenly emerged into bright sunshine and skimmed along the top of the cloud cover as though we were skiing across an endless snow-field. The pilot revealed his secret. He had returned from Belgium only a couple of hours earlier, had noted the height of the clouds and rightly thought I would enjoy the experience. Over the next year I made numerous flights between Stapleford and Brussels, sometimes entirely on instruments when the weather was really dirty, and learned to appreciate the difference between flying the unpretentious single-engined Cessna and Eric Thurston's 'real aircraft'. I was disappointed when towards the end of 1978 the Ministry of Defence had to end this agreeable arrangement.

❖

Weekends, when no meeting of the Council was scheduled for the beginning of the working week, provided opportunities for other activities. Some members of our staff expressed an interest in the history of the First World War and so we arranged a number of visits to the battlefields and war cemeteries. In order to make the best use of our time, one member of our group would circulate a brief account of the events on a particular sector of the western front. We copied contemporary maps from histories of the war, and colleagues in the embassy in Paris, who were keen to take part in the visits to the battlefields in France, brought with them up-to-date maps published by the French ordnance survey.

Our first excursion was to the Ypres salient. The party consisted of members of UKrep and their wives and friends; these included Dieter von Brühl of the German Representation and his wife, Mariotty. We arranged to meet in a cafe in the centre of Ypres, now known by its Flemish name – Ieper. After coffee and briefing by our volunteer guide for this tour, we set off for Messines, south of Ieper. The siege-war masterpiece, as the military historian Liddell Hart described it, was an offensive planned by General Plumer, commanding the British Second Army, which led to the capture of the strategically important Messines ridge. The attack was preceded by the simultaneous explosion at 3.10 a.m. on 7 June 1917 of nineteen mines containing 600 tons of explosives. Although the Ypres battlefield is now speckled with modern farms and villages, many of the huge craters can still be seen. They are now circular ponds, in some cases used as watering holes for cattle. The largest, Spanbroekmolen, was known to soldiers of the Second Army as 'Lone Tree Crater' and is now 'The Pool of Peace'. It is kept as nature remade it by Toc H, an organisation set up after the First World War to counter hate and foster comradeship. 'Toc H' was the phonetic alphabet equivalent of 'T H', which stood for Talbot House, the original headquarters of the society in Poperinghe in Belgium. Across the ripples on the surface of the water framed by bulrushes, we could see Mount Kemmel to the south and the spires of Ypres to the north.

By contrast, the Somme battlefields were virtually unaltered and we could find our way by using the 1916 maps. On either side of the road between Albert and Bapaume which divided the battlefield, many of the sites of the battles have been preserved. The trenches, now grass-covered, still contained barbed wire – of a much heavier gauge than today's equivalent – as well as pickets and pieces of weaponry. The woods of dreadful memory to the south of the road – Delville, Mametz, Bazentin – were wired off. These contain so many unexploded shells and grenades that they are considered unsafe. Every autumn, those who farmed the surrounding fields ploughed up barrowloads of shrapnel pellets, cartridges, grenades and heavier relics, such as artillery shells, which they would stack by the side of the road to be collected and detonated by French army engineers. Shells with copper rings for setting the fuse are identified as British because, as one farmer told us, "the British were richer in those days than us French".

On one of our visits to the Somme battlefield Dieter von Brühl was accompanied by his father, who had taken part in the battle in July 1916. We drove along the road towards Bapaume to where the German front line had been. We left Dieter, Mariotty and his father at this point and moved on. Later in the day Dieter told us that his father had found the site of his trench. This upset him and Dieter asked if he was recallimg his comrades. "No," the elder von Brühl replied, "I remembered what it was like to be here."

In the southern Belgian town of Mons, through an introduction by one of our Belgian friends, we were able to visit the Bell Tower, which looms over Castle Square, and climb up to see the carillon in action; this had miraculously survived two world wars. From Castle Square we went to the railway station at Obourg, from the roof of which Corporal Thomas of the Royal Irish Dragoon Guards fired the first shot by a soldier of the British Expeditionary Force on 22 August 1914. The small cemetery contains British and German graves and, a short walk away, a plaque marks the spot where a soldier of the Canadian army fired the last shot in November 1918.

Having spent time on the Ypres salient and on the Somme, Jean and I were anxious to make a pilgrimage to the site of the other great cauldron of the Western Front, Verdun. I asked my driver, Theo Maes, to work out a route for our next visit to the European Assembly in Strasbourg which would enable us to do this on the way. When we left Brussels the sky was overcast and we ran into thick mist as we approached the Ardennes. We made slow progress; at times the mist was so thick that we had to stop to check that we were still on the right road. When we reckoned that we were only a kilometre or so from Verdun I told Theo that I feared our detour had been in vain; we would not see a thing. A minute later we rounded a bend in the road and suddenly were in bright sunshine. Theo said: "It seems someone wants you to make this visit." Ahead of us, on the edge of the Bois de Caures, stood the memorial to Colonel Driant and his two depleted battalions of Chasseurs who, for two days in February 1916, had withstood the full weight of the German assault before they were overrun. Driant's warnings about the enemy build-up had been ignored and resented by his superiors. To the people of France his heroism became a legend. The sun continued to shine as we inspected Fort Vaux and Douaumont, walked through the forest of white crosses in the French cemetery, and looked down on the 'Voie Sacrée' along which for months on end buses brought up fresh lambs to the slaughter.

Shortly before we left Brussels Theo Maes learned from one of his friends of a recent discovery which he felt sure would interest us. Jean and I accepted his suggestion that he and his friend take us at the weekend to Wijtschate, a village at the southern edge of the Messines ridge. There we were shown a German shaft, wood-lined and over forty feet deep, which led to galleries where mines would have been laid. The entrance to this shaft had been discovered a few weeks earlier by the son of a museum curator when chasing a wounded rabbit which disappeared down a hole. Further excavations revealed trenches with human remains and the remnants of uniforms and personal equipment of the type worn in 1914. Of particular interest was that, according to the curator's researches, these trenches had at one time been occupied by the 16th Bavarian Reserve Infantry Regiment, one of whose messengers was Corporal Adolf Hitler.

In December 1977 I was told that the leader of the Opposition would be visiting Brussels and would like to meet me. I invited her and her party, which included Ian Gilmour, John Davies, Douglas Hurd and John Stanley to stay with us. Mrs Thatcher had a number of speaking engagements and meetings with Belgian politicians, but we arranged for her to visit Ukrep on her last day in Brussels. At a working dinner at our house the previous evening I rehearsed with senior members of the staff the points we intended to cover and tried to anticipate the questions Mrs Thatcher would raise. This turned out to be a needless exercise. As soon as she entered our conference room and before I could set the scene by telling her what was happening in the Community, Mrs Thatcher began to tell us what should be happening and continued to do so throughout the meeting. As she left, her companions led us to believe that this performance, brilliant as it was if not wholly realistic, was not unusual.

Less turbulent were private weekend visits by Edward Heath, and a formal visit in November 1978 by the Prince of Wales who, to the delight of my Coreper colleagues, spent over an hour at one of our regular meetings. Meanwhile, the Council had been continuing the laborious brick-upon-brick construction of Europe. In the autumn of 1977, after skilful lobbying in Community capitals, Culham was accepted as the site for the JET project. At the same time, Roy Jenkins, who had succeeded Ortoli as President of the Commission, delivered a lecture at Florence in which he recommended that the next phase in the development of the Community should be a leap towards economic and monetary union. This initiative was one inspiration for the proposal by Chancellor Schmidt and President Giscard at the European Council in Bremen in July 1978 that a zone of monetary stability be established in western Europe in response to the breakdown of the Bretton Woods system and the economic disturbances which followed the oil price rises of 1973 and 1974. The debate this provoked resulted in the establishment of the European Monetary System.

While Roy Jenkins' proposals on economic and monetary union attracted the attention of the world press, another passage in his Florence lecture, which I thought could be of comparable importance in the long term, was ignored. In this he argued that the Community should be given only those functions "which will, beyond reasonable doubt, deliver significantly better results because they are performed at a Community level . . . we must equally leave to member States functions which they can do equally well or better on their own." That this was not picked up by the press was a disappointment. When drafting the Florence lecture, Crispin Tickell,[6] Roy Jenkins' chef de cabinet, had consulted me privately about certain passages. He and I shared the view that the Commission was often too ready to seek ways of extending the competence of the Community and in so doing caused unnecessary irritation to ordinary citizens. This early definition of subsidiarity was one product of our discussion. Although Roy Jenkins was able to persuade his colleagues at their annual retreat the following year that the Commission should in future submit proposals to the Council only if, among other things, the action proposed could not be undertaken as well, or better, at national level, there was little evidence in subsequent years that this agreement was being strictly observed. Although opportunities arose to do so, for example when the Single European Act was agreed in 1986, it was not until 1991 at Maastricht that the principle of subsidiarity was enshrined in a Treaty. This reflects little credit on attitudes and priorities in Brussels then and later.

The negotiations with Greece dragged on. The Commission had from the beginning expressed misgivings about the effect on the Community of the accession of Greece, but President Giscard and, to a lesser extent, Genscher, the German foreign minister, seemed determined to bring them to a quick conclusion. Concessions were made against the better judgment of the Commission and several members of the Council and an agreement was finally concluded. In disregard of past practice and without consulting his colleagues, Giscard announced that the signature ceremony would take place in Athens in May 1979. What personal interest if any Giscard had in making such an arrangement no one knew. One of my more cynical colleagues said that we should realise that the mantle of European civilisation once borne by Greece had fallen on the shoulders of the French president.

❖

On the morning of 22 March 1979 I received the dreadful news of the murder of my friend and colleague Richard Sykes, our ambassador in The Hague. Later in the day we heard that the Belgian neighbour of a senior member of the NATO delegation had also been killed – a tragic instance of mistaken identity. Once again we were conscious of the stench of evil.

Security measures were immediately put in place to protect the three ambassadors in Belgium, the other two being John Killick, my NATO counterpart, and Peter Wakefield, the ambassador to Belgium, as well as other Britons in prominent positions. The fact that a Belgian had been murdered outside his home in Brussels outraged opinion throughout the country. Naturally our freedom of movement was circumscribed but, on the basis of the expert advice we were given, Jean and I were able to carry out our duties without serious inconvenience. On one or two occasions the Council secretariat received telephone calls during meetings of Coreper threatening my life.

The Belgian security services provided me with two bodyguards. One was blond, the other dark, and to Theo, Jean and me they were Starsky and Hutch. They accompanied us everywhere – to and from Ukrep by as many different routes as we could devise, to social events and on our occasional walks in the Forêt de Soignes, through which Wellington's army marched on their way to Waterloo. Marc and Jean-Claude, as they were called, gradually became members of the household. When the Council met in Luxembourg we stopped at the border so that they could hand over their responsibilities to the local security service. Of my two new bodyguards one was short and thin and the other somewhat overweight. As they escorted us into the city, Theo remarked: "I think Starsky and Hutch have been replaced by Laurel and Hardy."

At the end of 1978 David Owen discussed with me the appointment he wanted me to take up when my tour at Ukrep ended. He recognised that the first six months of 1977 when we held the presidency had been arduous and he planned to relieve me in the summer of 1979. However, the political situation at home created problems and in the spring he told me that it would not be sensible for the time being to move me to the post he had in mind. He hoped I would be willing to carry on rather longer. The result of the general election in May 1979 created a new situation and, in the end, it was decided that I should remain in Brussels until the end of October and then return to the Foreign and Commonwealth Office as deputy to the permanent under secretary, Michael Palliser. The Conservative victory brought a new British cast on to the European stage. I accompanied Mrs Thatcher when she made her first appearance at a meeting of the European Council in Strasbourg in June 1979.

❖

During my remaining months in Brussels I had time to reflect on the evolution of the Community and the role the United Kingdom had played over the previous four years.

Much of the work of Coreper and the Council of Ministers was concerned with points of detail, and it was all too easy, but unwise, to lose sight of the underlying political purpose. In choosing a common market as their instrument for integrating the countries of western Europe, the leaders of the European movement in the 1950s drew inspiration from the contribution that the 'Zollverein' – the customs union – had made to the process of unifying Germany in the nineteenth century, as well as from the more recent benefits of trade liberalisation in the three Benelux countries. However, since solutions to many of the Community's problems lay beyond its control, a common market and a customs union had proved an inadequate platform for confronting contemporary and future challenges. This had obliged the Community to move into territories uncharted in the Treaty of Rome – almost always under the pressure of external events.

I was not persuaded that the common market, the subsequent extensions of Community competence and the still immature system for political cooperation would provide a secure platform on which to mobilise Europe's potential, or enable it to recapture the imagination of the citizenry. 'Brick-upon-brick' I could understand. But were the foundations deep and broad enough? It was time, I believed, to extend the area of cooperation beyond the fields of energy, industry, transport and economic and monetary policy. Against the background of uncertain leadership in Washington and the threats to our security and prosperity and to the stability of our societies, I felt that closer collaboration in defence, especially between Britain, France and Germany, would enhance the Community's international stature and provide a more solid and credible basis for 'ever closer union of the peoples of Europe'.

As for the United Kingdom's contribution to the enterprise, I was convinced that, if we were to wield influence when and where we wanted, we had to make greater allowance for the differences in member states' approaches to work in the Community. Because of our involvement in continents beyond Europe, we were inclined to think in global rather than continental terms. The fact that for nine hundred years British sovereignty had not been compromised by defeat in war made us slow to realise that the steady globalisation of the world economy was invalidating traditional concepts of national sovereignty. Then again, Westminster spends weeks and months perfecting proposals for new legislation to take account of every imaginable interest or eventuality, in the expectation that the resulting law or laws will be observed. This contrasts with the continental attitude to the law which is often idealistic in tone. When it was proposed that the Community reach a particular goal by a particular date, the inclination of the cautious British was to seek to establish beyond reasonable doubt that the objective was attainable, whereas our continental partners, no less realistic in practice, were content to treat the stated objective as an aspiration.

These differences in historical experience, tradition and attitude did not alter the essential truth; our destiny was linked to that of our partners in continental Europe. How many graves of British service men and women on continental soil were needed to remind us where our interests lay and where our influence had to be applied? After our own misjudgments in the late 1940s and early 1950s and the rebuff we suffered in 1963, it seemed to me essential that we exploit the opportunity then on offer to play a leading role in shaping the new Europe.

A few days before we left for home, Jean and I stood on a ridge in Artois. The autumn sun was slowly burning off the mist which hung over the village and the farms in the valley. We stood on hallowed ground. Behind us, amid rows of graves aligned with military precision, rose a monument to the young men of many nations who had perished in another great battle. On it was inscribed an appeal for unity among nations and humanity among men which could serve as a motto for all who contribute to the European enterprise:

"Nations, soyez unies; hommes, soyez humains."

18

Power Games

In need of refreshment before what we assumed would be my last post in the public service, Jean and I flew to Kathmandu with two friends at the beginning of December 1979. I had known William Hook, a judge of the Sheriff Court in Scotland, since boyhood. Margo Hook was a leading figure in the British travel industry. On arrival we met our guide and spent the rest of the day sightseeing in the Nepalese capital. In an open window on the upper floor of an old house we saw the solemn face of a young girl who, we were told, had been identified soon after birth as a goddess and would so remain until her tenth or eleventh year. The next day we flew to Pokhara, where we were joined by our porters and immediately began our trek in the foothills of Annapurna.

We climbed steadily for the next several days, camping overnight on the edge of villages with mysterious names – Hengja, Dhampus, Naudanda, Kare – and magnificent views of the Annapurna massif and the forbidding peak of Macchapuchre. The temperature, which was ideal during the day for hill walking, fell rapidly as the sun set and we were glad to wrap up in our sleeping bags as soon as our evening meal was over. The track we followed on the second last day dropped down the side of a steep escarpment to the lake shore at Phewa. From there we walked back to Pokhara to join our flight to Kathmandu and on to Agra. Settled a few hours later in our hotel, we looked out towards the glistening dome of the Taj Mahal framed in the window against a sky reddened by the setting sun. Over the next week, in completing the Agra–Jaipur–Delhi triangle, Jean and I achieved one of our modest ambitions – to share an experience of India. As the aircraft taking us back home gained height and we could see the vast expanse of Delhi below, it was not in my mind that in a matter of weeks I would return, but in a different capacity.

❖

My main responsibility as deputy to the permanent under-secretary was to supervise the conduct of our relations with the developing world. I was due to begin work at the beginning of January 1980, but this plan was brutally interrupted by the Soviet invasion of Afghanistan. On Christmas Day 1979 Soviet troops were airlifted into the capital, Kabul. Two days later, what was portrayed as a coup d'état took place in Kabul. The then president, Hafizullah Amin, was executed. He was succeeded by Babrak Karmal, who had emerged mysteriously from exile in eastern Europe and was believed to be better disposed towards the Soviet Union than his hapless predecessor. In Washington, President Carter denounced Soviet military intervention which, he said, threatened world peace. To this the Russians replied that they had acted in response to an urgent request for help from the Afghan government. By the end of the year Soviet tanks had been seen close to the Khyber Pass on the north west frontier of Pakistan. This induced the Americans to warn that they would defend Pakistan against any aggression.

My immediate task was to offer Peter Carrington, the foreign secretary, an assessment of Soviet intentions and to recommend ways in which we should respond. For this purpose I asked Kelvin White, the head of the south Asian department, to form a small task force to manage the new crisis. It was a fortunate coincidence that at this moment the department directly concerned was led by someone who was especially well informed about the tribal structures and traditions in Afghanistan. Our preliminary assessment was that Soviet intervention had been precipitated by fears in Moscow that the puppet regime of Hafizullah Amin was about to collapse. Apart from the consequences in Afghanistan itself, this could have caused unrest among the Soviet Union's Muslim minorities. As for our response to these events, we believed that the most urgent need was to steady the nerves of other governments in the region who would be feeling exposed. On 2 January 1980 Peter Carrington accepted this advice and preparations were made for him to tour the region. This would provide an opportunity not merely to offer reassurance, but also to assess the impact of the Soviet action in the Middle East and south Asia. I was anxious for two reasons that India be included in the secretary of state's itinerary. First, the Indian government could well have been alarmed by the possibility of additional American military aid being sent to Pakistan; secondly, any criticism of Soviet intervention by India could have a helpful influence on opinion in the rest of the non-aligned world.

On 9 January we flew to Ankara, where we found that the Turkish assessment of Soviet motives coincided broadly with our own. The speed with which Peter Carrington's visit to the Gulf region had been arranged was appreciated both in Muscat by the Sultan and in Riyadh by Prince Faisal, the Saudi foreign minister. More work had to be done when we reached the subcontinent. In Islamabad we had a full day of discussions on 15 January at the ministry of foreign affairs before calling on the president of Pakistan, Zia ul-Haq. During this meeting Peter Carrington offered Pakistan increased development aid.

Early the following morning we flew to Peshawar, where we were briefed on the situation on the Afghan border by the Governor of the North West Frontier Province. From there we were flown by helicopter along the Khyber Pass to a camp which had been established to cater for the large number of refugees who had crossed into Pakistan since the Soviet invasion. Afghan troops manned the frontier which was marked by a large red notice bidding 'Welcome to the Democratic Republic of Afghanistan' in Urdu and English. We then flew to the fort at Landikotal where we witnessed a *jirga* – an assembly of tribespeople in which, in theory, each member of the tribe could take part on an equal basis, it being acknowledged that in practice some participants were more equal than others. The Commissioner for Refugees briefed us on the measures the government of Pakistan were taking to cope with the flow of tribespeople which he expected to continue for some time. After lunch in the Officers' Mess of the Khyber Rifles, we were entertained by the regimental pipe band and tribal dancers. Peter Carrington had disclosed to the commanding officer that I had served during the war on another part of the frontier. This led to my being bombarded with questions, mostly on the theme 'what is different today?' My reply was that the main difference was in the physique of the troops. But, I added, some things had not changed; for example, the pipers still played some tunes too fast.

Later that afternoon we flew from Peshawar to Delhi, where Peter Carrington called on Indira Gandhi in her home. She looked tired and preoccupied. The secretary of state began with a brief account of our visit earlier in the day to the Afghan frontier and the refugee camp. He then set out the reasons for our deep concern at the Soviet action in Afghanistan. In the first place, by the use of overwhelming force, the Soviet Union was seeking to impose on a non-aligned country a style of regime which suited the Soviet Union. But more serious was the risk that Soviet intervention would provoke a response from the other superpower; this would serve neither the interests of the superpowers nor those of the countries of the region. Indira Gandhi did not demur. Indeed, she made no attempt to conceal her own anxieties. Her main fear was that East–West confrontation, hitherto a somewhat distant threat to stability, was being brought to the frontiers of the subcontinent; an increase in Western military aid to Pakistan could disturb the delicate balance. She categorised Soviet action in Afghanistan as 'inadmissible' but, characteristically, was tempted to attribute to the Russians and Americans equal blame for the increase in tension in the area. This, however, did not detract from her evident appreciation of Peter Carrington's initiative in visiting her to share his concerns.

On our return to London on 18 January, the task force reviewed the results of the tour. Our conclusion was that, even though it was likely that before long Soviet forces would be sucked into a guerrilla war they could not win, some signal of our disapproval of their action was needed; at the same time, an effort should be made to rally opposition in the non-aligned world. We had kept in close touch throughout with the Americans and were not surprised when President Carter announced in his State of the Union Message to the Congress on 23 January that any attempt by outside forces to gain control of the Gulf region would be regarded as an assault on the vital interests of the United States. On the following day, in a statement in the House of Lords, Peter Carrington hoisted our signal of disapproval. He announced that export credits for the Soviet Union would not be renewed when these expired in February; that the transfer of sensitive technology would be more tightly controlled; and that food sales and high level contacts would be suspended.

At this point I was able to take advantage of an old acquaintance. Nearly thirty years earlier, David and Jean Newsom had sat on our terrace in Baghdad watching smoke and flames rising from the information office of the United States Embassy which had been attacked by a mob. We had remained in touch since those days. David was now the under-secretary for political affairs in the State Department and was in London comparing assessments of the implications of the Soviet intervention in Afghanistan. Over lunch I briefed him on the results of the foreign secretary's tour and we went on to discuss how best to mobilise the support of non-aligned nations. We concluded that the most effective method would be to present a proposition which the Russians could not reasonably refuse and which should appeal to opinion in the developing world. We drew up a three-point proposal: first, Afghanistan should be recognised as a neutral and non-aligned state; secondly, its neutral and non-aligned status should be guaranteed by neighbouring states, other states in the region and the superpowers; and thirdly, Soviet troops should be withdrawn. David and I agreed that we would each submit this idea to our respective secretaries of state.

Peter Carrington reacted with some enthusiasm and I invited the task force to consider ways of launching this initiative. While options were being examined, we were reminded that we still had some way to go to concert western reactions to the Soviet intervention; the French had expressed reluctance to take part in a meeting the Americans wanted to hold in Bonn on 20 February with representatives of the United Kingdom, France, Germany and Italy to discuss the crisis. In the light of this, we decided that a meeting of foreign ministers of the European

Community due to take place in Rome on 19 February offered the best opportunity to present the proposal which we were confident would be acceptable to the French.

In Rome Peter Carrington told his colleagues that his formula was in line with a resolution of the United Nations General Assembly which had called for respect for the sovereignty, territorial integrity, political independence and non-aligned character of Afghanistan. He added that there was a historical precedent. After the Afghan Wars of the nineteenth century, Afghanistan had acquired what he termed 'unwritten neutrality', guaranteed by both Tsarist Russia and British India. However, this tacit understanding had lapsed with the withdrawal of the imperial presence from the subcontinent in 1947.

The foreign secretary's initiative was warmly endorsed by all his European colleagues and it was published immediately after the meeting as a European Community proposal. The initially lukewarm reaction in Washington suggested that David Newsom had not yet been able to persuade the White House of the merits of the neutrality proposal but, at dinner in London on 21 February, Peter Carrington managed to convince Cyrus Vance, the United States secretary of state, of its tactical value. When ministers of Algeria, Yugoslavia and India – the three radicals in the non-aligned movement – met in Delhi early in March, they reacted negatively to our initiative. Their criticism related ostensibly to our emphasis on 'neutrality' rather than 'non-alignment', but of course their real objection was that the European Community had stolen their clothes.

❖

Although European affairs fell outside my area of responsibility, the prime minister asked me to undertake a particular task in connection with the United Kingdom's contribution to the Community Budget. At the turbulent meeting of the European Council in Dublin at the end of November 1979, Mrs Thatcher had said she was not afraid to precipitate a crisis over this issue. On that occasion no solution had been found, and it had been agreed that another attempt would be made when heads of government met in Luxembourg at the end of April 1980. Following the Dublin Council, Mrs Thatcher had said more than once that she was ready to see progress on a number of outstanding Community issues. She now wanted me, with due discretion, to convey her current thinking to Francesco Cossiga, the prime minister of Italy, who would be in the chair at Luxembourg, and to President Giscard and Chancellor Schmidt.

I travelled to Rome on the morning of 16 April and spent the afternoon with Signor Berlinguer, Cossiga's diplomatic adviser. My message was that what Mrs Thatcher would be prepared to accept on agricultural prices, on fisheries and the regime for sheepmeat – the three other current topics – would be linked to the prospects for an equitable solution of the budget problem. I went on to suggest in outline what the United Kingdom's position on these subjects might be. Berlinguer said that, while he could not commit Cossiga, what I had said would contribute to the personal efforts Cossiga would make to find a solution at Luxembourg.

I breakfasted the following morning at the Quai d'Orsay with Bernard Reymond and Jacques Wahl, the two principal advisers to President Giscard on Community matters. Bernard Reymond's immediate reaction to my opening remarks came straight out of the Couve de Murville diplomatic lexicon. There was clearly a wide gap between our positions, he said; doubts remained about the readiness of the United Kingdom to accept the principles and disciplines of the Community – doubts nourished by our frequent demands for special financial arangements and apparent efforts to undermine the principles of the common agriculture policy and the own resources system. Having fired this salvo, Bernard Reymond, with generally constructive interjections from Wahl, then discussed in detail possible approaches to all the issues which would feature on the Luxembourg agenda. At the end of the meeting I said that the working of the common agriculture policy produced absurdities which everyone acknowledged; seeking to deal with these was not to be construed as an attack on the policy. Likewise, our partners had to understand that the inequitable budget situation coloured the thinking of British ministers about the Community. It was in the general interest that a solution be found as soon as possible.

In Bonn on 18 April, I was obliged to perform in three Acts, which I suppose was appropriate on the banks of the Rhine; Act I with State Secretary Lahnstein at the Finance Ministry; Act II at the Foreign Ministry with State Secretary Lautenschlager; and Act III at the Federal Chancellery with Herr von Staden, the diplomatic adviser to Chancellor Schmidt. All three responded to my opening statement by sharing their ideas about possible solutions to the outstanding problems. What was needed now, they argued, was the will to reach agreement. Lack of flexibility in the recent past had caused the Chancellor concern, but my remarks suggested that we were now entering 'the phase of flexibility'.

In the event, a more generous formula for settling the budget problem was rejected by Mrs Thatcher in Luxembourg only to be accepted a month later, with minor modifications, by Peter Carrington when foreign ministers met in Brussels.

❖

Soon after I had submitted my report on these conversations to Number 10, the prime minister's private secretary crossed Downing Street to call on me. He said that Sir Jack Rampton, the permanent under-secretary at the Department of Energy, was due to retire in July. Would I agree to have my name put forward to succeed him? A reply within the week would be helpful. On reflection over the next few days, the pros seem to outweigh the cons. My new appointment was announced at the end of April 1980.

As a head-of-department-designate I was invited to the dinner the prime minister gave for permanent secretaries at Number 10 on 6 May. I was seated well below the salt and was not required to contribute to the discussion. This was an uncomfortable occasion. My toes curled as my future colleagues raised one objection after another to the prime minister's propositions. Over the four years I had spent in Brussels I had learned from my European Community colleagues the virtues of the 'Yes, but . . . ' as opposed to the 'No, because . . . ' preface to a contrary opinion. If the prime minister had heard more of the former and less of the latter, she might have taken away a slightly less unfavourable impression of the top ranks of the civil service.

On 27 June I left the Foreign and Commonwealth Office for the last time as a member of the Diplomatic Service and Jean and I headed north for a brief holiday hill-walking in the Highlands.

I began work in Thames House on 4 August. As the Department of Energy was one of the smaller ministries, it did not take me long to meet all the staff in their offices. Over the next few weeks I visited energy installations of one kind or another. These included the coal-fired power station at Didcot, the nuclear stations at Windscale and Dounreay, the national control of the Central Electricity Generating Board (the CEGB) and the Thistle Field in the North Sea, owned by the British National Oil Corporation (BNOC). I also met the staff of the Department's Offshore Supplies Office in Glasgow, the Gas Standards Branch in Leicester and the Atomic Energy Authority at Harwell. Sir Derek Ezra, the Chairman of the National Coal Board, invited me to accompany him when he visited Thoresby Colliery in north Nottinghamshire; the installation of new machinery had enabled the colliery to increase production to three thousand tonnes of coal a day. This was my first visit to a coal mine. After we returned to the surface we met managers and representatives of the trade unions from all the pits in the area. Derek Ezra told them that, while the industry faced short term problems, he had no doubt that it had a big future. As was soon to become apparent, he understated the difficulties and overstated the prospects.

One of the first problems I had to tackle was the structure of the department. Pressure was being exerted from the centre to reduce costs and increase efficiency. A Chain of Command Review and the scrutinies conducted by Sir Derek Rayner and his team were important instruments for reform. However, central initiatives which could produce substantial benefits in large departments with numerous executive functions were not necessarily suitable for small policy-oriented departments.

These might in any case have their own ideas for improvements. Within a matter of months I had reduced the complement of under-secretaries and cut the number of deputy secretaries from four to two. In so doing I exceeded the target I had been set by the centre. This did not satisfy the Treasury. They attempted to impose on me a new target to compensate for the failure of other departments to achieve theirs. I refused; it was unacceptable that virtue should be punished and vice condoned. I heard no more. A Rayner scrutiny of the department's international work – always an attraction for sceptical outside economisers – cost some £14,000 and identified potential savings of some £40,000. Meanwhile, a personal initiative by the department's vigorous establishment officer reduced the department's travel and subsistence budget by £300,000 in one year. The only cost to the department was his own intellectual effort.

I inherited no central co-ordinating mechanism and set up a steering committee to concert advice to ministers on policy issues, and a management board to handle staffing and organisational questions. The steering committee consisted of the deputy secretaries, the chief scientist, the economic and legal advisers, the head of the energy policy division and other under-secretaries directly concerned with the subjects under discussion. The secretary of state, David Howell, had brought with him to the department a political adviser from Conservative Central Office. I thought his membership of the committee would serve two purposes: first, having heard the arguments, he would be able to draw on these when advising David Howell; secondly, he could shed light on ministers' thinking. My senior colleagues were uneasy, but in the end agreed with some reluctance. Over the months Michael Portillo proved a useful contributor to the work of the steering committee.

In one of my first conversations with him, David Howell said that I would be disappointed if I imagined I would spend my time thinking strategic thoughts about the long term security of the nation's energy supplies, or ways in which we might develop our relations with other oil-producers. I was more likely to find myself arguing with the nation-alised industries on matters of detail. He was exaggerating, of course, but only slightly. At that time the secretary of state for energy had a statutory responsibility "for securing the effective and coordinated development of coal, petroleum and other minerals and sources of fuel and power in Great Britain and in the Continental Shelf and for promoting economy and efficiency in supply, distribution, use and consumption of fuel and power". So far as the oil industry was concerned, the secretary of state was able to discharge these responsibilities through the system of awarding licences for exploration offshore, even though, apart from the BNOC, that industry was in the private sector. The coal, gas and electricity industries, as well as parts of the nuclear industry, were owned by the state.

From my seat in Thames House, the awkwardness in the relationship between government and state-owned industries was painfully obvious. This derived, it seemed to me, from the original Morrisonian concept of an arm's-length relationship – a relationship in which the enterprise is neither within the embrace of the state nor standing on its own. An arrangement designed to have the best of both worlds had probably, over the years, had the worst. The chairmen of the nationalised industries, who guarded their operational independence with zeal, would complain that their freedom of action had been circumscribed by a shift in policy or a new financial constraint. For his part, the secretary of state could, and from time to time did, find himself obliged to defend actions which were part and parcel of the day-to-day management of the industry. There was tension too within the government – and not always creative – between the Treasury, which controlled the purse strings, and the department of energy which was charged with defining the policy objectives for each industry within the framework of the government's economic strategy. Unlike the harlot in Rudyard Kipling's dictum, it was the secretary of state's prerogative to carry responsibility without adequate power.

❖

In the autumn of 1980 Derek Ezra telephoned to me and to David Howell to warn that a serious situation faced the coal industry. The economic recession had caused a severe drop in the demand for coal and the viability of the industry could come under threat. Without a ban on imports and more support, some pits would have to be closed. This assessment, so far removed from the talk a few weeks earlier of certain 'short term problems' was alarming. While we considered the implications, David Howell alerted the prime minister and other ministers concerned. We knew that pit closures would be opposed by the miners and the memory of the events of 1974 which had led to the fall of the Heath government was still fresh. We were also aware that, although Joe Gormley, the miners' leader, was a comparative moderate, he would not wish to see the industry in rapid decline; and Arthur Scargill was looking over his shoulder from his redoubt in Yorkshire.

David Howell's instinct was against precipitate action. On the other hand, John Moore, the junior minister in the department responsible for relations with the National Coal Board, was rigorously opposed to any concession; we should stand firm. Although stocks of coal at the surface were high because of the drop in demand, it seemed to me that we were not well placed to resist Ezra's demands for an import ban and fresh support to maintain the industry for the time being. Our situation would have been different if we had been warned of the impending crisis several months earlier. Debate in the department continued, but it was common ground that so long as no public reference was made to the scale of any pit closures, the problem might be manageable.

The Coal Board was due to meet leaders of the National Union of Miners on 10 February to discuss the situation. Despite Derek Ezra's assurance that on no account would mention be made of any specific number of pits which might be closed, a list of between twenty and fifty pits due for closure was being publicly discussed as soon as the meeting was over. Whether Ezra's undertaking was breached by accident or design we never learned. This disclosure gave the militants their cue. Strikes began in Kent and South Wales. At a meeting at Downing Street chaired by the prime minister, it was decided to meet the Coal Board's demands. Given the situation in which we had been placed, to suffer a Pyrrhic defeat was the only sensible course.

To escape from the domination of the National Union of Miners which had brought down one government and humiliated another, there was one overriding strategy – to prepare to withstand a prolonged strike. At our request the CEGB provided us with weekly reports on the size of coal stocks at power stations. Copies of these were passed to Number 10. Later we asked the CEGB to prepare a plan for adding substantially and rapidly to these stocks by road and rail and for increasing the use of oil-fired power stations. The advent of Nigel Lawson as energy secretary in the autumn of 1981 and the close interest of the prime minister provided fresh impetus for our operations. Before long coal from the pits was being transported to power stations twenty-four hours a day on the aptly named 'merry-go-round' system. Our aim was to accumulate as much coal at power stations as space would permit. When Arthur Scargill was elected President of the National Union of Miners in 1982, Nigel Lawson invited him to call at Thames House. Scargill's behaviour on this occasion sealed his fate. He painted an ambitious picture of the situation in the industry and its prospects so removed from reality that it was evident there could be no meaningful dealings with him.

My relations with another monolith – the gas industry – were coloured by the personality of the chairman of British Gas Corporation, Sir Denis Rooke. He regarded the gas industry as his personal fief and resented interference from any quarter. He argued that gas was a premium fuel too precious to burn in power stations. It was a tradition that from time to time the permanent under-secretary would discuss mutual concerns over dinner at the Corporation's headquarters in Rivermill House on the Embankment. These occasions provided Denis Rooke with the opportunity to castigate the department, individual ministers and the government in general for their policies and attitude on a range of issues. As the evening wore on I received the full force of his notoriously violent language. His reaction when Sally Oppenheim, the minister for consumer affairs, proposed the privatisation of gas showrooms was one of uncontrolled fury. At the end of these disagreeable encounters, Jack Smith, Rooke's forbearing deputy, would accompany me to the front entrance apologising on the way for his boss's behaviour. I told Jack I was the lucky one; I did not go to Rivermill House every day.

Sir Frank Tombs, the Chairman of the Electricity Council – the body which grouped the boards which distributed electricity – was restive and paid me an early call to explain why. He felt he had been misled when he had been appointed in 1977 by the then secretary of state, Tony Benn. He had been assured that legislation would be introduced to change the structure of the industry in such a way that the chairmanship of the Council would be merged with that of the CEGB to create a structure similar to that in Scotland. When David Howell became energy secretary, he abandoned this plan. Papers in the department confirmed this series of events and I arranged for Frank Tombs' wish to end his contract to be met and for him to be compensated.

We had two main problems with the electricity industry. These concerned the high level of prices industry had to pay for its supply, and the bulk supply tariff. This tariff, which was the price the regional boards who distributed electricity throughout the country paid to the CEGB, was the main element in the cost to the consumer, and the department had constant difficulty in ascertaining precisely how it was calculated. A similar problem was to arise some years later over the costs of de-commissioning superannuated nuclear power stations.

The British nuclear industry had led the world when the first station to supply the public with electricity generated by nuclear power came into operation at Calder Hall in 1956. This pre-eminent position had been lost through failure to consolidate success, ministerial indecision and argument within the industry over the choice of technology. The Steam Generated Heavy Water Reactors and, later, the Advanced Gas-Cooled Reactors (AGRs) had proved costly to build and less efficient than the American-designed Pressurised Water Reactors (PWRs), which had proved highly successful in France. Walter Marshall, the Chairman of the Atomic Energy Authority, whom Nigel Lawson was to bring in to chair the CEGB in 1982, had for long advocated investment in the PWR. He had his way when, after several fallow years, David Howell and George Younger, the secretary of state for Scotland, announced that, while work already in hand on one AGR at Heysham in Lancashire and another at Torness near Dunbar in Scotland would continue, a PWR would be built alongside an existing conventional power station at Sizewell in Suffolk; a public inquiry would be held before any contracts were let for work at Sizewell. Sir Frank Layfield, an eminent Queen's Counsel, was invited to conduct this Inquiry and he called on me for his initial briefing. After only a few minutes' conversation I was convinced that his appointment was inspired.

The future of our research at Dounreay into the next stage of nuclear power generation – the fast-breeder reactor – needed to be reviewed in the light of the decisions on the two AGRs and the projected PWR at Sizewell, escalating costs and changes in forecast demand for energy. In the department we accepted that there could still be a need for this technology in the early years of the twenty-first century. But there was a strong case for combining our research effort with others. This was the background to a visit I paid to Washington at the beginning of October 1982. When I met President Reagan's scientific adviser at the White House and spoke later to the chairmen of the relevant congressional committees, I stressed that we had not yet completed our study of the options for our fast reactor programme. We had noted, however, that a recent report of the Government Accounting Office in Washington had pushed back the date when the fast reactor would be needed. Even though we did not share all the views expressed in the report, the present seemed an appropriate time to re-examine the basis for international collaboration. It was clear from the responses I received that, while they would welcome collaboration at some stage, the Americans were in no hurry; in their opinion commercial development of the fast reactor was unlikely this century. They suggested that design work on a large demonstration breeder reactor should continue and ultimately be conducted on as broad an international basis as possible. They specifically mentioned the French and Japanese as eventual partners.

My visit to Washington coincided with a minor transatlantic crisis. A number of continental European countries had entered into contracts with the Soviet Union for the supply of Siberian natural gas. This had alarmed the White House who were fearful of the political implications of what could become undue dependence on Soviet gas. The Department of Commerce had been so hasty as to impose sanctions against the European companies concerned. No one I met supported the action which had been taken and discussion focused on how best to extricate the Administration. Before long good sense prevailed.

❖

The department of energy's relations with the oil companies posed few problems. Preparations for the periodical award of licences for offshore exploration naturally caused the companies some apprehension but, since both the procedure and the results met with general satisfaction, our relationships were not impaired. My meetings with representatives of the United Kingdom Offshore Operators Association rarely involved discussion of matters of principle, but these afforded an opportunity for complaints to be aired and dealt with at an early stage, and for improvements in procedures to be suggested. When I visited offshore platforms and other installations, I was gratified to receive unsolicited expressions of appreciation for the work of the department. However, we and the companies did suffer one disappointment. Much effort had been put into a proposal to lay a network of pipes in the North Sea to carry the gas then being burnt off at the various platforms to a terminal on the north east coast of Scotland. At a cost of £4 billion this environmentally-friendly 'gas-gathering pipeline' would add appreciably to our gas reserves. Planning was at an advanced stage when the Treasury withdrew their support and the project was abandoned.

The department's chief scientist, Tony Challis, who had already had a distinguished career with Imperial Chemical Industries, kept a close eye on the development of alternative sources of power. He and I agreed that research which seemed unlikely to produce results within a reasonable timescale should cease to be funded by the department. Windmills and solar power were the front runners; others proved disappointing. Tony was enthusiastic about the prospects for EOR – enhanced oil recovery. This was a process whereby the ten per cent of oil normally left in an oilfield when, in theory, it had been pumped dry could be extracted. This process, if feasible, would prolong the life of the North Sea oilfield. It was later to become an integral part of the oil companies' operations offshore.

Much attention was devoted to conservation – a term about which most of us in the department had reservations. It suggested discomfort, abstinence, even deprivation. There were other possibilities. The department organised regular conferences to convey our message to industry, commerce and the public sector; these had the more appealing title 'Energy Management Conferences'. When we came to consider establishing our energy conservation office as a separate entity, I suggested that it be called the Energy Efficiency Office. The staff concerned seemed to like their new name.

I had known Nigel Lawson when I was a government spokesman and he one of the journalists who asked the difficult questions. He thought the department could more aptly be described as the Department of Nationalised Industries, and I was not surprised when, soon after his arrival, he suggested that I set my steering committee to work on options for the future of the gas and electricity industries. This task brought out the best in my colleagues. We were not required to argue whether these industries should continue to be owned by the state or transferred to the private sector, as was happening to the BNOC. We therefore concentrated on the functions of the industries, on the connections between these functions, and the appropriate organisational and management structures.

The meetings Nigel Lawson held in his office to discuss the steering committee's conclusions provided entertainment and stimulus of a high order. He would have in his hand a rather untidy looking sheet of paper covered with notes. He would begin by asking a number of questions – some seemingly tangential, others designedly provocative. The atmosphere having been warmed up in this way, we would then review the steering committee's various propositions. Before drawing the meeting to a close, Nigel Lawson would ensure that all those who had not yet spoken had a chance to do so. He would then ask me to sum up and to propose the next steps. When others had dispersed, he often asked me and Julian West, his imperturbable private secretary, to stay behind not so much to conduct a post-mortem as to enable him to extend his own thoughts on the issues we had been discussing. These occasions were some compensation for the frustrations caused by the problems of the nationalised industries.

As no successor had been identified by the time I was due to retire, I agreed to a request from the head of the civil service that I stay on at the department until the end of 1982. As a last favour Nigel Lawson wanted me to join the board of Britoil as a government director. On privatisation the government had retained a substantial shareholding in the company. This gave it certain rights, one of which was to appoint two directors to the board of the company. I had seen enough of the chairman of the company to wonder whether he would welcome to his board someone who had worked so closely with the secretary of state, but I agreed, with little enthusiasm. The cabinet office were afraid that my appointment would be seen as a case of 'jobs for the boys' and prescribed an interval of several months before I could join the company. I was in no hurry.

During my remaining months in the department I tried an experiment. A number of members of the staff had been seconded for specified periods to private companies, either in the City or in industry. This scheme had worked well, even though in some cases our staff accepted offers from their temporary hosts of permanent jobs. I did not object to this, since I thought that any injection into the City or industry of people with experience of work in government was to the national good. At the same time I was keen to encourage inward secondments. The editor of the *Financial Times* agreed to my suggestion that Sue Cameron, one of his newspaper's energy correspondents, might work for some months in one of our divisions. When John Moore and other junior ministers heard about this they were alarmed. "She will come in, keep notes and write up lots of gossip about us when she leaves." I said that I was sure she would do nothing of the kind; she would leave the department with a far deeper understanding of how we worked and would thereafter see energy problems from a new and better-informed angle. Nigel Lawson shared my view and urged his colleagues to relax. When Sue Cameron began her secondment I asked her to let me have her impressions after, say, six weeks. When she returned she told me the experience so far had been quite different from what she had expected. She had been struck by the readiness with which she had been accepted, by the degree of commitment of her new colleagues, and by their willingness to work long hours day after day.

On the eve of my departure, Sue Cameron's *Financial Times* colleague, Ray Dafter, asked me if I thought the department of energy should survive as a separate entity. An awkward question. The energy sector was in a state of prolonged transition. The contribution coal made to meeting our energy needs had dropped from 50 per cent in 1970 to 35 per cent and was still falling. During the same period, the contribution of oil had risen from 9 per cent to over 40 per cent; natural gas now met nearly 20 per cent of demand. Fifteen oilfields were already in production offshore and eleven more were being developed. The role of the state sector had already been reduced by the conversion of BNOC into Britoil plc and, when the work my steering committee had begun on the structure of the gas and electricity industries had been refined, it was inevitable that these too would be transferred to the private sector. If at the time Nigel Lawson had been correct in describing it as the Department of Nationalised Industries, my answer to Ray Dafter's question had to be: "For the present, yes. But watch this space."

I left Thames House and the public service on 21 December 1982 and, as predicted by several colleagues from elsewhere in Whitehall who had preceded me, I did so with few regrets.

19

The Missing Link

Before my retirement from the public service, Jean and I had agreed that I would decline any offer of a Monday-to-Friday job. Experience had taught us that Monday-to-Friday could all too soon become Sunday-to-Saturday, and we had other interests to pursue. Our first task was to find somewhere to live. We stored our furniture, sold our London flat and used our weekend cottage in Berkshire as a base for our search.

We were not left undisturbed for long. The voice on the telephone said: "Out of sight you may be, but not out of mind." The British Council in Germany were organising a series of seminars at which middle-rank civil servants in the Land governments could discuss political, economic and cultural topics relating to contemporary Britain. They hoped I would be prepared to take part in some of these to talk on energy policy. Others would be speaking on such subjects as Britain and Europe, industrial strategy, education, administration and the media. I attended two of these seminars – the first at Schloss Hohenkammer north of Munich in March 1983, and the second at Lenzkirch-Saig in the Black Forest in May. What impressed me most was that these German civil servants, who worked for the governments of Bavaria and Baden–Württemberg, were able to debate a range of current issues in fluent and grammatical English and were well informed about the United Kingdom and international affairs generally. They were a splendid advertisement for the federal system of government in Germany.

❖

Late in March I received another telephone call which was to open the gate to a brave new world. An assistant secretary in the Department of Trade and Industry had a message for me from Kenneth Baker, the minister for industry and information technology. I might be aware, he said, that at a meeting in Nairobi in the autumn of 1982, the ITU – the International Telecommunication Union – had decided, given the critical role communications played in economic and social development, to establish an international commission to recommend ways of encouraging the expansion of telecommunications across the world. The commission, which would be of manageable size, was to be formed in May and, since I had experience of the United Nations and developing countries and had handled technical subjects in the recent past, Kenneth Baker hoped I would agree to be the British member of the commission. When I said that before replying I should need to know what this would entail, I was invited to visit the department to be briefed. But that was not all. The government wanted the United Kingdom to have the chairmanship of this commission; would I be prepared to assume this responsibility? I said that, once again, I should welcome more information about the implications; this too could be discussed. And there was one more thing. Someone was needed to chair the United Kingdom National Committee for World Communications Year; the Department would give me all possible support if I would take this on too. I asked when World Communications Year would be. Oh, was the reply, it began last January.

❖

When I visited the department a few days later, I met some of those who had been preparing the United Kingdom's contribution to World Communications Year. This had two main objectives – to offer developing countries increased training opportunities, and to promote greater awareness, especially among the young, of the importance of efficient communications. The communications industry in the United Kingdom was providing practical support. Various groups and companies were organising conferences, exhibitions, films and publications – many aimed at schools – which underlined not only the benefits modern telecommunications were bringing to the country, but also Britain's commitment to help in improving systems in the developing world.

I also learned more about the background. In November 1981 the General Assembly of the United Nations had 'recognised the fundamental importance of communications infrastructures as an essential element in the economic and social development of all countries'. The Assembly had also recorded its conviction that 'a World Communications Year would provide the opportunity for all countries to undertake an in-depth review and analysis of their policies on communications development and stimulate the accelerated development of communications infrastructures.' This convoluted prose expressed a serious concern. I was already aware that there had been a strong feeling in the General Assembly for some years that in many developing countries communications had been accorded too low a priority. When investment decisions had been taken at national level, preference had been given more often than not to industry and agriculture, the social services and the armed forces.

The Department of Trade and Industry provided me with an office and a private secretary. They also recruited as my special adviser John Harper who, as a former managing director of the Inland Division of British Telecom, had extensive experience of creating and managing telecommunications systems. He was to play the same role of candid adviser, acute commentator, tireless supporter and loyal friend as Janet Whiting had played during the three years I spent at Number 10.

Richard Butler, the Australian secretary general of the ITU, visited London in April to discuss plans for the commission. I learned during his visit that Jonathan Solomon, the under-secretary in charge of the telecommunications division in the department, had played a leading role in the events which led to the decision to set up the commission. At Nairobi the previous autumn a characteristic North–South dispute over development aid threatened to split the ITU. Developing country delegates were deeply concerned at the widening gap in the distribution of telecommunications world wide. Of the 600 million telephones in the world, three-quarters were concentrated in nine advanced industrialised countries. There were more telephones in Tokyo than in the entire African continent. To redress the imbalance, or at least narrow the gap, developing countries were seeking a substantial transfer of resources. The immediate tactical issue at Nairobi had been how best to respond to this demand. The solution – an independent commission to establish the facts and recommend remedies – owed much to Jonathan Solomon's diplomacy.

Butler had spent several months since the Nairobi conference recruiting members of the commission. He seemed to approve of my credentials and in May he was able to announce the names of the seventeen members of the commission – five from western industrialised countries, two from eastern Europe and the remaining ten from different regions of the developing world. Members were invited to assemble in Geneva on 24 October 1983 for the first meeting. The title the commission had been given was another example of convoluted verbiage – 'The Voluntary Independent International Commission for World-Wide Telecommunications Development'.

Before travelling to Geneva I had another task. To mark World Communications Year the ITU had arranged three regional conferences on the general theme of 'telecommunications for development'. The department suggested that, if I were to chair the independent commission, attendance at one of these would enable me to learn about the main concerns of developing countries at first hand. My experience at the Latin American regional conference at San José in Costa Rica in August 1983 proved the merit of this advice. In the first place, the Costa Rican Minister of Information and Communications, Armando Vargas Araya, who chaired the conference, was also to be a member of the commission. But, apart from this, the conference attracted a number of experts, both in the industry and in academia, who had been studying the link between investment in telecommunications and economic development in different parts of the world for some years. Heather Hudson, a professor at the University of Austin in Texas, had identified sectors in predominantly rural economies where improvements in telecommunications had brought perceptible benefits. John Gilbert of the Canadian Department of Communications had observed the enhancement of the quality of life of the Inuit people of the Arctic Circle. Listening to them and others accelerated my ascent of the learning curve.

This was my first visit to central America. The need to change flights at Miami entailed a tedious wait in the heat and humidity and it was dark as I entered my room in the Hotel Cariari in San José. When I turned on the light I saw in a corner of the ceiling a moth of dimensions appropriate to an extra in a science-fiction horror movie. I retreated to the reception desk where the clerk was reassuring. With the aid of a ladder and a towel he removed the docile creature and life improved from then on. Armando Vargas wanted me to see the effects of the policies his government had instituted and arranged for one of his staff to take me on a tour of the surrounding region. I saw none of the poverty or squalor I was expecting, only ordered activity and evidence of modest prosperity. As we turned into a small town, a large group of children in neat school uniforms were awaiting their turn in groups to cross the road; this might have been Switzerland. The town jail, I learned, might have to close for lack of prisoners. What was the secret, I asked; after all, across the border to the north, Nicaragua was in turmoil. The answer, I was told, was simple. For years it had been agreed policy in Costa Rica not to spend state income on armed forces but rather on services essential to the economy; and these included not only education and health, but also communications.

When I arrived in Geneva on the eve of the first meeting of the commission, I was assured that there would be wide support for my chairmanship of the commission. I spent the rest of that evening drafting the programme of work I thought the commission should set itself. This embodied ideas in the material I had read, suggestions by my advisers and the conclusions I had drawn from the conference in Costa Rica. In the afternoon of the following day, 23 October 1983, members of the commission and their advisers assembled in one of the small conference rooms in the headquarters of the ITU. I was elected chairman by a unanimous vote and four vice-chairmen from different regions of the developing world were also elected. The ostensible intention was that they would support me in steering the work of the commission; in the event this did not happen, but the gesture was appropriate and appreciated.

The membership of the commission was impressive. The four others from the industrialised world would bring valuable knowledge and experience to our work. Dr Koji Kobayashi was the founder, chairman and chief executive officer of the NEC Corporation of Japan. He had been among the first to exploit the marriage of the technologies of the computer and communications. William Ellinghaus had begun his career climbing telegraph poles and was now president of AT&T – the American Telephone and Telegraph Company; for him the American dream had become reality. Like Bill Ellinghaus, Louis-Joseph Libois, the chairman of the Caisse Nationale des Télécommunications, had been a telecommunicator throughout his working life. With the personal encouragement of his President and a generous budget, he had mounted the operation which had provided France with one of the most modern and efficient telecommunications networks in the world. Volkmar Köhler had been a member of the German federal parliament for over ten years and was now a state secretary with special concern for development cooperation.

The two members from eastern Europe were academics. Professor Alexandru Spataru was a specialist in applied electronics. Leonid Varakin was the rector of a national telecommunications institute in the Soviet Union. He was invariably accompanied by an 'adviser' who, because he was never observed to advise, was generally assumed to be his KGB 'minder'.

The representatives of the developing world included some political heavyweights. Dr Manuel Perez Guerrero, the Venezuelan minister of state for international economic affairs, had held numerous United Nations posts. As chairman of the UN commission on Aden in the 1960s, he had been obliged by George Brown to play clock-golf on the lawn at Dorneywood. John Malacela, the Tanzanian minister for communications, was another who, apart from a succession of ministerial posts at home, had held a variety of international appointments. Abdul Rahman al-Ghunaim, the Kuwaiti under-secretary for communications, had experience in the field of insurance and banking. General Achmad Tahir had won distinction in Indonesia's wars of liberation in the late 1940s and early 1960s and, since leaving the army, had held posts in the communications field. He was now minister of tourism, posts and telecommunications.

On taking the chair for the first time, I listed the tasks on which I thought the commission should concentrate at the outset of its work. These ideas corresponded with the thinking of other members and by the end of the second day I secured their agreement to an initial programme of work. Even before we did this we had to agree how to interpret this awkward Greek–Latin hybrid 'telecommunication'. We decided to exclude broadcasting and concern ourselves primarily with information transmitted through the telephone system. Having done this, we agreed that the essential tasks were to establish the facts about the situation throughout the world, to examine the role new technologies could play, the most appropriate methods of organising and managing telecommunications systems, and how the sums needed for investment could be raised. We saw no need to commission original research; recent studies by the ITU and the Organisation for Economic Cooperation and Development, by the firm of Arthur D Little and the World Bank had provided most of the statistical information we required.

This was a heavy programme and we decided it would be sensible not to meet again until it had been completed. Meanwhile, however, governments, international and regional organisations and the manufacturing industries should be invited to comment on the task we had been set. Members undertook to consult relevant organisations and individuals in their regions. Before I adjourned the meeting, we agreed with enthusiasm to delete the words 'voluntary' and 'international' from the title of the commission.

On returning to London I reviewed the results of this first meeting with the team of advisers and allocated tasks. Richard Butler had persuaded the Canadian Government to release John Gilbert, whose presentation at the Costa Rica conference I had admired, in order to act as secretary to the commission. He established an office in Geneva, but came frequently to London for consultation. Over the next few weeks I signed seven hundred and four letters seeking comments and advice from heads of government, posts and telecommunications authorities, captains of industry and presidents of international and regional organisations throughout the world. I also drew up a short list of those whom it would be best to consult in person. But first, there was unfinished World Communications Year business to attend to.

The centrepiece of the United Kingdom's contribution to the Year was a special conference at Leeds Castle in Kent in November which I chaired. This was attended by representatives from twenty-two Commonwealth countries and many of those involved in the communications industry in Britain. Three issues were addressed: the role of telecommunications in economic and social development; levels of communications technology; and means of financing investment in the expansion of telecommunications networks. This agenda sat well with the independent commission's programme of work. As regards the controversial issue of financing investment in this sector, an ingenious suggestion by the highly talented Jonathan Solomon was endorsed by the conference. He proposed the establishment of a revolving fund which would provide loans to finance the provision of consultancy and training and the purchase of equipment. Operators and equipment manufacturers in industrialised countries might contribute to the fund by annual instalments. The resources of the fund would be replenished by the repayment of the loans.

My final act as chairman of World Communications Year in the United Kingdom was to preside at a conference in London organised by the British Computer Society. This was designed to focus attention on the implications for trade of advances in information technologies. Leading figures in the industry described the economic and other benefits which would flow from the communications systems of the future, and prominent users, notably in publishing and the financial sector, described how they were exploiting the new technologies. If this conference did nothing else, it brought home to me that the gap in telecommunications between advanced societies and the developing world was likely to widen unless remedial action were taken soon.

❖

The British Government invited the commission to hold its second meeting at Leeds Castle in May 1984. Meanwhile, individual members and our advisers were preparing papers on certain aspects of our work. Dr Heather Hudson in Texas agreed to contribute a draft chapter for our report on the role of telecommunications in social and economic development. Papers on other subjects were written either by my team of advisers, or by the newly established secretariat. I thought it best that I should write the first draft of a paper on the crucial question of financing, since some of the ideas being put forward seemed over-ambitious in the current world economic situation.

In the early months of 1984, John Harper and I visited Washington for talks about the commission's mandate with Tom Clausen, the President of the World Bank, Mimi Dawson of the Federal Communications Commission and Secretary Baldridge at the Department of Commerce. While all three acknowledged the problem the commission was required to address and supported our approach, they confirmed my view that international public finance on the scale some of my colleagues had in mind would not be available. We had therefore to think in different terms.

When John Harper and I visited the commission secretariat in Geneva in March, John Gilbert arranged for us to meet senior officials in the ITU secretariat, including the heads of all the regional divisions, as well as Richard Butler. During our talks I detected some anxiety on the part of members of the ITU secretariat lest any recommendations we made might detract from what they were doing. I hoped that this did not portend future problems but thought no more about it at the time.

Our efforts were gathering momentum and we still had a long way to go.

An invitation to address an energy conference at Georgetown University in April provided me with an opportunity to share thoughts on the way with Bill Ellinghaus and his assistant, Larry Forrester, at the AT&T offices in New York and to address a lunch-time meeting of leaders of the United States telecommunications industry. Once again John Harper and John Gilbert accompanied me. We all felt that these encounters sharpened our ideas about the way in which the financing issue should be handled. We were less sure of the impact we made on our hosts. They understood the importance of the problem, but gave no sign at that stage of willingness to invest in measures to resolve it.

❖

When the commission met at Leeds Castle in May, it was of interest that the team from the ITU was led by the deputy secretary general, Jean Jipguep. He assured us that he was present merely as an observer and to offer any help we might want. When welcoming him in that capacity, I took the opportunity to emphasise the intellectual independence of the commission.

Members of the commission reported in turn on the consultations they had conducted in their regions since our first meeting at Geneva. Abdul Rahman al-Ghunaim, the Kuwaiti member and one of the four vice-chairman, tabled a proposal for a 'World Telecommunication Development Organisation', or 'Worldtel' for convenience, which would carry out a comprehensive programme aimed at achieving balanced telecommunications development world wide. He envisaged that all members of the United Nations would have shares in the organisation. First reactions were mixed and I invited members to consult opinion in their own regions with a view to a substantive discussion of Abdul Rahman's idea at the next meeting. We accepted offers from the governments concerned to meet in Munich in August, at Arusha in Tanzania in October, and in Indonesia in November.

The venerable Dr Kobayashi was anxious for help in enlisting the support of the Japanese government and telecommunications organisations for the work of the commission and invited me and John Harper to visit Japan for this purpose. Over three days in the middle of July, at meetings with ministers and senior officials in the Ministry of Posts and Telecomunications and the Foreign Ministry, with the chairmen of the domestic and international telecommunications organisations and representatives of the industry, I explained the commission's aims. Without anticipating its precise recommendations, I suggested ways in which Japan might contribute to narrowing the gap. As we expected, our hosts were non-committal, but the persistence of their questioning

indicated that the internal debate about the privatisation of the telecommunications operators had implications for Japan's external relations
especially in south east Asia.

Dr Kobayashi insisted that we should not leave Japan without visiting
Kyoto and Nara. His amanuensis, Tomio Kuriki, was our travelling
companion, and our guide was an amateur historian. When we admired
the deer roaming in the meadows at Nara she told us that, in the days
of the Shogun, anyone guilty of killing one of these protected deer
would be summarily executed. For this reason, in the early hours of
the morning, the father of the house would order his eldest son to go
out to ensure that there was no dead deer in the vicinity. If he found one,
he was to drag it to his neigbour's house. This, she told us with a straight
face, was the origin of the phrase 'passing the buck'. Her repertoire did
not end there. At Nijo Castle in Kyoto, she explained that the senior
concubine would order the junior concubine she had selected to spend
the night with the Shogun to offer him tea. If the Shogun did not
approve of the selection, he would decline the tea. This, our guide
claimed, explained the expression 'she's not my cup of tea'.

❖

At our third meeting in Munich at the begining of August, a number
of draft contributions to our final report, which had been prepared by
members of the commission and our advisers, were approved. When we
turned to the Kuwaiti Worldtel proposal, the considered reactions, based
on consultations in regions, were on the whole sceptical. Our conclusion
was that, while the concept had merits, it was too ambitious for this early
stage. In the light of my own discussions in London and Washington I
suggested that we should refer in our report to a variety of ways in which
investment in telecommunications systems in the developing world
might be financed. General Tahir gave me strong support. Those he had
consulted in south east Asia had underlined the fact that no two situations
were alike; solutions had to be tailored to the circumstances of each
country. I was asked to develop these ideas before our next meeting.

I then invited my colleagues to consider an idea prompted by the clear
messages that emerged in response to the letters I had sent out after the
Commission's first meeting in Geneva. It was evident that developing
country administrations felt at a disadvantage when negotiating with
international agencies and foreign commercial enterprises; they wanted
disinterested advice. Was there not a case for some form of advisory
service? This could help those responsible for telecommunications in
developing countries to review and audit their current activities and
assist them in preparing projects and applying for both public and private
finance. An important objective would be achieved if, by some means,
such advice could be provided free of charge.

❖

During our three days in Munich our German hosts arranged for us to see some of the Bavarian countryside and enjoy its fruits. A convivial evening, when members of the Commission, our secretariat, our advisers, secretaries and interpreters were entertained by the Siemens company in the Munich Ratskeler, contributed to what John Malacela was to describe later as the family atmosphere. We were satisfied with the progress we were making in the conference room, even on the most contentious subjects, but I was uneasy on two counts. First, while the representatives of the ITU had behaved impeccably so far, I wondered what the reaction would be when they reported to their colleagues in Geneva on the ideas that had been floated at this Munich meeting. I had no idea then how dramatically my anxiety was to be justified.

My other concern arose from information my team of advisers had gleaned in London. The department was apparently becoming alarmed at the trend of our discussions on financing and the conclusion was being drawn that the department would be wise to 'distance itself' from the commission. History seemed to be repeating itself. John Harper and the rest of the team were amused when I told them about my experience in Ottawa in 1975 as a member of the Commonwealth Group of Experts on Trade and Development when Whitehall seemed to think that, if left to myself, I would pawn the crown jewels. The pathology had not changed.

In the few weeks before the next meeting in Tanzania in early October, our secretariat, advisers and others produced a number of draft chapters for our final report. I added to Heather Hudson's draft on 'The Role of Telecommunications' material from the numerous case histories we had received; the argument she presented convinced all members of the commission beyond a peradventure that there was indeed a causal link between investment in telecommunications and economic and social advance. Drawing on his unique experience, John Harper wrote a chapter on 'Internal Organisation and Management of Telecommunications' and Larry Forrester, in his office at the headquarters of AT&T in New Jersey, contributed a draft on 'The Choice of Technology'. Others compiled notes on training and the possibilities of local manufacture of equipment.

As requested at Munich, I prepared a paper for discussion at Arusha on the financing issue. The argument I set out was based on three factors specific to the telecommunications sector. First, an effective telecommunications system which met demand not only was inherently profitable but also generated wealth; as soon as a telephone line was installed and used, it earned money for the operator and contributed to economic activity. Secondly, technological advances had widened the options for administrations wishing to improve and expand their networks and had driven down costs. Thirdly, developing countries represented a fast-growing, and potentially the largest, market for the manufacturers of telecommunications equipment.

Our host at Arusha, John Malacela, whose qualities all his colleagues had come to admire, demonstrated his courage when, despite the tragic death of his son in an accident just before our arrival in Tanzania, he insisted on remaining in Arusha to ensure the smooth functioning of the commission. He wanted members of the commission to see at first hand the kind of problem a developing country faced in the communications field and had arranged for us to visit two rural areas to inspect the telephone facilities. In the first small town we were met by a dispirited group of officials; the local exchange, which had been installed in colonial days, had chosen that morning to break down. A malfunction made John Malacela's point. We had better luck in the next town and were then taken to Lake Manyara and the Ngorongoro crater, where we were to spend the next twenty-four hours observing the magnificent wildlife. On our return to Arusha we met a number of John Malacela's ministerial colleagues and senior officials. They made little secret of their impatience with the political dogma which stultified their efforts. At weekends they could drive with their families across the border into Kenya, where they could see and enjoy the benefits of individual initiative and private enterprise. They described to us the projects they intended to promote as soon as the 'Mualimu' had left the scene. Members of the commission were due to meet the Mualimu – President Julius Nyerere – later in the week.

At Arusha the ITU was represented not by Jean Jipguep but by Richard Butler, the secretary general himself. Soon after our meeting began the debate took an interesting turn. Armando Vargas, the Costa Rican vice-chairman, reported on a meeting of the International Institute of Communications in Berlin which he and a small group of others connected with our commission had attended a few weeks earlier. This group had drafted a proposal for an 'Institute for Telecommunications Development' which, as an integral part of the structure of the ITU, would offer developing countries a wide range of advice and help. No sooner had Armando finished his report than Larry Forrester, speaking on behalf of Bill Ellinghaus, said that both the State Department and the Department of Commerce in Washington had welcomed the idea of an advisory service first aired at Munich. The French and German members reported similar favourable reactions when they had sounded opinion after our Munich meeting. Two points had been stressed by their interlocutors: if such an advisory body were to attract funds from the private sector, its management and staff would have to be of high calibre and it would have to be seen to be operationally independent of the ITU.

As a result of these reports a new paper was drafted at Arusha for detailed consideration at our final meeting in Indonesia. This recommended the establishment of a centre for the development of telecommunications which would contain three elements: the first would collect information about telecommunications policies and experience; the second would advise on creating and managing an efficient system; and the third would provide specific assistance, for example over preparing specifications for projects, training and management assistance. When this paper was first circulated, John Malacela asked if any names had been suggested for the head of such a centre. I told him we had not yet reached that stage. He then said: "We need a new McNamara." We were all aware that, as President of the World Bank, Robert McNamara had won the respect of many leaders in the developing world. There were murmurs of approval round the conference room.

On the financial question we made a similar leap forward. The draft I had prepared was received with more enthusiasm than I had expected. It contained a variety of recommendations including an invitation to industrialised countries to contribute a proportion of their revenue from traffic with developing countries to a development fund, and the creation, as early as possible, of a revolving fund, an investment fund, a commercial consortium and investment trusts. Worldtel, I suggested, should be left for study at a later stage. The essential messages in the paper were that far higher priority had to be given to investment in this sector not only by the governments of developing countries themselves, but also by donor governments and international organisations, and that developing countries had to create the conditions which would attract foreign private investment.

Before leaving Arusha members of the commission attended the inauguration of a new post office and telephone exchange at the Usa River. Richard Butler laid the foundation stone and I planted a tree which, it was said, would in due time provide shade for those waiting to make their telephone calls. We also called on President Nyerere at State Lodge. He listened politely to my account of our work, but it was obvious that he had reached the stage in his life when reminiscence gave him the greatest pleasure. On our last evening in Arusha we had supper in the garden of our hotel from where we could look out across the plain to Mount Meru. When the meal was over a group of musicians, singers and dancers entertained us. The combination of soft evening air, voices in harmony, the colour, the drum beat and movement had an unexpected effect. To everyone's delight and, no doubt, his own relief, Dr Varakin's assistant at long last dropped his 'minder' role and began to enjoy himself.

❖

The commission assembled in Jakarta in the second week of November

1984. This was to be the decisive moment. The welcome we received from President Suharto was not a formality. He had been well briefed by General Tahir. The president explained that no one could hope to govern a country containing literally thousands of islands, many with tiny communities, without an effective communications system. For this reason and to enable Indonesia to prosper as a member of the Association of South East Asian States, his government awaited our report with impatience. Nor was Ali Wardhana interested in platitudes. He was the minister responsible for coordinating policy on the economy, finance, industry and the supervision of development. At a reception in our honour, he shared with us his views on the opportunities, especially in the development field, presented by the new technologies. But, although he knew our mandate did not extend to broadcasting, he thought it right to express his concerns about the impact on social structures in a country such as Indonesia of the television invasion.

The following day, 13 November, we flew on to Bali where we were to complete our work. The draft texts of all the chapters were reviewed, amended as necessary and endorsed as regards substance. My colleagues invited me to revise the language of the texts in order to achieve uniformity of style. They also asked me to write a final chapter containing our conclusions and summarising our recommendations. A number of members proposed that we commit ourselves to an overriding objective. After discussion we agreed that this should be 'to bring all mankind within easy reach of a telephone by the early part of the next century'. John Malacela and General Tahir wanted a title for our report which our potential audience would remember. I disclosed that when taking a shower that morning the words 'The Missing Link' had come to mind. This, it was thought, would serve our purpose well.

When it seemed that our work was nearly complete Richard Butler, who had intervened in our discussions from time to time, detonated his bomb. He announced that, when the Administrative Council of the ITU met in July 1985, he would be unable to recommend that it accept our report if the chapter on the proposed Centre for Telecommunications Development remained in its current form. I immediately adjourned the meeting to allow everyone time to consider the implications of this extraordinary intervention. I asked Bill Ellinghaus and Gérard Corré, who was representing Louis-Joseph Libois, to accompany me to a meeting with Butler to clarify the situation. They agreed and we spent the next several hours closeted with Butler. We told him that the readiness of those we had consulted to support the Centre would depend on the degree to which it was independent of the ITU and on the calibre of the director. Despite this Butler insisted throughout that the Centre should be based in Geneva and linked organically to the ITU. We assumed that he feared that, if the Centre were established on the lines we proposed under 'a new McNamara' and in a place of its own choosing, it would be seen as a rival to the Union. We told him that the changes on which he insisted would transform the Centre from a slim, predominantly private sector enterprise into another arm of the bureaucracy. Such an entity would neither attract sufficient funding nor prove effective on the ground. After some hours of fruitless debate, I said that I had no option but to inform the other members of the commission that our work had been frustrated and that there would be no report.

John Malacela, Manuel Perez Guerrero, General Tahir and the others were dismayed. They at once undertook to talk to Butler and urged me meanwhile to go to bed. At breakfast they reported that they had succeeded in reducing the number of changes Butler wanted to what they considered acceptable. They hoped I would agree. The text they had negotiated was in my view just beyond the limit of what was reasonable, but to jettison all that we had achieved at this final stage would have been irresponsible. The price the commission paid to secure the secretary general's endorsement was that our proposal for the Centre, as set out in the Report, did not represent our original concept.

So it was thanks all round and goodbye. I would send members the final version of 'The Missing Link' for their approval within a few weeks and hoped to present the printed version to the secretary general of the ITU in January 1985.

The fate of the Centre for Telecommunications Development was settled when the Administrative Council of the ITU met in July 1985. Members of the Council were persuaded to establish the Centre in the form on which Richard Butler had originally insisted during the long night at Bali. A thoroughly competent and well-intentioned young German – the last person to consider himself the 'new McNamara' John Malacela was looking for – was eventually appointed 'executive director'. The constraints placed on him and his colleagues prevented them achieving anything significant on the ground, and in 1991 it was decided that the Centre should be absorbed into the development bureau of the ITU. On the eve of the Centre's disappearance I received a note from this frustrated man: "The challenge turned into a defeat."

Although the demise of the Centre was a disappointment, it did not weaken the impact of the commission's Report. As time passed evidence accumulated, notably from India, the Pacific and Latin America, that the two crucial messages it contained – higher priority for investment in this sector and the need to attract foreign entrepreneurs – had been received, understood and acted upon.

In the weeks following our return from Bali my office in London hummed with activity. While the numerous annexes to the Report were being compiled and statistics checked, I recast the text of our report, removing jargon and imposing a similar pattern and style on each chapter.

The Report reflected the course of our studies, consultations and debates over the previous year. We were in no doubt about the role of telecommunications in economic and social progress. Telecommunications were essential to the emergency and health services; they increased the effectiveness of public administration, commerce and other economic activities; they reduced the need to travel. But the benefits would be felt only if the network operated efficiently. Less tangible benefits were also available. An efficient network could contribute to national cohesion, enhance the quality of life and distribute more evenly the fruits of economic, social and cultural development. We therefore concluded that 'henceforward no development programme . . . should be regarded as balanced, properly integrated or likely to be effective unless it includes a full and appropriate role for telecommunications and accords a corresponding priority to the improvement and expansion of telecommunications'.

In order to achieve the objective of bringing 'all of mankind within easy reach of a telephone by the early part of next century', we proposed action in four areas: to ensure that investment in telecommuniucations was given higher priority; to make existing networks in developing countries commercially viable; to ensure that financing arrangements took account of the foreign exchange problems of developing countries; and, to improve international cooperation. Under each of these four headings we grouped specific recommendations addressed variously to governments in both industrialised and developing countries, international agencies, telecommunications operators, suppliers of equipment and finance houses.

The delivery of the final printed version of the Report to our office in London was an occasion for a modest celebration. I thought it would be right to report to his successor, Geoffrey Pattie, completion of the task Kenneth Baker had given me nearly two years earlier. He seemed to have other preoccupations and it was not until 8 January 1985 that I was given an appointment. Since the crown jewels were still intact, I looked forward to hearing his views. When I entered his office he said: "I have read your Report with interest." He then asked me a number of questions about the next steps. And that was it. Back in our office John Harper and the rest of the team were anxious to know the minister's reaction. I said: "Not even a Pattie on the back."

I presented the Report to Richard Butler at a formal ceremony in Geneva on 22 January 1985. The press conference which followed began a process of exposition and persuasion which took me over the next several months to Washington and Ottawa, to a specially arranged conference on World Telecommunications Development at Arusha, to Cannes and Tokyo. Even then the appetite for information and guidance was not satisfied. In March 1986 I addressed the annual conference of Caribbean telecommunications organisations in the Bahamas and a World Telecommunication Forum in Nairobi in September of the same year. And so it continued year after year. To mark the passage of ten years since 'The Missing Link' was published, I was invited to address conferences in Bangkok and Hawaii. At the Pacific Telecommunications Conference in Honolulu in January 1994, Pekka Tarjanne, Richard Butler's successor at the ITU, reviewed developments over the previous decade. The gap which the independent commission had found unacceptable had been narrowed; the more prosperous developing countries had made substantial progress. But those with low incomes still lagged behind. The gap was still too wide, and much remained to be done. Dr Tarjanne also said that the time had come to abandon the cumbersome title the commission had been given; henceforth it would be known as the 'Maitland Commission'.

Some reports remain on the shelf. 'The Missing Link' is still seen by many in the developing world as the essential guide to better communications. At the Nairobi conference in 1982 Jonathan Solomon had the right idea at the right time. It was an honour to be asked to lead an inquiry into a state of affairs which all seventeen members of the commission regarded as an international injustice. We believed that it was not right, in the latter part of this century, that a minority of the human race should enjoy the benefits of remarkable new technologies while a majority lived in comparative isolation. Neither in the name of common humanity nor on grounds of common interest was such a disparity acceptable. In focusing the attention of the international community on this situation and in advocating practical ways in which it might be remedied, 'The Missing Link' struck a chord all over the developing world.

20

Foothills and Foreign Fields

When the quarantine prescribed by the Cabinet Office ended in the summer of 1983, I joined the board of Britoil as one of the Government-appointed directors; the other was Alistair Frame, the chief executive of Rio Tinto Zinc. This provided me with my first view from the inside of the corporate sector at work and extended my knowledge of exploration for and extraction of oil and gas from the North Sea. In August 1985, when the Government sold the bulk of its remaining shareholding in the company, I resigned from the board as required by the company's articles of association.

I acquired further experience of the private sector as a non-executive director of two other companies. Slough Estates had an unusual history. At the end of the First World War, a group of businessmen bought the entire stock of surplus military vehicles which had been used on the Western Front. These were brought back to England, repaired at what was known as 'the Dump' at Slough, and sold to meet the growing demand for private motor cars and commercial vehicles. The buildings and machinery installed for this purpose and now unused were the base upon which the first industrial estate was created. Instead of having to buy land and buildings, new businesses could rent these from the Slough Trading Company, which also provided essential services. The modern Slough Estates, led by Nigel Mobbs, the grandson of one of the original entrepreneurs, is one of the largest industrial landlords in the world, with industrial estates not only in Britain but also in continental Europe, Canada, the United States and Australia. During the nine years I spent on the board of this company, I derived much satisfaction from monitoring commercial management of a high order.

In 1986, at the invitation of its chairman, Terry Harrison, I became one of two non-executive directors of Northern Engineering Industries – a coalition of heavy engineering companies manufacturing, among other products, power generators, bridges and heavy-lifting equipment.

Once a year the entire managerial staff of the company assembled at a weekend retreat, when corporate issues were debated and the managing director of each of the subsidiary companies gave an account of his stewardship over the previous year. This occasion generated a sense of solidarity. It also provided board members with a clear picture of the overall performance of the company as well as an opportunity to assess the quality of the management. A good performance at the retreat could lead to better things.

The world market for the company's products was highly competitive and costs had to be kept under rigorous control. I saw what this meant in practice when visiting company sites in Newcastle, Gateshead, Sheffield, Derby and Edinburgh. When the managing director of one of the companies was rather anxiously describing his plans for reducing the work force after the installation of new automated machine tools, the leader of the trade union took me aside. He told me not to pay too much attention to what the boss was saying; the lads understood the situation better than he thought and had no intention of doing anything that would harm the interests of the company. When an opportunity arose in the spring of 1989 for Northern Engineering Industries to merge with Rolls Royce on mutually beneficial terms, my fellow non-executive director and I gave enthusiastic support to what was a logical development and, in so doing, voted ourselves out of the company.

❖

In the autumn of 1984 the head of the South Asian department at the Foreign and Commonwealth Office invited me to call on him. He told an encouraging story. Rajiv, the son of Indira Gandhi, and Margaret Thatcher had established a good relationship based on mutual respect and, it was said, admiration. This had opened up possibilities for a general improvement in our relations. One immediate consequence was a decision, despite Indian resentment over what was seen as leniency towards Sikh extremists in Britain, to revive the non-official dialogue which had begun seven years earlier and had then faltered. The purpose would be the same – to provide a forum where informed persons from both countries, acting in their private capacities, could discuss a range of issues of common interest. The only change was the title; the Indo-British Exchange of 1978 was now to be called the Indo-British Colloquium. Would I agree to be the co-ordinator on the British side?

My Indian opposite number, I learned, would be none other than T. N. Kaul, who, as head of the Department of External Affairs, had made heavy weather of the arrangements for Edward Heath's visit to New Delhi in 1971. He was now a member of the Executive Board of the United Nations Educational, Scientific and Cultural Organisation (UNESCO) in Paris. The next meeting of the teams was to be held in India, but neither their composition, nor the agenda, nor the precise place and dates had been settled. Much remained to be done. This seemed a worthwhile assignment and, as Kaul had claimed in conversation with our High Commission in New Delhi that he was the personal choice of the late Mrs Gandhi, the Indian Government were told that I was Mrs Thatcher's personal nominee as co-ordinator of the British team.

Late in November I received a message from Kaul in Paris. He suggested that each team should number no more than ten and represent a range of disciplines. The agenda should cover economic and commercial relations, science and technology, education, culture and the media, as well as political issues. He envisaged a meeting lasting two and a half days towards the end of March 1985. Alan Nazareth, the director general of the Indian Council for Cultural Relations – the ICCR – would be responsible for the arrangements in India. I replied that I saw no difficulty with these proposals and promised definitive comments before the Christmas holiday.

Over the following months, with secretarial support from Grindlay's Bank and the assistance of the Foreign and Commonwealth Office, I assembled the British team. We left for India on the morning of 9 April 1985 and landed in New Delhi at half past three in the morning of the following day. The intention was that, after resting in a hotel, we would leave by coach that afternoon for Simla, where we would be accommodated in the former Viceregal Lodge. On arrival at New Delhi we learned that the meeting would be held not in Simla but in the former summer retreat of the Maharajah of Patiala at Chail, some thirty kilometers to the east of Simla. Chail had the distinction of having one of the highest cricket grounds in the world. We met our Indian counterparts shortly before boarding the coach and for the next eleven and a half hours we were imprisoned together as the reluctant vehicle groaned its way towards the foothills of the Himalayas. At the front of the bus a proud notice announced: 'COLD DRINKS AVILAVEL'. Cold drinks were indeed available throughout the journey, which we broke from time to time for refreshment and to stretch our legs. By the time we reached Chail the shared experience had already dismantled any barriers and it was as a band of friends and colleagues that we unloaded our baggage under the clear starlit sky. As British co-ordinator I had been allocated the Maharani's room.

In the morning we had a few hours to absorb the astounding natural beauty of Chail – the hillsides covered with pine and cedar and an uninterrupted view of the great snow-covered range in the distance. The high power of the British team was a clear indication to the Indians that we were taking this revived initiative seriously. My colleagues were Michael Donelan of the London School of Economics; Jean Floud of

Nuffield College, Oxford; John Hanson, who represented the British Council in the United Kingdom High Commission in New Delhi; Janet Morgan, the author and adviser to the director general of the BBC; Andrew Rowe, the Member of Parliament for Mid Kent; David Thomson of Lazards; and David Watt, one of the outstanding journalists of the day. The Indian team consisted of Professor Damodaran, a leading member of the planning staff of the Ministry of External Affairs, two economists and three journalists. One of the journalists, Inder Malhotra, was a senior figure on *The Times of India*; another was Dr Saryu Doshi, the editor of Marg publications and the wife of a prominent industrialist in Bombay.

Kaul and I chaired alternate sessions which covered the subjects Kaul had proposed the previous autumn. From the beginning both sides were at pains to discuss practical issues rather than theory and this determination persisted throughout the two and a half days. The opening statement by Professor Damodaran at our first session set the tone. His exposition of the bases of Indian foreign policy was eminently clear and reasonable. When the time came to draw conclusions, we found few points on which we disagreed. We saw opportunities for increased trade, for more joint ventures, for greater exchanges in the fields of art and music, dance and drama – both classical and folk – and more frequent contacts between educational and technical institutions. We proposed a British Festival in India and urged that more Indian films be shown on British television. We devoted particular attention to the role of the media. This was a matter of some concern to the Indian side, who wished the British press to present a more balanced picture of the new India.

This was achievement enough. We derived even greater satisfaction from the rapport which was so quickly established between the two teams. On our last afternoon in the hills we visited the Viceregal Lodge in Simla; this was of special interest to Janet Morgan, who was at that time working on her biography of Edwina Mountbatten. As we walked back to our coach the percipient and articulate Saryu Doshi put her arm through mine. "This is wonderful," she said, "you and we see so many things in the same way. If only our political leaders could have a dialogue like this."

We all felt the same. A possible exception was T. N. Kaul, whose selective summaries of the sessions he chaired seemed to embarrass those on his side of the table. However, when he addressed a press conference on his return the next day to New Delhi, he kept any reservations he may have had to himself. He told the press that he felt there was much more common ground between the two countries than the differences that seemed to arise from time to time; new India and new Britain presented a fertile field for greater co-operation and reducing past differences. Kaul announced that the next seminar would take place in Britain in 1986; further meetings would be held annually thereafter as part of a continuing high-level dialogue.

When my colleagues and I were asked by members of the High Commission in New Delhi before we boarded our return flight to London how we had fared at Chail, our unanimous response was: "S U double C E double S – 'pronounced success'". We shared Kaul's ambition that the dialogue should be resumed annually and, on my return home, I drew up plans for the next meeting in the early summer of the following year. In July 1985 I was in a position to propose dates both to T. N. Kaul and to the Indian Council for Cultural Relations and meanwhile I made provisional reservations of accommodation. When after some time I had received no reply I sent a further letter. Still silence. In February of the following year, I learned from our High Commission in New Delhi that Lalit Mansingh, the new director general of the ICCR, claimed not to have received my original letter. He had gone on to say that, in any case, the dates I proposed were inconvenient. Over the following months, despite alternative suggestions and reminders, further excuses of diminishing credibility were put forward by the Indian side. Our best guess was that elements in the Ministry of External Affairs in New Delhi, congenitally opposed to a closer relationship with Britain and concerned at the success of the encounter at Chail, were obstructing continuation of the dialogue. With the agreement of the Foreign and Commonwealth Office I abandoned this fruitless and humiliating exercise. Some years later the lion in the path was removed and this valuable dialogue was resumed under a new name and leadership of a different generation.

❖

As a member of Coastal Command during the war John Barraclough had piloted Catalina flying boats. He claimed, with the suspicion of a twinkle in his eye, that these aircraft could remain airborne so long that aircrew flew by the calendar, not the clock. After the war he was the first to fly in a single-engined jet aircraft non-stop to South Africa. When I first met him, in March 1983, this retired Air Chief Marshal was Vice-Chairman of the Commonwealth War Graves Commission. He wondered if I would fill a vacancy which would arise later in the year. I did not hesitate and in due course I received the Royal Warrant appointing me a Member of the Commission for four years from 1 December 1983.

The Commission was the brainchild of Fabian Ware, whose advocacy led to the creation in May 1917 of a new organisation to provide care for the graves of those who had lost their lives in 'The Great War', and commemoration for the missing. In 1922 King George the Fifth undertook a pilgrimage to war cemeteries on the Western Front. The tour ended at Terlincthun on the Channel coast. In his speech there the King articulated the principle on which all of the Commission's work was based – that there should be no distinction on any grounds in the treatment of the dead. He said: "We remember, and must charge our children to remember, that, as our dead were equal in sacrifice, so they are equal in honour, for the greatest and the least of them have proved that sacrifice and honour are no vain things, but truths by which the world lives."

Nearly one and three-quarters of a million men and women of the Commonwealth forces died in the two world wars of the twentieth century. The Commission maintains 2,500 cemeteries and plots in 140 different countries. There are other war graves in civil cemeteries and churchyards throughout the world. Those who have no known grave are commemorated on memorials. The Thiepval Memorial to the Missing of the Somme bears over 72,000 names and the Menin Gate – the Memorial to the Missing of the Ypres Salient – over 54,000. There are similar memorials at Rangoon in Burma and Runnymede; the latter commemorates more than 20,000 missing of the Air Forces.

The Members of the Commission, of which The Duke of Kent is President, include representatives of the partner governments – Canada, Australia, New Zealand, South Africa and India, as well as the United Kingdom. Costs are shared by these governments in proportion to the numbers of their graves.

Apart from attending meetings of the full Commission I was also a member of the Commonwealth–French Joint Committee, a trustee of the Superannuation Fund and a member of the Finance Committee. In this latter capacity I became familiar with some intriguing Commission usage. From time to time we were required, for legal reasons, to designate a member of the Commission staff a 'Proper Officer'. Where did this leave other members of the staff?

In the summer of 1984 I toured cemeteries in north-west Europe with the two Area directors concerned. At the headquarters of France Area at Arras, I learned about the arrangements for liaison with the local authorities and saw some of the Commission craftsmen repairing damaged headstones. At Ieper, the headquarters of North West Area, I discussed the effect of an innovation recently approved by the Commission. For many years the Commission gardeners had been responsible for the day-to-day maintenance of a number of cemeteries in the vicinity of their homes. It had been decided that it could be more cost-effective to form the supervisors and gardeners into mobile groups. These were equipped with vans which took them and their machines from one cemetery to another over a wide area. At each cemetery, in one concentrated effort, the whole group would carry out their maintenance tasks. When these had been completed the group would move on to the next cemetery and do the same. It was clear from the comments of the gardeners that this concentration of resources was proving even more effective than had been predicted. The morale of the staff had been further boosted by the arrival of more powerful mowing machines.

In all but name, it seemed, the gardeners in the two areas were Belgians, or Frenchmen who fitted perfectly into the landscape. But most of those with English names had proudly retained their British nationality. These were the grandsons of British soldiers of the First World War who had found their own 'mademoiselle from Armentières' and decided to make a new life and a new home for themselves.

When the Area director and I were visiting Tyne Cot on the Passchendaele Ridge, the largest cemetery in the Ypres Salient, three coaches arrived carrying boys from Gravesend High School in Kent. The master in charge told us that he had been preparing the boys for this tour for the previous few months. When they disembarked from their coaches, the boys were in high spirits, but, as they approached the rows of headstones, they fell silent. They formed into pairs or small groups and, before they left, one or two signed their names in the Visitors' Book. When they had set off for the Menin Gate, where they were to lay a wreath, I opened the Visitors' Book. One of the boys had written: "So many, and so young".

During trips abroad on other business I took the opportunity to visit cemeteries for which the Commission was responsible. My work on world telecommunications took me to Japan a few weeks after my tour in France and north-west Europe. The supervisor of the cemetery in Yokohama, Len Harrop, had made a unique contribution. Over several years he had collected hundreds of botanical varieties from the countries whose nationals were buried in the cemetery. These were now flourishing and linked the plots of graves which were grouped according to nationality. When the telecommunications commission was touring in Tanzania in October of the same year, I happened to notice a sign to the war cemetery in Moshi and diverted our convoy. The entire commission was astonished by the splendid condition of the cemetery despite a recent drought. In an adjacent park stood a monument to the Tanzanian soldiers who had lost their lives in the operations in Uganda which led to the overthrow of Idi Amin. When in Indonesia, pursuing a contract for Northern Engineering Industries in July 1986, I visited the cemetery in Jakarta without advance warning. John Jaya, the Javanese caretaker, and the three gardeners were hard at work weeding the borders and trimming the edges of the lawn. John greeted me as though he had been expecting my visit. He showed me where, on his own initiative, the areas between the gravestones had been planted with small ground-covering plants. His own house and the utility buildings were scrupulously neat. The story was the same everywhere I went – Singapore, Kenya, the Bahamas. Not only were the cemeteries immaculately maintained, despite harsh climatic conditions in some places, but the morale and dedication of the supervisors, caretakers and gardeners of different nationalities were exceptional. I had not encountered anywhere an international workforce so highly motivated by the work of their choice.

The high point of the four years I served as a Member of the Commission was the seventieth anniversary of the first day of the Battle of the Somme – 1 July 1916 – the day the British army suffered nearly 60,000 casualties. Scores of British and French survivors of that battle, supported by members of their families, assembled for the service of remembrance in front of the memorial at Thiepval. Many were in wheelchairs, others were remarkably spry. After the wreaths were laid, the Duke of Kent read the Lesson. It then fell to Frank Johnston, the Chaplain-General, to give the address. I had been wondering how he would approach this unique occasion and, when it became clear that he intended to address his remarks to the survivors, I was sure he had made the right choice. The memories of those days and weeks, he told them, would forever remain fresh and vivid since they affected each one in different ways. He recalled that only a few weeks earlier one veteran had confessed: "Every night as I go to bed, I think about it." Frank Johnston continued: "Those who fought and died on the Somme were not supermen; they were ordinary people but they embodied and exemplified the values of obedience, discipline and selfless regard for others, even unto death." From where I was standing I could see that many of the survivors were deeply touched by Frank Johnston's words, as though they had not realised with how much awe, respect and love they were regarded.

We had been told before the service began that, when it was over, the Duke of Kent would speak to a few of the veterans. This turned out not to be accurate. The Duke spoke to every single one of the survivors – in French and in English, as appropriate. George Younger, the secretary of state for defence and, as such, chairman of the War Graves Commission, David Williams, the admiral who had succeeded John Barraclough as Vice-Chairman, and I followed in the Duke's footsteps and marvelled at the modesty, courage and resilience of these old men. As we gathered later for lunch, the question in our minds was how those who took part in the battle had endured for week after week conditions and suffering which seemed beyond our comprehension. In his novel *The Middle Parts of Fortune*, Frederic Manning offered an explanation: "These apparently rude and brutal natures comforted, encouraged and reconciled each other to fate, with a tenderness and tact which was more moving than anything in life . . . They had been brought to the last extremity of hope, and yet they put their hands on each other's shoulders and said with a passionate conviction that it would be all right, though they had faith in nothing, but in themselves and in each other."

For years the ambitions of the German Kaiser, the irresolution of political leaders in France and Britain in the period leading up to the outbreak of the First World War, and the obstinacy of the generals, had been subjects of controversy. I hoped that the young who visited Tyne Cot, Thiepval and the countless other memorials would see these not simply as some corner of a foreign field irrigated by too much youthful blood. Those dreadful events demonstrated the frailty of the flesh and the invincibility of the human spirit. The same lesson was to be drawn from the sacrifice of those who died in the Second World War, for they exemplified the same values as those who had gone before.

21

Independent Channels

In the autumn of 1986 Douglas Hurd, who was then the home secretary, invited me to become deputy chairman of the Independent Broadcasting Authority – the IBA. At that time the IBA had four main functions. It selected and appointed the fifteen independent television companies which served each region of the country. It had a duty to ensure that the content of programmes was balanced, that news was accurate, that controversial issues were treated impartially and that good taste and decency were not offended. The Authority was also responsible for ensuring high standards in advertising. Finally, since it owned the transmitters, the IBA was the broadcaster of independent television and, as such, had the right to view programmes before they were broadcast. The members of the Authority included representatives of Scotland, Wales and Northern Ireland and of different sectors of our national life. The Authority's considerable collective wisdom was supplemented by the advice of committees on education, religion, medicine and advertising, and a general advisory council which helped the Authority to assess the quality of the programmes it broadcast.

I was pleased to be working once again with George Thomson, later Lord Thomson of Monifieth, who had been chairman of the IBA for five years. We had coincided at the Foreign Office and in Brussels, and now we were to work together at Brompton Road. He accepted my suggestion that I should visit the regional television companies as early as possible not merely to establish my credentials but, more important, to hear at first hand their reaction to the ideas which the government was known to be considering for a major reform of the commercially funded television system. These included proposals for a new method of awarding television contracts and a bigger role for independent producers of television programmes. Much of the government's thinking had been stimulated by the report of the Peacock Committee on the Financing of the BBC. This report, which had been published in 1986, contained a wide range of recommendations affecting much more than the financing of the BBC. It was expected that the government's considered ideas would be set out in a White Paper which would be followed by a new Broadcasting Bill.

Between February and October 1987 I discussed these and other issues with all fifteen television companies. I was relieved that throughout this series of visits little dissatisfaction was expressed with the way the IBA handled relationships. All of the companies were opposed to the idea of awarding contracts by auction. Some wondered how the IBA could be expected to judge between the merits of an established programme-maker and a new bidder. Others wanted to know how bids for contracts were to be composed. All felt that broadcasting standards would be jeopardised; the 'moguls', who coveted prestige and would willingly run the companies at a loss, would be let loose. As regards the contentious question of the portrayal of violence and sex, the unanimous view was that the solution lay in 'sensible portrayal' – an all-purpose phrase to which no one could object. However, as one highly experienced executive admitted, the problem was that it was not always easy to persuade directors to exercise restraint.

For a number of reasons, not least dissatisfaction with some of the practices of the unions in the television industry, the government wanted independent producers of television programmes to have better access to the network. There was talk of a quota of programmes – perhaps twenty-five per cent – which would have to be provided by independent producers. Most of the companies were prepared to see more independently produced programmes on the screen; many of these were original and creative. Others saw an inconsistency in the government's approach; on the one hand the government preached the virtues of market forces and, on the other, interfered with the play of these forces by introducing a compulsory quota.

On one subject there was unanimity. All the companies strongly supported the existing geographical structure of independent television. I had no problem understanding why. As I traversed the country – from Aberdeen to Plymouth, from Belfast to Norwich, from Cardiff to Newcastle upon Tyne – I became aware of the strong sense of regional identity stimulated by the companies. It seemed to me that when Robert Fraser, the first director general of the IBA's predecessor, the Independent Television Authority, devised the regional system, he had drawn a map of the United Kingdom which reflected, with sympathy and remarkable accuracy, the interests and sentiments of the inhabitants.

❖

The controversial nature of the government's ideas placed some strain on relations between the Authority and the Home Office. This was not eased by an incident in March 1988. Interviewed on Anglia

Television about the government's intentions towards commercially funded television, Douglas Hurd, normally courteous and sure-footed before cameras and microphones, made an extraordinary reference to the IBA. When he was asked whether cash would in future be the final arbiter when it came to choosing between rival companies bidding for a franchise, he said: "At the moment you have a system no one likes where people go behind closed doors and try to convince the IBA, which isn't elected by anybody, or responsible to anybody, who should have it." This statement did nothing to allay anxieties among the staff at Brompton Road. Inasmuch as members of the IBA were appointed by the home secretary and were responsible, through him, to Parliament to which the Authority submitted its annual reports, this was either an aberration or a Freudian slip. The squall this produced was nothing compared with the tempest which was to follow.

Early in April 1988 the staff of the IBA were told that, as part of their *This Week* series, Thames Television intended to show a programme on 28 April about the circumstances in which three members of the IRA were shot in Gibraltar. Certain facts were beyond question. First, there was no doubt that the three terrorists intended to carry out a murderous attack on the security forces in Gibraltar; the shootings frustrated this intention. However, it was also clear that when they were shot the three were unarmed and the parked car believed to contain explosives had no explosives. The explosives, together with detonating equipment were found in Marbella two days later by the Spanish police. Inevitably the Gibraltar incident was already the subject of controversy and a focus of media attention.

Thames Television were told that the Authority would wish to preview this programme and arrangements were made for this to be done on the day before transmission – 27 April. In the evening of 26 April Geoffrey Howe, the foreign secretary, spoke on the telephone to George Thomson. He had learned about the intention to broadcast this programme and expressed concern that it could prejudice the inquest into the deaths. This was expected to be held at the end of June. He asked that the showing of the programme be postponed. George Thomson said he would look into the matter and be in touch with the foreign secretary's office by the morning of 28 April.

In the course of 27 April, the programme – *Death on the Rock* – was seen by the staff of the IBA, by the director general and by George Thomson. Although I was at Brompton Road on that day, I was not made aware of the problem and did not see the programme in advance. The opinion of Counsel was obtained; this was that the programme was not in contempt and that it was for the IBA to decide whether or not to show it. The unanimous view of those who previewed it was that it should be shown. When I and other members of the Authority saw the programme later, we agreed with this decision.

The reaction of ministers was violent. Geoffrey Howe denounced what he said was an attempt to constitute a television programme as "judge, jury and prosecuting counsel". This, he said, was "grossly and wholly improper". The prime minister, asked whether she was furious, confessed that her anger over the programme went "much deeper than being furious". Thus inspired, sections of the tabloid press set out to vilify a number of those who had described on the programme what they had seen; some of the more scurrilous of these allegations were found to be totally false and their authors and publishers had to pay substantial libel damages when this matter came to court. The broadsheets for the most part supported the Authority's decision to transmit the programme. Not only were they opposed in principle to government intervention in matters of this kind, but they were also mindful of the fact that, at the time of the shootings, the writing press had sent their own investigators to Gibraltar to try to establish the facts and their findings had been extensively reported.

The effect of the ministerial outbursts was to ensure that the programme received more attention than would otherwise have been the case. George Thomson was robust in defence of the Authority's decision to transmit the programme. In his view the "over-reaction" of ministers had been ill-judged; the government's intervention could threaten the independence of television and the IBA.

In an undated letter to George Thomson which was received at Brompton Road a week after the programme appeared, Geoffrey Howe repeated his concern over prejudice to the inquest and quoted in aid a statement made by Lord Salmon at the inquiry into the Aberfan disaster. This was to the effect that, once any type of tribunal has been appointed, it would be inappropriate for the press, radio or television to conduct anything in the nature of a parallel inquiry. This quotation gave rise to the only light moment in this strange episode. Interviewed by The Independent about the contempt issue, the legal adviser to Thames Television argued that the government was probably aware that it did not have the protection of the law in this instance and might have been trying to create a legal case where none existed. She added: "Bringing Salmon into the argument was a red herring."

A few days after the programme was transmitted Ian Trethowan, the chairman of Thames Television, told me that, with the benefit of hindsight, he would have made three minor amendments to the programme, which he did not specify. However, he did not believe that these would have diminished the wrath of ministers, which he considered quite unreasonable. As a former political editor of Independent Television News and director general of the BBC, Ian Trethowan had developed highly sensitive political antennae. His main anxiety, which I shared, was that this affair could prejudice the debate about the future of commercially funded television which would reach a crucial stage when the promised White Paper appeared.

The board of Thames Television invited Lord Windlesham and Richard Rampton, QC, to conduct an inquiry into the preparation of the programme. In their report they criticised the company for its handling of the evidence of one witness and for one passage in the commentary. But their closely argued conclusion was that the programme was responsibly made and did not create any real risk of prejudicing the Gibraltar inquest.

The Windlesham/Rampton Report was a substantial piece of work. The detailed account of the measures the producers took to ensure accuracy and impartiality was enlightening. However, I felt it was unfortunate that the passions aroused by *Death on the Rock* prevented serious consideration of those passages in the report which were of wider application, and especially Chapter 12, which the authors called 'A Child of its Time'. My experience in the Authority had persuaded me that certain aspects of the treatment of current affairs by this most powerful of media raised more serious issues for the nation than, for example, the portrayal of violence and sex. However wise the judgment of members of the Authority might be, their difficulty in performing their duty was that human nature made controversy inevitable. 'Balance', 'accuracy' and 'impartiality' in news reporting were no easier to judge than what does, or does not, give offence. The opinions of individual viewers were not always balanced, accurate, or impartial. Journalists were often over-sensitive to criticism and too ready to perceive threats to the freedom of the press. For their part, politicians could resent what they saw as the self-serving interests of television interviewers ambitious to establish themselves as a force in the eyes of the public. I thought there was material here for fruitful discussion between the Authority and the television companies. But the moment passed.

As for the deaths on the Rock, I concluded that, in the light of the controversy which had been provoked, the truth about what happened would probably never be known. In the end, the inquest in Gibraltar was not prejudiced by the transmission of the Thames Television programme. George Thomson said that he had done his duty and Geoffrey Howe had done his. That seemed as reasonable and as generous a way as any of drawing a line under this affair.

It was a pity that in his last year as chairman of the Authority George Thomson should have been so publicly at odds with the government. More important issues had to be settled, but not in his time. The gossip columns predicted that he would be succeeded by either a politician more in tune with the government's approach to the broadcasters, or a captain of industry. Speculation ended when the appointment of George Russell as chairman from 1 January 1989 was announced; he had been a member of the Authority for several years until 1986. Following an approach from our near neighbour, Chris Patten, the Member of Parliament for Bath and, at that time, minister of overseas development, I had meanwhile been offered a post as chairman of a health authority. It was agreed with the Home Office and the Department of Health that I would remain at the IBA until the end of March 1989 in order to support George Russell during his first three months at Brompton Road. The government's White Paper, which bore the provocative title *Broadcasting in the 90s: Competition, Choice and Quality*, was published in November 1988. Comments on the proposals it contained were required by the end of February 1989, but we successfully negotiated an extension until the end of March. As I had been co-ordinating the Authority's response, George Russell asked me to complete this task before I left.

As foreshadowed, the White Paper proposed that the Authority be replaced by an Independent Television Commission, which would not be the broadcaster, and that contracts would be awarded, through a tendering process, to the highest bidder. The rationale for such radical reforms was set out in the introduction to the White Paper. This rightly drew attention to the impact on broadcasting policy of technological and other developments, and notably the availability of new channels. The aim was to open the doors so that individuals could "choose for themselves from a much wider range of programmes and types of broadcasting". The government believed that, "with the right enabling framework, a more open and competitive broadcasting market can be attained without detriment to programme standards and quality. Its single biggest advantage will be to give the viewer and listener a greater choice and a greater say."

I could not decide whether these words were mere expressions of dogma, conscientious expectations of what would happen in practice, or pious hopes. I was even more puzzled when I failed to find any clear reference to provision for documentaries, drama, the arts and science, nor to programmes for children, nor any positive commitment to continue religious programmes. What concerned me most was the absence of any undertaking to preserve the networking arrangement, which enabled the best regional programmes to be seen nationally. This, in my view, was the supreme virtue of the independent television system.

It was obvious that a closely argued response to the White Paper would be needed if what the IBA regarded as the defects in the government's proposals were to be remedied in the Broadcasting Bill to be presented to Parliament. Staff and members of the Authority gave priority to the preparation of our response.

Understandably, the television companies were most concerned about the proposal to allocate licences through a tendering process. I and others in the Authority would have preferred a different approach. I saw no objection to, and indeed many advantages in, the replacement of the Authority with a Commission with more limited responsibilities and powers. The consequent changes in the content of the licences under which the companies would broadcast in future seemed equally reasonable. Apart from anything else, there would be no repetition of the fuss over *Death on the Rock*. However, I should have preferred a system under which existing franchise holders were invited to apply for new licences and allowed to operate under these for, say, two years, after which takeovers or mergers would be allowed, subject to limits to prevent excessive concentration of ownership. However, given the apparent strength of the government's commitment to the tendering process, which would contribute large sums to the Exchequer, we had to consider whether anything was to be gained at this stage by suggesting an alternative.

In the end the staff responsible for collating the views of members and divisions of the Authority produced an authoritative, closely argued and readable document. George Russell paid particular attention to the Authority's proposal for the selection of licensees, to which he contributed the notion of the 'quality of money'. The IBA's Response was well received by the press and the industry and, in the end, the Broadcasting Bill, which became law in November 1990, kept the barbarians much further from the gates of Rome than some had feared when the White Paper first appeared.

Nonetheless I was still unconvinced by the main element in the government's policy. There was an absolutism about the reference in the White Paper to the central position of the viewer and listener which bordered on the disingenuous. In practice, the only choice available to the viewer and listener is to switch from one channel or station to another, or to switch off. This has always been so and, for as far ahead as one can see, will always be so. In practice the range of choice is dictated by the broadcasters and, since the new system for allocating licences placed such a heavy financial burden on the successful companies, it seemed inevitable that they would be tempted to concentrate on the cheaper and more profitable programmes at the expense of those with narrower appeal. I wondered whether in the end the viewer's choice would lie between home-grown and imported sit-coms, game shows, police serials, science-fiction, old movies and late-night sex. It would be tragic if our screens were never again to be adorned with a Jewel in the Crown.

22

Health of the Nation

When Chris Patten asked me in the summer of 1988 whether I would consider a post in the National Health Service, he was under the impression that what was on offer was chairmanship of a regional health authority. He had sounded me on behalf of John Moore and Tony Newton, who were at that time ministers in the Departments of Social Security and of Health. When it emerged at the end of July that the organisation in question was the Health Education Authority, Chris Patten said: "There have been problems. It's highly political." This comment was prompted by public controversy the previous year over a report by the Authority on the link between deprivation and health.

Until 1987 responsibility for educating the public on health matters lay with the Health Education Council, which had the legal status of a company limited by guarantee. Norman Fowler, then secretary of state for health, decided to replace the Council with a new statutory body. In April 1987 the Health Education Authority was set up as an integral part of the National Health Service. The Order under which it was established placed a number of obligations on the new Authority. In essence these required the Authority to provide information and advice about health directly to members of the public throughout England; to assist others who provided such information to the public; and to advise the secretary of state on health education matters.

Norman Fowler's initiative was prompted by a specific challenge – the AIDS epidemic. In November 1986 he reminded the House of Commons that there had been no known cases of AIDS before 1981 and that the first case of transmission of the virus by blood transfusion had been reported in the United States in 1983. He stressed the importance, among other measures, of a campaign of public education and quoted a telling comment by the United States Surgeon General: "Information is the only vaccine we have." He then announced the start of an advertising campaign advising against promiscuity and warning drug users not to share needles. To be effective, he said, these advertisements would have to use language which some might find offensive; but the danger was that the essential message might not be understood. Unless action were taken, the infection could spread to the heterosexual population, as had happened elsewhere. So a linguistic balance had to be struck. Norman Fowler added that the education campaign, once launched, would have to continue. He then announced that a new body, the Health Education Authority (the HEA), would be established for this purpose and would, at the same time, continue the wide-ranging health education programmes then being undertaken in England by the Health Education Council. But there was one important difference; so far as the AIDS campaign was concerned, he intended that the new Authority's responsibilities would embrace not merely England, but the whole of the United Kingdom.

I joined the board of the Authority as a member in December 1988 and became chairman in April 1989. My letter of appointment assumed that my duties would take about two days a week. This was to prove a spectacular underestimate.

When I paid my first, and only, call on Kenneth Clarke, then secretary of state for health, he made a modest but unsuccessful effort to disguise his lack of enthusiasm for health education. My meeting with his deputy, David Mellor, was more fruitful. We had become acquainted when he joined the Department of Energy as a junior minister in 1981 and we had further contacts over broadcasting policy when he has minister of state at the Home Office. He had two immediate concerns. First, he thought it essential that I keep in close touch with the chief medical officer, Donald Acheson, on whose advice the Authority's education projects had to be based, and he arranged for us to meet over lunch. He also wanted the respective responsibilities of the Department and the Authority to be clarified. This led to the preparation by an official in the department and the chief executive of the Authority of a Memorandum of Understanding which, while acknowledging the operational independence of the Authority, was prudently designed to ensure that neither side took the other by surprise.

The board of the Authority contained representatives of a wide range of interests as well as a few who worked in the fields of medicine, or public health. As the term of office of some of the members was due to end immediately before I took over as chairman, David Mellor discussed with me his suggestions for new recruits and asked for mine. This consultation resulted in the accession to our boardroom of two pillars of the media and education, Esther Rantzen and Heather Brigstocke.

❖

The HEA was a comparatively small entity – a staff of under two hundred and an annual budget of about £30 million, of which one third was earmarked for the AIDS campaign. It was evident from the beginning that the structure of the organisation needed attention. The impression it gave of a collection of 'baronies' was undesirable on a number of grounds. Above all, coherence of aim was essential. Health education and health promotion attract highly motivated people, many with a strong attachment to particular causes. However, the HEA was not a lobby or a pressure group. As one of the few Special Authorities, the HEA was an integral part of the National Health Service and had to operate within the framework of government policy. But it had a unique distinction – not merely the right, but the obligation, to advise the secretary of state on health education matters. No one in the Authority could expect to enjoy privileged access to the inside track one day and, on the next, set off in another direction in pursuit of a separate objective.

This was my first close encounter with the social sector and I had to learn its customs and traditions. I also had to overcome the language barriers. There were two of these since, in addition to 'health-speak', the reforms being carried out in the National Health Service – the NHS – had a bearing on our work and this called for knowledge of 'management-speak'. I learned, for example, that results were not achieved and that services were no longer provided; they, and many other things, including babies, were delivered. I marvelled at the insensitivity of whoever it was that introduced the terms 'purchasers' and 'providers' into a service which so intimately concerned the ordinary citizen. Apart from the fact that the identity of purchasers and providers was not immediately obvious to the public, nor indeed to countless thousands in the NHS, I wondered how long it would be before patients, like passengers on the railways, became 'customers', or even, when treated, 'products'. Health-speak had its own rules. One was to avoid use of the possessive whenever possible. Thus,'the results of the review of the assessment of needs' became even more obscure when translated into 'the needs assessment review result'. Anything even mildly important was 'key'. More mysterious, however, was the convening of meetings to discuss 'issues centring around teenage smoking', or any other topic. My pleas for plain English were received politely, and ignored.

❖

An opportunity to create a greater corporate sense in the organisation was at hand. In May 1988 the Authority had circulated a 'consultation document' to over four thousand health, educational and professional organisations, local authorities and others in both the public and private sector. This document summarised the aims and future plans of the Authority and invited comments and suggestions. In the light of the responses, work began on the Authority's future plan. The framework was set by the 'Health for All' strategy drawn up by the World Health

Organisation in 1978 and enshrined in the Alma Ata Charter. This expressed certain beliefs about the needs and rights of all people to expect basic standards of health and health care. At the first annual retreat of members and senior officers of the Authority which I attended at Torquay in June 1989, we discussed the main elements of what was to become our strategic plan for the next five years. This was warmly endorsed by David Mellor on behalf of the Department of Health in October and published in November. On 28 November, in launching what was the first national plan of its kind anywhere in the world, I said that it reflected the Authority's ambition that by the year 2000 the people of England would be 'more knowledgeable, better motivated and more able to acquire and maintain good health'. Apart from its publications and advertising, the Authority would concentrate its efforts on schools and colleges, the workplace and primary health care.

Having completed work on the strategic plan we were able to reconstruct the Authority. The 'baronies' came under the control of a small team of executive directors and work was grouped under seven headings – HIV/AIDS and sexual health, coronary heart disease, smoking, cancers, alcohol, nutrition and family and child health.

Of these seven programmes, two required especially sensitive treatment – sexual health and smoking. The first of the HEA's press and television campaigns on HIV and AIDS had been launched in February 1988. A second in June of that year was aimed at holiday makers. The evaluation of these campaigns was positive. Awareness of the risks was being raised. However, we became increasingly concerned about the vulnerability of young heterosexual people and decided in April 1989 that this should be addressed in a mass media campaign, including television advertisements, at the end of that year. We knew it would not be easy to devise a message advocating 'safer sex'. All members of the Authority took the view that a caring relationship was the proper context for a sexual relationship. But we had to accept that many young people had a different attitude. David Mellor defined our problem in clear terms: " . . . we have to give practical advice based on behaviour patterns we know about, not necessarily behaviour we approve of". For the purposes of our television campaign we sought to compose a message which would alert young people to the risk without alarming them and, at the same time, place this message in a context which would not appear to condone, or be readily misrepresented as condoning, promiscuity. My colleagues and I felt that the wisdom of Solomon would have been helpful at this time.

Following our normal practice, in July and October 1989 we conducted research into the effectiveness of our proposed television advertisements. The findings failed to provide the clear guidance we wanted. It appeared that, while many young people were indeed concerned about the risk, doubts were expressed about the effectiveness of the message in the form we proposed. So we went back to the drawing board. However, this was not our only problem. First, the press reported – correctly as it turned out – that the prime minister, Mrs Thatcher, who, as we learned later, found the whole subject of sexual health distasteful, had intervened to stop a £1 million national survey of sexual behaviour which the HEA proposed to commission in the light of a pilot study. This was followed by a campaign by influential sections of the press against the AIDS programme. On 7 November, Sir Reginald Murley, a former president of the Royal College of Surgeons and therefore someone who should have known better, wrote an article in the *Daily Mail* under the title 'Phoney Face of the War on AIDS'. In this he argued that it was wrong to address the general population; he disclosed that he had advised Mrs Thatcher that only drug users and gay men were at risk. A week later, Lord Kilbracken, whose interests lay in journalism and nature study, claimed in the House of Lords that "the chance of catching AIDS from normal sexual contact is statistically invisible". This statement was widely reported in the press.

I concluded that these events, combined with the lack of dramatic statistics about the spread of HIV infection and the incidence of AIDS, created an atmosphere in which our intended message would be discounted. Ministers in the Department of Health accepted our advice that the campaign be deferred. Public awareness of the risk to heterosexuals had to be raised if our messages to the young were to be effective.

We did not delay. On 24 November the HEA and the Department of Health jointly hosted a symposium in central London attended by over two hundred delegates. Six eminent figures in the field of public health drew on their professional experience to contradict the irresponsible assertions of Reginald Murley and Lord Kilbracken. Virginia Bottomley, who had meanwhile succeeded David Mellor, told the symposium: "No one can afford the luxury of complacency . . . The essence of prevention is to act before a new and serious condition reaches epidemic proportions."

The stark message which emerged from the symposium stimulated a generally sensible public debate and inspired a number of mass media programmes broadcast on World AIDS Day – 1 December. The scene was now set for the HEA's television campaign. In this series of advertisements, which we launched in February 1990, a number of experts, including some of those who had spoken at the symposium, set out the facts in straightforward and sometimes moving terms. I hoped then that the tide of scepticism about the threat to heterosexuals might have been stemmed. Over the following years we reinforced the message in a variety of ways. Despite an extraordinary campaign by the *Sunday Times* which, in the face of overwhelming evidence, sought to deny the existence of an AIDS epidemic in Africa, awareness of the risk was raised and behaviour influenced to the extent that the impact of the epidemic became manageable. A report by the Public Health Laboratory Service in June 1993 showed that the number of AIDS cases would soon plateau among homosexual men and that HIV infection was declining among drug users. But a steady increase in new cases of AIDS among heterosexuals was expected to continue for some time. Julia Cumberlege, the minister who carried responsibility in this field, said that these findings vindicated the policies put in place to fight the disease. Britain had the lowest estimated prevalence rates of HIV in western Europe; the rate in France was six times higher, in Spain four times and in Italy three times. When I left the Authority I felt that, while there were no grounds for complacency, a modest victory against heavy odds could be claimed.

The Authority's smoking programme required sensitive handling for a different reason. The facts were not in dispute. Every year over 110,000 people in the United Kingdom died before their time from diseases attributable to smoking, and over 7,000 hospital beds were occupied every day by patients suffering from smoking-related diseases. The treatment and care of these patients cost the National Health Service more than £325 million every year. Ministers accepted the medical consensus that smoking could cause distress, painful illness and premature death, and agreed that the warning to this effect on cigarette packets should be given more prominence. They argued that a regular increase in the price would be the most effective way of discouraging the consumption of tobacco products. The HEA agreed and I wrote to the chancellor of the exchequer each year when he was preparing his budget to urge a further increase in duty.

Our problem arose from the reluctance of ministers to contemplate a ban on tobacco advertising. Leaders of the medical profession favoured such a ban as did the members of the board of the HEA. However, we were reminded from time to time that the Authority operated within the parameters of government policy and that it would be improper for us to adopt a public position on this, or indeed any other issue, which contradicted government policy.

In the HEA we took the view that tobacco was a special case in that it was the only product legally on sale which, when used in the manner manufacturers intended, could cause distress, painful illness, or premature death. Since tobacco had been legally on sale for centuries and a substantial minority of the population still smoked, it would be unreasonable and unrealistic in any foreseeable future to attempt to outlaw the consumption of tobacco products. But surely it was unethical to promote their sale.

Even without the legal or voluntary ban on advertising that we would have preferred, the Authority's advertising and other campaigns, assisted by the ever-increasing number of organisations banning smoking on their premises, contributed to a steady reduction in the number of smokers. We scored a particular success in October 1992, when the *World in Action* television series broadcast a documentary programme to coincide with the publication of the results of an investigation we had commissioned into the effects of passive smoking. Despite this sustained campaign and the efforts of countless other organisations, the number of teenage smokers continued to rise steadily.

The objective of enabling the people of England to acquire and maintain good health set out in the strategic plan was the Authority's response to a perceived challenge. Although health in England was better than ever, the health record was poor in comparison with our neighbours in Europe. While the death rate from coronary heart disease and stroke had fallen over the previous decade, it was still the highest in the industrialised world. A National Fitness Survey – a joint venture with Allied Dunbar and the Sports Council – published in June 1992 showed that 48 per cent of men and 40 per cent of women were overweight. A study by the Royal College of Physicians in the late 1980s found that many deaths caused by fire, drowning, homicide, suicide and traffic accidents were attributable to smoking or alcohol misuse, or both.

The response to this challenge which we conveyed through our various programmes could be summarised in a five-point code of conduct for good health: do not smoke; drink sensibly and enjoyably; follow a balanced diet; take plenty of exercise; and learn to manage stress.

One of our consistently successful programmes was called *Look After Your Heart*. This programme, which was funded jointly by the HEA and the Department of Health, had been launched in 1987. Organisations of all kinds were awarded a certificate if they adopted four out of the ten measures specified in the 'Look After Your Heart Charter' to improve the health of their employees and undertook to adopt the rest within a fixed timescale. These included no-smoking policies, provision of healthy food, facilities for exercise, and regular professional advice on healthy living. Among the organisations to whom I awarded certificates were the Metropolitan Police, Norwich Union, the Midland Bank, the Royal Air Force and the Royal Navy. Surveys of firms which had subscribed to the programme showed not only improved morale among the workforce and their families but also fewer working days lost through ill-health. In April 1994, seven years after the campaign was launched, HP Foods in Birmingham became the one thousandth organisation to sign the Charter.

A good idea, efficiently brought to reality, can produce spectacular results. David Bedford, who was in charge of our press and public relations, produced good ideas at regular intervals. One in particular seemed to have considerable potential. He was convinced we could reach a mass audience through a 'phone-in' show on television. To obtain a second opinion Jean and I invited David and his family to lunch with us at our home in West Wiltshire one Sunday in June 1991; Esther Rantzen, Desmond Wilcox and their family were to join us. As David developed his concept, he was closely interrogated by Esther who added suggestions and modifications. In the end she agreed to commend the idea to the programme planners at the BBC. The proposal was accepted in principle. An experienced member of the HEA staff was attached to the producion team to advise on public health aspects of the programme. After four months intense work, the one and a half hour *Health Show*, hosted by Terry Wogan, was broadcast at peak viewing time on Sunday, 26 April 1992. Apart from various sketches and a quiz, the show featured the successful efforts of three families over a short period to change their way of life by giving up smoking, taking more physical exercise and eating healthy food. Over nine million people watched the programme and 1.6 million – over one-third of viewing households – asked for a copy of the accompanying *Health Show Guide* produced by the HEA. The BBC told us that this level of response was unprecedented. The outstanding success of this joint venture led to further collaboration with both BBC television and radio.

The effectiveness of the Authority's efforts depended crucially on the relevance and quality of its publications. Each year the Authority distributed some 50 million items and introduced about 150 new titles. These covered a wide range of subjects. *The Pregnancy Book* and *Birth to Five* were distributed free of charge to all first-time parents. *Enjoy Healthy Eating*, which William Waldegrave (Kenneth Clarkes's successor) enthusiastically endorsed, was a popular version of an authoritative scientific report by the Committee on Medical Aspects of Food Policy, the title of which – 'Dietary Reference Values for Food Energy and Nutrients for the United Kingdom' – would not have moved it into the best-seller list. The HEA's booklet, which contained appetising pictures on every page, was an attempt to dispel some of the confusion about diet and to show that healthy food could also be tasty.

In 1992 we reviewed our publishing function and decided that the service would be more sensitive to the market and more cost-effective if we established a simulated trading company which would operate under a managing director. Once they were satisfied about the financial implications, the Department of Health raised no objection. I felt that if this experiment were successful other discrete activities could be treated in the same way. I knew that the staff concerned were keen to assume more responsibility and to be released from existing constraints.

❖

In June 1991 the Department of Health published a Green Paper entitled *The Health of the Nation*. This well-constructed and lucidly drafted document was a model of how governments should present their proposals for public discussion. In his introduction William Waldegrave said that his purpose was to focus attention on the role of the National Health Service in 'improving and protecting health'. The principal themes in the document were the prevention of ill-health and the promotion of good health; the need for people to change their behaviour; and the merits of setting targets for improvements in health. In the light of responses to the Green Paper, the government intended to publish a health strategy for England. Parallel action would be taken in other parts of the United Kingdom.

The government's intention to devise such a strategy caused excitement and much satisfaction in the HEA. A few weeks after his announcement William Waldegrave asked if I would be willing to serve a further term as chairman from April 1992. At that time I was finding the work both interesting and rewarding and the prospect of contributing to the fashioning of the new national strategy was appealing. Had I known of the changes and problems ahead, I would have declined. In the event, I said I was ready to continue for another year. William Waldegrave pressed for more and we settled for two years – making a total of five.

The HEA was closely involved in the preparation of the White Paper version of the national strategy. The task of preparing our response brought out the best in our staff. We addressed each of the points on which the Department had invited comment. We also proposed a comprehensive strategy for reducing smoking, through fiscal policy; a ban on the advertising and promotion of tobacco products; the creation of more smoke-free environments; and a national programme of health education.

Because it had been subjected to close scrutiny by various other departments in Whitehall, the final version of *The Health of the Nation* lacked the verve of the Green Paper. The arrangements for its publication were interrupted by the general election, which led to ministerial changes at the Department of Health, and it was not presented to parliament until July 1992. The White Paper called for improvement in five areas – coronary heart disease, cancers, mental illness, HIV/AIDS and sexual health, and accidents. The HEA was required to review 'its strategic aims and objectives in the light of the priorities and targets in this White Paper'. We responded immediately and our new strategy for

the years 1993 to 1998 was approved by Virginia Bottomley, the new
secretary of state, in December 1992. However, in endorsing it she
informed me of her intention to commission an independent review
of the work of the Authority.

This news was unwelcome both to the board and to the staff.
Following David Mellor's approval of our first five-year Strategic Plan
in 1989, the 'baronies' had been replaced by a more coherent structure
which enabled the Authority to coordinate work on seven health topics.
Two years later this had been amended to accommodate the priorities in
the White Paper. A review so soon after this was bound to lead to further
changes, but I hoped that, if the review could be completed swiftly, the
disturbance would be limited. However, it was not until May 1993 that
I had a chance to comment on the scope of the review. The composition
of the review team and their terms of reference were announced in July.
These were to review the future role and responsibilities of the HEA in
the light of the new structure of the NHS, the strategy in *The Health of
the Nation*, government policy on market-testing and contracting out,
and the need for cost-effectiveness.

John Lee, a former minister, was appointed to lead the review. He and
his three colleagues wasted no time. They took evidence from the HEA
and others during September and October and submitted their report to
ministers at the end of November 1993. Time passed. Rumours spread
about the Lee team's recommendations and I became anxious about the
effect on the morale of our staff, who by this time had known for over
a year that the future of the Authority was under review.

The cause of the delay in announcing the government's decision
appeared to be argument within Whitehall. Meanwhile, my extended
term as chairman was due to expire on 31 March 1994 and no successor
had been appointed, nor even approached. I was pressed to stay on. This
time I set a limit of six weeks, in the hope that I would still be on
hand when the government announced its decision about the future of
the HEA. This hope was not fulfilled. It was not until 19 December
1994 that the new minister for health announced the government's
conclusion: after a brief transitional period, the HEA would be funded
largely by contracts rather than directly by the Department. This
statement ended two years of uncertainty during which some of the
Authority's most prized staff left to make their way elsewhere. When I
heard of the minister's announcement, I asked myself why this eminently
sensible solution could not have been achieved two years earlier through
the normal process of direct discussion between the Authority and the
department.

❖

The language William Waldegrave had used in presenting the lucidly
drafted Green Paper version of *The Health of the Nation* had encouraged

me and my colleagues to believe that ministers had decided that the time had come to respond positively to the challenge laid down in the Alma Ata Declaration of 1978 on 'health for all by the year 2000'. This impression appeared to be confirmed by the reference in the introduction to the White Paper by his successor, Virginia Bottomley, to 'the need to concentrate on health promotion as much as health care'. After all, 'as much as' means 'fifty-fifty'. The secretary of state seemed to go even further in her foreword to *Managing the New NHS* – the government's response to Kate Jenkins' review of structure, functions and manpower. In this she said: "We must not lose sight of the overall objectives of the NHS – promoting health, preventing disease and providing high quality services and patient care".

Public health had had a chequered history in Britain. At the beginning of the nineteenth century, Jeremy Bentham articulated the philosophy of 'the preventive way' and made 'preventive medicine' a speciality. Other dominant figures were Thomas Southwood Smith, who drew attention to the condition of children in factories, the dwellings of the industrial classes and the value of quarantine, and Edwin Chadwick, who inspired the creation of the General Board of Health in 1848. In 1871 the Royal Sanitary Commission recommended combined responsibility for the sanitary and poor laws. A Report of the Commission on the Poor Law in 1909 stimulated the introduction of national insurance and in 1919 the Local Government Board became the Ministry of Health. It was this last development that William Waldegrave had in mind when he pointed out that his predecessor was required under the 1919 Act to "take all such steps as may be desirable to secure the preparation, effective carrying out and coordination of measures conducive to the health of the people".

Between the wars the Ministry of Health was occupied with housing, town and country planning and day nurseries and it was only after the Second World War that it became concerned with administering the National Health Service. In January 1988 the report of a Committee of Inquiry into the Future Development of the Public Health Function was published. This document, known as the Acheson Report, was one of the inspirations of *The Health of the Nation*. In the HEA we were fortunate that one of the members of our board, Professor Alasdair Geddes, had been a member of Donald Acheson's committee and was steeped in the subject.

I assumed that preoccupation with the reforms to the NHS set in train by the White Paper 'Working for Patients' had delayed ministers' response to the Acheson Report. This was understandable. I was somewhat surprised, however, by what seemed to be a lack of urgency on the government's part in gaining public acceptance of the strategy in *The Health of the Nation* once it was published. Like others who had been invited to advise on the strategy, I began to wonder about the government's level of commitment. The resources put at the disposal of the small, hard-working team of officials in the department charged with implementing the strategy were meagre; and the impression of commitment was not enhanced when one of the senior advisers at her side defiantly smoked a cigarette while the secretary of state was addressing a press conference.

❖

The concerted assault on the major causes of early death, disease or disability and the combined effort to bring about substantial improvements in health and well-being contemplated in *The Health of the Nation* made sense in social, political and economic terms. The population was ageing. New drugs and treatments were available which added life to years and years to life. As in every other industrialised country, the cost of health care was reaching unaffordable levels. Part of the solution lay in reducing the number of our fellow citizens needing treatment and care who were suffering from avoidable illnesses.

Those who worked in the fields of prevention of disease and the promotion of good health faced serious obstacles. Principal among these were ignorance, complacency and prejudice. Ignorance could be overcome by education, publicity and advice. Complacency was more difficult to dispel. The research we carried out into the impact of our sexual health programmes demonstrated time and again that heightened awareness of risks to health did not always lead to changes in behaviour. Where HIV and AIDS were concerned, thinking 'not me' could be a tragic delusion.

Prejudice created intractable problems. Throughout the years I spent at the HEA I failed to find a convincing reason for the perverse attitude of some commentators to public health issues, nor could any of those who had spent a lifetime labouring in this particular vineyard. I was forced to accept, as they had done before me, that, for reasons deeply embedded in our culture, health education in Britain would inevitably arouse criticism, if not outright hostility. There were a number of possible explanations. Health education called for change – changes in attitude, in habits and in behaviour. Making such changes was not easy and those who advocated them were seldom popular. There might be a deeper explanation. Perhaps it was our spirit of tolerance, our attachment to individual liberties and our irreverent attitude to authority which inclined us to scorn what could be portrayed as 'nannying'. There was, of course, another side to our national character; we were often too slow to face unpleasant facts and too eager to identify extenuating circumstances where none existed.

In a democracy such as ours it was right that the consensus on health matters should be challenged and that those who subscribed to it should be required to defend their position. But when we were dealing with matters of life and death, as was the case with coronary heart disease, with smoking, and with AIDS for which there was no known cure, it seemed to me that those who chose to challenge the consensus had an obligation to do so responsibly.

The charge of 'nannying' assumed that health education sought to deny the right of individuals in a free society to behave as they wished. By supporting health education, the argument ran, the government was interfering with individual liberties. 110,000 deaths each year from smoking and 28,000 from alcohol misuse were tragic proof of the falsity of this accusation. Health education did not deny any individual rights. On the contrary, it honoured an important right – the right of individuals to be made aware of essential facts so that they could make an informed choice about the way they lived their lives. In his foreword to the *Citizen's Charter* John Major said: "Citizenship is about our responsibilities – as parents, for example, or as neighbours – as well as our entitlements. The *Citizen's Charter* is not a recipe for more state action; it is a testament of our belief in people's right to be informed and choose for themselves." There is no obvious reason why this right should not apply in matters of health and a reference in the introduction to *The Health of the Nation* to John Major's statement might have muted some of the libertarians.

Although there were moments when I thought of asking the Home Office to carry out forensic tests on the chalice I had been handed by Chris Patten, I valued the opportunity I had been given for over five years to work with people and organisations concerned with aspects of public health – for instance, those concerned with the health and well-being of families and children, the black and ethnic minorities, the aged, the disabled, the pharmaceutical profession – as well as numerous colleagues in the NHS. The salt of the earth is sprinkled liberally throughout the social sector.

To mark the end of my chairmanship the staff of the Authority arranged a valedictory concert at St Giles Church in the Barbican, noted for its excellent acoustics. The London Concert Sinfonia played Vivaldi, Handel, Clarke, Purcell, Pachelbel and Telemann. This was a splendid gesture on the part of the staff whose dedication and resilience had won my admiration from the beginning. It had not been easy for them to operate in a constantly changing environment, nor for the senior executives to sustain morale in conditions of prolonged uncertainty. I should have preferred to take leave of an organisation which had a clear role and an assured future, but time ran out.

Postscript

The years I spent in one form of public service or another coincided with a period of unprecedented change: in international relations, in the world economy, in the way we live and in the means of communication. Fifty years ago the people of Britain emerged, wounded and exhausted, from an experience without parallel in our history. We embarked then on a social revolution. We set about rebuilding our economy and dismantling the greatest empire the world had known. We consciously embraced a programme of radical change. Today we are a different nation with a different role in the world.

Fifty years ago, despite our weariness, a kind of contentment settled on the people of this country. We were fortunate. We thought we knew where we were going. Today we are an anxious, inward-looking society. The catalogue of public concerns is forbidding: crime and fear of crime; drug abuse; unemployment and fear of unemployment; disparities in wealth; homelessness; threats to our environment; disillusion with politics and politicians; misbehaviour in high places. We wonder what we have done to deserve this and seek to identify the causes – fallen standards in education; decline of the family; excesses of the media; preoccupation of politicians with the short term; progressive vulgarisation of our society.

If, for the time being, our national self-confidence has faltered, there are good reasons. It has not been easy for society to absorb the changes which have affected us directly. Their impact has no precedent. Television has opened our eyes to the realities of the world, but it has also provided those on the other side of the screen with an instrument with which we can be subjected to potent influences in our own homes. The transistor and the micro-chip have enabled each section of society to remain constantly in tune with the culture of its choice. The contraceptive pill has offered women a wider role. Innovations in medical treatment and care have altered the demographic structure. Through advances in communications and information technology, we are more than ever part of a community of nations and cannot live in isolation from events and opinions elsewhere in the world. Yet certain factors which influence our lives are within our control and, as enfranchised citizens, we cannot escape responsibility for the consequences of the choices we make, especially in the political field.

In the 1970s organised labour enjoyed too much power. When this was abused, the economy suffered and the nation decided, after the winter of discontent, that enough was enough. Different theories began to affect our lives. Responsibility, it was argued, rested with the individual, not the state. Market forces would determine the conditions of trade. Competition would increase efficiency. Greater efficiency would generate greater rewards. The greater wealth created would trickle down to all levels of society.

After an initial period of severe economic and financial turmoil, this prescription seemed to be curing the patient. Then doubts arose. When allowed free rein, market forces and competition – in themselves admirable concepts – began to look like the survival of the fittest. In the same way, the profit motive, undoubtedly a powerful incentive, began to look like greed. This was not what was intended. Had some ingredient been omitted from the prescription? Experience suggested that the insistence of the classical economists on social justice as a prerequisite for the proper working of the market had been overlooked. The missing ingredient was adequate provision for the effects of the economic prescription. What was to be done with those who proved not to be the fittest was not clear; nor what would happen to those unable even to enter the competition – the deprived, the less well endowed, those less capable of fending for themselves, those more likely to succumb to peer pressure or malign influences. What Abraham Lincoln meant at Gettysburg was that all men had equal rights, not that they were equally capable of exercising those rights and enjoying their fruits.

What we may come to regret most about the 1980s was the systematic denigration of the idea of public service. The consequences were inevitable. Morale and, with it, standards of performance and conduct declined. It is right that the role and effectiveness of our great national institutions should be reviewed in the light of new circumstances and that reforms should be introduced when these are shown to be necessary. But the reviews and reforms should be carried out in a measured and humane way which does not undermine the basis of mutual trust and respect between the government and those who serve it. This has been a notable characteristic of the British system for a century and a half, and much admired across the world. For hundreds of thousands of our people the public service is a vocation, and the national interest will be better served when this is once again more widely acknowledged.

The relationships I enjoyed in central government with ministers of different parties – right back to that bear hug in Ernest Bevin's office when we concluded the Nile Waters Agreement in 1949 – had a quality which not even Peter Hennessy, in his masterly history and analysis of Whitehall, was able to capture. Government consists to a great extent of responding to today's bad news and choosing between options of barely distinguishable shades of grey. The joint intellectual effort of assessing the importance of the relevant factors, of identifying flaws in the argument and anticipating the unexpected, created bonds which were valued by all concerned. How often did I wait anxiously for news from the cabinet room? If our argument prevailed there were congratulations all round, and commiseration if we lost. That pride in joint endeavour seems not so common today.

As a nation we are inclined to carry some of our virtues to extremes. We often confuse liberty with licence, tolerance with indifference and thrift with parsimony. Nevertheless, as our self-confidence returns, so the pluses in our situation will once more exceed the minuses. Although they are subject to unprecedented pressures, the young today have choices and opportunities not available to any of their predecessors. When news of the French Revolution reached him in 1789, William Wordsworth thought it bliss to be alive. How would the poet of today celebrate the fortunes of the young who stand on the threshold of a new century? What new concepts for living and governance will be devised? How will a better balance be struck between individual rights and responsibilities? How will our environment and heritage best be protected? What role should Britain play in Europe and in the world? How will the wealth of nations be harnessed and distributed for the general good? What law of nations will preserve the peace? Since in the end the human spirit always prevails there can be no doubt that new generations, drawing on the unique genius of this nation, will find answers to these and many other questions.

❖

In the green hills on the north-east frontier of India where this story began fifty years ago, there is a monument to those who died when the Japanese advance into India was halted in 1944 and the tide of the war in Burma turned. It bears a message on behalf of those it honours:

> When you go home, tell them of us and say
> For your tomorrow we gave our today.

As the years passed in enjoyment of the blessings of this life, I thought more and more of the friends of my youth who had also left home to go to war, but had not returned. I was more than ever persuaded, as I know were many of my contemporaries, that devoting my today and my tomorrow to the service of the public good was the best way in which I could hope to make their sacrifice worthwhile.

BURMA 1945

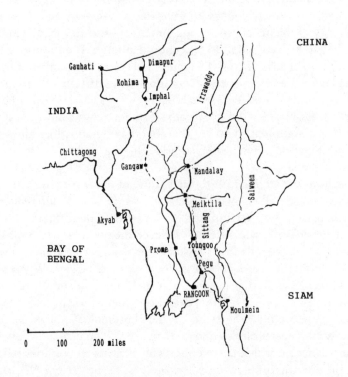

CHINA

Gauhati
Dimapur
Kohima
Imphal

INDIA

Chittagong

Gangaw

Mandalay

Meiktila

Akyab

Sittang

Salween

BAY OF
BENGAL

Prome
Toungoo

Pegu

RANGOON

Moulmein

SIAM

Irrawaddy

0   100   200 miles

CENTRAL BURMA   1945

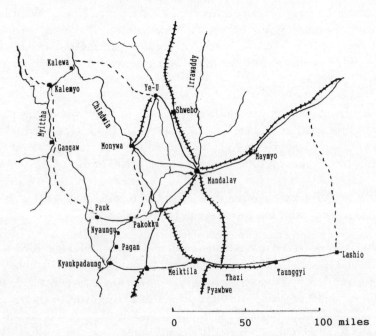

Kalewa

Kalemyo

Ye-U

Irrawaddy

Shwebo

Myittha

Chindwin

Gangaw

Monywa

Mandalay

Maymyo

Pauk

Pakokku

Nyaungu

Pagan

Kyaukpadaung

Meiktila

Thazi

Pyawbwe

Taunggyi

Lashio

0   50   100 miles

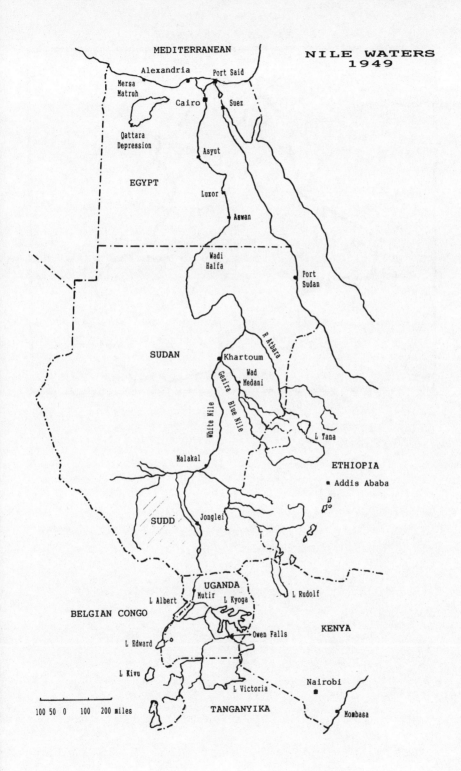

NILE WATERS
1949

MEDITERRANEAN

Alexandria
Port Said
Mersa
Matruh
Cairo
Suez

Qattara
Depression

EGYPT

Asyut

Luxor

Aswan

Wadi
Halfa

Port
Sudan

SUDAN
Khartoum
R Atbara
Wad
Medani

White Nile
Gezira
Blue Nile

L Tana

Malakal

ETHIOPIA

Addis Ababa

SUDD
Jonglei

UGANDA
L Albert
Mutir
L Kyoga
L Rudolf

BELGIAN CONGO

Owen Falls

KENYA

L Edward

L Kivu

Nairobi

L Victoria

100 50 0   100   200 miles

TANGANYIKA

Mombasa

IRAQ   1950

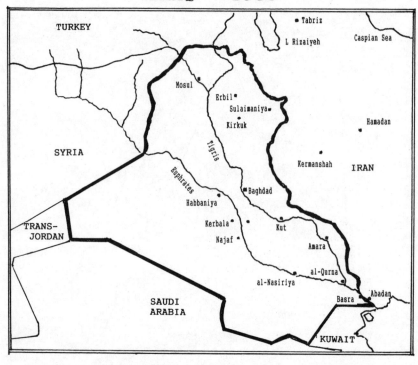

Notes

1 Preparation for War

1   Dr Lewis Penny. Later Senior Lecturer in the Geology Department of the University of Hull.
2   Bernard Fergusson (Lord Ballantrae). Later UK High Commissioner in New Zealand.

3 Rock, Domes and Desert

1   John Rae. Later Head of the BBC Monitoring Service at Caversham.
2   Peter Tripp. Later Ambassador to Libya and Thailand and UK High Commissioner in Singapore.
3   Edward Henderson. Later spent many years in the Gulf. Political Agent and Ambassador in Qatar.

4 Nile Waters

1   Sir Daniel Lascelles. Later Ambassador to Ethiopia, Afghanistan and Japan.
2   Ian Bell. Later held a number of senior consular posts. Ambassador to the Dominican Republic.
3   Geoffrey McDermott. Later British Minister in Berlin.
4   George Clutton. Later Ambassador to Poland.
5   Gordon Campbell (Lord Campbell of Croy). Later Secretary of State for Scotland in Edward Heath's government.
6   Anthony Montague Browne. Later left the Foreign Service to become private secretary to Sir Winston Churchill.
7   Sir Michael Stewart. Later Minister in the British Embassy in Washington and Ambassador to Greece.

5 Rivers and Tribes

1   Humphrey Trevelyan (Lord Trevelyan). Later Ambassador to Egypt, Iraq and the Soviet Union and High Commissioner in South Arabia.
2   Sir Geoffrey Arthur. Later Ambassador to Kuwait and Political Resident in the Persian Gulf.
3   Professor Robert Drew. Later Lieutenant-General Sir Robert Drew.

6 Oriental Secretary

1   Sir Herbert Gamble. Later Ambassador to Ecuador and Bolivia.
2   Sir John Richmond. Later Political Agent and Ambassador to Kuwait and to the Sudan.
3   Morgan Man. Later Ambassador to Saudi Arabia.
4   Sir Richard Beaumont. Later Ambassador to Morocco, Iraq and Egypt.

5   Hon. David Newsom. Later US Ambassador to Libya and Under Secretary at the US State Department.

6   Guy Clarke. Later Ambassador to Liberia, Guinea and Nepal.

7 A Most Honourable Marquess

1   Sir John Coulson. Later Minister in the British Embassy in Washington and Ambassador to Sweden.

2   Sir Denis Allen. Later Ambassador to Turkey.

3   Sir Evelyn Shuckburgh. Later Ambassador to Italy.

8 Centre for Arab Studies

1   John Henniker-Major (Lord Henniker). Later Ambassador to Jordan and Denmark and Director-General of the British Council.

2   Sir James Craig. Later Ambassador to Syria and Saudi Arabia and Director General of the Middle East Association.

3   Sir Terence Clark. Later Ambassador to Iraq and Oman.

9 A French Love Affair

1   Sir John Russell. Later Ambassador to Ethiopia, Brazil and Spain.

10 Frustration in Europe

1   SirEricRoll(LordRollofIpsden).LaterChairman,thenPresident,ofSCWarburgGroup.

2   Rev Sir Herbert Andrew. Later Permanent Under Secretary of State for Education and Science.

3   Sir Roderick Barclay. Later Ambassador to Denmark and Belgium.

4   Sir Christopher Audland. Later Deputy Secretary-General of the European Commission and Pro-Chancellor of Lancaster University.

5   John Robinson. Later Ambassador to Algeria and Minister in the British Embassy at Washington.

6   Sir Michael Butler. Later UK Permanent Representative to the European Communities and Chairman, City European Committee, British Invisibles.

7   Sir Harold Evans. Later Chairman, Health Education Council.

8   Sir Michael Hadow. Later Ambassador to Israel and Argentina.

11 Nasser's Egypt

1   Michael Hannam. Later Consul-General, Jerusalem.

2   Sir Colin Crowe. Later Ambassador to Saudi Arabia, UK High Commissioner in Canada and UK Permanent Representative to the United Nations.

3   Sir John Wilton. Later Ambassador to Saudi Arabia.

12 Michael and George

1   John Harris (Lord Harris of Greenwich). Later Minister of State, Home Office.

2   Murray Maclehose (Lord Maclehose of Beoch). Later Ambassador to Vietnam and Denmark and Governor and Commander-in-Chief, Hong Kong.

3   Sir Edward Youde. Later Ambassador to China; Governor and Commander-in-Chief Hong Kong.

4   Sir Derek Day. Later Ambassador to Ethiopia, Chief Clerk at the Foreign Office, UK High Commissioner in Canada and Member of the Commonwealth War Graves Commission.

5   Sir Nicholas Barrington. Later UK High Commissioner in Pakistan.

6   Sir Christopher Soames. Later Lord Soames.

7   Sir Denis Greenhill. Later Lord Greenhill of Harrow.

8   Sir Robin Haydon. Later High Commissioner, Malta; Ambassador to the Republic of Ireland.

13 Qaddafi's Libya

1   Sir John Leahy. Later Ambassador to South Africa, UK High Commissioner in Australia and Chairman Lonrho.
2   Sir George Jefferson. Later Chairman British Telecomunications.
3   Sir Peter Wakefield. Later Ambassador to Lebanon and Belgium and Director, National Art-Collections Fund.
4   Marrack Goulding. Later Ambassador to Angola and Under Secretary-General, Special Political Affairs, at the United Nations.
5   David Gore-Booth. Later Ambassador to Saudi Arabia.
6   Keith Haskell. Later Ambassador to Peru and Brazil.
7   Sir Peter Terry. Later Air Chief Marshal and Governor and Commander-in-Chief, Gibraltar.

14 Number 10

1   Robert Armstrong (Lord Armstrong of Ilminster). Later Secretary of the Cabinet.
2   Anthony Royle. Later Lord Fanshawe of Richmond.
3   William Staveley. Later Admiral of the Fleet Sir William Staveley, First Sea Lord and Chief of the Naval Staff.
4   Hugh Cudlipp. Later Lord Cudlipp of Aldingbourne.
5   Sir Morrice James. Later High Commissioner to Australia.

15 Resolution on First Avenue

1   Louis de Guiringaud. Later French Minister of Foreign Affairs.
2   Sir Michael Weir. Later Ambassaor to Egypt.
3   Sir Anthony Parsons. Later Ambassador to Iran and UK Permanent Representative to the United Nations.

16 Harold Wilson's Second Thoughts

1   Sir James Hamilton. Later Permanent Under Secretary of State, Department of Education and Science.
2   Sir Peter Preston. Later Permanent Secretary, Overseas Development Administration, Foreign and Commonwealth Office.
3   Sir Kenneth Stowe. Later Permanent Under Secretary of State, Northern Ireland Office, and Permanent Secretary, Department of Health and Social Security.

17 One of Nine in Europe

1   Sir Rodric Braithwaite. Later Ambassador to the Soviet Union.
2   Brian Crowe. Later Ambassador to Austria.
3   Jean Dondelinger. Later Member of the European Commission.
4   Niels Ersbøll. Later Secretary General of the Council of Ministers of the European Union.
5   Sir Terence Streeton. Later UK High Commissioner in Bangladesh.
6   Sir Crispin Tickell. Later Ambassador to Mexico and United Kingdom permanent representative to the United Nations.

Index